Concise Dictionary of
and Cultural Anthrop

Concise Dictionary of Social and Cultural Anthropology

Mike Morris

WILEY-BLACKWELL

A John Wiley & Sons, Ltd., Publication

This edition first published 2012
© 2012 Michael Ashley Morris

Blackwell Publishing was acquired by John Wiley & Sons in February 2007.
Blackwell's publishing program has been merged with Wiley's global Scientific, Technical,
and Medical business to form Wiley-Blackwell.

Registered Office
John Wiley & Sons Ltd, The Atrium, Southern Gate, Chichester, West Sussex,
PO19 8SQ, UK

Editorial Offices
350 Main Street, Malden, MA 02148-5020, USA
9600 Garsington Road, Oxford, OX4 2DQ, UK
The Atrium, Southern Gate, Chichester, West Sussex, PO19 8SQ, UK

For details of our global editorial offices, for customer services, and for information about
how to apply for permission to reuse the copyright material in this book please see our
website at www.wiley.com/wiley-blackwell.

The right of Michael Ashley Morris to be identified as the author of this work has been
asserted in accordance with the UK Copyright, Designs and Patents Act 1988.

Wiley also publishes its books in a variety of electronic formats. Some content that appears
in print may not be available in electronic books.

Designations used by companies to distinguish their products are often claimed as
trademarks. All brand names and product names used in this book are trade names, service
marks, trademarks or registered trademarks of their respective owners. The publisher is not
associated with any product or vendor mentioned in this book. This publication is designed
to provide accurate and authoritative information in regard to the subject matter covered.
It is sold on the understanding that the publisher is not engaged in rendering professional
services. If professional advice or other expert assistance is required, the services of a
competent professional should be sought.

Library of Congress Cataloging-in-Publication Data

Morris, Mike (Michael Ashley)
  Concise dictionary of social and cultural anthropology / Mike Morris. – 1st ed.
    p. cm.
  Includes bibliographical references.
  ISBN 978-1-4443-3209-4 (hardback) – ISBN 978-1-4443-6698-3 (paperback)
1. Ethnology–Dictionaries. I. Title.
  GN307.M67 2012
  301.03–dc23

                                                    2011036442

A catalogue record for this book is available from the British Library.

Set in 10/12pt Sabon by SPi Publisher Services, Pondicherry, India
Printed in Singapore by Ho Printing Singapore Pte Ltd

1 2012

To Matthew

Contents

Acknowledgments

I'd like to thank the following people for their various contributions towards making this dictionary.

Rosalie Robertson and Julia Kirk at Wiley-Blackwell, and the several reviewers whose helpful comments they supplied, as well as Hazel Harris for copy-editing. Stephanie Ogeneski and Daisy Njoku at the Smithsonian for help with pictures.

In Oxford: David Zeitlyn at ISCA, for his suggestions and comments on the draft (errors and omissions remain mine). Nadine Beckmann for supplying fieldwork photos and advice. Mark Dickerson of the Pitt Rivers Museum, for assistance with references and sources. Margaret Robb, formerly Social Sciences Librarian, for encouraging me to complete this book, and Louise Clarke, her successor, for further support. The staff of the Oxford Kidney Unit, Churchill Hospital, who have worked hard to keep me alive and functional for many years. Vicky Dean at ISCA, for patient and loyal friendship. Louise Trevelyan and Matthew Morris, for providing a life away from work.

Lastly, I acknowledge Meg Douglas, who died when this book was in its earliest stages, and whose kindness, intelligence, and compassion enlightened her many friends.

Introduction

Anthropology is a relatively young discipline with a complex history. In a world that is increasingly accessible and globalized, the new student needs a quick guide to help them even begin to untangle the web of allusions that academic anthropology may often evoke. Having come to the subject unprepared myself, many years ago, I empathize with readers struggling to make sense of what should be a vital and vibrant area of study.

I hope this text provides the beginner with a starting point for comprehension; in addition to the necessarily brief definitions of terms (which chiefly focus on concepts rather than particular peoples or places), I provide bibliographical references to a mixture of anthropological classics, related works from outside the field, and current ethnology, for both background reading and further research.

Terms referred to in the text that have their own separate entries are shown in SMALL CAPITALS.

List of Illustrations

A

AAA. See AMERICAN ANTHROPOLOGICAL ASSOCIATION.

Aboriginal. The earliest known occupant (or feature) of a region; often (capitalized) specifying INDIGENOUS peoples of Australia. "Aborigine" is often considered offensive. Early anthropologists and sociologists such as RADCLIFFE-BROWN and DURKHEIM were greatly interested in Australian Aboriginal societies. These have been examined by specialists such as B. Spencer and F. J. Gillen; and, more recently, by such writers as Howard Morphy and Ian Keen.

Abu Sunbul (Egypt). See BURCKHARDT.

acculturation. A process by which one group of people's IDENTITY is modified by meeting another: one CULTURE introduces elements that are accepted or resisted by the other, leading to the weaker group remaining partially autonomous, the ASSIMILATION of the weaker group into the stronger unit, or occasionally a merged culture. Members of the dominant culture may be physically present or act on the other remotely. Even when acculturated, the weaker group may not totally assimilate. In general use, acculturation and assimilation may be used synonymously. See also SYNCRETISM, the adoption of elements of one religion into another.

acephalous. Having no head; of a STATE or people, having no formal leader (as in foraging cultures—see HUNTER-GATHERER).

achievement/ascription. A distinction made by PARSONS, one of five such PATTERN VARIABLES, or sets of alternative social strategies. Achieved STATUS derives from competition with one's peers; ascribed status comes through

Concise Dictionary of Social and Cultural Anthropology, First Edition. Mike Morris.
© 2012 Michael Ashley Morris. Published 2012 by Blackwell Publishing Ltd.

one's birth. While it may be claimed that "traditional" (see TRADITION) societies ascribe status and "MODERN" societies favor achievement, certain areas (e.g. GENDER roles) may be more complicated.

acquisition. See LANGUAGE ACQUISITION.

act. To perform a deed, or the deed itself. The definition of an "act" has been much discussed in SOCIOLOGY. See also AGENCY (the ability to act), BROKER, COLLECTIVE CONSCIENCE, ROLE, SPEECH ACT. In common use, of course, "acting" often implies theatrical ROLE-playing.

Further reading: Hastrup (2004).

action anthropology. A form of APPLIED ANTHROPOLOGY in which the anthropologist works for the interests of a minority CULTURE that is in difficulty of some kind, facilitating that culture's decisions. Pioneered by Sol TAX from the 1930s onward.

actor/network theory (ANT). A sociological approach associated with Bruno Latour, John Law, Michel Callon, and others that has influenced several SOCIAL SCIENCES. It stresses the *performative* nature of networks, and, controversially, can be said to ascribe AGENCY, the ability to act, to non-human elements of a network—people and the things they use interact to perpetuate the network. Critics have argued that ANT underplays the real political and POWER relations involved in its area of study. ANT is a branch of SCIENCE AND TECHNOLOGY STUDIES.

Further reading: Latour (2005).

adaptation. In biology and anthropology, the response of a population or INDIVIDUAL to new environmental (see ENVIRONMENT) factors. Individuals develop physically in differing ways according to local conditions; over a longer period populations evolve (see EVOLUTION). Adaptation also operates at various cultural levels, through behavior and SOCIAL ORGANIZATION.

adat. Customary law in Islamic (see ISLAM) South-East Asia, as distinct from religious law, or SHARI'A.

Further reading: Davidson & Henley (2007).

address terms. Relationship terms used directly with their subject, to talk *to* them. May be employed more loosely than REFERENCE TERMS (terms used to talk *about* others), as when calling an older COUSIN "uncle."

adelphic polyandry. A form of POLYANDRY—marriage to multiple husbands—in which the husbands are brothers (or are regarded as such). From Greek, *adelphi* ("brothers").

adivasi. A member of the ABORIGINAL tribal peoples of India. From Sanskrit, "original inhabitant."

adolescence. See YOUTH.

adoption. The voluntary extension of KINSHIP ties to people outside one's immediate biological FAMILY, most often involving adults adopting children. It may be mainly understood as a legal commitment, a more permanent step than fostering.

Legal adoption derives from ancient Rome; the Romans distinguished between beneficial "changes" of parent and cases in which birth parents had died. In NON-WESTERN societies the anthropologist may find such distinctions less useful, as a fluid range of practices and attitudes may present themselves. One area of interest is transnational adoption (see TRANSNATIONALISM), with issues such as questions of ETHNICITY and IDENTITY.

Further reading: Bowie (2004).

Adorno, Theodor (1903–69). German philosopher, influenced by MARX; member of the Frankfurt School (see CRITICAL ANTHROPOLOGY). He adopted a critical stance toward the mass MEDIA and POSITIVISM, attacking the "culture industry" on the grounds that it twisted art to its own repressive ends, and toward spurious rationalism. His works include *Minima moralia* (1974 [German 1951]), *Prisms* (1967 [German 1955]), and *Negative dialectics* (1973 [1966]). See also HABERMAS.

advocacy. The PRACTICE of speaking for another (the Latin root means "called to [support]"). The notion of advocacy in the SOCIAL SCIENCES and the ethical questions surrounding it have become issues in areas such as APPLIED ANTHROPOLOGY, DEVELOPMENT, HUMAN RIGHTS, and particularly ACTION ANTHROPOLOGY.

aesthetics. A term originally taken from the Greek for "things perceptible," the precise meaning of which was contested by Alexander Baumgarten and Immanuel Kant in the eighteenth century. Its English use encompasses both the THEORY of sense PERCEPTION and the investigation of the principles of beauty in the arts (see ART). For anthropologists, key questions include what criteria are valid in the study of art of NON-WESTERN cultures (see CULTURE), what the function of art is, and what it may mean.

Further reading: Weiner (1994).

affect. Generally used as a verb; as a noun, "affect" refers in psychology to emotional response to stimuli or thoughts. Its consideration is an issue in anthropology of the BODY.

affiliation. Used generally to describe ADOPTION (literally or metaphorically), affiliation also has two meanings in anthropology. It describes the relationship of a child to its parents, and hence to lines of DESCENT (the relationship to the parent *alone* being known as FILIATION), and also covers voluntary social ASSOCIATION between wider groups.

affine. See AFFINITY.

affinity. KINSHIP held through MARRIAGE (e.g. "in-laws") as opposed to BIRTH (CONSANGUINITY). Those connected by affinity are termed "affines."

affluent society. See ORIGINAL AFFLUENT SOCIETY.

afterology. A term adopted by Marshall D. SAHLINS (from a phrase by Jacqueline Mraz) to describe disparagingly POST-MODERNISM, POST-STRUCTURALISM, and similar phenomena.

Further reading: Sahlins (1999).

Agamben, Giorgio (1942–). See SOVEREIGNTY.

agamy. A MARRIAGE CUSTOM whereby people are free to marry members of their own group as well as members of another group. Compare the narrower expectations involved in ENDOGAMY and EXOGAMY.

age-class system or **age system.** A means of organizing men (seldom WOMEN) into groups based on common age and ROLE ("age sets" passing through the same "age grades" together), typically in East Africa or the Americas. The most common distinction is the separation of young men from their ELDERS.

ageing. The last stages of physical maturity; later adulthood. A folksy image of the kinds of peoples studied by anthropologists would involve revered ELDERS dispensing wisdom to the young, but this is not necessarily accurate. In some ways people are just as constrained by societal expectations (and factors such as GENDER) in old age as in YOUTH. It is certainly true, however, that in industrialized societies people quite often regard the elderly as a burden, requiring expensive medical and personal care. A further aspect of ageing is the occasional emergence of a GERONTOCRACY.

Further reading: Myerhoff (1978).

agency. The ability of an INDIVIDUAL ("agent") or group to ACT of their own volition, without constraint by STRUCTURE. Certain schools of social thought stress agency (see POLITICAL ANTHROPOLOGY). Contrast CULTURAL DETERMINISM.

Further reading: Wisnewski (2008).

aggression. Of particular interest in psychology (see PSYCHOLOGICAL ANTHROPOLOGY). Anthropologists have uncovered a wide range of aggressive practice, including conventions regarding who is likely to be a victim, and under what circumstances. Aggression may result in full-blown VIOLENCE or the capitulation (or flight) of the target. It is often studied in relation to young males (see YOUTH), in relation to children, and in relation to situations that provoke aggression.

A lot of work has been done on aggressive behavior among other ANIMALS, for instance PRIMATES. The theories of the Austrian ethologist Konrad Lorenz, who regarded aggression as inbuilt, were popular in the 1960s but have latterly been rejected in favor of more culturally nuanced explanations.

agnate. See AGNATIC.

agnatic. In KINSHIP, a term for relation by DESCENT from the father's side of the family; a person so related is an "agnate." The mother's-side equivalent terms are ENATE and UTERINE; see also COGNATIC, PATRILINEALITY.

agricultural involution. See INVOLUTION.

agriculture. Literally, the cultivation of the soil (for FOOD and so on), but usually understood to include wider PRACTICES such as raising livestock. Studied particularly by anthropologists interested in DEVELOPMENT issues (e.g. RURAL politics and economics) but issues also include large-scale land use in technologically sophisticated ways.

agronomy. The study of land management, RURAL economy and related areas.

AIDS. Acquired immune deficiency syndrome, which develops from the human immunodeficiency virus (HIV) to allow infection, was first identified around 1982 and has had major impacts around the world, particularly in sub-Saharan Africa, where mortality rates remain high. As the PANDEMIC developed, judgmental attitudes toward some early victims hampered efforts to treat and prevent it. See also DISEASE, RISK, SEX.

Further reading: ten Brummelhuis & Herdt (1995); Fassin (2007).

alcheringa. See DREAMING.

alcohol. The general name for a number of chemical compounds with assorted uses (for example ethanol) produced naturally or artificially. Ethanol is the basis of "alcoholic" DRINKS. Naturally fermented drinks have a long history of recreational use, use in RITUAL, and use other contexts, in many CULTURES, although not everywhere: for instance, they are forbidden according to Islamic (see ISLAM) and Sikh CUSTOM. Even in the US, Prohibition in the 1920s criminalized alcohol.

Alcohol works on the BRAIN to alter mood and lower inhibitions, which can create social problems (such as CRIME and VIOLENCE), ILLNESS, and long-term dependency. Many social scientists have investigated methods of treatment and rehabilitation for alcohol abusers.

Further reading: Wilson (2005).

Figure 1 Alcohol. Anthropologist Nadine Beckmann tasting *pombe*, a local beer, Ulugura mountains, Tanzania. Photo copyright: N. Beckmann.

Ali ibn Abi Talib, Caliph (c. 600–661). See SHIA.

alliance. A relationship created by MARRIAGE, not just between the spouses but encompassing "in-laws." From the French scholarly TRADITION as elaborated in LÉVI-STRAUSS' classic work on ELEMENTARY STRUCTURES. "Alliance systems" may involve SYMMETRICAL ALLIANCE or ASYMMETRICAL ALLIANCE (that is, differing forms of MARRIAGE exchange); "alliance theory" stresses these connections and their social importance rather than, as in some anthropological writings, viewing connections of DESCENT as being central to social cohesion (see DESCENT THEORY). As with much THEORY, alliance theory tends to describe ARCHETYPES that do not always appear so neatly in reality. See also CROSS-COUSIN.

Further reading: Lévi-Strauss (1969[b]); Héritier-Augé & Copet-Rougier (1990–4).

alliance systems. See ALLIANCE.

alliance theory. See ALLIANCE.

allograph. In LINGUISTICS, either a particular written form of a given letter-SYMBOL (GRAPHEME) or one of a number of letters or combined letters representing a PHONEME.

allometry. In biology, the study of relative growth rates among parts of a BODY, human or otherwise, especially where one feature appears out of proportion with what may be expected (e.g. where a human baby's head develops faster than other parts). From Greek, "other" and "measure."

allopathy. A term used in homeopathy to describe conventional medical approaches (compare BIOMEDICINE). It refers to treatment inducing a reaction in the sufferer which *counters* their symptoms; "homeopathy," by contrast, specifies treatment that would, if given in sufficient amounts, *induce* these symptoms.

allophone. In LINGUISTICS, a variant form of the same sound (compare PHONE); for example, "p" in "span" and "p" in "pan" are regarded as distinct allophones since "p" is only aspirated (produced with a breath) in the second case.

Al-Qaida. See TERRORISM.

alter. (noun) A term used when discussing relationships: a person to whom EGO stands in some relationship. From Latin, "another".

alterity. The state of "otherness," difference; a PROPERTY of what one group conceives of as the "OTHER." For example, a migrant group of South Asians living in London may be conceived of as marked by alterity.

Althusser, Louis (1918–90). French structuralist (see STRUCTURALISM) philosopher (born in Algeria), influenced by GRAMSCI and a critical disciple of MARX. Althusser popularized the idea of the "ideological STATE apparatus": social elements (e.g. the MEDIA) that promulgate the dominant IDEOLOGY. A sufferer of bipolar disorder, he strangled his wife in 1980 and died in an institution. Major works include *For Marx* (1969 [French 1965]) and *Lenin and philosophy* (2nd ed. 1977 [French 1969]).

altruism. Concern for the wellbeing of others rather than oneself. Coined (in French) by COMTE in the nineteenth century. Altruism is an issue in such areas as GAME THEORY, and numerous explanations for its development and forms (e.g. KIN SELECTION ALTRUISM, RECIPROCAL ALTRUISM) have been advanced.

Further reading: Ridley (1996).

Amazonia. The region around the Amazon river, home to outstanding resources in terms of RAINFOREST, PLANTS, and ANIMALS, and a shrinking and diverse number of INDIGENOUS peoples. About half of Amazonia is in Brazil, and much interest has been generated by the struggle of local peoples with its GOVERNMENT.

Amazonia has been investigated by LÉVI-STRAUSS and by specialists such as John Hemming, David Maybury-Lewis, and Peter Rivière. It continues to exert a powerful fascination for the ordinary reader as much as the expert.

Further reading: Lévi-Strauss (1961); Nugent (2007).

ambilineal. A term first used by Edmund LEACH to denote a KINSHIP system in which one may claim membership of the matrilineal (see MATRILINEALITY) or patrilineal (see PATRILINEALITY) group (the mother's or father's side of the FAMILY), though not both. FIRTH and others have occasionally discussed "ambilateral" relations (the prefix "ambi" comes from Latin, "of both sides").

ambilocality. In POST-MARITAL RESIDENCE, the CUSTOM of a married couple residing with, or near to, *either* the husband or wife's relatives, as opposed to, for example, NEOLOCAL residence (setting up home in a new place).

American anthropology. The North American tradition in anthropology is characterized historically by a division into FOUR FIELDS, including CULTURAL ANTHROPOLOGY, itself distinct from the British tradition of SOCIAL ANTHROPOLOGY.

An age of gifted amateurs and evolutionary theorists, such as MORGAN, in the mid-nineteenth century led, in both the US and in Britain, to the birth of an academic discipline under the guidance of figures such as Franz BOAS. The AMERICAN ANTHROPOLOGICAL ASSOCIATION formed to represent the new profession, which eventually gained popular attention through the writings of BENEDICT, Margaret MEAD and others. Theorists such as SAPIR developed new insights into the cultural dimension of LINGUISTICS. Many of this generation had been taught directly by BOAS.

In the latter part of the twentieth century, the influence of LÉVI-STRAUSS and STRUCTURALISM was felt, as well as a concern with REFLEXIVITY, as anthropologists began to take full account of their own cultural backgrounds and biases. American anthropology has also absorbed POST-MODERNISM (see *WRITING CULTURE*), a development now old enough to inspire retrospective analysis and lead to a plethora of new theoretical avenues.

Further reading: Boas (1974); Stocking & Handler (1983–2010).

American Anthropological Association. A major anthropological organization, with over 10,000 members. Founded in 1902, it has numerous sections and runs an annual meeting. Its many publications include *American anthropologist, American ethnologist,* and *Anthropology news,* and its titles are accessible via the AnthroSource online portal (http://www.aaanet.org).

American Indian. An inaccurate (see INDIAN) but not generally offensive term that has been steadily replaced in American English by NATIVE AMERICAN.

American Museum of Natural History. The AMNH (http://www.amnh.org) houses a vast collection that includes a substantial anthropology section, formed in 1873. Several major figures, principally BOAS and Margaret MEAD, have worked here.

Amerindian. INDIGENOUS (person, group, or LANGUAGE) to North, South, or Central America; NATIVE AMERICAN. See also INDIAN.

amitalocality. See AVUNCULOCAL RESIDENCE.

AMNH. See AMERICAN MUSEUM OF NATURAL HISTORY.

amoral familism. A term coined by Edward Banfield to describe a supposed prioritizing among MEDITERRANEAN societies of the material, short-term interests of one's family over those of the COMMUNITY. The concept has since been challenged. Compare LIMITED GOOD.

Further reading: Banfield (1958).

Amritsar (India). See SIKHISM.

Anansi. See TRICKSTER.

ancestor. One from whom a person or group claims DESCENT. The ancestor usually pre-dates the descendant's grandparents or may be a mythical person or creature. There is a wide variety of attitudes and PRACTICES relating to ancestors, for example concerning who is considered important, how they are remembered, and for what. Anthropologists such as Maurice BLOCH have studied these practices. See also ANCESTOR WORSHIP, DESCENT GROUP.

ancestor worship. In several parts of the world, groups of people of the same lineage, CLAN, or other relationship group venerate ANCESTORS, and perform rites to them. This can be seen as an exercise in POWER, strengthening the FAMILY against outsiders; it is also tied up with the belief that ancestors influence the lives of their descendants. The phrase "ancestor worship" is itself contentious owing to its origins in a nineteenth-century view of human development, and to the diversity of practices that it covers.

Further reading: Weber (1951).

Andamanese. See NEGRITO.

Andes. The largest mountain range in the world, running along the western coast of South America through countries such as Colombia, Peru, and Chile.

androcentrism. A viewpoint placing men at the centre; early anthropologists have been criticized for what are now perceived as androcentric assumptions (e.g. that men are "naturally" superior to WOMEN).

androgyny. The condition of possessing both male and female sexual characteristics; being a HERMAPHRODITE. From the Greek for both "man" and "woman."

anglophone. English-speaking (person, country, or other community).

animal. Animals can be studied in at least three main ways. They may be viewed as physical resources to be exploited: for FOOD in such areas as AGRICULTURE; entertainment (as in fox hunting, cock fighting, horse racing, and other SPORTS); for scientific and medical research; or for RITUAL purposes (see also SACRIFICE). On a more abstract level, animals are SYMBOLS or METAPHORS by which to classify the world (see e.g. TOTEMISM). In a third way, people can be insulted if they are compared to certain animals.

Some animals develop significance (e.g. in TABOOS regarding FOOD) in particular cultures—as in those that abstain from eating pigs, and those that ascribe special STATUS to cattle (see CATTLE COMPLEX, HINDUISM). Such processes involve an element of CLASSIFICATION.

See also AGGRESSION, ANTHROPOMORPHISM, DARWINISM, ETHNOBIOL-OGY, ETHNOZOOLOGY, ETHOLOGY, EVOLUTIONARY ANTHROPOLOGY, FOLK CLASSIFICATION, HUNTING, NATURE AND CULTURE, PASTORALISM, PRIMATE, PROPERTY, SHAMAN, SOCIOBIOLOGY, TERRITORIALITY, TRANSHUMANCE.

Further reading: Leach (1964); Morris (1998); Kalof & Fitzgerald (2007).

animism. The belief that inanimate objects and natural phenomenema have SOULS. Animism was viewed by nineteenth-century religious theorists as part of a PRIMITIVE outlook that might be supplanted by RATIONALISM.

anisogamy. MARRIAGE between partners of unequal STATUS—either HYPER-GAMY ("marrying up" to a higher group) or HYPOGAMY ("marrying down"). Marriage between social equals is ISOGAMY.

Année sociologique. A pioneering journal founded by DURKHEIM and associated with his influential school of SOCIOLOGY.

anomie. A sociological term to describe a condition characterized by breakdown or disregard of NORMS. First used in this way by DURKHEIM in *Suicide* (1897): societies regulate desires by setting frameworks for goals; when such frameworks are broken, goals become unobtainable and anomic conditions result, with rising instances of suicide.

A social system may also become anomic when norms are applied unevenly or unclearly, or during WARS (for example), when norms may be waived. See also URBANISM.

ANT. See ACTOR/NETWORK THEORY.

anthropocentrism. The assumption that mankind is the centre of existence. Compare ETHNOCENTRISM.

anthropogeography. A type of HUMAN GEOGRAPHY principally associated with Ratzel in the late nineteenth century. Ratzel regarded geography not simply as a natural science but as one also partly concerned with cultural and political elements. Compare GEOGRAPHICAL DETERMINISM, GERMAN ANTHROPOLOGY.

anthropological linguistics. Anthropologists have had an interest in LANGUAGE from the earliest beginnings of the discipline, for example Sir

William Jones' work on Sanskrit in the eighteenth century. Many writers compiled dictionaries and GRAMMARS of colonies in which they worked, and key early twentieth-century figures such as BOAS and MALINOWSKI began to develop insights into how language reveals the underlying outlook of a society.

A little later, the WHORFIAN HYPOTHESIS—loosely, the argument that a particular WORLDVIEW is closely tied to the linguistic means available for its expression—allied language to a cultural understanding of the world. By the 1960s, ETHNOSCIENCE or the "new ethnography" had led to a greater interest in FOLK CLASSIFICATION.

Following the work of CHOMSKY, anthropologists and linguists have diverged: while linguists (mostly) view language as a discrete system capable of independent study, anthropologists are keen to see it as something that operates primarily in a *social* setting.

Areas such as SOCIOLINGUISTICS, the ETHNOGRAPHY OF SPEAKING, and DISCOURSE theory (see THEORY) have been fertile ground for Dell Hymes, John Gumperz, and many others, and for sympathetic linguists such as Deborah Tannen. Recent work also encompasses METAPHOR, and the expression of relations of POWER, GENDER differences, linguistic minorities, and so on. Since the turn of the millennium the Internet has begun to emerge as a field of interest.

Further reading: Ottenheimer (2009).

Anthropological Survey of India. See INDIAN ANTHROPOLOGY.

anthropology. The scientific study of humankind, including human origins, institutions, beliefs, and social and cultural forms. The word comes from Greek, "speaking of man," and seems to be late sixteenth century, though a growing interest among western writers concerning the peoples encountered by travelers, traders, and explorers is evident much earlier (and goes back at least to HERODOTUS).

Anthropology emerged as a distinct field in the later nineteenth century, at which point it began to grow from a by-way of earlier disciplines (HISTORY, philosophy, and later LINGUISTICS and especially SOCIOLOGY), or the pursuit of amateurs (see ARMCHAIR ANTHROPOLOGY), into a recognized academic endeavor as practiced by TYLOR, BOAS, and other leading scholars.

During the twentieth century, figures such as MALINOWSKI, EVANS-PRITCHARD, and RADCLIFFE-BROWN in Britain; Margaret MEAD, BENEDICT, and KROEBER in the US; and numerous others advanced the standing and scope of anthropology. The subject developed different concerns in different countries, from American CULTURAL ANTHROPOLOGY, with its FOUR FIELDS orientation, to British SOCIAL ANTHROPOLOGY, German VÖLKERKUNDE, and so on (see also CHINESE ANTHROPOLOGY, DUTCH ANTHROPOLOGY, FRENCH

ANTHROPOLOGY). In the same way, the theoretical leanings of early anthropologists (such as EVOLUTIONISM and DIFFUSIONISM) yielded over time to a more nuanced understanding of what had been called PRIMITIVE peoples. Influences from related areas such as the SOCIOLOGY of DURKHEIM or WEBER, or the LINGUISTICS of SAUSSURE and SAPIR, opened new and radical perspectives.

As the twentieth century progressed, European anthropologists became more aware of their own ties with COLONIALISM; the multidisciplinary influence of STRUCTURALISM spread, as did political currents such as MARXIST anthropology.

With the advent of POST-MODERNISM and REFLEXIVITY, the subject entered a period of introspection (see also *WRITING CULTURE*). Today new branches continue to emerge, from MEDICAL ANTHROPOLOGY to the investigation of new technologies. See also ETHNOGRAPHY, ETHNOLOGY, HISTORY OF ANTHROPOLOGY.

Further reading: Harris (1990); Eriksen (2004); Rosman et al. (2009); Strang (2009[b]).

anthropology at home. The ethnographic study of one's own SOCIETY. Of particular interest to European anthropologists in the 1980s, as funding for travel became tighter and as a way of circumventing access difficulties. See also AUTOETHNOGRAPHY.

Further reading: Jackson (1987).

anthropometry. Comparative measurement of the BODY to determine average dimensions in different ages, groups, and so on. Measurements might include height, weight, and ratios. Generally more studied in the nineteenth and early twentieth century, anthropometry is now often associated with outmoded theories on RACE and physical difference, but is still used with fossil records and in public health.

Further reading: Ulijaszek & Komlos (2010).

anthropomorphism. The attribution of human-like feelings or motivations to non-human entities: most obviously ANIMALs but also God.

apartheid. In politics, the policy in twentieth-century South Africa (from Afrikaans and Dutch, "apartness") of "separate development" for non-white ethnic groups. Enshrined in law following the election of the National Party in 1948, it was vociferously opposed in the wider world and most of its laws were repealed in 1991.

apical ancestor. An ANCESTOR (real or supposed) shared by members of a SEGMENTARY SOCIETY; the one who sits at the apex (top) of any GENEALOGY.

Apinayé. See PARALLEL DESCENT.

Appadurai, Arjun (1949–). Indian anthropologist long resident in the US; a leading writer on GLOBALIZATION. Born in Bombay (Mumbai) and educated at Brandeis University and Chicago, he has held professorships at Yale, Chicago, and Pennsylvania and is currently with the New School, New York. He co-founded the leading journal *Public culture* in 1988 and his own writings include *The social life of things: commodities in cultural perspective* (ed., 1986), *Modernity at large: cultural dimensions of globalization* (1996), *Globalization* (ed., 2001), and *Fear of small numbers: an essay on the geography of anger* (2006).

applied anthropology. A field in which the anthropologist deals with a practical issue concerning a population or region, either by informing social policy or by direct action. This often takes place outside academia. Many US anthropologists have preferred the term "practicing anthropologist." See for example the National Association for the Practice of Anthropology (http://practicinganthropology.org). Compare (in their various implications concerning the anthropologist's involvement or detachment) ACTION ANTHROPOLOGY, ADVOCACY, DEVELOPMENT.

Further reading: *Anthropology in action* [journal].

appropriate technology. TECHNOLOGY suited to the cultural and ecological context in which it will be used. Typically thought of as simple, cheap tools and machines that can be employed in DEVELOPMENT. Compare INTERMEDIATE TECHNOLOGY.

Arabia Felix. The old Roman name for the Arabian peninsula; "Arabia the fortunate."

archaeology. The scientific study of the remains and ARTEFACTS left by the cultures of the past, from comparatively recently to as far back as PREHISTORY. Inasmuch as it frequently concerns ancient (rather than modern) societies, it is a sister discipline to anthropology. For terms relating to archaeology see ETHNOGRAPHIC ANALOGY, FOUR FIELDS, LITHIC, MATERIAL CULTURE, PROCESSUAL, QUATERNARY, SALVAGE ETHNOGRAPHY, SERIATION.

archaeology of knowledge. A particular approach to the HISTORY of thought developed by FOUCAULT: the products of differing disciplines in a particular age are compared, to give a picture of the kind of understanding available *at that time*. Knowledge is linked to POWER structures. Compare HISTORY OF IDEAS.

Further reading: Foucault (2002).

archetype. A first model, a prototype. Archetypes may appear as stock characters in stories or NARRATIVES ("heroes," "villains," and so on), or may otherwise represent particular things or situations. Often associated with the psychologist Carl Jung.

archipelago. A group of (often volcanic) islands, or the sea area enclosing them; for example, the Malay Archipelago.

architecture. The ART and science of designing and constructing buildings, as well as other edifices, such as bridges and ships. One aspect of MATERIAL CULTURE. The cultural significance of *house* design is one area studied: as well as the practical aspects of architecture, which will be modified according to purpose (for dwelling, for storage, as places for particular activities), built forms make symbolic statements about the conception of SPACE (see SYMBOLIC ANTHROPOLOGY).

Further reading: Carsten & Hugh-Jones (1995).

Ardener, Edwin (1927–87). British social anthropologist and linguist; born London. Educated at the London School of Economics (1945, under FIRTH, LEACH, and Audrey Richards), he did fieldwork in Cameroon(s). Ardener lectured in social anthropology at Oxford from 1963 to 1987. He co-founded the *Journal of the Anthropological Society of Oxford*. He edited the collection *Social anthropology and language* in 1971; his own articles are collected in *The voice of prophecy* (ed. M. Chapman, 2007 [1989]).

Further reading: *Journal of the Anthropological Society of Oxford* (1987), special issue.

Argonaut. A legendary Greek hero; the Argonauts accompanied Jason in their ship, the *Argo*. MALINOWSKI alludes to them in the title *Argonauts of the Western Pacific*.

Aristotle (384–322 BCE). See BINARY OPPOSITION, CATEGORY, COMMODITY, MIMESIS, OLIGARCHY.

armchair anthropology. The "armchair" PREFIX in general use refers to critics who air views based on reading or speculation rather than first-hand knowledge of a subject (hence "armchair general," one who theorizes about the conduct of a war). Pioneers such as FRAZER, who did not do their own FIELDWORK, were sometimes later dismissed as "armchair anthropologists."

arranged marriage. MARRIAGE between partners who are chosen by other people, typically parents. In British DISCOURSE, often regarded as a "problem" to do with families with origins in South Asia.

art. The skill or technique required to produce aesthetically meaningful WORK using objects, spaces, and/or bodies; and the products of this work. In Western TRADITIONS, art typically encompasses literature, painting, sculpture, DANCE, DRAMA, and film. In anthropology, art is particularly the province of MATERIAL CULTURE. Art can aid understanding of a culture's

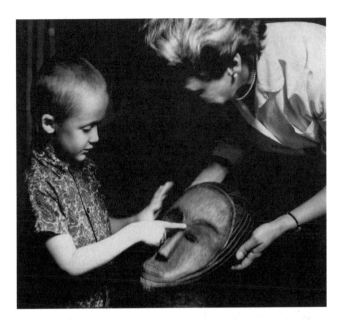

Figure 2   **Art.** A wooden mask from the Fang people of West Africa shown at an American exhibition, 1960. Photo: US Information Agency; National Anthropological Archives, Smithsonian Institution NAA INV 0600 3500.

conventions and concerns, and writers such as LEACH and LÉVI-STRAUSS have discussed its symbolic significance (see SYMBOLIC ANTHROPOLOGY). See also LITERARY ANTHROPOLOGY, SCRIMSHAW, VISUAL ANTHROPOLOGY.

Further reading: Coote & Shelton (1992); Morphy & Perkins (2006).

artefact or **artifact.** Anything produced by people, as opposed to naturally occurring: utensils, TOOLS, weapons, ART, and crafts. Often used in the context of historical or archaeological finds. From Latin, "made by skill." See also MATERIAL CULTURE, MUSEUM, TECHNOLOGY.

artisan. A skilled manual worker or craftsperson (e.g. a carpenter, ceramicist, or plumber), sometimes regarded as socially intermediate between the professional and laboring classes.

Aryan (languages). See INDO-EUROPEAN.

ASA. See ASSOCIATION OF SOCIAL ANTHROPOLOGISTS.

Asad, Talal (1932–). Saudi Arabian anthropologist, raised in Pakistan and educated at Oxford, where he gained a doctorate in 1968. As of 2011 he teaches at the City University of New York. An early critic of COLONIALISM in anthropology, he has since concentrated on issues of RELIGION and secularism in the context of notions of modernity (see MODERN), with a focus on the MIDDLE EAST. His works include *Anthropology and the colonial encounter* (ed., 1998 [1973]), *Genealogies of religion: discipline and reasons of power in Christianity and Islam* (1993), and *Formations of the secular: Christianity, Islam, modernity* (2003).

ascendant. A KINSHIP term for those *preceding* EGO: father, grandfather, great-grandfather, and so on going backwards, including COLLATERAL relatives such as uncles. Compare DESCENDANT.

ascription. See ACHIEVEMENT/ASCRIPTION.

ashram. An Indian religious retreat, associated with self-denial and austerity. A famous example was Gandhi's ashram near Nagpur. From Sanskrit, "toward religious exertion."

Asia, southeastern. See SOUTHEAST ASIA.

Asiatic mode of production. A type of economic system characterized by MARX as one in which villagers possessing no private PROPERTY co-exist with non-productive "parasitic" cities and a "despotic" STATE. The villagers have no CLASS relationship with these groups. The THEORY has been criticized for its Eurocentric (see EUROCENTRICISM) viewpoint. See also MODE OF PRODUCTION.

assimilation. A term to describe how immigrant communities adapt to, or are absorbed into, the host CULTURE. Originally conceived as a simple matter of the newcomer adopting majority ways, it is now viewed as a two-way process by which both parties are modified. See also ACCULTURATION, CULTURAL PLURALISM.

assisted reproduction. See REPRODUCTIVE TECHNOLOGIES.

association. A group of people with a common IDENTITY, purpose, or cause. Associations are usually characterized by having some degree of organization, for instance rules and set procedures, and by exclusivity (an association for WOMEN will not be open to men). They may be drawn together by a common TRADE or profession (e.g. the AMERICAN ANTHROPOLOGICAL ASSOCIATION); ETHNICITY or RACE (e.g. the National Association for the Advancement of Colored People); GENDER (e.g. the Women's Rights Project); or a combination of factors. MAINE famously observed that associations based on STATUS—usually of FAMILY—have gradually given way to those based on CONTRACT—that is, one chooses to belong to them. One popular form is the "voluntary association." See also RELATIONS OF RELATIONS.

A more abstract meaning of association (as introduced by the philosopher Locke) refers to "association of ideas" and similar meanings.

Further reading: Ardener & Burman (1995).

Association of Social Anthropologists (ASA). British organization for professional anthropologists (http://www.theasa.org), founded by EVANS-PRITCHARD and others in 1946. It publishes the conference series *ASA monographs*.

asylum seeker. A person desiring permission to live in a country to which they have no prior ties, on the basis that they would face danger or persecution at home. The term is often used in contemporary British political DISCOURSE, frequently with a pejorative or emotive implication.

asymmetrical alliance or **exchange.** MARRIAGE exchange in which indirect or GENERALIZED EXCHANGE takes place—that is, between two or more groups, as opposed to DIRECT EXCHANGE between two groups. Asymmetrical exchange is associated with HYPERGAMY and HYPOGAMY. See ALLIANCE.

atheism. Lack of belief in God, or a god. In western thought, atheism grew during the ENLIGHTENMENT; the scientific advances of the nineteenth century were further held to weigh against traditional (see TRADITION) theistic views. Twentieth-century states such as the Soviet Union entrenched MARXIST IDEOLOGY by espousing atheism. Care should be exercised in deciding whether, for example, some eastern religions are "atheist" or actually operate from a separate PARADIGM. Compare HUMANISM.

atom of kinship. LÉVI-STRAUSS' term for the simplest possible relationship structure, including not just the NUCLEAR FAMILY but also a representative of the group giving the woman in MARRIAGE, for example the maternal uncle (MB in KINSHIP terms).
Further reading: Lévi-Strauss (1977[a]).

atomism. In its social sense (as opposed to the scientific THEORY), the idea that SOCIETY is constituted of INDIVIDUALS, whose actions are more significant and worthy of scrutiny than the whole society: the opposite of HOLISM.

augury. The PRACTICE of divining the outcome of future events from observing natural phenomena, such as the behavior of birds (such a sign can itself be described as an augury). The term comes from the Romans, but the ancient Greeks, and many other cultures since, have practiced augury. See also DIVINATION.

Austin, J. L. (1911–60). See LOCUTION, PERFORMANCE, PERLOCUTION, SPEECH ACT.

Australasia. An imprecise term for Australia and some of its neighbors, usually including New Zealand and Papua New Guinea; compare OCEANIA.

Australian anthropology. A good deal of study in Australia has focused on ABORIGINAL peoples: from the early works of Baldwin Spencer and

F. J. Gillen, which helped engender an evolutionist (see EVOLUTIONISM) vision of supposedly PRIMITIVE mankind, to FIELDWORK by RADCLIFFE-BROWN, W. L. Warner (see YOLNGU), and on to work by academics such as Ian Keen and Howard Morphy. Much interest has accrued around local KINSHIP systems and religious practice. It is worth noting that many ethnologists, especially early on, were born outside Australia—for example, Spencer and Radcliffe-Brown were British; Warner was American.

As Aboriginal peoples have asserted rights in law, anthropologists have been involved as advisors; anthropology itself has not escaped critical attention (nor ethical questions for self-reflection) and writers of Aboriginal DESCENT are beginning to make themselves heard in the academy.

Further reading: *Oceania* [journal].

Austronesian. A LANGUAGE group (and the peoples who use the relevant languages) of the South Pacific—Indonesia, Malaysia, MELANESIA, New Zealand, and elsewhere (including, owing to MIGRATION, Madagascar).

authority. The POWER to have one's will or viewpoint prevail, either in terms of politics, LAW, RELIGION, or in such areas as expertise ("he is a world authority on the subject"). WEBER distinguished between several kinds of authority: traditional (see TRADITION), legal, and charismatic (see also CHARISMA, the capacity to exert personal authority). Authority may derive from SOVEREIGNTY.

autarchy. In politics, self-government without constraint from outside, or absolute rule of a STATE by a leader or faction.

autochthonous. Native to a PLACE, INDIGENOUS. From Greek, "sprung from that land." Thus, an "autochthon" was an ABORIGINAL person. The same idea can extend to PLANTS, diseases, and so on.

autoethnography. A form of ETHNOGRAPHY in which the author is a member of a particular group who is writing about that group or about themselves as part of it, or is an external anthropologist writing about their personal experience of doing research. Allied to POST-MODERNISM, autoethnography develops such concerns as REFLEXIVITY and ANTHROPOLOGY AT HOME. It has been criticized for its lack of objectivity. Autoethnography has been used in SOCIOLOGY and literature as well as anthropology.

Further reading: Reed-Danahay (1997).

auxology. In fields such as human biology and paediatrics, the study of growth and development. From Greek, "increase." See also BIOLOGICAL ANTHROPOLOGY.

avoidance relationship. A KINSHIP practice by which a family member will attempt not to meet or address another family member. Most commonly this applies between a son-in-law and mother-in-law. Often compared with the JOKING RELATIONSHIP and theorized as similarly reducing CONFLICT.

Further reading: Radcliffe-Brown (1952: chapters 4 & 5).

avunculate. A feature often associated with matrilineal (see MATRILINEALITY) societies in which the mother's brother (in KINSHIP terms, MB) exercises the parental control over her son that other groups assign to the father. The son also inherits from the MB. When the son marries, the couple may live with the uncle (AVUNCULOCAL RESIDENCE). The son/MB may also have a JOKING RELATIONSHIP.

avunculocal residence. The POST-MARITAL RESIDENCE practice of a couple living with, or close to, an uncle, usually the husband's maternal uncle (MB in RELATIONSHIP TERMINOLOGY). See also AVUNCULATE. The opposite, amitalocality, involving the paternal aunt, is little heard of.

axiom of (kinship) amity. A convention of altruistic behavior (see ALTRUISM), working in favor of one's relatives and close neighbors, in a TRADITIONAL SOCIETY.

Further reading: Fortes (1969).

ayahuasca. A hallucinogenic (see HALLUCINOGEN) DRINK made from *Banisteriopsis caapi* (or other PLANTS), sometimes known as "yagé." Widely used in healing and shamanic activities (see SHAMAN) in the Amazon and Orinoco basins.

Further reading: Luna & White (2000).

ayllu. A social and political unit among Andean peoples (see ANDES) based around KINSHIP or other factors, dating back to Inca times (circa thirteenth century onward).

ayurveda. An Indian MEDICAL SYSTEM dating back to 5000 BCE and derived from the *Vedas* (see VEDA): its aim is to restore bodily balance by means of regulated DIET, massage, aromatherapy, meditation, and medicines. From Sanskrit, "life knowledge." Compare UNANI.

Azande. See ZANDE.

B

B or Br. In RELATIONSHIP TERMINOLOGY, the abbreviation for "brother."

Bachofen, J. J. (1815–87). See MOTHER-RIGHT.

Bakhtin, M. M. (1895–1975). Influential Russian theorist whose ideas about LINGUISTICS and literature—especially the assertion that dialogue is central to communication—became popular in several fields around the time of his death. Works issued in translation include *The dialogic imagination: four essays* (1981 [Russian: 1975]) and *The Bakhtin reader* (ed. Morris, 1994). Compare DIALOGIC.

Balfour, Henry (1863–1939). British pioneer of MUSEUM ethnography. Educated at Oxford, he worked under TYLOR. He was the first curator of the Pitt Rivers Museum (from 1891 to 1939) and an officer of several national societies. His writings include *The evolution of decorative art* (1893).

band. A band SOCIETY is a relatively small foraging group, which can vary in size from around 30 to 300 people. Bands move around frequently (compare NOMAD) and are HUNTER-GATHERERS. In early anthropology the band was believed to be an evolutionary stage between the simple FAMILY unit and the TRIBE. See also HEADMAN. Modern theorists such as Julian STEWARD and Elman Service have debated the structure of the band society.

Bantu. A LANGUAGE group, and by extension those who use it, incorporating many diverse peoples of East, Central, and Southern Africa. Bantu speakers may have spread originally from the area of Cameroon; among them are many groups who have been widely studied by ethnographers, including the Bemba, Xhosa, and Zulu.

Concise Dictionary of Social and Cultural Anthropology, First Edition. Mike Morris.
© 2012 Michael Ashley Morris. Published 2012 by Blackwell Publishing Ltd.

barbarism. Rudeness, lack of culture; in nineteenth-century EVOLUTIONARY ANTHROPOLOGY (e.g. MORGAN's *Ancient society*), "barbarism" was the term given to the phase of SOCIETY that came between SAVAGERY and CIVILIZATION; it was characterized by AGRICULTURE. The term was actually first used in this way by MONTESQUIEU in the eighteenth century.

barter. A form of economic EXCHANGE in which goods or services are *directly* traded for each other, as opposed to an indirect transaction involving MONEY, or GIFT exchange (a gift implies further obligations; barter does not).

Barth, Fredrik (1928–). Norway-based social anthropologist; a major theorist in ethnic IDENTITY. Born in Leipzig, Barth was educated at Chicago (in paleontology), did archaeological fieldwork in Iraq in 1951, and then anthropological fieldwork with Iraqi Kurds (he later also visited Pakistan and Iran). He was taught at the London School of Economics by FIRTH, gained his doctorate at Cambridge, and held professorships at Bergen and Oslo between 1961 and 1985. His wife, Unni Wikan, is also an anthropologist.

  Principally celebrated for editing and introducing *Ethnic groups and boundaries* (1969, new preface 1998), a key text on ethnic IDENTITY, Barth also wrote *Political leadership among Swat Pathans* (1959), *Nomads of South Persia* (1961), and *Balinese worlds* (1993).

Further reading: Gronhaug et al. (1991).

Barthes, Roland (1915–80). French literary critic and social theorist; a central figure in SEMIOTICS and associated with STRUCTURALISM. Barthes was influenced by anthropology and in turn influenced it himself, particularly in his work on MYTH as well as on the IDEOLOGY underlying seemingly innocuous elements of everyday life, such as advertising. His publications include *Mythologies* (1957; revised English ed., 2009) and *Eléments de sémiologie* (1964; *Elements of semiology*, 1967).

base and superstructure. A concept in MARXIST thought: in the same way as the foundation of a building underlies its superstructure, the base of a society's economic system supports its INSTITUTIONS, CULTURE, and IDEOLOGY. Frequently criticized as simplistic or deterministic (see DETERMINISM). See also INFRASTRUCTURE.

Bastian, Adolf (1826–1905). See GERMAN ANTHROPOLOGY, PSYCHIC UNITY.

Batavia. The former name (1619–1949) of Jakarta, Java, the capital of Indonesia. As Batavia it was the center of operations of the colonial Dutch rulers and the Dutch East India Company ("VOC").

Bateson, Gregory (1904–80). See CYBERNETICS, EIDOS, ETHOS, MEAD [M.], PLAY, SCHISMOGENESIS.

Bateson, William (1861–1926). See GENETICS.

Baudrillard, Jean (1929–2007). French philosopher and social theorist, critic of POST-MODERNISM and SEMIOTICS. His central ideas include the notion that modern MEDIA have made SOCIETY "hyperreal," falsifying genuine social relations. His works include *La société de consommation* (1970; *The consumer society*, 1998) and *Simulacres et simulation* (1981; *Simulacra and simulation*, 1994).

Baugh, John (1949–). See VARIATION.

Beattie, John (1915–90). British social anthropologist of Africa; born Liverpool and educated at Dublin and Oxford. Having trained for the Colonial Service he was posted to Tanganyika (now Tanzania); he subsequently studied and taught anthropology at Oxford, doing further fieldwork in Uganda. He went on to hold the Chair of African Studies at Leiden. His books include *Bunyoro: an African kingdom* (1960), *Other cultures* (1964), and *The Nyoro state* (1971). He also co-edited *Studies in social anthropology: essays in memory of E. E. Evans-Pritchard* (1975).

behavioral level. An aspect of (usually) KINSHIP analysis dealing with what people *actually* do as opposed to what they may be expected to do by cultural "rules." Compare CATEGORICAL LEVEL (what cultures prefer them to do) and JURAL LEVEL (what cultures prescribe that they should do).

behaviorism. An approach in psychology (and philosophy, where it is associated with J. B. Watson) that emphasizes the analysis of a subject's behavior rather than of internal processes. Compare SYMBOLIC INTERACTIONISM.

Bemba. See BANTU.

Benedict, Ruth (1887–1948). American cultural anthropologist, a leading figure in the CULTURE AND PERSONALITY movement and associate of Margaret MEAD. Born New York City, she was educated at Vassar (in English); she also studied anthropology at the New School of Social Research, with Goldenweiser. At Columbia she studied under BOAS, taking a Ph.D. in 1923; she joined the teaching staff, eventually becoming a full professor. Her fieldwork was conducted mostly in the south-western US. Her works include *Patterns of culture* (1934), *Race: science and politics* (1940, rev. ed. 1943), and the popular classic on Japan, *The chrysanthemum and the sword* (1946.)

Further reading: Mead (2005).

Bentham, Jeremy (1748–1832). See DEEP PLAY, UTILITARIANISM.

Berber. Any of several peoples inhabiting the north coast of Africa. At various times nomadic (see NOMAD) and sedentary. Specific groups include the KABYLE and TUAREG. Studied by Pierre BOURDIEU. The term derives from Arabic (as in "Barbary"—compare BARBARISM).

berdache. In some North American Indian societies, a person (usually male) who assumes the GENDER attributes appropriate to the opposite SEX (see also TRANSVESTISM). Socially accepted as a discrete CATEGORY. A few writers have questioned the conception of the berdache recently.

Bergson, Henri (1859–1941). See *HOMO FABER*.

Béteille, André (1934–). See INDIAN ANTHROPOLOGY.

bifurcation. The process of splitting something in two. While the term is used descriptively in areas such as MATERIAL CULTURE, it also occurs notably in KINSHIP and RELATIONSHIP TERMINOLOGY, where members of the father's and mother's sides of a family may be known by *different* terms—they are bifurcated.

Bifurcate collaterals are ASCENDANTS of EGO who are COLLATERAL to each other. They are distinguished in two ways: from LINEAL (direct) relatives and from each other. Thus we find specific terms used to *separate* (lineal) father (F in KINSHIP terms) from (collateral) *father*'s brother (FB) and *mother*'s brother (MB).

Bifurcate merging, conversely, brackets together in the *same* terminological CATEGORY ascendants on one of the two sides (M or F) who are of the same SEX and distinguishes them from others (thus F=FB—that is, they are known by the same term—but F≠MB).

CROW TERMINOLOGY, IROQUOIS TERMINOLOGY, and OMAHA TERMINOLOGY all use bifurcate merging. See also SKEWING.

big man or **bigman.** A local leader in MELANESIA, in some ways similar to a CHIEF, but usually selected on the grounds of skill rather than accorded STATUS by HEREDITY. There is some debate about this distinction. SAHLINS was an early popularizer of the label, and regarded chiefs as essentially Polynesian.

Further reading: Sahlins (1963); Godelier & Strathern (1991).

bigamy. MARRIAGE to a second spouse while the first survives; usually a criminal offence in the western world, though some societies practice POLYGAMY.

bilateral. Involving two sides, as in BILATERAL DESCENT.

bilateral descent or **bilateral kinship.** A term for a KINSHIP system in which both matrilineal (see MATRILINEALITY) and patrilineal (see PATRILINEALITY) DESCENT (the father's and mother's side of the family) are considered relevant for the purposes of calculating social STATUS, rights, and so on.

bilineal descent. A rarer synomyn for DOUBLE DESCENT.

bilingualism. Ability to communicate in two LANGUAGES. Bilingualism may be of interest with regard to social issues such as the dominance of an official language and consequent withering of the alternative. This has political dimensions in countries such as Canada and Wales. "Bilingualism" may also be an official political policy instituted in order to counter such language erosion.

Further reading: Heller (2007).

bilocal. Being in two places. In RELATIONSHIP TERMINOLOGY, an occasional synonym for ambilocal (see AMBILOCALITY).

binary opposition. The division of experience into contrasted pairs of concepts (e.g. good and bad, RIGHT AND LEFT) goes back at least as far as Aristotle (see DUALISM). In structural anthropology (see STRUCTURALISM) it is an analytical device used by LÉVI-STRAUSS as a clue to the workings of MYTH and wider CULTURE. Oppositions such as edible/inedible, raw/cooked, and so on are held to point to deeper divisions or categorizations (nature/culture, etc). Compare PURITY.

bioethics. The field of ethical considerations arising from biological science, as in the application of new techniques (e.g. REPRODUCTIVE TECHNOLOGIES, cloning, human embryo research). Studied under this name since the late 1960s, though of course such considerations go back to classical times in various forms. See also ETHICS.

Further reading: Bosk (2008).

bioanthropology. Synonym for BIOLOGICAL ANTHROPOLOGY.

biological analogy. Synonym for ORGANIC ANALOGY.

biological anthropology. The British term for the study of humans and other ANIMALS, usually PRIMATES, from an evolutionary viewpoint. "Bioanthropology," as it is also called, encompasses such specialisms as human evolution, primatology, human GENETICS, HUMAN ECOLOGY, human growth, DEMOGRAPHY, MORPHOLOGY, and PALEONTOLOGY. Studies of EVOLUTION and primatology may also be termed PHYSICAL ANTHROPOLOGY. Confusingly, this is the term sometimes used in American institutions for the *whole* field of biological anthropology. See also the emerging field of EVOLUTIONARY ANTHROPOLOGY.

Further reading: Boyden (1987).

biomedicine. Medicine taking into account aspects of biological sciences; specifically used in MEDICAL ANTHROPOLOGY as a non-judgmental way of referring to conventional western medicine.

Further reading: Lock & Nguyen (2010).

biopolitics. FOUCAULT's term for politics worked on the BODY, stemming from a shift in the way POWER operates in the modern era. Instead of rulers having the simple ability to take life (from individuals or groups), they exercise administrative control over its maintenance. This "biopower" has been theorized by several writers to include torture, biomedical interventions, and public health initiatives, and the paraphernalia of "security" measures.

Further reading: Foucault (1990: 140).

biotechnology. The use of living organisms in the creation of FOOD and DRINK, medicines, and REPRODUCTIVE TECHNOLOGIES, and in other industries. Anthropologists, who may be au fait with traditional methods of production using micro-organisms (e.g. in cheese and yoghurt) may have to consider newer forms of genetic engineering and their cultural and psychological impact. Much attention has been given recently to the debates on the use of genetically modified ("GM") crops.

Further reading: Rabinow (1996); Bamford (2007).

birth. Anthropological interest in human childbirth has uncovered a variety of social PRACTICES, and a number of aspects demanding attention, from the purely technical to personal and GENDER politics. In recent years traditional birth methods have gained support over the assumption that western procedures are automatically best. Many recent studies focus on new REPRODUCTIVE TECHNOLOGIES.

Further reading: Jordan (1983); Davis-Floyd & Sargent (1997).

birth control. See CONTRACEPTION.

black. As used to denote ETHNICITY, black or Black became the generally acceptable term for dark-skinned people, and to discuss issues concerning them ("Black politics in the new era") from the later twentieth century. Initially sometimes implying militancy—as in Black Power—it gradually passed into more neutral use. Compare COLORED, NEGRO.

Further reading: Alexander (1996).

black economy. See INFORMAL ECONOMY.

Bloch, Maurice (1939–). Cognitive anthropologist born in France and educated at Cambridge; professor of anthropology at the London School of Economics from 1984 to 2005. His many writings (often based on FIELD-WORK in Madagascar) include *Marxism and anthropology* (1983) and *How we think they think* (1998). Bloch helped to advance MARXIST theory in Britain and has studied RITUAL extensively. See also ORATORY.

blood brotherhood. See BLOOD COVENANT.

blood feud. A type of FEUD based on the obligation to avenge murdered or wronged kin by killing or physically chastising the wrongdoer. See also VENDETTA, a prolonged feud.

blood covenant or **pact.** An agreement made between two or more men (or occasionally with WOMEN) involving the mingling of blood from their bodies (see BODY), making them "blood brothers." A surrogate (such the blood of an ANIMAL, or FOOD) may replace actual blood. Most anthropological case studies have focused on African examples.

Further reading: Evans-Pritchard (1962); Tegnaeus (1952).

Boas, Franz (1858–1942). German-born anthropologist, FIELDWORK pioneer, and social activist. A central figure in twentieth-century American CULTURAL ANTHROPOLOGY, he took the discipline away from the untested theorizing of

Figure 3   Boas. Franz Boas poses for a figure in an exhibition showing a Kwakiutl ceremony, c. 1895. National Anthropological Archives, Smithsonian Institution, negative MNH 8300.

ARMCHAIR ANTHROPOLOGY and from biological DETERMINISM toward an understanding of the complexity of CULTURES.

Born in Minden, Westphalia, Boas obtained a doctorate in physics at Kiel in 1881 and secured a geography position at Berlin. After initial field research on Inuit culture in Baffin Land from 1883 to 1884, he made a total of twelve field trips to the north-west Pacific coast (studying AMERICAN INDIANS) from 1886 onward. He took up residence in the US from 1887, teaching at Clark University; he was later attached to the AMERICAN MUSEUM OF NATURAL HISTORY (1895 and 1901–5). Boas also taught at Columbia, becoming a professor from 1899 to 1936, and he was President of the AMERICAN ANTHROPOLOGICAL ASSOCIATION (1907). His many celebrated students included KROEBER, SAPIR, BENEDICT, and Margaret MEAD. Among his works are *The social organization and the secret societies of the Kwakiutl Indians* (1897), *The mind of primitive man* (1911), *Anthropology & modern life* (2004 [1932]), and *Race, language and culture*, 1940.

Further reading: Boas (1974); Stocking (1982); Cole (1999).

bodhisattva. See BUDDHISM, LAMA.

body. At least since MAUSS' work on "body techniques," sociologists and anthropologists have understood that the body is a social as well as a physical entity. Increasingly, they have departed from the classic philosophy of Descartes—Cartesian DUALISM—to see the individual not as a MIND and a body yoked together but as a single *embodied* organism. The body is of general interest to medical and physical anthropologists; in its specifically social guise it is the focus of work on the symbolism of RIGHT AND LEFT, understandings of body and SOCIETY (or the cosmos) as images of each other, and (following FOUCAULT) the control or punishment of the body by AUTHORITY. Anthropologists have long understood the body as a site for ART, such as RITUAL markings, TATTOOS, and incisions.

Feminist critics have also examined narratives of the female body: its construction as "weak" and "delicate," or prone to hysteria; societal pressures to shape and subjugate it ("body image"); and so on.

See also AFFECT, DEATH, FLAGELLATION, MENSTRUATION, OBESITY, PURITY.

Further reading: Mauss (2006); Turner (2008); Mascia-Lees (2011).

Bohannan, Paul (1920–2007). See SPHERES OF EXCHANGE.

border. The line dividing countries, states, or regions. Borders are symbolically important to notions of IDENTITY and may become locations for disputes involving MIGRATION or outright WAR. Compare FRONTIER.

Further reading: Donnan & Wilson (1999).

botany. See ETHNOBOTANY, TAXONOMY.

Botswana. See PROTECTORATE, SCHAPERA.

Bourdieu, Pierre (1930–2002). French sociologist and anthropologist, influential both in the academy and, latterly, with the wider French public. He was born in Denguin, Pyrenees, and educated at the École Normale Supérieure in Paris. Bourdieu undertook fieldwork in Kabylia, Algeria, from 1958 to 1964; having worked at EHESS, he held the Chair of Sociology, Collège de France, from 1981. His large written legacy includes *Sociologie de l'Algérie* (1958; *The Algerians*, 1962), *Esquisse d'une théorie de la pratique* (1972; *Outline of a theory of practice*, 1977), *Le sens pratique* (1980; *The logic of practice*, 1990), and *La misère du monde* (ed., 1993; *The weight of the world*, 1999). See also CULTURAL CAPITAL, DOXA, FIELD THEORY, HABITUS, PRACTICE THEORY, REPRODUCTION, SYMBOLIC CAPITAL, SYMBOLIC VIOLENCE, TASTE.

Further reading: Wacquant (2003).

bourgeoisie. See CLASS.

Br. See B.

brain. The organ in the human skull (or its equivalent in certain other animals) that controls many of the BODY's functions and is the seat of thought. Of particular interest in BIOLOGICAL ANTHROPOLOGY, COGNITIVE ANTHROPOLOGY, and MEDICAL ANTHROPOLOGY. See also COGNITION, MIND, NEUROANTHROPOLOGY (the anthropological study of the nervous system).

Further reading: Reyna (2002).

bricolage. A concept developed by LÉVI-STRAUSS in *The savage mind*. In the same way that a *bricoleur*—a kind of handyman—improvises from materials at hand, so cultures adapt existing SYMBOLS and other elements to make "new" forms.

Further reading: Lévi-Strauss (1966).

bride capture. A marital CUSTOM in which the bride is supposedly abducted by the groom or his allies from her family. Symbolic "capture" is sometimes practiced in contemporary cultures, but McLennan went further and regarded it as a survival of actual capture in past societies.

Further reading: McLennan (1865); Barnes (1999).

brideprice or bridewealth. A form of MARRIAGE payment in which the groom's family transfers MONEY, PROPERTY, and/or labor ("brideservice") to the bride's family, in compensation for her labor. Although some view the PRACTICE (and term) as retrograde, it is not simply a kind of purchase but carries symbolic significance; for example, creating ties between the participating families and facilitating further ties. Some would argue that "price" is misleading for this reason, and "bridewealth" is now the more usual term. Bridewealth is common in some areas of Africa, Asia, the Pacific, and Americas. Compare DOWRY.

Further reading: Goody & Tambiah (1973).

British anthropology. The bulk of the British TRADITION can be characterized as SOCIAL ANTHROPOLOGY, at least until the later twentieth century. It can be distinguished from the CULTURAL ANTHROPOLOGY practiced in the US by a narrower focus on social institutions and organization.

The ROYAL ANTHROPOLOGICAL INSTITUTE has represented British practitioners since the 1870s; university departments began to appear (e.g. Oxford, Cambridge, Liverpool) a few years later. British social anthropology is associated historically with EVOLUTIONISM, DIFFUSIONISM, and FUNCTION-ALISM. It also has ties to the British Empire, for instance in the interconnection between anthropology and colonial administration (hence a particular concern with parts of Africa, India, and so on—see COLONIALISM).

Under the influence of STRUCTURALISM and MARXISM (partly influences from France, echoing the original sociological influence of DURKHEIM and his school), later British scholars moved further from these roots, and the international nature of anthropological DISCOURSE tends in any case to blur distinctions nowadays. The British tradition, despite criticism from American anthropologists (for example) and indubitable periods of parochialism, has produced some of the central figures of world anthropology—among them J. G. FRAZER, TYLOR, EVANS-PRITCHARD, RADCLIFFE-BROWN, Raymond FIRTH (a Commonwealth anthropologist), and Edmund LEACH. Practitioners such as MALINOWSKI adopted Britain as their base for significant periods. See also ASSOCIATION OF SOCIAL ANTHROPOLOGISTS.

Further reading: Urry (1993); Goody (1995); Kuper (1996).

broker. An INDIVIDUAL who acts as an intermediary between parties trying to reach an agreement. In anthropology, brokers may be viewed as social agents (see AGENCY). Robert Paine compared their role to that of patrons (see PATRON–CLIENT RELATIONSHIP). The term "culture broker" or "cultural broker" specifically refers to the member of an INDIGENOUS group who acts as a go-between or interpreter with other cultures—for instance, NATIVE AMERICANS who dealt with settlers.

Further reading: Paine (1971).

Bromlei, I. V. (Yu. Bromley; 1921–90). See RUSSIAN ANTHROPOLOGY.

Buddhism. The belief system of followers of the Buddha ("enlightened," from Sanskrit), who was active in Northern India in the fifth century BCE. Buddhism normally entails a belief in KARMA and the practice of meditation, along with actions demonstrating personal morality and wisdom, in order that one may break the cycle of REINCARNATION and achieve NIRVANA (compare HINDUISM). The two main divisions are Theravada Buddhism, the older and more conservative form, and Mahayana Buddhism, which is more liberal. The so-called "Pali [language] canon" is of central value to the former; the latter recognizes more TEXTS and emphasizes *bodhisattvas*, the saintly figures who ACT as examples. Writers such as Gombrich have made major studies of Theravada Buddhism, which is found in Thailand, Burma, and Sri Lanka; later anthropologists such as David Gellner have shifted the focus to Mahayana strains in Nepal, Tibet, China, and Japan.

Further reading: Gellner (2001); Gombrich (2006); Prebish & Keown (2010).

buildings. See ARCHITECTURE.

bull-roarer. A sound-making device usually composed of a small piece of wood attached to a thong that is then swung to produce a whirring effect. Associated with RITUAL uses among the ABORIGINAL peoples of Australia.

Burckhardt, J. L. (John Lewis, pseudonym of Johann Ludwig; 1784–1817). Swiss explorer, born Lausanne. With British support he travelled in North Africa, often disguised as a MUSLIM; he was the first European to visit the archaeological site at Petra, to journey to Mecca, and to see the Egyptian temple at Abu Sunbul ("Abu Simbel"). His works include *Travels in Arabia* (1829) and *Notes on the Bedouins and Wahábys* (1830).

Bureau of American Ethnology. A pioneering US organization, established by Congress in 1879. It was responsible for early fieldwork among NATIVE AMERICANS and for several important publications, for example *Contributions to North American ethnology*. In 1965 it was merged into what is now the Department of Anthropology, National Museum of Natural History, part of the SMITHSONIAN INSTITUTION.

bushman. See SAN.

C

C or Ch. In RELATIONSHIP TERMINOLOGY, an abbreviation for "child."

cadre. In military and organizational terms, the permanent staff of a regiment. In Communist systems, it is applied to cells of workers (sometimes INDIVIDUALS), for example office-holders in recent Chinese SOCIETY. Originally derived from Latin, "quadrum" ("square").

caliph. In the Islamic (see ISLAM) TRADITION, a civil and religious ruler. The title was first used by Abu Bakr, who succeeded Muhammad. It derives from Arabic, "successor." See also SUNNI.

Callon, Michel (1945–). See ACTOR/NETWORK THEORY.

candomblé. An Afro-Brazilian urban RELIGION based on African PRACTICES but incorporating elements of CATHOLICISM and spiritualism.

Further reading: Matory (2005).

cannibalism. The eating of human flesh, not only as FOOD but for RITUAL or magical (see MAGIC) ends. From the old Spanish, *Cannibales* (derived from CARIB). Heavily TABOO in many societies. Arens suggests that reports of cannibalism are often based on misapprehensions and prejudice, and that its incidence has been greatly overstated.

Further reading: Arens (1979); Obeyesekere (2005).

cant. Of language: the jargon of a particular group, often to enforce secrecy among, for instance, beggars or thieves.

Concise Dictionary of Social and Cultural Anthropology, First Edition. Mike Morris.
© 2012 Michael Ashley Morris. Published 2012 by Blackwell Publishing Ltd.

capitalism. An economic system that emerged in Europe in relatively recent times, preceding the Industrial Revolution. It is characterized by the operation of a free MARKET, private ownership of enterprises, and relations of EXCHANGE in which profit is a key motive.

In the SOCIAL SCIENCES, the workings of capital have been extensively analyzed by MARX, for whom the social relations it created were of great importance—for example, the worker has to sell their labor as a COMMODITY to an employer. WEBER saw a desire for profit as less specific to capitalism and argued that a spirit of RATIONALISM was a key factor. Anthropologists in the more radical climate of the later twentieth century were sometimes swayed by MARXIST approaches and also by the work of POLANYI. Much work recently has been concerned not with ECONOMIC ANTHROPOLOGY but with the consequences that ensue when a SOCIETY comes to capitalism after using other systems (often, following the collapse of STATE-run SOCIALISM); other topics include the rise of corporations, GLOBALIZATION, and economic TRANSNATIONALISM.

Further reading: Polanyi (2001); Hann & Hart (2009).

cargo cult. A form of MILLENARIANISM—belief in a future golden age— usually in MELANESIA, characterized by a belief that goods will come to one via RITUAL. It sprang up in the late nineteenth century as a response to contact with affluent colonialists, and sometimes involves belief in the return of one's ANCESTORS. An example is the JOHN FRUM MOVEMENT.

Further reading: Lawrence (1971); Worsley (1968).

cargo system. A MAYA religious INSTITUTION involving rotating offices ("cargos") held by the men of an area temporarily; they then have the economic duty to pay for the celebration of Catholic SAINTS. The expense raises their STATUS but moderates wealth overall.

Further reading: Cancian (1965).

Carib. The Caribs were native peoples of Northern South America, after whom the Caribbean is named. Following contact with Spanish explorers, their name became linked with CANNIBALISM.

Caribbean. The region of the tropical sea, part of the Atlantic Ocean, that is bounded by the Caribbean islands, Central America, and the northern edge of South America. See CARIB, HANNERZ, KITLV, LATIN AMERICA, MATRIFOCALITY, NEGRITUDE, PIROGUE, PLURAL SOCIETY, VOODOO.

carnival. A period of festivity often taking place immediately before Lent (in Roman Catholic CHRISTIANITY) marked by feasting, celebration, and the inversion of social order. Usually centered on Mardi Gras ("Fat Tuesday," or Shrove Tuesday), it can be viewed as a social RITUAL with political overtones.

Famous carnivals include those in Rio de Janeiro and Notting Hill, London. The name is derived from Latin, "putting away flesh." Compare FIESTA. See also TRANSVESTISM.

Further reading: Cohen (1993).

carrying capacity. In ECOLOGY, the maximum population (human, ANIMAL, or plant) that can be borne sustainably, given the resources of a particular area.

case study. A method in SOCIAL SCIENCES that focuses on a single example of a phenomenon (or compares a small number of examples). Good for the detailed assessment of a subject and for testing hypotheses and approaches that can later be applied to larger groups. A disadvantage is that results may not be generalizable.

cash crops. Agricultural products grown for sale to outsiders, rather than for SUBSISTENCE. Associated particularly with countries that were once colonized, and that may be trying to service debts; crops include coffee, sugar, cotton, and flowers.

cassava. See MANIOC.

Cassirer, Ernst (1874–1945). See PHILOSOPHICAL ANTHROPOLOGY.

Castaneda, Carlos (1931?–98). South American cultural anthropologist and popular author, about whom biographical details are uncertain (place and exact date of birth, for example—he may have been born in São Paulo or Cajamarca, Peru). Educated at the University of California, Los Angeles, he found popular success with countercultural writings such as *The teachings of Don Juan: a Yaqui way of knowledge* (1968), which proved controversial when questions were raised as to whether they were anthropology or works of fiction.

caste. The hereditary and hierarchical (see HIERARCHY) division of SOCIETY in (usually) India, associated there with HINDUISM. Members of a caste share the same profession and STATUS and traditionally avoid physical contact with members of other castes. Subdivisions of castes ("jatis") are linked to particular obligations and rights (the "jajmani" system). Anthropologists disagree on whether caste should be read in ways similar to SOCIAL STRUCTURES outside India or as something unique. The nature of jajmani conventions has also been disputed. The word "caste" derives from Spanish and Portuguese, *casta* ("race").

Further reading: Dumont (1980); Béteille (1996).

categorical level. An aspect of (usually) KINSHIP dealing with implicit INDIGENOUS CLASSIFICATION as it is shown by how RELATIONSHIP TERMINOLOGY is used. The categorical level implies what cultures prefer people to do; compare BEHAVIORAL LEVEL (which covers what they actually do) and JURAL LEVEL (what cultures prescribe that they should do).

category. A division within a system of CLASSIFICATION. The term derives from the Greek for "assertion" and its underlying implications have been a philosophical area of debate since Aristotle; Kant notably investigated it. Anthropologists have often studied INDIGENOUS categories as a key to FOLK CLASSIFICATION.

Catholicism. Broadly the oldest and most traditional branch of CHRISTIAN-ITY, although "protestant" churches sometimes incorporate what appears to be Catholic doctrine ("Catholic," from Greek, simply means "universal"). Very influential in many places (notably, for instance, LATIN AMERICA); Catholic anthropologists have included DOUGLAS and EVANS-PRITCHARD (see also MISSIONARY). See also CANDOMBLÉ, CARGO SYSTEM, CARNIVAL, DRINK, EXORCISM, FICTIVE KINSHIP, SAINT, SODALITY.

Caton, Steven C. (1950–). See POETICS.

cattle complex. A term invented by Herskovits in a 1926 thesis. It refers to a set of beliefs among certain pastoral peoples (see PASTORALISM) according to which they valued cattle as social, rather than economic, goods; refrained from killing them except at certain ceremonies; and became strongly attached to them. Subsequent writers have shown that these PRACTICES have rational bases, and that there is a wide array of meaning to be derived from the study of cattle ownership. See also ANIMAL.

Further reading: Herskovits (1926); Galaty & Bonte (1991).

celebrations. See CARNIVAL, *FIESTA*, RITUAL.

central place theory. A geographical THEORY advanced by Walter Christaller concerning the way SETTLEMENTS tend to be distributed in regular patterns and the way in which they are influenced by economic considerations (e.g. by people's requirement to travel to MARKETS). Each "central PLACE" is associated with its surrounding area, and size hierarchies are evident. Christaller's work influenced (for example) notions of SPACE.

Further reading: Christaller (1966).

centralized systems. Arrangements for controlling assets, either tangible or otherwise (e.g. goods, information), within complex societies (see COMPLEX SOCIETY). The control of such assets generates political POWER.

center (or core) and periphery. A sociological term with two related meanings: E. Shils used it in the 1970s to discuss the distribution of privileges between social groups, and their connection. Perhaps more significantly it was used earlier by MARXIST writers in a similar way to that finally elaborated by Wallerstein in WORLD-SYSTEM theory, delineating an opposition between a dominant (typically) capitalist group of industrialized nations (core) and weaker countries, that provide them with labor and raw materials (periphery).

Centre for Contemporary Cultural Studies, University of Birmingham, UK. See CLASS, CULTURAL STUDIES.

Centre national de la recherche scientifique. See CNRS.

ceremonial exchange. A synonym for gift EXCHANGE. See GIFT.

Césaire, Aimé (1913–2008). See NEGRITUDE.

Ch. See C.

Chagnon, Napoleon (1938–). American anthropologist famous for numerous studies of the YANOMAMI; emeritus professor, University of California at Santa Barbara. Chagnon was accused of helping to exacerbate an outbreak of measles among the Yanomami by Patrick Tierney in *Darkness in El Dorado* (2000); he was criticized by his peers but later partially exonerated. Books include *Yanomamö* (5th ed. 1997) and the co-edited *Adaptation and human behaviour* (2000).

chaos theory. See COMPLEXITY THEORY.

charisma. In SOCIOLOGY, a POWER of personal AUTHORITY such as to allow one to lead people or inspire devotion. The term derives originally from THEOLOGY but was adapted by WEBER in *Wirtschaft und Gesellschaft* (*Economy and society*, 1922). Authority derives from the volition of the leader's followers, rather than from legal STATUS or TRADITION. The process by which charismatic authority may later acquire stability is called ROUTINIZATION. Anthropologists tend to focus on the social consequences of charismatic movements, while psychologists take a more personal approach.

Further reading: Weber (2009).

Chayanov slope, Chayanov's rule. The early-twentieth-century theories of the Soviet writer Alexander Chaianov (or Chayanov) regarding PEASANT economies were taken up by SAHLINS, who formulated "Chayanov's rule" ("the greater the working capacity of the household, the less its members WORK") in studying the DOMESTIC MODE OF PRODUCTION. A "Chayanov slope" is a line drawn on a graph demonstrating the labor intensity required to meet the differing needs of household consumers. See also RUSSIAN ANTHROPOLOGY.

Further reading: Sahlins (2004).

Chicago School. Several separate groups at the University of Chicago have been known as the "Chicago School." Apart from a notable anthropology department, Chicago has been associated with the urban SOCIOLOGY of Robert Park and Louis Wirth in the 1930s (see also PLACE, URBANISM) and, most generally, the free-market economics of Milton Friedman (late twentieth century).

chief. Leader of a chiefdom, a fairly centralized SOCIETY. The chief acts as a focus of POWER, controlling economic and political activity (e.g. waging WAR) over a relatively wide area. Chiefs usually also claim AUTHORITY. Power is often hereditary. Contrast BIG MAN (SAHLINS held that big men were essentially Melanesian, chiefs Polynesian).

childbirth. See BIRTH.

childhood. The period between infancy and puberty. It has been argued that western notions of childhood as a discrete entity emerged during the eighteenth century with the rise of private schooling outside the home. Later, a sentimental view of children led to attempts to shield them from adult-oriented life, for instance by improving their working conditions in industry.

In anthropology, the major pioneer of a non-homogenous approach to childhood—one that recognized the variables produced by CULTURE—was Margaret MEAD, whose popular works on young people in Samoa and New Guinea advanced the relativist agenda of the CULTURE AND PERSONALITY school. Among those who followed, notably, was the American sociologist and psychologist John W. M. Whiting with research such as the Six Cultures project.

As studies of attitudes toward childhood (both among adults and among children themselves) in separate cultures grew in number and sophistication, questions emerged about the previously dominant conception of the child's experience. Instead of being viewed as passive recipients of adult-imposed SOCIALIZATION, children were studied on their own terms, their WORLDVIEW given prominence. They came to be seen as possessing HUMAN RIGHTS, which might be compromised by child abuse, EXPLOITATION, and POVERTY.

Compare BIRTH, YOUTH and see also ADOPTION, EDUCATION, INCEST, INFANTICIDE, TRAFFICKING.

Further reading: Mead (1930); Whiting (2006); Montgomery (2009).

Chinese anthropology. Early Chinese anthropologists were relatively open to European and American influences. As in RUSSIAN ANTHROPOLOGY, they developed an abiding interest in local MINORITY CULTURES. A few are widely known outside China—e.g. Fei Xiaotong and Francis L. K. Hsu. Following the establishment of the communist (see COMMUNISM) People's Republic under Mao Zedong in 1949, conditions became difficult for anthropologists, who were obliged to flee or "rebrand" themselves. Official interest in minorities increased; conversely, foreign anthropologists were obliged to work on expatriate Chinese groups. China nevertheless remained an area of interest to a number of anthropologists, for example Maurice Freedman. James L. Watson and Frank Dikötter are among more recent authors to investigate Chinese society.

Following Mao's death in 1976, conditions improved. As with post-communist Eastern Europe, there is a good deal of interest in the issues thrown up by China's ambiguous position in the twenty-first century.

Further reading: Guldin (1994).

Chomsky, Noam (1928–). American linguist, philosopher, and polemicist, born in Philadelphia. He gained his doctorate at the University of Pennsylvania in 1955, thereafter working at the Massachusetts Institute of Technology. He is primarily renowned for developing TRANSFORMATIONAL-GENERATIVE GRAMMAR and is the author of many influential works including *Syntactic structures* (1957; 2nd ed., 2002) and *Aspects of the theory of syntax* (1969). He has been a persistent critic of US politics and MEDIA. See http://www.chomsky.info.

choreometry. A method for recording and studying DANCE.

Christaller, Walter (1893–1969). See CENTRAL PLACE THEORY.

Christianity. A world RELIGION centered on the divinity of Jesus Christ (d. circa 29 CE). Anthropology developed in European and American societies, which largely took a Christian understanding of the world as a given; thus, Christianity can be discerned at the root of some of the discipline's (earlier) assumptions.

While it has attracted the attention of sociologists such as WEBER, Christianity is mostly of interest to ethnographers where it intersects with local PRACTICES and beliefs, for instance in a MISSIONARY context (see e.g. SYNCRETISM). Essentially Western religious TRADITIONS (derived from roots in the MIDDLE EAST) have adapted to INDIGENOUS concerns as Christianity has been taken abroad in Africa, Asia, and elsewhere. Other issues that have attracted investigation include Christian RITUALS, PILGRIMAGE, and, latterly, the impact of Christian FUNDAMENTALISM in the United States. See also CATHOLICISM.

Further reading: Comaroff (1985); James & Johnson (1988); Hefner (1993).

Cicero, Marcus Tullius (106–43 BCE). See ORATORY.

cinema vérité. See ROUCH.

circulating connubium. "Connubium" derives from the Latin for "CO-MARRIAGE." Circulating connubium is a system of marriage EXCHANGE identified by Dutch experts and associated with SOUTHEAST ASIA, in which women circulate by GENERALIZED EXCHANGE, passing in one direction only between groups, rather than directly between two groups exclusively. It has been studied by scholars of the region such as LEACH and NEEDHAM.

circumcision. In several groups (e.g. Jews, Muslims), male circumcision (removal of the foreskin) is a religious requirement; other groups (e.g. ABORIGINAL Australians) may cut other parts of the penis as a RITE OF PASSAGE. Female "circumcision" (most common in Northeast Africa) varies from removal of the clitoral prepuce to INFIBULATION. Although there are cultural explanations for such interventions, they can have serious health consequences, and there is growing resistance to them.

civil society. A term commonly used in eighteenth-century philosophy and political THEORY to distinguish the way of life of western nations, in opposition to "barbarous" OTHERS. Used by MARX and GRAMSCI to describe a sphere that is separate from the apparatus of the STATE; the term has been taken up again to describe the alternative to state control in post-communist societies.

civilization. A highly developed phase of SOCIETY. In nineteenth-century EVOLUTIONARY ANTHROPOLOGY, the ultimate destination for societies that had evolved from SAVAGERY and BARBARISM. Civilization might be recognized by such features as the use of IRRIGATION, writing, or complex structures. Peoples in different stages of this posited DEVELOPMENT might be studied for clues as to how civilizations arose. See also CULTURE.

cladistics. Cladistic TAXONOMY of organisms is based on the idea of *clades*—groups whose members share characteristics derived from a common ancestor. From Greek, "branch."

clan. A UNILINEAL KINSHIP group of people claiming common ancestry and heritage; similar to TRIBE. The assumed FAMILY connections in a clan are usually unclear or mythical; compare LINEAGE (in which members trace themselves to a specific ANCESTOR). Clans are often made up of a number of smaller groups; a larger group of clans may be called a PHRATRY.

"Clan" is commonly used to describe family groups in such cultures as those of the HIGHLANDs of Scotland. See also SIB and GENS for usage.

clash of civilizations. An idea deriving from a book (originally an article) by Huntington suggesting that *cultural* differences are key to understanding political discord; the THEORY has been controversial.

Further reading: Huntington (1996); Besteman & Gusterson (2005).

class. Apart from related meanings (e.g. in ANIMAL or plant CLASSIFICATION), "class" is commonly used to refer to the ordering of a SOCIETY by rank, wealth, and POWER. In the nineteenth century, MARX made a basic distinction between PROPERTY owners and proletariat, which was further elaborated by WEBER to encompass administrators and petite bourgeoisie. For a long time in British SOCIETY the upshot of such thought has been a basic assumption that one is either upper (aristocratic, rich, and/or landed), middle (educated, "comfortable" financially), or working class. American sociologists have sometimes, by contrast, delineated a "classless" structure in the US, where traditional factors are less important than other signs of STATUS. More recently, writers have analyzed the growing complexity of employment relations, and how they blur class dynamics.

Anthropologists, especially Marxists, have sometimes struggled to impose a western template for class on regions without a classic industrial-relations framework (e.g. in Africa). They have had some success in charting the rise of new bourgeois formations. See also the wider (less narrowly political) concepts of STRATIFICATION, ELITE, INEQUALITY. A halfway point between anthropological and sociological views of class might be found in some of the work of the CCCS at Birmingham, UK, and other proponents of CULTURAL STUDIES.

Further reading: Durrenberger & Erem (2005); Brosius (2010).

classification. The arrangement of things or concepts into categories, organized by common characteristics. Synonymous with TAXONOMY. Anthropologists, following the lead of DURKHEIM and MAUSS, have studied classification in many areas, including such "universal" fields as COLOR TERMS and RELATIONSHIP TERMINOLOGY. The work of Brent Berlin encompasses notable examples (see also FOLK CLASSIFICATION). Occasionally social scientists have encountered problems (for instance regarding KINSHIP) when they have adhered to their own classifications too rigidly; in practice classification is best seen as a tool to aid comprehension rather than as fixed and solid. See also DUAL CLASSIFICATION, FAMILY RESEMBLANCES, POLYTHETIC CLASSIFICATION, PROTOTYPE THEORY.

Further reading: Durkheim & Mauss (1969); Ellen (1993).

classificatory cross-cousin. A relative who is classed by the same term as a CROSS-COUSIN. The classificatory cross-cousin may be a more distant relative. This convention is important for studies of ALLIANCE, since the classificatory cross-cousin is thus considered marriageable. See also SISTER'S DAUGHTER'S MARRIAGE.

classificatory kinship. Early anthropologists such as MORGAN realized that in some relationship systems LINEAL and COLLATERAL KIN (in other words, both direct and indirect relatives) are grouped together under common terms. Morgan contrasted such "classificatory" kin terms with DESCRIPTIVE

KINSHIP terms, which distinguish between such relatives. See also GROUP MARRIAGE.

Further reading: Morgan (1997).

client. See PATRON–CLIENT RELATIONSHIP.

climatic determinism. A type of DETERMINISM stressing the effect of climate on human achievement, associated particularly with Ellsworth Huntington (early twentieth century).

clinically applied anthropology. See MEDICAL ANTHROPOLOGY.

closed system/open system. A system is closed when it is complete in itself, impervious to externals, and open when it is incomplete or modifiable. The terms can be used in hard sciences or computing in a fairly literal way, and in several fields in a more metaphorical sense ("his beliefs are very fixed, and may be seen as a closed system").

cloth. See TEXTILES.

clothing. One aspect of MATERIAL CULTURE: anthropologists have studied the significance of clothing in RITUAL, its symbolism, how designs express IDENTITY (as in SUBCULTURES), or how designs follow the dictates of fashion. The "exotic" dress of some cultures is a key indicator of their otherness in the western imagination, where it is usually shorn of precisely the meanings that give it resonance to its wearers. Choice of dress may be ethnically sensitive, as when a person operates between two cultures and is faced with deciding between the "uniform" of one or the other. In recent years issues around Islamic dress have been notable in western social DISCOURSE. Arguments about "appropriate" dress have long been a staple of GENDER relations, particularly assumptions about women's ETHICS (compare HONOR). See also TEXTILES.

Further reading: Banerjee & Miller (2003); Bowen (2007); Eicher et al. (2008).

CM. See CULTURAL MATERIALISM.

CMA. See CRITICAL MEDICAL ANTHROPOLOGY.

CNRS (Centre National de la Recherche Scientifique). A large French GOVERNMENT-run organization (http://www.cnrs.fr/index.php) that conducts research in areas including anthropology. See also FRENCH ANTHROPOLOGY.

code. A set of SIGNS operating within stated or implicit rules by which a CULTURE communicates meaning. A code can take many forms, from the CLOTHING worn by a group or individual (perhaps conforming to an explicit "dress code," violation of which has consequences), to particular gestures or bodily comportment, or (most especially) LANGUAGE.

Obviously many languages have formal rules, which can be taught, but most speakers also acquire a sense of the TONE and choice of words that are appropriate to certain situations. In other words, they gradually understand CODE-SWITCHING.

The work of the Russian theorist Vladimir Propp has been an influence on anthropology. He suggested that NARRATIVE codes operated in folk tales: elements of character (compare ARCHETYPE) and incident were recurrent and even interchangeable between stories, serving as a code by which the audience understood them. See also DIGLOSSIA.

Further reading: Propp (1968).

code-switching. In LINGUISTICS, the ACT of changing one's LANGUAGE style (CODE) according to audience: for example, to another language, or another DIALECT, or a different level of formality. Compare BILINGUALISM, DIGLOSSIA.

cognate. Cognate entities are those that are related: two particular meanings are relevant. Humans referred to as cognates are CONSANGUINE (blood) relatives, those of common DESCENT or FILIATION. This may imply relation on the mother's side (ENATE, UTERINE) rather than the father's (agnate, see AGNATIC). In LINGUISTICS, LANGUAGES or words deriving from a common source are cognate. See also GLOTTOCHRONOLOGY, LEXICOSTATISTICS. The term comes from the Latin for "born together."

cognatic. Having relationship through a common ANCESTOR; as in COGNATE. Relationship on the father's side of a family is termed AGNATIC; relationship through the mother's side is ENATE or UTERINE.

cognition. The action or faculty of knowing; the processes involved in dealing with information, including PERCEPTION, awareness, judgment. Cognition, which relates closely to how we acquire and understand our own CULTURE, is in the purview of both anthropology and psychology.

cognitive anthropology. The ethnological study of the workings of the MIND: particularly how different cultures reason and formulate categories. In general, cognitive anthropology represents a more biological approach to the field than, for instance, SOCIAL ANTHROPOLOGY, and arguably has less in common with the humanities than it has with traditional sciences. See also ETHNOSCIENCE, PERCEPTION.

Further reading: Bloch (2005); Whitehouse & Laidlaw (2007); Kronenfeld et al. (2011).

Cohn, Bernard S. (1928–2003). See INDIAN ANTHROPOLOGY.

cohort. In SOCIOLOGY and DEMOGRAPHY, a group of INDIVIDUALS with a shared characteristic, often their year (or period) of BIRTH.

Cold War. See COMMUNISM.

Coleridge, Samuel Taylor (1772–1834). See HEURISTICS.

collateral. In KINSHIP, a collateral relative is one whose connection to EGO, while based on blood relationship (CONSANGUINITY), is at one remove from the straight line of DESCENT. Thus one's father is LINEAL kin, but one's uncles, aunts, and cousins are collateral—literally, "to the side" of him.

collective conscience or **consciousness.** According to DURKHEIM, the shared moral framework and beliefs of a SOCIETY, within which INDIVIDUALS must ACT and by which they are constrained. See SOCIAL SOLIDARITY.

Further reading: Durkheim (1933).

collective representation. A label from DURKHEIM: a shared SYMBOL or concept (e.g. the idea of God) that is understood by the INDIVIDUAL but also has wider meaning external to that individual as a kind of SOCIAL FACT. Although initially formulated with regard to religious PRACTICE, the term has wide use.

Further reading: Durkheim (1995).

Collingwood, R. G. (1889–1943). British philosopher and historian; influential in his contention that the "absolute presuppositions" underlying intellectual inquiry are variable rather than fixed (*An essay on metaphysics*, 1940 [rev. ed. 1998], ch. 4). A fellow of Oxford University (1912–35), Collingwood was involved in archaeological research from 1919, and was professor of metaphysics at Oxford from 1935 to 1941. His books include *Religion and philosophy* (1916), *An essay on philosophical method* (1933), *The idea of nature* (1945), and *The philosophy of enchantment* (ed. D. Boucher et al., 2005).

colonialism. A set of PRACTICES associated with political dominance by a large, powerful (see POWER) nation of a smaller, separate people; usually derogatory in general use. Colonized peoples may find settlers from the colonial power living among them (e.g. British governors in Africa and the Indian RAJ during the early twentieth century) and find their economic interests subsumed into those of their rulers. They may also find that they encounter DISCRIMINATION. Like many other politically sensitive issues, colonialism became an area of intense debate in the 1970s. Compare IMPERIALISM, INTERNAL COLONIALISM.

Further reading: Asad (1998).

color terms. Colors can be described in many ways, though Berlin and Kay famously argued for a good deal of equivalence in the understanding of color values across cultures. Nevertheless, words for particular "colors" in one language may not exist in another. The Munsell color chart, based on hue, intensity, and light, is widely used in the study of this field.

Further reading: Berlin & Kay (1991); MacLaury et al. (2007).

colored. An ethnic CLASSIFICATION for people of non-"white" parentage. It generally superseded NEGRO as the "acceptable" term in this context around the early-mid twentieth century, and was later supplanted by BLACK or more ethnically specific terms. In certain contexts it can have particular meanings, as in "Cape Colored," a South African term for "mixed-race" people.

Comaroff, John L. (1945–) and **Jean** (1946–). South African-born anthropologists who, following periods in Cape Town and Manchester, settled in 1978 in Chicago, where both now hold professorships. Well known for their work on COLONIALISM, MISSIONARY activities, and processes of HEGEMONY, especially as they affect the Tswana people of South Africa, they have produced several notable volumes separately and together: *Rules and processes: the cultural logic of dispute in an African context* (John with Simon Roberts, 1981); *Body of power, spirit of resistance: the culture and history of a South African people* (Jean, 1985); *Of revelation and revolution: Christianity, colonialism, and consciousness in South Africa* (together; two volumes, 1991–7); *Ethnography and the historical imagination* (together, 1992); and *Ethnicity, Inc.* (together, 2009).

commensality. The practice of eating together (from Latin, "together" and "table"). Social rules often govern who eats with whom, who sits where, and other points of etiquette, depending on factors such as relative STATUS. Commensality is a component of some types of SACRIFICE.

commodity. In economics, an item produced specifically for the purposes of TRADE; anything so produced when considered in light of its EXCHANGE VALUE. MARX formulated a distinction familiar as far back as Aristotle between USE VALUE (the value attached to an item produced to meet a SOCIETY's immediate needs) and EXCHANGE VALUE (that given to it by a MARKET, where it is sold by intermediaries to others). In this light, goods *become* commodities, with both use and exchange values.

It is important to remember that labor (see CAPITALISM) and services are viewed in many cultures as commodities. Thus they may have undergone a process of "commodification."

Anthropologists have contrasted commodity exchange with GIFT exchange, which can be seen as more personal, with different obligations, though opinion varies as to details. See also PETTY COMMODITY PRODUCTION.

commodity fetishism. A phrase of MARX (in *Capital*) to describe the mental displacement by which people engaged in the EXCHANGE of a COMMODITY come to regard the commodity itself as the seat of the social relation between producer and consumer, rather than any more personal connection (which under CAPITALISM may not exist outside the transaction). The thing, in other words, is a kind of FETISH. Compare REIFICATION, the process of turning people into "things."

Further reading: Taussig (2010).

communication. A general term for all transmission of information between organisms. Human communication often involves a LANGUAGE of some kind (or symbolic behavior), and takes place through speech, GESTURE, writing, and/or electronic MEDIA. Anthropologists have been influenced by the groundbreaking work in this area of linguists such as SAUSSURE, and later SAPIR. Numerous theorists such as JAKOBSON have attempted to draw up models of the communication process, and specify the possible variations involved in it. In the 1960s, Hockett identified the design features of all ANIMAL communication, including those (such as the ability to discuss objects that were not physically present) that appeared to be unique to humans. There was some interest around this time as to whether, for instance, chimpanzees could "communicate." A separate outgrowth of anthropological interest in this period was the ETHNOGRAPHY OF COMMUNICATION. Latterly, anthropologists have become more interested in ambiguity and complexity, with attention shifting to a study of DISCOURSE and a willingness to see communication as a collaborative, mutable process rather than as a simple series of messages sent and received. See also HABERMAS.

Further reading: Hockett (1960).

communism. A political and economic doctrine associated with the work of MARX and ENGELS in the mid nineteenth century, specifically the *Communist manifesto* of 1848, although similar ideas were popular prior to this and go back to, for instance, early Christianity. Communist THEORY intersects with SOCIALISM, which was also taking shape during this period. The aim of communism is the common ownership of the MEANS OF PRODUCTION so that all workers derive the benefits of their labor; SOCIETY in such a condition is free of CLASS distinctions such as those that exist between workers and owners. The communist ideal involves (in Marx's original vision) an intermediate stage of socialism leading to the eventual overthrow of CAPITALISM.

In practice, the most famous attempt to implement a communist regime—in Soviet Russia between the 1917 Bolshevik revolution and 1991—had disastrous consequences for many citizens and finally collapsed under the weight of its own contradictions; first Lenin and then Stalin altered MARXIST theory for their own ends. Stalin was responsible for purges of ideological enemies and caused millions of deaths. Nevertheless, the communist system had been adopted by China in 1949 and also taken up (or imposed from outside, by Russia in particular) in many other places in Eastern Europe,

LATIN AMERICA, SOUTHEAST ASIA, and Africa. The "cold war" between the communist bloc and the US and Western Europe developed after World War II. Although many communist systems fell apart around the same time as Soviet Russia, the influence of communism remains a topic of concern to anthropologists, particularly as in the "post-communist" era people who were used to living under controlled economies encountered a free MARKET, with varied consequences, such as OSTALGIA. See also CHINESE ANTHROPOLOGY, POLITICAL ANTHROPOLOGY, RUSSIAN ANTHROPOLOGY.

Further reading: Marx & Engels (2008); Alexander et al. (2007).

communitas. A state defined by TURNER as a social relationship or sentiment arising between people who experience certain crucial events—for example, moments of LIMINALITY or PILGRIMAGE—together. This bond temporarily unites them in a way that is outside normal SOCIAL STRUCTURE.

Further reading: Turner (1974).

community. A social group usually understood to be small-scale (between the FAMILY and the STATE), drawn together by common interests and self-defined as separate from other communities. Important work in this area has been done by Tönnies (see *GEMEINSCHAFT* AND *GESELLSCHAFT*). Whereas the community was once studied as an entity bound to a particular locale—e.g. a VILLAGE—it is now often treated as nearer to being a shared IDEOLOGY, irrespective of the location of its members. There is a good deal of debate about the specifics of what the term entails. Compare SPEECH COMMUNITY.

Further reading: Cohen (1985); Creed (2006).

compadrazgo. A ritualized relationship found mainly in Spain and LATIN AMERICA in which a child acquires GODPARENTS who thereby form a significant bond with the child's parents. The godparent is often of a higher STATUS and may feel obliged to accept the "HONOR" implied; one godparent may be tied to numerous families in this way. See also RITUAL KINSHIP.

comparative linguistics. The study of LANGUAGE families (see LANGUAGE CLASSIFICATION), involving comparison of similar words or COGNATES in different languages with the aim of determining whether they are descended from a common PROTOLANGUAGE. The protolanguage ancestor may be hypothetically reconstructed, and subgroups within several related languages may be conjectured. Words appearing to be similar in different languages can also be explained by other reasons than language relationship (e.g. by linguistic borrowings). Comparative linguistics overlaps with HISTORICAL LINGUISTICS.

comparative method. Originally, in nineteenth-century anthropology, a way of using ethnographic information to place societies within an evolutionary scheme (see EVOLUTIONISM). Such approaches fell out of favor as anthropology grew in sophistication. More generally used to mean studying different cultures together, as in the standard method of classic British SOCIAL ANTHROPOLOGY. There has been some disagreement about how valid such comparisons might be, the conditions for comparison, and so on.

Further reading: Evans-Pritchard (1963); Holy (1987).

comparative musicology. An early term for ETHNOMUSICOLOGY.

competence. In LINGUISTICS, a speaker/hearer's competence is what they implicitly understand about the LANGUAGE, considered as a kind of system. This is contrasted with PERFORMANCE, their actual use of it. Introduced by CHOMSKY.

Further reading: Chomsky (1965).

complementary dualism. A form of DUALISM based on complementarity on the symbolic level—as seen in moieties (see MOIETY).

complementary filiation. A THEORY developed by Africanists such as Meyer FORTES to describe certain relationship ties in UNILINEAL DESCENT groups. Although children derive social STATUS from their membership of one LINEAGE, they maintain an emotional connection to the parent of the other lineage and thus to that parent's relatives (e.g. in a patrilineal system, the mother's brother). This theory has been challenged by writers who see the parents' MARRIAGE ties as of more importance. See also FILIATION.

complex society. A SOCIETY that is comparatively large and stratified in various ways, as opposed to what is sometimes called a SIMPLE SOCIETY. "Complex societies" may well be developed STATES with significant urban populations (see URBAN ANTHROPOLOGY) whose arrangements tend to engender INEQUALITY. It should be understood, however, that *all* societies, however "simple," can be read as complex in certain ways. See also SOCIAL SOLIDARITY.

complex structures. In LÉVI-STRAUSS' THEORY of KINSHIP rules, the opposite of ELEMENTARY STRUCTURES: rather than positive, *pre*scriptive expectations of those who are going to marry, the choice of spouse is influenced more by negative, *pro*scriptive rules (e.g. forbidding INCEST) as well as by personal preference. See also PRESCRIPTION/PROSCRIPTION, CROW-OMAHA (a label for "semi-complex structures").

complexity theory. A development from such areas as chaos THEORY: natural and social phenomena are not "naturally" inclined to harmony and simplicity but actually tend toward adaptive change and complex patterns. Of interest in numerous fields since the close of the twentieth century, for instance SOCIOLOGY, HISTORY, GEOGRAPHY. See also SYSTEMS THEORY.

Further reading: Urry (2005).

componential analysis. In LINGUISTICS, the breaking down of language into its basic distinct elements of meaning (components, or "significata"): for example, the word "boy" = male, young, human. Developed in anthropology by such writers as Goodenough, it was found particularly useful in dealing with RELATIONSHIP TERMINOLOGY, and was mooted as revealing the underlying thought patterns of particular cultures. Associated with NEW ETHNOGRAPHY, ETHNOSCIENCE, and the beginnings of COGNITIVE ANTHROPOLOGY.

Further reading: Goodenough (1956).

Comte, Auguste (1798–1857). French philosopher and pioneer of SOCIOLOGY and POSITIVISM (terms he was the first to use; see also ALTRUISM). Comte worked for SAINT-SIMON between 1817 and 1824, and later developed the *Cours de philosophie positive* (1830–42). He was a major influence on DURKHEIM.

concubinage. In general use, a concubine is a "common-law" wife—a woman cohabiting, or acting as a sexual partner, with a man to whom she is not married. In anthropology the term may also refer to a facet of polygynous MARRIAGE, by which a man may have a "major" wife, with greater rights and obligations, and a "minor" wife (or wives), with lesser ones.

Condorcet (Jean-Antoine-Nicolas de Caritat, marquis de Condorcet, 1743–94). French aristocrat and progressive philosopher, whose radical ideas concerning social evolution and the potential for human perfectibility and equality influenced later theorists such as COMTE and SAINT-SIMON. *Esquisse d'un tableau historique des progrès de l'esprit humain* (*Outlines of an historical view of the progress of the human mind*) was published posthumously. He was a moderate participant in the French Revolution and died in prison.

configurationism or **configurationalism**. Any THEORY that stresses the whole rather than the parts, especially GESTALT THEORY. In anthropology, associated with the ideas of Ruth BENEDICT, who saw cultures as having coherent "personalities" whose configurations could be analyzed. The notion has been criticized but has echoes in some later writers, such as Clifford GEERTZ. See also CULTURE AND PERSONALITY and compare HOLISM.

Further reading: Benedict (1934).

conflict. Conflict can arise between any groups or INDIVIDUALS with opposing aims: how much impetus they have to resolve their differences depends on such factors as the strength and durability of their social ties. Anthropological studies have contributed to wider research in conflict resolution (see e.g. MANCHESTER SCHOOL). Compare LAW, VIOLENCE, WAR.

Confucianism. A Chinese philosophy based on the words of Confucius (Kung Fu-tzu), who was active in the sixth century BCE, and on the system developed by his early followers. Confucianism was taught in Chinese institutes of higher EDUCATION until the mid twentieth century. Kung Fu-tzu encouraged a concern with balance; respect for ANCESTORS was also developed to a high degree later on. These guiding principles were swept away under Communist rule in the mid twentieth century. See also DAOISM.

Further reading: Weber (1951).

conjectural history. The attempt to hypothesize the way a CULTURE has developed in the absence of historical records. RADCLIFFE-BROWN used the term to contrast early anthropological method with the empirical observation current by the early twentieth century. Compare CULTURE HISTORY.

Further reading: Radcliffe-Brown (1929).

conjugal family. Synonymous with NUCLEAR FAMILY ("conjugal": joined by MARRIAGE).

connubium. See CIRCULATING CONNUBIUM.

consanguine (noun and adjective). An INDIVIDUAL related to another by BIRTH; that is, sharing CONSANGUINITY. Compare affine (see AFFINITY).

consanguine family. A conjectural early form of MARRIAGE suggested by MORGAN in which brothers and sisters intermarried in a group. The idea was refuted by Andrew LANG.

Further reading: Morgan (2000).

consanguinity. KINSHIP attributed through one's BIRTH (literally, shared blood) as opposed to through MARRIAGE (AFFINITY).

consociate. In the work of GEERTZ and others, a consociate is someone with whom one has a social relationship.

conspicuous consumption. Ostentatious use of expensive goods and services, for the purpose of enhancing social STATUS. Coined by Thorstein Veblen in relation to the top strata of American society, but can be generally applied. Conspicuous CONSUMPTION is similar to a form of POTLATCH.

Further reading: Veblen (2007).

constant. In general and SOCIAL SCIENCES, a feature or quantity that is fixed or invariable, as opposed to a VARIABLE.

consumption. The process of eating, drinking, or otherwise using a resource. While consumption of goods and services has long been a theme of economics (often distinguished from PRODUCTION), it has increasingly grown in interest for social scientists as western cultures have become "consumer societies." Thinkers such as BOURDIEU have noted the prestige attached to what one wears or eats and the arts one patronizes (novelists such as Bret Easton Ellis have frequently satirized such concerns). Thanks to GLOBALIZATION, consumerism has spread and spawned new forms in new MARKETS. Even where INDIGENOUS cultures have not been modified, their existing patterns of FOOD or DRINK use (for example) remain significant. For instance, a RITUAL may require the consumption of particular items at set times.

An older meaning of "consumption" refers to wasting DISEASES, which "consume" the sufferer.

See also CONSPICUOUS CONSUMPTION, OBESITY.

Further reading: Miller (1994); Bourdieu (1999).

contagious magic. One of the forms of SYMPATHETIC MAGIC.

contested concepts. See ESSENTIALLY CONTESTED CONCEPTS.

contract. An agreement, sometimes legally binding, between parties to do (or not do) something specified. In the nineteenth century, MAINE suggested that a major indication of social EVOLUTION was that modern societies had moved from relationships between people who had a fixed STATUS—set for them through FAMILY or similar connections—to ones based on discrete contracts freely undertaken by independent agents.

Further reading: Maine (2006).

contraception. Any method (natural or artificial) of preventing conception. In the twentieth century artificial contraceptive methods became increasingly available in western societies and their use less subject to stigma (or legal restriction). Issues surrounding what was later termed "family planning" include questions of GENDER, POWER, and EUGENICS.

Further reading: Russell et al. (2000).

controlled comparison. A study using a COMPARATIVE METHOD (in the later sense) in such a way that VARIABLES are minimized—either by studying similar societies in highly comparable settings or examining the same features in different societies.

conversion. A change of nature or character. A term with a large number of applications, most often (in anthropology) to do with the switching of religious affiliation, either between religions or from non-belief to belief. Often discussed in the context of MISSIONARY work.

Further reading: Hefner (1993); Robinson & Clarke (2003).

Cook, James (Captain; 1728–79). See POLYNESIA, SAHLINS, TABOO, TATTOO.

Figure 4   **Cooking**. A kitchen with an open fire, Eastern Tanzania. Photo copyright: N. Beckmann.

cooking. Preparing FOOD by heating it; said to be found everywhere (raw food is also a significant area of study). Among others, LÉVI-STRAUSS drew conclusions concerning the cultural meanings of cooking (drawing attention to the BINARY OPPOSITION of raw/cooked).

In cultures where food supply is abundant, quality can be said to be more significant than quantity: a culture of "cuisine" develops, with CLASS or TASTE overtones, marking off those with the means to enjoy "fine dining" rather than merely satisfy HUNGER.

Further reading: Lévi-Strauss (1969[a]); Goody (1982); Bourdieu (1999).

Coon, Carleton S. (1904–81). See RITE OF INTENSIFICATION.

Copperbelt. A region of Zambia famous for some of the world's largest copper deposits, which are extensively mined. The area has been studied by A. L. Epstein, among others.

Further reading: Epstein (1992).

cordillera. Spanish: a mountain chain (comprising parallel ridges), specifically the ANDES. In American use cordilleras may include the Rockies or the Sierra Nevada.

core. See center and periphery.

corporate group or **descent group** or **kin group**. A social group based on common relationship (e.g. a LINEAGE) that usually is recognized as a legal entity, may impose obligations on its members, and sometimes holds common PROPERTY.

corroboree. An Australian ABORIGINAL gathering involving dancing and singing at night.

Corsica (France). See VENDETTA.

cosmogony. An account of the origin and evolution of the universe, or parts of it, and the study of such accounts. A cosmogony (from Greek, "birth of the world") may be a creation myth (as in the opening of the Book of Genesis) or a theory such as the "big bang." Compare COSMOLOGY.

cosmology. The study of the universe, *or* a particular cultural model of it. Anthropologists such as LÉVI-STRAUSS have examined NON-WESTERN peoples' conceptions of how the cosmos is ordered, and some have drawn inferences from these to various forms of social organization.

Further reading: Spencer (2003).

courtship. The process of attempting to acquire a spouse or sexual partner, often understood as a man paying attention to a woman. In western SOCIETY more formal courtship behavior (visits to the family home, chaperones) has been superseded by more relaxed attitudes, which may be based on greater freedom for women, and easy access to CONTRACEPTION.

cousin. A child of the brother or sister of a parent of EGO.

couvade. A term first used by TYLOR to describe a BIRTH CUSTOM in which the father imitates or shares in aspects of the mother's experience during childbirth. From French, "couver," to hatch.

Further reading: Rival (1998).

co-wife. One of two or more WOMEN married to the same husband.

cowrie or **cowry**. The shell of a marine snail, common in the Indian Ocean and sometimes used as MONEY in regions of Africa, the Pacific Islands, and South Asia.

Creationism. See FUNDAMENTALISM.

creole. A person in certain areas (e.g. West Indies, Mauritius) born in that place but of European or African extraction. The term may also be applied to their LANGUAGE, or other similarly formed languages; a creole language starts as a PIDGIN and becomes a creole by virtue of being adopted as a native tongue by new generations.

crime. An action that violates the law of a given CULTURE. There are many types of criminal ACT, of varying degrees of severity, and the amount of serious crime in any one place will usually depend on historical and economic factors, on the one hand (relative social INEQUALITY and POVERTY are sometimes considered to be contributory), and the culture's changing perceptions of what is criminal on the other. For instance, if a STATE or POWER regards HOMOSEXUALITY as a crime, then it may be treated as such. Anthropologists have often worked in regions suffering from high levels of crime. See also ALCOHOL, DEVIANCE, DRUGS, HOMICIDE, VIOLENCE.

Further reading: Volkov (2002).

critical anthropology. Depending on context, the critical perspective of anthropology, as used to challenge western assumptions when describing another SOCIETY (or one's own); the post-World War II (see WAR) MARXIST anthropology dealing with such themes as CAPITALISM and POWER; or post-1960s anthropology following the agenda of the Frankfurt School, a pre-war group of German intellectuals (e.g. ADORNO) working on similar issues.

Further reading: *Critique of anthropology* [journal].

critical medical anthropology. Broadly, the application of a CRITICAL ANTHROPOLOGY perspective (in its second sense) to health issues, placing them in a political context and adopting a skeptical approach to the assumptions implicit in BIOMEDICINE. Sometimes abbreviated to "CMA."

Further reading: Baer et al. (2003).

cross. In RELATIONSHIP TERMINOLOGY, a relation traced to EGO by opposite-SEX links—as in the case of CROSS-COUSINS. Compare PARALLEL COUSIN, PARALLEL DESCENT.

cross-cousin. A COUSIN (of either SEX) linked through parents who are brother and sister (e.g. one's father's sister's daughter or FZD). Compare PARALLEL COUSIN. Cross-cousins may be expected to take spouses from particular sets of corresponding cousin and have been much studied in ALLIANCE theory. See also CLASSIFICATORY CROSS-COUSIN.

cross-cultural. Much anthropological research is cross-cultural in nature: it implicitly or explicitly compares how things are done in one SOCIETY with the state of affairs in another. Writers since HERODOTUS have used this COMPARATIVE METHOD; it was later used by nineteenth-century anthropologists to attempt an evolutionary plan of humankind. In the twentieth century, MURDOCK pioneered more rigorous methods, such as STATISTICS and SAMPLING. Much anthropological interest has recently focused on the ways in which data can be collected and used in order to make valid cross-cultural comparisons, including the use of secondary material in databases such as the HUMAN RELATIONS AREA FILES. See also GALTON'S PROBLEM.

cross-cutting ties. Connections a person has that pull his/her loyalties in more than one direction. For instance, a person may belong to a particular PLACE and feel an allegiance to others there, but also to a particular religious group, membership of which may cause CONFLICT with the first allegiance group. It has been suggested that cross-cutting relationships can foster social cohesion, as there is an incentive for the individual to work to lessen conflicts that arise.

Crow. See CROW-OMAHA, CROW TERMINOLOGY, LOWIE.

Crow-Omaha. A term covering any RELATIONSHIP TERMINOLOGY character- ized by features (for instance bifurcate merging of some categories—see BIFURCATION) that are common to both CROW TERMINOLOGY and OMAHA TERMINOLOGY. Crow-Omaha systems have been studied since L. H. MORGAN and their significance has been extensively debated. Anthropologists' views have tended to be colored by their perspective: whether subscribing, for instance, to DESCENT THEORY or the alternative ALLIANCE tradition—within which the Crow-Omaha MODEL may be seen as a "semi-complex" third way between ELEMENTARY STRUCTURES and COMPLEX STRUCTURES.

crow terminology. A RELATIONSHIP TERMINOLOGY characterized by *bifurcate merging* of categories (see BIFURCATION), so EGO's parents' same- sex SIBLINGS and PARALLEL COUSINS are termed as in IROQUOIS TERMI- NOLOGY: mother's sister and mother share a term, for instance (MZ=M); and there is merging of separate GENERATIONS such that Ego's father's sister and father's sister's daughter share a term (FZ=FZD). Associated with MATRILINEALITY; compare IROQUOIS TERMINOLOGY and OMAHA TERMI- NOLOGY and see CROW-OMAHA. First discussed (as part of a group) by MORGAN; later identified by Spier and MURDOCK.

Further reading: Spier (1925); Murdock (1949).

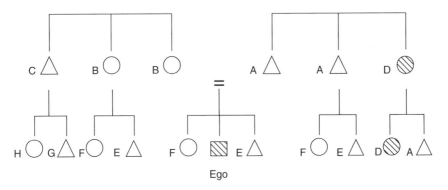

Ego

Figure 5   Crow terminology.

cuisine. See COOKING.

cult. A non-mainstream religious movement usually centered on a particular person or idea. Given that the term generally has pejorative connotations, anthropologists usually prefer terms such as "new RELIGION"; they typically study them through such issues as the relation between social deprivation and cult membership, the use of SYMBOLS, and healing RITUAL. Leading writers include Bryan Wilson and Paul Heelas. See also SECT.

cultural anthropology. The American TRADITION that is equivalent to SOCIAL ANTHROPOLOGY (see also BRITISH ANTHROPOLOGY), although it places greater emphasis on aspects such as MATERIAL CULTURE and is less concerned with the ethnographic analysis of particular elements (e.g. law or KINSHIP) than with presenting a rounded portrait of all aspects of its subject.

Cultural anthropology has its intellectual roots in the work of figures such as BOAS, who drew away from the nineteenth-century evolutionary tradition toward a focus on CULTURE as the paramount determinant of people's lives: as MALINOWSKI was doing in social anthropology (with different priorities), Boas foregrounded the workings of "PRIMITIVE" social systems *on their own terms*, adopting a relativist position (see RELATIVISM) as distinct from the implied ETHNOCENTRISM and RACISM of some of his forebears.

Boas had a great influence on the development of the subject in America in his own right and through his students, such as BENEDICT and KROEBER. The most notable writer to emerge from his coterie in this context was probably Margaret MEAD, who popularized the field and ensured its crossover into public policy.

From the mid twentieth century there were some fraught doctrinal arguments about the differences between social and cultural anthropology, and their relative merits. To a large extent the distinction has been diminished in recent years.

Further reading: Eller (2009); Rosman et al. (2009).

cultural broker. See BROKER.

cultural capital. A sociological term for the intangible assets possessed by those who have absorbed the dominant CULTURE in terms of knowledge, ways of speaking, manners, and modes of CONSUMPTION. Associated with the work of BOURDIEU. See also SYMBOLIC CAPITAL.

Further reading: Bourdieu & Passeron (1990).

cultural change. The processes by which people adapt to new conditions or circumstances. Historically, anthropologists have moved from an early assumption that "savage" societies changed slowly and inexorably toward

CIVILIZATION to more enlightened theories of CULTURE CONTACT, involving such ideas as DIFFUSIONISM and ACCULTURATION, and on to a realization that the world is increasingly bound together by such developments as GLOBALIZATION, so that change both from within a CULTURE and from outside it is inevitable.

cultural core or **culture core**. According to STEWARD, the features of a given CULTURE that relate most nearly to its SUBSISTENCE and economic life.

Further reading: Steward (1976).

cultural determinism. A belief that CULTURE determines the way peoples live, with little scope for the INDIVIDUAL to exercise AGENCY. One variety of DETERMINISM.

Further reading: Spiro (2001).

cultural ecology. An early name for ECOLOGICAL ANTHROPOLOGY.

cultural economy. A strand of ECONOMIC ANTHROPOLOGY. The full range of cultural factors involved in economic activities is stressed: how people comprehend what they are doing, the nature of networks they form, and the cultural effects of what began as purely economic contacts (for instance the consumption of American television shows in other societies). Cultural economists stress the limits of classical "rational" MARKET theories, disputing that western economic models can be applied easily to NON-WESTERN contexts and pointing out that alternative concepts of economic ETHICS (for instance the Islamic system, prohibiting usury—see MONEY) are of equal validity to large numbers of people.

Further reading: Amin & Thrift (2004); Gudeman (2008).

cultural materialism (CM). An anthropological PARADIGM chiefly developed by HARRIS in the 1960s that builds on MARX but rejects the Hegelian assumptions of DIALECTICAL MATERIALISM in favor of a view that accounts for REPRODUCTION and environmental factors. Introducing *Cultural materialism*, Harris posits social life as primarily a rational response to practical issues, and stresses CM's emphasis on "womb and belly and earth and WATER" over "words, ideas, high moral values and ... beliefs." In CM, infrastructure (loosely: TECHNOLOGY, population, and production factors) determines structure (domestic and political economy) and superstructure (thought and behavior). ("Cultural materialism" in literature is an unrelated school of thought also with MARXIST ancestry.) See also MATERIALISM, ECOLOGICAL ANTHROPOLOGY.

Further reading: Harris (1996, 2001[a], 2001[b]).

cultural pluralism. A form of PLURALISM whereby a particular SOCIETY holds within it a number of diverse ethnic groups, each with their own CULTURE. Ideally, there is no pressure toward ASSIMILATION, nor is there DISCRIMINATION, though many minority groups experience such things in reality. The analysis of cultural pluralism developed from that of the PLURAL SOCIETY.

cultural relativism. The notion that the WORLDVIEW of a SOCIETY is culturally constructed within it; thus it is invalid to judge it outside its own context (e.g. by imposing one's own moral standards). In anthropology the idea derives from the work of BOAS, which stood in opposition to the nineteenth-century evolutionary view that societies operate on universal principles. Cultural RELATIVISM becomes a thorny issue in debates over such matters as female CIRCUMCISION, or the ASSIMILATION or otherwise of immigrant populations, where differing sets of values may come into CONFLICT.

cultural studies. An interdisciplinary field particularly associated (originally) with the Centre for Contemporary Cultural Studies at the University of Birmingham, UK (1964–1991) and such figures as Richard Hoggart, Stuart Hall, and Paul Gilroy. Another major influence was the author Raymond Williams. Cultural studies broadens the common understanding of "CULTURE"—in its non-anthropological sense—as an ELITE pursuit involving, say, literature or opera, to encompass also "popular culture"—as in movies, television, and popular newspapers. It questions the political meanings (for instance issues of POWER and INEQUALITY) behind such MEDIA, and their relation to their audiences. Matters of CLASS, RACE, and GENDER are similarly important. Anthropologists have sometimes been critical of the approach of cultural studies, which is generally less tied to hard data and more theoretical.

Further reading: Gilroy (2002).

culturalism. A theoretical approach emphasizing CULTURE. The term has been used in a number of ways; in British anthropology of the mid twentieth century it may be used to disparage a perceived over-reliance on culture as an explanatory factor (as might be seen in the views of BOAS and others).

culture. In general use, "culture" is usually treated as an attribute of the quality of refinement in the MIND, which can be accumulated or exercised through reading, attending the theatre and classical MUSIC concerts, and similar pursuits. While the strictly anthropological sense of the term encompasses some of this meaning, it also refers to something wider, less Eurocentric (see EUROCENTRISM), and less dependent on formal EDUCATION.

The first real appearance of "culture" in anthropological writing is in the opening of Tylor's *Primitive culture* (1871), where it is regarded as interchangeable with "civilization": "that complex whole which includes knowledge, belief, art, morals, law, custom, and [other traits] acquired by man as a member of society." Allowing for the context of its time, this might be a good shorthand for the larger reading of culture: pretty much everything a SOCIETY believes, thinks, or does. In America, however, where CULTURAL ANTHROPOLOGY gradually developed as a discrete field of study, a different set of assumptions was fostered by BOAS, whose relativistic understanding of *many* cultures (rather than one monolithic whole), operating contemporaneously by their own criteria, ultimately derived from the German ENLIGHTENMENT tradition of such authors as J. G. Herder.

As anthropology developed differently in the US and Britain, there thus developed a gulf between the British focus, influenced by SOCIOLOGY, on society—SOCIAL ORGANIZATION and SOCIAL STRUCTURE, exemplified by authors such as RADCLIFFE-BROWN—and the American concentration on culture as the unifying concept. Such a focus is notable in figures such as GEERTZ. To a great extent, the "social versus cultural" debate has been superseded by other concerns in recent years.

Whatever one's take on culture, it is a term that needs handling with care—as in many other areas of thought, it is important to remember that the idea of culture is a tool by which we reach understanding, not an empirical fact. There is not (for instance) a neatly defined "Turkana culture" floating apart from the Turkana people. People *make* culture.

Further reading: Tylor (1871); Kroeber & Kluckhohn (1952); Baumann (1996).

culture and personality. A school within American ethnology from the late 1920s onward associated with SAPIR, Margaret MEAD, BENEDICT, and others. These writers suggested, for instance, that the different characteristics among various CULTUREs could be attributed to variations in methods of SOCIALIZATION, and criticized attempts to construct universal theories of human psychology. In keeping with the original influence of the field of psychology on them, these anthropologists' work later fed into PSYCHOLOGICAL ANTHROPOLOGY. See also CONFIGURATIONISM, NATIONAL CHARACTER, WORLDVIEW.

culture area. The site of a CULTURE COMPLEX. Associated with diffusionist THEORY, which was superseded by new approaches (see STRUCTURAL-FUNCTIONALISM) and a recognition of the validity of the idea of INDEPENDENT INVENTION. Compare DIFFUSIONISM, *KULTURKREIS*.

culture bearer. A person regarded as carrying, and therefore spreading, certain values and traits representative of their own CULTURE.

culture-bound syndrome (CBS). A medical condition said to be specific to a particular CULTURE and usually related to anxiety: for example "koro" (characterized by fear that the genitals will shrink into the abdomen) in SOUTHEAST ASIA and "susto" (associated with loss of the soul following a shock) in Central America. Also known as "ethnic psychosis." The label is historically associated with some use as a convenient "explanation" for behavior which did not comply with expected standards under COLONIAL-ISM, and is still debatable—for instance, as to whether a CBS is a kind of "distress signal" or a "genuine" condition.

culture broker. See BROKER.

culture complex. A connected group of CULTURE TRAITS or PRACTICES that are held to be functionally related. The English-speaking version of *KULTURKREIS*, associated with early American anthropology in particular, following Fritz Graebner in Germany.

culture contact. Any circumstance in which peoples of different CULTURES interact such that new traits emerge in one or both cultures. It may also be regarded as an older euphemism for domination of one culture by another, since it is often associated with contact where there is a disparity of POWER—between European settlers and NATIVE AMERICANS, for example.

culture core. See CULTURAL CORE.

culture history. The reconstruction of a CULTURE's past through the study of related cultures. Associated with DIFFUSIONISM and Boasian approaches, in reaction to CONJECTURAL HISTORY. Boas is sometimes called the founder of a "culture history school."

culture of poverty. A THEORY developed by the anthropologist Oscar Lewis that in some societies (such as in Mexico) people in entrenched POVERTY became accustomed to their way of life and did not expect to be able to improve it, effectively perpetuating their own poverty. It has been challenged on the grounds that it blames the poor for social deprivation, rather than the system itself, and largely superseded in anthropological writing by later explanations. Also called the "cycle of deprivation."

Further reading: Lewis (1959; 1961).

culture trait. The smallest unit of a given CULTURE capable of being analyzed, which, when assembled with other such traits, was held, in early theory, to form a CULTURE COMPLEX.

cuneiform. Literally, wedge-shaped. The characters used in the WRITING SYSTEMS of early Mesopotamia between about 4000 and 1000 BCE. Cuneiform was derived from Sumerian PICTOGRAMS and was used in several languages (e.g. Akkadian). It bore some similarities to Egyptian HIEROGLYPHS.

Cushing, Frank Hamilton (1857–1900). Pioneer of FIELDWORK with NATIVE AMERICANS, born in Pennsylvania. Associated with the Bureau of American Ethnology, he lived with the Zuñi for five years and was an expert in their technologies. He died suddenly after choking on a fishbone. A good introduction to his work is *Zuñi: selected writings of Frank Hamilton Cushing* (1979).

custom. Habitual PRACTICES of an INDIVIDUAL or CULTURE, the traditional way of doing things or thinking about them, as passed down the generations. Custom is learned but often erroneously perceived as "natural," and affects decisions regarding all areas of social life, for instance FOOD practices, MARRIAGE, living arrangements, CLOTHING, and DEATH RITUAL. One area of particular interest to anthropologists in the colonial period was CUSTOMARY LAW.

customary law. In general legal use, laws that derive from ancestral TRADITION rather than formal policy. Anthropologists use the term to signify schemes historically existing among INDIGENOUS groups, as distinct from imported post-colonial legal codes.

cybernetics. A term coined by Norbert Wiener and defined in the title of his 1948 book *Cybernetics: or, control and communication in the animal and the machine.* The term derives from the Greek for "helmsman." Systems (of whatever kind: living organism, machine, or social) require FEEDBACK and data about their environments in order to function. The ideas involved in cybernetics were partly taken up by Gregory Bateson, and still survive in descriptions of the Internet. See also STRUCTURALISM.

Czaplicka, Marie (1884–1921). Polish anthropologist, born and educated in Warsaw. She became the first female Mianowski Fellow of Ethnology, at the London School of Economics in 1910, and then studied at Oxford from 1911 to 1912. A pioneering woman in the discipline, she advanced the study of Siberia and shamanism (see SHAMAN), undertaking fieldwork from 1914 to 1915 and publishing *My Siberian year* (1915) and *The Turks of Central Asia* (1918). She lectured at Oxford and Bristol. She encountered personal difficulties and committed suicide.

Further reading: Collins & Urry (1997); Czaplicka (1999).

D

D or Da. In RELATIONSHIP TERMINOLOGY, the abbreviation for "daughter."

dalit. A Hindu term (Sanskrit: "oppressed") for a member of the lower orders of South Asian SOCIETY, below the categories of the traditional CASTE system. Dalits were once called "untouchables" but Gandhi renamed them "Harijans" ("children of God"); they are also known as "scheduled castes."

dance. Any kind of patterned, rhythmical movement, usually to MUSIC and with consciously aesthetic intentions. Dance is sometimes associated with RITUAL (e.g. the North American ghost dance) or physiologically "altered states." It may be viewed as an essentially social form of expression, either reinforcing cultural expectations of participants or audience (for instance to do with GENDER roles or MARRIAGE) or conversely subverting them (dance can be a "safe" outlet for politically unacceptable impulses). More recently, anthropologists have focused less on the functional aspects of dance and begun to treat it as a complex bodily event, to be notated, filmed, and investigated as a kinetic process that may be loaded with symbolism.

Further reading: *Journal for the anthropological study of human movement*; Spencer (1985).

danwei. A Chinese "work unit": the evolving cultural concept of the *danwei* is significant in recent Chinese history.

Further reading: Bray (2005).

daoism or taoism. A Chinese RELIGION or philosophy (compare CONFUCIANISM and BUDDHISM) derived from teachings attributed to Laozi ("Laotse") (604–531 BCE). WEBER differentiated between Confucianism, the ruling class' philosophy, and Daoism, the popular religion. From Chinese "dao" or "tao," "the right way, the path."

Further reading: Pregadio (2008).

Darfur. Region of western Sudan with a recent history of considerable CONFLICT and disruption. Since 2003 there has been (arguably) civil WAR between the indigenous farmers (who are from the FUR and other ethnic groups) and their Arab neighbors, who include the Janjaweed militia, a group suspected of receiving support from the Sudanese government and linked to war crimes such as rape and MURDER on a scale approaching GENOCIDE.

Following a government ceasefire with the Justice and Equality Movement, a referendum gave Southern Sudan (i.e. the region south of Darfur) independent status, which was adopted in July 2011. Darfur's fraught condition, and the plight of its numerous displaced people, has attracted the attention of regional historians, anthropologists, and aid workers, and powerful monographs have been produced by writers such as M. W. Daly, Gérard Prunier, and Alex de Waal.

Further reading: De Waal (2005); Flint & de Waal (2008).

Darwin, Charles (1809–82). British naturalist, born Shrewsbury and educated at Edinburgh and Cambridge. Darwin journeyed to South America on *The Beagle* from 1831 to 1836 and, drawing on numerous antecedents, refined existing notions of EVOLUTION to a new level. He was influenced by the work of, among others, his grandfather Erasmus Darwin (who anticipated LAMARCK) and Alfred Russel Wallace. His major works include *On the origin of species by means of natural selection* (1859) and *The descent of man, and selection in relation to sex* (1871). See also DARWINISM, SOCIAL DARWINISM.

Further reading: Milner (2009).

Darwinism. The biological THEORY of EVOLUTION as propounded by Charles DARWIN in works such as *On the origin of species* (1859). Building on ideas associated with others, Darwin posited a common ancestry for apparently discrete sets of PLANTS and ANIMALS. According to the theory, different species inherit certain characteristics that then undergo ADAPTATION to their ENVIRONMENT through "natural selection." Natural selection suggests that the specimens of a species with the most advantageous characteristics for that creature are most likely to reproduce successfully, thus passing on inherited strengths. Over time the species evolves in accordance with the development of these traits.

Darwinism was enormously controversial, encountering fierce opposition, especially from those who saw it as a challenge to established religious beliefs, but it came to revolutionize contemporary thought. Subsequent developments in GENETICS (for example) have shown the original theories to be in need of further modifications. See also the separate strand of thought in SOCIAL DARWINISM.

Das, Veena (1945–). Indian anthropologist, a professor at Johns Hopkins University since 2000. Her influential work incorporates themes of IDENTITY, VIOLENCE, and SUFFERING. These have been examined in publications such as *Structure and cognition: aspects of Hindu caste and ritual* (2nd ed. 1987), *Mirrors of violence: communities, riots and survivors in South Asia* (ed., 1990), and *Social suffering* (1997), which she co-edited with KLEINMAN and Margaret Lock.

Davis, John (1938–). British social anthropologist of MEDITERRANEAN societies; born London and educated at Oxford and London. He did fieldwork in Southern Italy and, later, Libya. He was professor of social anthropology at Kent (1982–90) and Oxford (1990–5). Writing mainly on economics, KINSHIP, and MARRIAGE, he has published *Land and family in Pisticci* (1973), *People of the Mediterranean* (1977), *Libyan politics* (1987), and *Exchange* (1992).

Dawkins, Richard (1941–). See MEME.

death. Every aspect of death is subject to social construction, from when exactly the person is said to "die" to how the BODY is treated (e.g. burial, cremation, CANNIBALISM) to whether, and how, an "afterlife" is conceived. Similarly, the appropriate responses of those left behind, and the roles they must play, vary widely, and depend on the IDENTITY and STATUS of the deceased. An interesting contrast might be drawn, for instance, between the elaborate and codified RITUAL attending death in some parts of the world and the apparently more detached form that Christian burial can take in modern Britain. See also FUNERAL RITES, MOURNING, SATI.

Further reading: Hertz (1960); van Gennep (1960); Bloch & Parry (1982); Metcalf & Huntingdon (1991).

deconstructionism. A philosophical and literary technique associated with Jacques Derrida (late twentieth century) in which TEXTS are subverted by "deconstruction" to challenge the notion that they have a fixed meaning; critical analysis may reveal many possible meanings and expose hidden authorial assumptions. In a more general way, the term has been applied to similar techniques in other fields. Associated with POST-MODERNISM.

deep play. A phrase originally coined by the utilitarian philosopher Jeremy Bentham to describe a game involving stakes that are too high to make participation rationally worthwhile. Adapted by GEERTZ in a 1972 essay (2000 [1973]: chapter 15) to describe wagers in which other issues, such as cultural STATUS, took priority. See also PLAY.

Further reading: Geertz (2000 [1973]: chapter 1).

deep structure. In LINGUISTICS, the component identified by CHOMSKY that underlies "surface structure" and sets essential meanings, as opposed to the superficial manifestation above it (deep structure pertains to the SYNTAX under the SEMANTICS and PHONETICS of a statement). See also TRANSFORMATIONAL-GENERATIVE GRAMMAR.

deixis. In LINGUISTICS, a deictic word relates other sentence elements to their context—to space (as in "here/there") or time ("before/after"), or speaker to audience ("I/you"). From Greek, "reference." In logic, a deictic approach proves something by direct argument.

delayed-return. A term from a useful distinction made by James Woodburn. In describing HUNTER-GATHERER societies, Woodburn differentiates "immediate-return" systems—those in which WORK is focused on *present* concerns, with FOOD and other resources being used soon after they are acquired, disposable TOOLS and weapons being employed in ways requiring little labor, and few assets being held—from "delayed-return" systems— those that focus on *past and future* as well as the present, holding long-term assets such as livestock, food PLANTS, and storable food, as well as technical equipment, which will yield provisions over an extended time period, and in which there is the right of men to give their female KIN in MARRIAGE.

Further reading: Woodburn (1988).

Deleuze, Gilles (1925–95). French philosopher and critic of conventional MODELS of western thought. His works include the two-volume *Capitalisme et schizophrénie* (*Capitalism and schizophrenia*), co-authored with Félix Guattari (original French eds. 1972 and 1980, translated 1977 and 1987), which took on FREUD; *Nietzsche et la philosophie* (*Nietzsche and philosophy*, 1962; new English ed. 2006); and *Différence et répetition* (*Difference and repetition*, 1968, translated 1994). Deleuze developed the analogy of the rhizome—literally, an underground root—for thought patterns that are non-hierarchical or horizontal rather than "vertical." An associate of FOUCAULT, he has had a similar influence on some anthropologists.

deme. A COGNATIC (related by blood) local DESCENT group practicing ENDOGAMY (marriage *within* the group), such as was found in early Greek SOCIETY. G. P. MURDOCK reclaimed this previously used term for anthropology. From Greek, "district." Compare RAMAGE.

Further reading: Murdock (1949).

demographic transition. A shift in the demographic make-up (see DEMOGRAPHY) of a given area that is believed to be linked to industrialization or economic DEVELOPMENT. Broadly, a SOCIETY undergoing economic growth moves from a high birth rate and a high death rate to, first, high births and low deaths and, second, low birth and low deaths. The idea developed from Warren S. Thompson's work on comparative population growth among different nations.

demography. The systematic study of human population change by means of STATISTICS covering, for example, BIRTHS, DEATHS, DISEASE, and MIGRATION. Of considerable use to social scientists since the seventeenth century, and also to GOVERNMENTS in terms of areas such as social planning and healthcare. Anthropologists such as Ester Boserup and W. Penn Handwerker have studied the cultural effects of demographic factors. Named in the late nineteenth century, from Greek, "people-writing."

demon. See EXORCISM, JINN, VOODOO.

dependency theory. An idea associated with SOCIOLOGY and HISTORY from the 1950s to the 1960s. Dependency theory posits underdevelopment (see DEVELOPMENT) in the THIRD WORLD as the consequence of reliance by these countries on FIRST WORLD capitalist nations for goods, investment, and expert help. Aid in this context is viewed as a tool of further oppression. Associated with authors such as Andre Gunder Frank. Although criticized for presenting too simplistic a dichotomy, dependency theory influenced WORLD-SYSTEM theory.

Derrida, Jacques (1930–2004). See DECONSTRUCTIONISM, DIFFÉRANCE, POST-STRUCTURALISM.

dervish. A member of a type of Muslim order committed to POVERTY and austerity; some of the orders perform dances or have similar rituals. Compare SUFISM. The term derives from Persian, "poor."

Descartes, René (1596–1650). See BODY, RATIONALISM.

descendant. A KINSHIP term for those *succeeding* EGO; for example, son, grandson, great-grandson, and so on. Compare ASCENDANT.

descent. The ancestry of INDIVIDUALS, usually in order to determine their social standing: which groups they belong to, what offices they may hold, and other rights and responsibilities. The degree to which ancestry is traced, and the privileges it confers, vary according to social convention. Descent is a key theme in the study of KINSHIP.

descent group. A group whose members all share common DESCENT from a (real or mythical) ANCESTOR. Descent groups encompass both CLANS and LINEAGES, and may be reckoned in various ways (see e.g. UNILINEAL, MULTI-LINEALITY, DOUBLE DESCENT). The concept is generally less significant in western than NON-WESTERN societies.

descent theory. An approach to the organization of non-STATE societies—those based around UNILINEAL KINSHIP groups—associated with the work of EVANS-PRITCHARD, FORTES, and others in Africa. Their focus on DESCENT contrasts with ALLIANCE theory, which foregrounds MARRIAGE, and whose proponents disputed with the descent theorists and argued for the paramountcy of affinal ties. Even other British anthropologists attacked the rigidity of descent THEORY, arguing that reality is more complicated than MODELs found in theory. See also SEGMENTARY LINEAGE SYSTEM.

Further reading: Fortes (1953); Kuper (2005).

descriptive kinship. In descriptive KINSHIP systems (the label comes from MORGAN), each individual relative is known—described—by a *specific* term of their own, rather than being grouped with others under the same term (as happens in CLASSIFICATORY KINSHIP). The descriptive term used is usually best understood as an exact combined form—"mother's brother" (MB) rather than the more ambiguous "uncle," for instance. SUDANESE TERMINOLOGY has good examples of the use of descriptive kinship terms. As with other examples of kinship and TRANSLATION, descriptive kinship may be less straightforward than it appears. An alternative label for this type of labeling is "individualizing" terminology; compare ZERO-EQUATION.

descriptive linguistics. The branch of LINGUISTICS concerned with LANGUAGE use at a particular time, without historical comparison or comparison with other languages. Also called "synchronic linguistics"; contrast HISTORICAL LINGUISTICS. This approach is associated with SAUSSURE, Leonard Bloomfield, and SAPIR.

determinism. The belief in philosophy and similar fields that human actions, and natural events, are determined by what preceded them, in a way that is theoretically completely predictable (thus free will would be an illusion). The alternative view may be labeled "indeterminism"—or, in some contexts, POSSIBILISM. As Newtonian views of the world have been challenged by twentieth century developments, a less ordered MODEL of existence has emerged, and thus the argument for determinism has run into some difficulties. For specific forms see CLIMATIC DETERMINISM, CULTURAL DETERMINISM, ENVIRONMENTAL DETERMINISM, GEOGRAPHICAL DETER-MINISM, LINGUISTIC DETERMINISM, TECHNOLOGICAL DETERMINISM.

development. In the context of SOCIAL SCIENCES and politics, development usually refers to activities aimed at improving the living conditions of people in poorer regions (e.g. the THIRD WORLD) through GOVERNMENT and agency projects involving the introduction of TECHNOLOGY, higher educational standards, or similar improvements. Development raises numerous issues, for example concerning what "underdevelopment" is. In the post-World War II era, many western agencies promoted initiatives that were attacked by later MARXIST critics for being in thrall to MODERNIZATION THEORY (loosely, the belief that poorer nations would "develop" along western lines naturally) and for pursuing programs that were more likely to entrench POVERTY than to alleviate it. In some quarters, development anthropology (or APPLIED ANTHROPOLOGY) was looked down upon. More recently, development work has shifted away from economics and toward improving quality of life more generally, and toward SUSTAINABLE DEVELOPMENT. This has renewed anthropological engagement.

Further reading: Hobart (1993).

developmental cycle (of domestic groups). A concept from the work of a group around Meyer FORTES at Cambridge University in the 1950s: the size of the domestic unit, rather than being static, fluctuates over time—for example, as new members are born, mature, and leave, and older dependents are added and later die.

Further reading: Goody (1958).

deviance. "Deviant" behavior is socially defined and can represent a wide spectrum of departures from the NORM, encompassing CRIME, challenges to the status quo, and unconventional modes of living (e.g. membership of certain SUBCULTURES, HOMOSEXUALITY). It is possible for conformist behavior in one place or time to be deviant in another. The concept of deviance can be traced as far back as DURKHEIM, but is primarily found in later SOCIOLOGY. Compare DYSFUNCTION, STIGMA.

diachronic. A term derived from the linguistic work of SAUSSURE that indicates a concern with developments *through* time in the area of study, rather than at one particular point; in other words, a "historical" approach. Compare DESCRIPTIVE LINGUISTICS, SYNCHRONIC.

diachronic linguistics. Synonym for HISTORICAL LINGUISTICS.

dialect. A non-standard variety of a LANGUAGE. Commonly thought of as found in diverse regions, or among particular classes (see CLASS), of a country (for instance, the way a Liverpool cab driver uses English may not be same as the mode of speech of an opera singer being interviewed by the BBC). It is useful to recognize that languages are themselves not intrinsically "better" than dialects: arguably they simply represent the idiom of those in POWER. See also SOCIOLINGUISTICS, SPEECH COMMUNITY.

dialectical materialism. A philosophical THEORY associated with MARX and ENGELS (developing ideas from Hegel): phenomena are considered not in isolation but as dynamic parts in a process, with contradictory elements possessing the potential for various outcomes. Social change is the end product of two opposing views synthesizing an outcome. See also MATERIALISM.

dialogic, dialogical. Characterized by dialogue. Although the importance of dialogue (in a general sense of interplay of meanings) had already been stressed by BAKHTIN, *dialogical anthropology* developed in the later twentieth century as a way of giving greater weight to input from the people studied; for example, giving them a more prominent VOICE in ethnographies.

Further reading: Tedlock (1987); Tedlock & Mannheim (1995).

diarchy. Rule by two people or two other entities, for instance as in the later stages of the British colonization of India (see RAJ).

diaspora. Originally a term to describe the scatterings of the Jews of ancient Israel (see JUDAISM); by extension any dispersal of a people from their common home (often against their will), such as African-Americans owing to SLAVERY, or South Asians living in Britain and other foreign countries. See also MIGRATION, TRANSNATIONALISM.

Further reading: *Diaspora: a journal of transnational studies*; Cohen (2008).

diet. The FOOD and DRINK an INDIVIDUAL or group customarily consumes. As well as attempting to acquire sustenance, most people will usually choose a diet that expresses cultural preferences—avoiding TABOO items, favoring the familiar or culturally prestigious. In recent times anthropologists have noted modern phenomena associated not just with HUNGER and FAMINE but also issues of superabundance, as in dysfunctional diet and OBESITY. Factors such as GLOBALIZATION increase the availability (for some) of hitherto unavailable items, but also discourage traditional choices that often provided better-balanced sustenance. See also FOOD, FOOD SYSTEM, NUTRITIONAL ANTHROPOLOGY.

Further reading: Harrison & Waterlow (1990).

différance. A literary term coined by Jacques Derrida (playing on the suggestive similarity of "difference" and "defer-ence"). In Derrida's view we cannot apprehend a definitive "meaning" in a TEXT because that meaning is always "deferred": the relationship that exists between SIGNs is not fixed, but generates an indefinite process of slippage whereby meaning eludes us.

Further reading: Derrida (1982).

diffusionism. "Diffusion" is the appearance of elements of one people's CULTURE or practices in another; it was first mentioned by TYLOR in *Primitive culture*. For a long time early British anthropologists in particular argued over the merits of diffusion or its alternative, INDEPENDENT INVENTION, as the explanation for similarities between diverse peoples. The major proponents of diffusionism included Elliot SMITH and W. J. Perry. In America, following BOAS, ethnographers were less concerned with subscribing to one view or the other. The new focus on FUNCTIONALISM of MALINOWSKI and his peers had rendered these distinctions pretty redundant by the 1930s.

Further reading: Boas (1924); Smith et al. (1928).

diglossia. Use of two variations of the same LANGUAGE ("high" and "low" in social terms) according to context; often involving division between a formal written academic style and a more demotic spoken form (as in Arabic). Compare CODE-SWITCHING.

Further reading: Ferguson (1959).

Dilthey, Wilhelm (1833–1911). See HUMAN SCIENCE(S), *VERSTEHEN*, *WELTANSCHAUUNG*.

dimorphism. The condition of occurring in two distinct forms (of PLANTS, ANIMALS, and words). The sexual division of some creatures into male and female is an example of dimorphism.

Dinka. A south Sudanese Nilotic people (known to themselves as "Mounyjaang"). The subject of LIENHARDT's *Divinity and experience*.

direct exchange. Also known as "restricted exchange." A form of MARRIAGE exchange associated with ELEMENTARY STRUCTURES in which wives are exchanged directly *between* two groups (thus, women of group A marry into group B, and those of group B marry into group A; contrast GENERALIZED EXCHANGE, also known as indirect exchange). Direct exchange is symmetrical (see SYMMETRICAL EXCHANGE); indirect or generalized exchange is asymmetrical (see ASYMMETRICAL EXCHANGE).

direct rule. A method of GOVERNMENT in colonial societies (see COLONIALISM): the ruler is a member of the colonizing ethnic group rather than of the subject people (the opposite case is INDIRECT RULE).

disaster. A sudden and destructive event, often involving major damage to property and loss of life. "Natural disasters" such as large-scale fires, earthquakes, floods, and tsunamis are of great interest to anthropologists both for what they reveal about the attitudes toward a catastrophe within the affected population and how such incidents are handled by their GOVERNMENTS, and any outside agencies (such as NGOs) involved. See also FAMINE.

Further reading: Hoffman & Oliver-Smith (2002); Benthall (2010).

discourse. How people talk or write about a subject. In LINGUISTICS, discourse was originally understood as a unit of speech or writing longer than one sentence. For anthropologists it has become a concern of ETHNOMETHODOLOGY and, through the influence of BAKHTIN (see DIALOGIC) and especially FOUCAULT, a subject of debate. TEXTS and speech of every kind derive meaning from their cultural *context*, and they are not value-neutral: a particular discourse advances a view of the world; in doing so it places speaker and audience in POWER relations, advancing a "reality" that may restrict as well as enable. Anthropological texts are as capable as any of this. (Similar ideas inform some political fiction, e.g. Orwell's *Nineteen eighty-four*.) See also ETHNOGRAPHY OF SPEAKING.

Further reading: Foucault (1977); Marcus & Fischer (1999).

discrimination. Treating people unequally (see INEQUALITY) through prejudice against their ETHNICITY, GENDER, sexuality, RELIGION, age, or beliefs. Examples might be taken from the pre-Civil Rights American South or APARTHEID-era South Africa. As minorities have grown more vocal in the west, anti-discrimination laws have become more common, and have expanded in scope to cover disability, MARRIAGE rights, and so on.

A second sense refers to personal TASTE ("he has a discriminating palate").

disease. An observable, measurable condition of the BODY associated with physical dysfunction or infection; compare the more subjective idea of ILLNESS. Disease and illness are the major concern of MEDICAL ANTHROPOLOGY. Disease as a concept is especially linked to the TRADITION of BIOMEDICINE.

Aspects of disease have many intimate ties to CULTURE. Where people live, the work they do, their DIET, their recreational habits, and their economic standing all modify their likely exposure to disease. For example, some sexual preferences (as in aversion to the use of condoms, even since the spread of AIDS) make the RISK of infection greater but persist through cultural choice. See also ENDEMIC, EPIDEMIC, PANDEMIC, SUFFERING.

Further reading: Eisenberg (1977); Landy (1977).

disembedded. Understood as separate from a cultural context (as opposed to "embedded"). For instance, POLANYI made this division between different types (western and NON-WESTERN) of economy. See also FORMALIST/SUBSTANTIVIST DEBATE.

Further reading: Polanyi et al. (1957).

disharmonic. See HARMONIC.

disposition. A habit or tendency to a certain kind of action that is unconscious. In the thought of BOURDIEU, a system of dispositions comprises the HABITUS.

Further reading: Bourdieu (1977).

distinctive feature. In PHONOLOGY, a term associated with the work of JAKOBSON, referring to those linguistic elements distinguishing otherwise indistinguishable forms (for instance, the voicing that marks "s" from "z"). Distinctive features may be found within a PHONEME. This idea influenced LÉVI-STRAUSS when he developed MYTHEMES. See also VOICE.

divination. A general term for a variety of strategies used to uncover hidden knowledge—either of the future or of wrongs already committed that require redress. Methods include consulting an ORACLE, AUGURY, interpreting some other random event, astrology, and so on. Divination is more often accepted as genuinely useful to its participants (if only in terms of healing rifts, for example) now than it once was. Famous case studies include EVANS-PRITCHARD's work on the ZANDE and Victor TURNER's on the Ndembu of Zambia. Compare SHAMAN.

Further reading: Evans-Pritchard (1937); Turner (1975).

divine kingship. The belief that a SOCIETY's ruler is an embodiment or agent of the SACRED realm. Many societies have or had such a belief. The figure of an ancient sacrificial king who must be killed was of particular interest to FRAZER. The sacred king was taken up in classic studies by EVANS-PRITCHARD—examining the *reth* of the Shilluk of Sudan—and several others. Evans-Pritchard and later writers tended to be skeptical about suggestions concerning traditions of REGICIDE. See also KINGSHIP.

Further reading: Evans-Pritchard (1948); Feeley-Harnik (1985).

division of labor. The distribution of parts of a WORK process between different employees, who then specialize in particular areas; more generally, the separation of different parts of social life, for example factory and home. The phrase was first used by the economist Adam Smith (*An inquiry into the nature and causes of the wealth of nations*, 1776) and subsequently developed by DURKHEIM.

Social scientists examine how societies divide up the various parts of their common life for which all the members are responsible: FOOD provision, ensuring social stability, meeting religious needs, and other necessities. Since the late twentieth century, much attention has focused on questioning roles assumed to be the "natural" domain of WOMEN. See also INDUSTRIAL SOCIETY.

Further reading: Durkheim (1933).

divorce. Ending a MARRIAGE by means legally or socially recognized in a particular CULTURE. In PRACTICE, divorce methods and CUSTOMS vary greatly and are closely related to marriage conventions. Key questions involve who is permitted to divorce and in what circumstances, the provision to be made for children, and whether marriage payments have been made and need to be repaid (see BRIDEPRICE and DOWRY).

domestic cycle. Synonym for DEVELOPMENTAL CYCLE.

domestic mode of production. A MODE OF PRODUCTION identified by Marshall SAHLINS as geared to the immediate needs of households and thus underproductive relative to potential.

Further reading: Sahlins (2004).

double descent. A double DESCENT system in KINSHIP is one in which a person's mother's *and* father's sides of the FAMILY are *both* relevant, for separate reasons, regardless of the person's own GENDER (compare MATRILIN-EALITY, PATRILINEALITY); the specific rights and obligations involved will vary from group to group. See also DESCENT GROUP, MULTILINEALITY, PARALLEL DESCENT.

Douglas, Mary (1921–2007). British anthropologist (born San Remo, Italy). Raised Catholic, she studied under EVANS-PRITCHARD at Oxford. She did fieldwork in the Belgian Congo (producing *The Lele of the Kasai*, 1963) and taught in London and later in the US. She is famous for *Purity and danger* (1966) (see PURITY), but also wrote about a wide range of other interests including CONSUMPTION (*The world of goods*, with Baron Isherwood, 1979), RISK (e.g. *Risk and culture*, with Aaron Wildavsky, 1982), and RELIGION.

doula. A person (other than a midwife) who assists a woman giving BIRTH: a doula may be a close relation, friend, the father of the child, or a health professional.

dowry. MONEY or PROPERTY brought to a MARRIAGE by the bride that derives from her family. Principally found in Eurasia and practiced by the wealthy. "Indirect dowry" is supplied by the groom's family, either straight to the bride or via her family, who then give an equivalent to her (this form has become more common in the MIDDLE EAST). Compare BRIDEPRICE.

Further reading: Goody & Tambiah (1973).

doxa. In the THEORY of BOURDIEU, "doxa" describes the base from which a CULTURE persuades itself that the socio-political form it inhabits is "natural" as opposed to being only one among a range of possibilities. Those with an interest in the doxa construct an *orthodoxy* to protect it and to disparage "heretical" viewpoints.

Further reading: Bourdieu (1977: 159–71).

drama. A performing ART typically associated in the west with the theatrical TRADITION descending from ancient Greece and Rome (with links to celebration and RITUAL) through such forms as "mystery plays," to the works of Shakespeare and Molière in the seventeenth century, the naturalism of Ibsen and Chekhov, and the formal experiments of Artaud and Brecht in the twentieth century. Drama can be a visceral medium for examining cultural issues or ethical dilemmas, and anthropologists such as TURNER have studied drama as a social force. The word derives from Greek, "action, deed"—which emphasizes the *performative* nature of drama.

Further reading: Turner (1986); Peacock (1987); Hastrup (2004).

Dravidian kinship. A KINSHIP system characteristic of parts of Southern India (but also found elsewhere) that focuses on CROSS-COUSINS and the expectation of their MARRIAGE.

Further reading: Trautmann (1981).

dreaming. Dreams have been associated with PROPHECY since the classical-era Egyptians and Greeks. For much of the twentieth century, FREUD's work on dreams as clues to the unconscious influenced western thought significantly. Dreams have been primarily thought of as the province of psychologists rather than social scientists.

Early researchers into the lives of Australian ABORIGINAL peoples described The Dreaming or Dreamtime, believed in these peoples' MYTHS to be the time of their creation, sometimes called "alcheringa" (from the Aranda term).

Further reading: Tedlock (1992).

dress. See CLOTHING.

drink. As with FOOD, the varieties of cultural significance attached to drinks have attracted anthropological interest. Apart from issues of availability of adequate and wholesome liquids to drink (see WATER), specific drinks (e.g. milk) may be more or less acceptable in a particular CULTURE, or associated with particular social settings or uses (tea ceremonies, RITUAL wine—as in Catholic mass). In such settings, drinking may well require an etiquette—who drinks and when, what is appropriate behavior, and so on.

A good deal of interest centers on the use and abuse of ALCOHOL, a substance so central to notions of conviviality in some cultures that the very term "drink" frequently implies its use specifically, and there are vast numbers of colloquial expressions referring to it.

Further reading: Douglas (1987); de Garine & de Garine (2001).

drugs. A wide number of substances, both naturally occurring (as PLANTS, for instance) and synthetically produced, can be regarded as drugs. When taken into the BODY (by whatever means), they alter it—temporarily and sometimes permanently. They may be categorized in various ways, for instance as HALLUCINOGENS or NARCOTICS. While widely used for medical (see ETHNOPHARMACOLOGY) and RITUAL purposes (see e.g. SHAMAN) in many societies, drugs may also be linked to social problems through their misuse. As with ALCOHOL, a good deal of sociological investigation has gone into the study of dependency and addiction.

Attitudes are at least partly dependent on CULTURE. Western societies commonly regard the use of cannabis or heroin as criminal, but tolerate NICOTINE and alcohol as part of normal social life. In some parts of the world—LATIN AMERICA and Asia, for instance—drug PRODUCTION is economically significant, and the illicitly created TRADE links stretch into

North America and Europe. Maintaining illegal activities may involve people in wider CRIME and VIOLENCE. Accordingly, the relative merits of legalizing certain drugs are often discussed both by academics and in wider social fora. See also AYAHUASCA, KHAT, PSYCHOTROPIC, TOBACCO.

Further reading: Goodman et al. (2007).

dual classification. The practice in a given CULTURE of dividing the elements of its experience on the basis of DUALISM or BINARY OPPOSITION. Tcherkézoff has shown how the Nyamwezi of Tanzania operate such taxonomies, and NEEDHAM is among the other anthropologists who have built on HERTZ's initial work on RIGHT AND LEFT.

Further reading: Needham (1973); Tcherkézoff (1987).

dual organization. A common feature of many societies, past and present, is to divide INDIVIDUALS into separate halves (moieties), with membership of a given MOIETY determining who an individual may marry, their ritual responsibilities, and so on. Certain societies (e.g. of Australian ABORIGINALS) may be highly given to dual organization. A measure of wider DUALISM (or BINARY OPPOSITION) is reflected in many areas of human thought. See also COMPLEMENTARY DUALISM, DUAL CLASSIFICATION.

dualism. A system of thought based on recognizing two principles or forces. These may be good and EVIL, MIND and BODY (as in Cartesian dualism), nature and nurture, feminine and masculine, or a similar pairing. Modern thinkers may shy away from too strict a division in using these terms. A number of aspects of dualist thought have, however, been the focus of anthropological studies of CLASSIFICATION, and an understanding of BINARY OPPOSITION is an important component of STRUCTURALISM. Compare COMPLEMENTARY DUALISM, MONISM, PLURALISM.

du Bois, W. E. B. (1868–1963). American writer and activist of mixed ETHNICITY; a famous campaigner against RACISM. Du Bois gained a doctorate from Harvard in 1895, and was closely associated with the National Association for the Advancement of Colored People. *The souls of black folk* (1903) is among his many works.

Dumont, Louis (1911–98). French anthropologist, born Salonika (now in Greece). Having been influenced by MAUSS as a student, he eventually began lecturing at Oxford (in 1951), in the circle around EVANS-PRITCHARD. He conducted fieldwork in Southern France and Tamil Nadu, India and wrote *La Tarasque: essai de description d'un fait local d'un point de vue ethnographique* (1951, new ed. 1987) and *Une sous-caste de L'Inde du Sud* (1957; *A South Indian subcaste: social organization and religion of the Pramalai Kallar*, 1986). In 1957 he co-founded (with David Pocock) the journal *Contributions to Indian sociology*. Thereafter a director of studies at what became EHESS, he published his landmark study of CASTE, *Homo hierachicus*, in 1967 (revised English ed., 1980). He also studied western individualism, producing several volumes on "*Homo aequalis*." See also HIERARCHY, INEQUALITY, PURITY.

Further reading: Celtel (2005).

Dundes, Alan (1934–2005). See FOLKLORE.

duolineal. Involving two lines: an occasional KINSHIP synonym for DOUBLE DESCENT; that is, relationship systems under which both the mother's and the father's sides are reckoned important.

duolocal. Involving two places: the custom of a married couple residing separately, each in their own birthplace. Few cultures practice duolocal residence.

Durkheim, Émile (1858–1917). The founder of modern French SOCIOLOGY; enormously influential in the development of the subject and related fields both in France and ANGLOPHONE countries. Born in Épinal, Durkheim was admitted to the Ecole normale supérieure in 1879, subsequently teaching at Bordeaux and the Sorbonne. He founded the journal L'*ANNÉE SOCIOLOGIQUE* (first issue in 1898) and gathered a group of scholars around him who included his nephew, MAUSS. His publications include *De la division du travail social* (*The division of labor in society*, 1893), *Les règles de la méthode sociologique* (*The rules of sociological method*, 1895), *Suicide* (1897), and *Les formes élémentaires de la vie religieuse* (*The elementary forms of the religious life*, 1912). These works have been translated many times, and introduced or made familiar a number of key concepts such as ANOMIE, COLLECTIVE CONSCIENCE, COLLECTIVE REPRESENTATION, SOCIAL FACTS, and types of SOLIDARITY. The British Centre for Durkheimian Studies publishes the journal *Durkheim studies*.

Further reading: Lukes (1992); Alexander & Smith (2005).

Durkheimian. In the manner of Émile DURKHEIM.

Dutch anthropology. The Dutch anthropological TRADITION is historically associated with study of the Dutch East Indies (modern Indonesia) and a version of STRUCTURALISM focusing on particular areas ("fields of ethnological study"). From the colonial tradition major figures such as J. P. B. and P. E. de JOSSELIN DE JONG arose. More recently, anthropologists have begun to shift their emphasis to the "SOCIOLOGY of non-western societies." Major Dutch publishers include the KITLV; universities of note include Leiden. See also BATAVIA.

Further reading: de Josselin de Jong (1984); Kloos & Claessen (1991).

Figure 6   Durkheim. Emile Durkheim was a seminal figure in sociology and anthropology. Photograph used by permission of Oxford University, School of Anthropology.

Dutch East India Company (VOC). See BATAVIA.

dyad. A group with two parts or members. In SOCIOLOGY, associated with Georg SIMMEL. Compare TRIAD.

dyarchy See DIARCHY.

dysfunction. Abnormal or disturbed function, either in a medical sense (e.g. "renal dysfunction") or of people or groups behaving in a manner other than the "expected" one. While the term was used in SOCIOLOGY in the mid twentieth century the therapeutic notion of dysfunctional attitudes has since permeated general DISCOURSE. Compare DEVIANCE.

E

e. A comparative KINSHIP abbreviation to denote that an INDIVIDUAL is "elder"; that is, older than EGO. For example, an older brother might be "eB."

E or Sp. In RELATIONSHIP TERMINOLOGY, the abbreviation for "spouse" (from French, "*épouse*").

Earth Summit (UN). See SUSTAINABLE DEVELOPMENT.

EASA. See EUROPEAN ASSOCIATION OF SOCIAL ANTHROPOLOGISTS.

École des hautes études en sciences sociales. See EHESS.

ecological anthropology. A specialism that focuses on the mutual influence of humans on their ENVIRONMENT and vice versa. A growing area since the mid twentieth century, ecological anthropology, initially called "cultural ecology," encompasses writers such as Julian STEWARD and Roy Rappaport, and a variety of strands, from its influence on CULTURAL MATERIALISM to historical, taxonomical, and other approaches. See also ECOSYSTEM, ENVIRONMENTALISM.

Further reading: Moran (2006); Rappaport (2000).

ecology. The study of the relationship between organisms and their ENVIRONMENT. The term was coined by Ernst Haeckel in 1866 (from Greek, "study of the dwelling"). Ecological concerns are of particular interest to anthropologists for reasons including the human effect on environments—in industries such as LOGGING, for instance in AMAZONIA and SOUTHEAST ASIA—and because of wider moral and political implications, for instance concerning the treatment of INDIGENOUS peoples.

Concise Dictionary of Social and Cultural Anthropology, First Edition. Mike Morris.
© 2012 Michael Ashley Morris. Published 2012 by Blackwell Publishing Ltd.

economic anthropology. Economic anthropology, building on antecedants such as the work of MAUSS on EXCHANGE, developed as a separate field from the mid twentieth century, and has expanded classical economic THEORY in several ways. While taking account of the traditional MODEL of rational MARKET-based activity (see e.g. ECONOMIC MAN), anthropologists have widened the focus of the subject to include not just MONEY transactions but also BARTER, GIFT exchange, and so on. They have also specialized in such areas as the POWER relations implicit in economic ties (sometimes adapting MARXIST theory), the social contexts of economic change (following the work of POLANYI), and the other ways in which people relate to each other through commodities and services (see CULTURAL ECONOMY). They recognize the ways in which economic factors moderate daily life, and the methods by which people can provide for themselves—from SUBSISTENCE-level AGRICULTURE to raising CASH CROPS, undertaking WORK for others, or a combination of means.

Recently, there has been some interest in the economic impacts of GLOBALI-ZATION (e.g. on migrating workers), the fate of citizens after SOCIALISM, and the events leading up to the worldwide financial crisis ("credit crunch"). See also CAPITALISM, COMMODITY FETISHISM, CONSPICUOUS CONSUMPTION, CONSUMPTION, FORMALIST/SUBSTANTIVIST DEBATE, HUNTER-GATHERER, INDUSTRIAL SOCIETY, INFORMAL ECONOMY, POTLATCH, PRODUCTION.

Further reading: Polanyi (2001); Carrier (2005); Gudeman (2009); Hann & Hart (2011).

Figure 7   **Economic anthropology.** A vegetable stall in Ngongoro village, Uluguru mountains, Tanzania; its owner also sells gold and rubies. Photo copyright: N. Beckmann.

economic man. An ideal INDIVIDUAL who, for the purposes of economic analysis, is assumed to behave in a perfectly rational manner, so as to maximize his/her own returns. Sometimes referred to by the Latin, "*Homo economicus.*" MALINOWSKI, in *Argonauts*, refers to the more obscure equivalent belief in "primitive economic man."

Further reading: Malinowski (2002).

ecosystem. A biological network comprising all the living organisms (including humans) in a given ENVIRONMENT, which exist in a state of interaction between themselves and with that environment; the dynamic relationships involved include energy flow and material exchange between these elements in a cyclical manner. Of interest in ECOLOGICAL ANTHROPOLOGY.

education. The process by which learning is achieved, either with children and young people or, in some cases, adults. The modern conception of a formal school system masks a cultural and historical reality: for much of humanity, processes of SOCIALIZATION and/or ENCULTURATION have usually taken place in other settings, often through means such as learning at home (and while performing WORK of some kind), through apprenticeship, and so on. In whatever setting, such formal education as exists is reinforced by (and reinforces) the "lessons" of the wider CULTURE.

Formal education has historically been associated with developing ETHICS and spiritual values; it has also been used to promote practical skills and, latterly, economic growth. In this regard, education mirrors wider cultural concerns. The conception of education as a process residing in a system of schools and colleges open—even compulsorily—to all has developed in INDUSTRIAL SOCIETY (e.g. Europe, Japan, the US) only in the last few centuries; but it is a legacy of far more restrictive institutions generally available only to rich males. This bureaucratized form of education was exported by COLONIALISM to many parts of the world; it has benefitted millions of people, but may nevertheless thus be viewed as a vehicle of political POWER. Such issues, including what the educator does in terms of endorsing the status quo (or even the STATE), are of great interest to thinkers such as BOURDIEU.

Further reading: Bourdieu & Passeron (1990); Spindler & Spindler (2000).

egalitarianism. The doctrine of social and economic (and so on) equality of all humankind. In western SOCIETY it offered a radical alternative to existing POWER structures in—for example—France and the US from the late eighteenth century onward. The idea of equality continues to play a large part in political RHETORIC in some cultures. Anthropologists have studied NON-WESTERN societies that were once assumed to be "naturally" egalitarian

Figure 8 Elder. Nadine Beckmann accompanies her research assistant, Aysha, to meet the latter's prospective grandmother-in-law, Mwanasalehe. Photo copyright: N. Beckmann.

and pointed out contradictions in this assumption; for example, in the treatment of WOMEN. See INEQUALITY.

Ego. In RELATIONSHIP TERMINOLOGY and KINSHIP, the person at the centre of the system, the "one" (real or posited) from whom other relations are described.

EHESS (École des hautes études en sciences sociales). Large French GOVERNMENT-backed research organization (http://www.ehess.fr/fr) with many branches, some run in conjunction with the CNRS. Established (from an earlier form) in 1975. See also FRENCH ANTHROPOLOGY.

eidos. In philosophy, the term for a Platonic ideal form. In anthropology, used by Gregory Bateson to describe the cognitive character (see COGNITION) of a given social group and thus its CULTURE. Also taken up by the sociologist Charles Madge and others. See also ETHOS.

Further reading: Bateson (1958).

elder. A high-ranking member of a TRIBE or other community (for instance a RELIGION) who has senior STATUS or AUTHORITY based at least partly on advanced age. Especially important where AGE-CLASS SYSTEMS are found. The term is often used in American English as a general synonym for "older person" ("elder care in the twenty-first century"). See also GERONTOCRACY.

elementary family. Synonymous with NUCLEAR FAMILY.

elementary structures. According to LÉVI-STRAUSS, societies adhering to an "elementary KINSHIP structure" define who is KIN and who is an affine (see AFFINITY) clearly. Only certain relatives are *positively* permitted as possible spouses. Alternatively, everyone is defined as a relative, but they are then divided into marriageable (see MARRIAGE) or not marriageable (see also MOIETY). By contrast, in COMPLEX STRUCTURES, such as many western societies, other factors (such as social, economic, or romantic ones) are more important in partner selection and the emphasis switches to who is *negatively* forbidden as a spouse. Elementary structures are associated with DIRECT EXCHANGE (or restricted exchange) and GENERALIZED EXCHANGE. See also CROW-OMAHA.

Further reading: Lévi-Strauss (1969[b]).

Eliot, T. S. (1888–1965). See FRAZER.

elite. The elite of any SOCIETY or group is that part that occupies positions of privilege, at the top of a HIERARCHY. These positions confer POWER unavailable to ordinary group members. The elite may include the rich or those in the upper CLASS, business leaders, or religious leaders. Theorists such as Gaetano Mosca, PARETO, and C. Wright Mills have analyzed elites.

Further reading: Mills (1999).

Elwin, Verrier (1902–64). See INDIAN ANTHROPOLOGY.

embedded. See DISEMBEDDED.

emic. A term derived by Kenneth Pike in 1954 from LINGUISTICS: an emic representation of the ideas or actions of the members of a CULTURE is drawn from the views of its own participants; an *etic* one is drawn from outside. For example, the external observer may regard certain phenomena as symptoms of a DISEASE—this is an *etic* judgment. But the cultural group in question may recognize other symptoms as characteristic of a particular ILLNESS that is not recognized elsewhere—this would be called an *emic* explanation.

Further reading: Headland et al. (1990).

emigration. See MIGRATION.

emotion. A strong feeling, such as LOVE, hate, anger, or fear. Emotions are subjective and may be characterized (cautiously) as essentially opposed to rational thought, though informing both thought and action. Anthropological interest has challenged the notion that people experience emotions in the same way everywhere; to some extent, emotions may be culturally constructed.

Further reading: Lutz (1988); Wulff (2007).

empiricism. A position in many fields (e.g. medicine, philosophy, and SOCIAL SCIENCES) that emphasizes the importance of experience and observation over THEORY. It was favored, for example, by some Chicago sociologists and by the proponents of ETHNOMETHODOLOGY. See also POSITIVISM.

enate. A KINSHIP term for a relation on the mother's side (contrast with AGNATIC).

enculturation. A similar process to SOCIALIZATION: the way in which an INDIVIDUAL acquires the thought and behavior patterns that embody their own CULTURE, normally in childhood. First used by Melville J. Herskovits in *Man and his works* (1948).

endangered. Commonly used of ANIMALS under threat of extinction. Also used by linguists in reference to LANGUAGES that are spoken by few people, or rarely, and are thus similarly imperiled. Compare LANGUAGE DEATH.

endemic. Constantly found in a PLACE or a people. Used in two main senses: of PLANTS and ANIMALS, to mean they are INDIGENOUS to an area, and of DISEASES, to mean they are usually present in low levels within a population (as opposed to arising in EPIDEMICS or PANDEMICS).

endogamy. Customary MARRIAGE *within* a group or social category. Contrast EXOGAMY: marriage outside the group.

Engels, Friedrich (1820–95). German revolutionary social theorist and businessman. Best known as a collaborator with MARX, though his own substantial works include *The origin of the family, private property and the state* (1884; see MORGAN). A major advocate of COMMUNISM. See also DIALECTICAL MATERIALISM, MATERIALISM, PRIMITIVE COMMUNISM, PROPERTY, and SOCIALISM.

Enlightenment, the. An eighteenth-century intellectual movement that developed from such strands as HUMANISM and was associated with a scientific, rational approach to issues. Exemplified by thinkers such as MONTESQUIEU, ROUSSEAU, Voltaire, Hume, and Kant. This period saw the first stirrings of modern anthropology as a distinct field, with several writers beginning to investigate "savage" peoples and common terms such as "anthropology" itself first being used significantly. Many key figures for modern ethnography (such as DURKHEIM and EVANS-PRITCHARD) have cited authors of this period as influences.

Further reading: Evans-Pritchard (1981); Wolff & Cipolloni (2007).

entitlement. "Entitlement theory" is an approach to FAMINE developed by the economist Amartya Sen that takes the view that such events arise not from absolute shortage of FOOD but from those in need not being culturally "entitled" to sufficient resources: that is, they may not produce, TRADE for, or otherwise legally acquire them within their own SOCIETY.

Further reading: Sen (1982); Sen & Drèze (1990).

environment. Literally, that which surrounds something; the totality of the external conditions affecting an INDIVIDUAL or organism, including physical factors, climate, and also other beings. See ENVIRONMENTALISM.

environmental determinism. A synonym for GEOGRAPHICAL DETERMINISM. See also POSSIBILISM.

environmentalism. A term covering perspectives that prioritize the ENVIRONMENT in some way. Loosely associated (since the 1970s) with efforts to preserve the natural world from degradation, usually as a result of human TECHNOLOGY. See also ECOLOGICAL ANTHROPOLOGY.

epidemic. An outbreak of DISEASE that arises in a particular area, affecting many people over a brief period, and at unusually high levels. Epidemiologists have been notably interested in major outbreaks of influenza (some of them large enough to count as PANDEMICS), cholera, and malaria. See also ENDEMIC.

Further reading: McNeill (1998); Herring & Swedlund (2010).

episteme. A system of knowledge, such as may determine one's outlook. First used in the context of classical Greek scholarship; picked up as a term by FOUCAULT.

epistemology. Study of the THEORY of knowledge. In SOCIOLOGY, it may be used to refer to methods by which knowledge is gained.

Epstein, A. L. (1924–99). See COPPERBELT.

equality. See EGALITARIANISM.

Erasmus, Desiderius (c. 1466–1536). See HUMANISM.

Erklärung. See VERSTEHEN.

Eskimo terminology. A RELATIONSHIP TERMINOLOGY in which SEX and GENERATION are distinguished for immediate relatives (the NUCLEAR FAMILY) but others (notably COUSINS) are more vaguely defined. Found in several places (e.g. Britain and the US); one of several variant types of system formally identified by Leslie Spier (although MORGAN had discussed Eskimo or Inuit systems) and later refined by G. P. MURDOCK.

Further reading: Spier (1925); Murdock (1949).

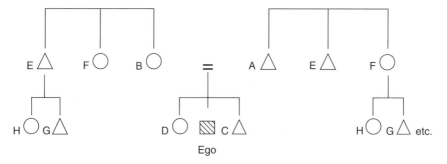

Figure 9 Eskimo terminology.

essentialism. In philosophy and SOCIAL SCIENCE, a belief that phenomena can be explained by defining their essence. It now has negative connotations, being considered an approach that is too simplistic and that ignores historical and cultural processes. A form of REDUCTIONISM.

essentially contested concepts. The British philosopher W. B. Gallie's label for terms (such as "art" or "democracy") that are so inherently disputable in their meaning that no "correct" way of using them can be agreed.

Further reading: Gallie (1968).

esthetics. See AESTHETICS.

ethics. The consideration of how one ought to behave; morality. Ethical concerns have been central to human thought for millennia: many religions have a keen focus on them, and philosophers since Socrates have studied ethical issues.

Ethics are significant for anthropologists in at least two ways: they will be interested in the moral systems of the people they study, and they themselves may well be obliged by formal and/or personal constraints to behave in certain ways in the course of their own research. FIELDWORK, for instance, requires the establishment of trust between anthropologist and subject, a trust the ethnographer needs to nurture.

Anthropologists may be working in areas that themselves give rise to ethical questions—as in studies of CRIME or VIOLENCE in a CULTURE. Organizations such as the ASSOCIATION OF SOCIAL ANTHROPOLOGISTS and the AMERICAN ANTHROPOLOGICAL ASSOCIATION have published their own ethical codes from time to time. See also BIOETHICS.

Further reading: American Anthropological Association (1998); Meskell & Pels (2005).

ethnic cleansing. A euphemism for the eradication of one ethnic or religious community by another within a particular region, either by FORCED MIGRATION or simple extermination. The term was first used regarding the Balkan

CONFLICT in the 1990s and later of events in Rwanda, but describes an activity that has occurred throughout HISTORY.

ethnicity. The quality of belonging to an ethnic group, in other words a people distinguished by discrete linguistic, cultural, or national features (an *ethnos* in ancient Greek). Similar in meaning to RACE, although ethnicity need not be defined by "race" alone. In anthropology, the modern study of ethnicity has turned on how meaningful it is to separate ethnic groups analytically, what membership of such a group means to those involved (see BARTH), and latterly on how ethnicity is used by modern states to mark difference, which can lead to CONFLICT and a sense of DISCRIMINATION. Barth's work in particular has been influential in turning concepts of ethnicity away from older constructions of it as something inherent, and toward a more fluid view.

Further reading: Banks (1996); Barth (1998); Guibernau & Rex (2010).

ethno-. PREFIX meaning "of a people or CULTURE." From Greek, *ethnos* ("nation").

ethnobiology. The branch of biology that studies the use made by different CULTURES of the ANIMALS and PLANTS in their ENVIRONMENT. It encompasses ETHNOBOTANY and ETHNOMEDICINE.

ethnobotany. INDIGENOUS knowledge and CUSTOMS concerning PLANTS in a particular ENVIRONMENT, and the scientific study thereof—of FOLK CLASSIFICATION, FOOD, healing (see ETHNOPHARMACOLOGY), and religious uses. Ethnobotanists have also been employed to locate plants of medical interest to pharmaceutical firms, raising issues of ETHICS and INTELLECTUAL PROPERTY.

Further reading: Minnis (2000).

ethnocentrism. The belief that one's own cultural values are natural and superior to others'. The term was given currency by William Sumner in *Folkways* (1907). "Secondary ethnocentrism" refers to the uncritical acceptance of the attitudes of another people by the anthropologist.

Further reading: Sumner (1979).

ethnocide. Intentional and systematic destruction of the CULTURE of an ethnic group, or of the group itself. See also GENOCIDE.

ethnographic analogy. The use of information about the practices of currently-living CULTURES, such as ABORIGINAL peoples, to infer the way of life of earlier communities. Principally used in ARCHAEOLOGY, where its limitations are recognized—for example, a manifest lack of "proof" in most cases. See also PROCESSUAL.

ethnographic present. The convention of writing up one's observation of a CULTURE in the present tense, whether or not this reflects its current state (since time will have passed since the FIELDWORK was done). Associated originally with early American ethnography and later criticized for encouraging a static, "pre-contact" view of NON-WESTERN societies.

ethnography. The written description of different peoples and their CUSTOMS (literally, "nation-writing," from the Greek): including articles, FIELDNOTES, monographs, and websites. The term covers both the object produced ("she has written an ethnography of the Arawak people") and the processes and methods of producing it ("what is the future of ethnography?"). The ethnographic monograph has long been a staple vehicle of anthropological research and THEORY, and the earliest genuine ethnographies, in this sense, developed in the mid nineteenth century through the work of such writers as MORGAN. See also WRITING CULTURE.

Further reading: Hammersley (2007); O'Reilly (2009); Melhuus et al. (2010).

ethnography of communication. An extension or relabeling of the ETHNOGRAPHY OF SPEAKING, widening its concerns with LANGUAGE use in context, and associated with the work of John Gumperz, Dell Hymes, Joel Sherzer, and others.

Further reading: Gumperz & Hymes (1964); Saville-Troike (2003).

ethnography of speaking. A development of ANTHROPOLOGICAL LINGUISTICS first formalized by Dell Hymes in the early 1960s that studies how LANGUAGE is used in its cultural context: the social nature of DISCOURSE. It swiftly expanded to draw in wider concerns, such as the ETHNOGRAPHY OF COMMUNICATION. See also SOCIOLINGUISTICS.

Further reading: Hymes (1962); Bauman & Sherzer (1989).

ethnohistory. A possibly contentious label for anthropological HISTORY: for the early part of the twentieth century, "ethnohistory" was regarded as the documentation of NON-WESTERN peoples by outsiders; later it shifted meaning to encompass, for example, oral histories from the peoples themselves. Questions raised include how history is perceived in different CULTURES—for example, non-chronologically—and how it is reworked according to contemporary needs.

Further reading: Tonkin et al. (1989).

ethnology. The scientific attempt to construct explanations for social and cultural phenomena by the comparative study of different peoples: essentially, what anthropologists do. Note that, as with many terms, "ethnology" may mean different things to different people at different times—it may be synonymous with SOCIAL ANTHROPOLOGY rather than PHYSICAL ANTHROPOLOGY to some European writers, for instance.

ethnomedicine. The traditional (see TRADITION) healing PRACTICES of particular ethnic groups, and the study of them, for instance in comparison to BIOMEDICINE.

Further reading: Kleinman (1980).

ethnomethodology. A sociological style associated with Harold Garfinkel that emphasizes the analysis of INDIVIDUAL assumptions about the nature of the world—people's "common sense" beliefs—over the study of wider SOCIAL STRUCTURES. See also EMPIRICISM, PHENOMENOLOGY.

Further reading: Garfinkel (2010).

ethnomusicology. Study of the MUSIC of different CULTURES. Originally the focus was on NON-WESTERN music specifically; later the field expanded to include all areas. Known as "comparative musicology" in the early twentieth century; "ethnomusicology" was coined by Jaap Kunst in 1950. Other notable contributors to the field include Alan Lomax.

Further reading: Post (2006).

ethnopharmacology. The study of the use of medicinal PLANTS and DRUGS in specific cultures. Ethnopharmacology intersects with ETHNOMEDICINE and ETHNOBOTANY.

ethnopoetics. The branch of POETICS dealing with (usually) non-western TEXTS and paying special attention to performance and context. The term comes from the American poet Jerome Rothenberg; other writers include Dell Hymes and Dennis Tedlock.

Further reading: *Alcheringa* [journal]; Hymes (2004).

ethnopsychiatry. The study of INDIGENOUS MODELS of mental ILLNESS and related states. The term comes from Louis Mars (Haiti, mid twentieth century) but was popularized by Georges (or George) Devereux. Much debate has since turned on what "ethnopsychiatry" means, along with its scope and perspective. As in many areas of anthropology, an understanding has arisen that framing other CULTURES in purely western terms may not be helpful: for instance, the characterization of the SHAMAN as a "mentally ill" person.

A number of leading social scientists have contributed in this area since the late twentieth century, using diverse approaches. Among them are Arthur KLEINMAN and Roland Littlewood.

Further reading: Littlewood & Dein (2000).

ethnopsychology. The study of INDIGENOUS MODELS of human thought and behavior. Associated with an ETHNOSCIENCE-derived perspective and the work of writers such as Catherine Lutz and Roy D'Andrade. A subdivision of PSYCHOLOGICAL ANTHROPOLOGY.

Further reading: Lutz (1988).

ethnoscience. Can be used as a general synonym for ETHNOGRAPHY. In anthropology, ethnoscience is specifically the study of different CULTURES' systems of knowledge about and CLASSIFICATION of the world, with the emphasis on an EMIC perspective—that is, the cultures' own viewpoints. Such INDIGENOUS KNOWLEDGE can be studied on an INDIVIDUAL basis or comparatively. Ethnoscience can also be described by the term NEW ETHNOGRAPHY, and is associated with a movement of early cognitive and linguistic anthropologists in the US from the early 1960s, including Harold C. Conklin and William C. Sturtevant. Latterly it has been of particular concern to those working in DEVELOPMENT.

Further reading: Ellen et al. (2000).

ethnozoology. The study of the way different CULTURES classify and interact with ANIMALS. See also FOLK CLASSIFICATION, TOTEMISM.

ethology. The branch of natural history dealing with ANIMAL behavior, and grounded in evolutionary THEORY. In contrast to BEHAVIORISM, which stressed deductive laboratory experiments, ethologists concentrate on an inductive study of animals in their natural environment. This approach has been used with human societies, for instance by Lee and DeVore.

Further reading: Lee & DeVore (1976).

ethos. The characteristic spirit of a person or group; used by Gregory Bateson in *Naven* to specify a people's emotional character, as distinct from their EIDOS.

etic. See EMIC.

etiquette. See COMMENSALITY, DRINK.

eugenics. The scientific study of the conditions under which better offspring (particularly human) are produced, with the aim of improving the stock. Promoted by Sir Francis Galton in the late nineteenth century (though the original idea goes back to Plato); in Galton's era the aims of eugenics were widely accepted as desirable in Europe and the US, but they later became controversial after adoption by the Nazi regime. *Positive* eugenics encourages more children among "desirable" subjects; *negative* eugenics discourages "undesirable" breeding.

eunuch. A man who has been castrated. Historically, eunuchs often guarded harems in eastern CULTURES; in some of these cultures (China, India, etc) they became powerful.

Eurocentrism or **Europocentrism.** Exclusive focus on Europe; the assumption that European values are naturally superior to those of other CULTURES; compare ETHNOCENTRISM.

Further reading: Goody (2010).

European Association of Social Anthropologists (EASA). Professional organization (http://www.easaonline.org) for anthropologists who qualified in, or are working in, Europe. The EASA publishes a monograph series, the journal *Social anthropology*, and holds conferences.

Evans-Pritchard, E. E. (1902–73). British anthropologist; a major figure in the development of social anthropology. Born in Crowborough, Sussex. E-P, as he became known, was educated at Winchester College and Oxford (1921–4). He attended the London School of Economics under SELIGMAN and MALINOWSKI. Pursuing fieldwork with the Azande (see ZANDE) in the Southern Sudan, he took a Ph.D. at the University of London in 1928. In 1930 he did fieldwork with the NUER. He was professor of sociology at King Fuad I University, Cairo, from 1932 to 1934, then reader in social anthropology at Cambridge and finally professor at Oxford from 1946 to 1970. E-P was the first (life) president of the ASSOCIATION OF SOCIAL ANTHROPOLOGISTS. He converted to Roman CATHOLICISM in 1944. His works include classics of ethnography such as *Witchcraft, oracles and magic among the Azande* (1937), *The Nuer: a description of the modes of livelihood and political institutions of a Nilotic people* (1940), and *Kinship and marriage among the Nuer* (1951). He also edited *African political systems* (1940) with FORTES. Later works often show his interest in the HISTORY OF ANTHROPOLOGY (see also ENLIGHTENMENT).

Further reading: Beattie & Lienhardt (1975); Douglas (2003); Burton (1992).

Evenki. See SHAMAN.

evil. That which is not good. In most contexts, evil is associated with morally wrong choices that cause SUFFERING to SELF and/or others. Evil is a major concern of many RELIGIONS; most advance explanations for the presence of evil in the world (see e.g. THEODICY). Evil is also a wider topic to secular thinkers. In an anthropological context, it is associated with the study of areas such as WITCHCRAFT, though, as with many ideas, one should beware of assuming that other cultures share western conceptions very exactly.

Further reading: Parkin (1985).

evil eye. A folk belief in the POWER of a person to do harm to others (or their PROPERTY) with a look—a widespread and ancient belief in peoples of the MEDITERRANEAN region and MIDDLE EAST. It shades into a more general wariness of incurring "bad luck" by provoking EVIL thoughts in others, or by giving praise to loved ones so as to "tempt fate."

Further reading: Dundes (1992); Migliore (1997).

evolution. In its best-known sense, the THEORY that species of living things develop from previous versions of themselves, as opposed to being created. Made famous (or notorious) by DARWIN (see also DARWINISM), though the word had this sense from at least the 1830s. "Social evolution" is the anthropological concept of directional change in a SOCIETY. In late-nineteenth-century studies it was supposed that "primitive" societies gradually evolved to greater levels of complexity, but a less ethnocentric view came to prevail among anthropologists and it was no longer assumed that social evolution is a rigid progression through EVOLUTIONARY STAGES; it was also accepted that societies can regress or remain static at times. Theories of evolution also now acknowledge that it cannot be directly willed by individuals: that is, that the consequences of social change may not ultimately be anything like what their original proponents intended. For more detail see EVOLUTIONISM.

evolutionary anthropology. A recent (late twentieth century) development of anthropology in which an avowedly biological perspective is paramount (compare BIOLOGICAL ANTHROPOLOGY). Evolutionary anthropology studies the impact of biological and ecological factors on thought and behavior. It is a wide field, encompassing not only human CULTURES—examining, for example, use of TOOLS, DIET preferences, relations to ANIMALS, and so on—but also much research on PRIMATES (in particular) and other creatures, from a number of specialist perspectives (e.g. PALEO-ANTHROPOLOGY, COGNITIVE ANTHROPOLOGY). In terms of wider disciplinary development, evolutionary anthropology may be seen as distinct from mainstream social and cultural anthropology, by whose practitioners it has been criticized—sometimes vociferously—as, for example, overly reduc-tionist in its "scientific" approach. See also NATURE AND CULTURE.

Further reading: *Evolutionary anthropology* [journal]; Dunbar (2004).

evolutionary stages. Theoretical steps in the EVOLUTION of a CULTURE: an early example is MORGAN and others' notion of the progression from SAVAGERY to BARBARISM to CIVILIZATION.

evolutionism. A perspective grounded in belief in theories of EVOLUTION. Nineteenth-century anthropologists such as TYLOR and MORGAN advocated what became known as *unilinear* evolutionism: the idea that evolution followed pretty much the same path in every society, with the same stages of development discernible. With the rise of FIELDWORK-centered anthropology at the start of the next century, authors such as BOAS (see also HISTORICAL PARTICULARISM) and MALINOWSKI rejected this MODEL and evolutionism fell from favor. It revived in a less straitjacketed form with the work of anthropologists such as WHITE in the 1930s (*universal* evolutionism); STEWARD proposed a PARADIGM in which different societies evolved differently in response to their particular circumstances (*multilinear* evolutionism). *Neo*evolutionism (or neo-Darwinism) is a term that generally applies to modern revivals of evolutionism; in SOCIOLOGY it is associated with the theories of Talcott PARSONS. See also EVOLUTIONARY ANTHROPOLOGY.

Further reading: Carneiro (2003).

evulsion. Pulling out or extraction, as in the voluntary removal of teeth among some peoples.

exchange. Exchange is a central concern for many anthropologists. All societies exchange goods, services, and other entities (including people—as in the transfer of brides for marriage ALLIANCE), but a particular exchange can mean one of a number of things. The main types are "GIFT exchange," in which the inherent value of the gift is less significant than its effect of consolidating social ties, and "COMMODITY exchange," which is nearer the capitalist model of purely economic activity, with little social meaning being necessary. Famous ethnographic examples of exchange practices include the KULA of MELANESIA and the North American POTLATCH. See also COMMODITY FETISHISM, SOCIAL EXCHANGE.

Further reading: Davis (1992).

exchange theory. A social THEORY with antecedents in economics and philosophy (for instance UTILITARIANISM) that was developed in SOCIOLOGY by Peter M. Blau and anthropology by George C. Homans. Broadly it sees SOCIAL EXCHANGE as a primarily rational activity in which one behaves in the way most likely to achieve a return in the form of rewards (of whatever kind); thus one is led to repeat one's most effective actions.

Further reading: Homans (1958).

exchange value. In economics (often in MARXIST theory), the value of a COMMODITY or service as shown by what it can be exchanged for. This is distinguished from its USE VALUE. Gold, for example, has certain practical uses but its exchange value is disproportionately high against these alone. In such cases capitalists gain the benefits of the SURPLUS value.

exegesis. A critical exposition of a TEXT, generally the Bible. In anthropology, it can mean a local explanation of a phenomenon.

exogamy. Customary MARRIAGE *outside* a group or social category; contrast ENDOGAMY, marriage within a group.

exorcism. The expulsion of a demon or EVIL SPIRIT. Associated with POSSESSION and a RITUAL of certain RELIGIONS (e.g. Catholic CHRISTIANITY).

Further reading: Kapferer (1991).

expert. Anthropologists may both serve as experts themselves, for example by giving evidence to legal inquiries, and also observe the expertise of the people they study—by, say, watching participants conducting a RITUAL. The term, at least as applied in everyday or familiar contexts, is not uncontentious—we may debate what "makes" one an expert.

Further reading: Morris & Bastin (2004).

exploitation. Making use of a resource of some kind (minerals, PLANTS, ANIMALS, or people), often with the implication that the user is self-centered or ethically questionable. In a political context, associated with MARX's view of CAPITALISM—a system for creating profit (see SURPLUS) from the efforts of poorly rewarded others. In different contexts "exploitation" covers not just economic but also GENDER and other relations. More neutrally, it may be applied without suggesting opprobrium ("plant exploitation for food is centered on the yam").

extended family. A domestic unit composed of a series of related nuclear families (see NUCLEAR FAMILY): for example where married children share a parental home. Extended families may extend "lineally" (as in parents and children) or "collaterally" (where the unit is composed of SIBLINGS—see JOINT FAMILY).

F

F or Fa. In RELATIONSHIP TERMINOLOGY, the abbreviation for "father."

Facebook. See SOCIAL NETWORK.

fait social. See SOCIAL FACT.

family. A group of people who have a common residence and/or relationship, and who share economic and reproductive ties. Traditional understandings of what makes a family may be brought into question by new ways of living—for example gay and lesbian relationships, ADOPTION, and FERTILITY issues—and there is growing recognition among social scientists of the effect of cultural and ideological influences on such social groupings. See also NUCLEAR FAMILY, KINSHIP.

family resemblances. In the *Philosophical investigations* (paragraphs 66ff), WITTGENSTEIN argues that there are no sharply defined concepts behind a CLASSIFICATION such as "games": the qualifications for being a game are so nebulous that they form instead a "network of similarities" that overlap in at least some particulars in the same way as family resemblances do in people. Among anthropologists influenced by Wittgenstein, NEEDHAM espoused the similar notion of POLYTHETIC CLASSIFICATION. See also LANGUAGE GAMES, PROTOTYPE THEORY.

Further reading: Wittgenstein (2009).

famine. A major shortage of FOOD in a region, often occurring quickly, and with significant consequent DEATHs from starvation and DISEASE. Famine may be immediately caused by WAR or natural DISASTER, or may come about from STATE mismanagement; it has been argued that its effects are

Concise Dictionary of Social and Cultural Anthropology, First Edition. Mike Morris.
© 2012 Michael Ashley Morris. Published 2012 by Blackwell Publishing Ltd.

exacerbated by cultural factors (see ENTITLEMENT). Anthropologists have investigated particular famines and contributed to the debate among NGOS and politicians as to how best to alleviate them. See also HUNGER, SCARCITY.

Further reading: De Waal (2005).

farming. See AGRICULTURE.

fasting. See HUNGER.

fecundity. See FERTILITY.

feedback. A term originally used in electronics, to describe a returning output signal, and subsequently in CYBERNETICS and other areas. Feedback is the information that systems derive from their ENVIRONMENT that allows them to adjust and maintain their performance. See also SYSTEMS THEORY.

Fei Xiaotong (1910–2005). See CHINESE ANTHROPOLOGY.

female circumcision. See CIRCUMCISION.

feminist anthropology. Anthropology with a particular concern with WOMEN's roles in SOCIETY: particularly since the 1960s, feminist anthropologists have taken issue with the historical male bias (ANDROCENTRISM) in earlier works and have striven for a more rounded picture of social life. Recent studies tend to focus on such issues as the relation of GENDER and POWER. The Association for Feminist Anthropology has been a section of the AMERICAN ANTHROPOLOGICAL ASSOCIATION since 1988.

Further reading: Moore (1994); Lewin (2006).

fertility. Derived from Latin, "to bear." Productiveness; specifically, a woman's ability to produce children successfully (distinguished from *fecundity*, the state of being able to conceive). Anthropologists have explored several areas in this field, from the study of fertility rites and cults to the vexed question of who controls WOMEN's fertility. See also REPRODUCTIVE TECHNOLOGIES.

Further reading: *Human fertility* [journal]; Loizos & Heady (1999).

fetish. An object believed in NON-WESTERN societies to have special POWERS, or to be imbued with a spirit (contrast "idols," which are valued for what they represent rather than their own qualities). The term gained currency in the nineteenth century. Now equally found in more general use ("he fetishizes this theory"). See also COMMODITY FETISHISM.

feud. A social institution for regulating VIOLENCE by which killings are avenged and HONOR maintained. Two groups in a SMALL-SCALE SOCIETY reciprocate attacks until a resolution is reached (e.g. by payment of compensation); characteristically, this activity is conducted by family members against another family. Fear of inciting a feud may deter violence. See also BLOOD FEUD, VENDETTA.

Further reading: Turney-High (1971); Black-Michaud (1975).

feudalism. The political system that developed in northern Europe in the Middle Ages; characterized by a pyramidal POWER structure, at the apex of which was the king, who was answerable only to God. The king dispensed land to feudal lords in exchange for military and other support. The lords in turn granted the means of livelihood, and protection, to PEASANTS. MARX, WEBER, and others made studies of feudalism; Marx in particular viewed it as as preceding CAPITALISM. Much discussion has been made of (e.g. Asian) polities that appear to be "feudal" (compare ORIENTAL DESPOTISM).

Further reading: Bloch (1989).

fictive kinship. A PRACTICE by which non-related INDIVIDUALS are treated as if they were part of a FAMILY. College fraternities and Catholic religious expressions ("Father," "Sister," etc) are examples. Compare RITUAL KINSHIP.

field theory. A field, at its broadest, is any sphere of action or investigation, literal or metaphorical, from a field of battle to a FIELDWORK site or, at a more abstract level, an area of academic study (e.g. "the field of hermeneutics"). In the work of BOURDIEU a field is primarily a domain within which people *compete*; they obey the principles of that field, and each of the separate fields (among them ART, EDUCATION, and politics) has its own particular logic and priorities.

fieldnotes. A crucial part of FIELDWORK in anthropology (though also used in other SOCIAL SCIENCES). An ethnographer will normally make quick notes while studying a situation or interviewing a subject, later augmenting them when writing up. The form can be very flexible. The use of fieldnotes raises issues of confidentiality and context—for instance, the posthumous release of MALINOWSKI's unguarded comments in the field created controversy.

Further reading: Malinowski (1989); Sanjek (1990); Emerson et al. (1995).

fieldwork. Many SOCIAL SCIENCES involve fieldwork: few make it as crucial to their PRACTICE as does anthropology. Characteristically, fieldwork involves a long period—several months or years—living among the people studied (see PARTICIPANT OBSERVATION), speaking their language and absorbing their CUSTOMS (as well as conducting more formal kinds of research). The most notable early anthropologist to champion fieldwork was MALINOWSKI. In recent years there has been some debate as to the problems associated with fieldwork—for instance, the dangers of assuming that data taken from the field will have much value outside their immediate context.

Further reading: Dresch et al. (2000); Rabinow (2007).

Figure 10 Fieldwork. Nadine Beckmann talking with Aysha and Mwanasalehe (see also ELDER). Photo copyright: N. Beckmann.

fiesta. Spanish for "feast": in Spain and LATIN AMERICA, a celebration of a SAINT's day or other holiday, marked by processions and dancing. *Fiestas* may be seen (along with similar occasions—see e.g. CARNIVAL, RITUAL OF REBELLION) as opportunities for reaffirming social order or IDENTITY.

filiation. A process by which children are recognized as bound to their parents, with attendant rights. Note that the French word "*filiation*" covers both this sense and what in English is called DESCENT. Compare AFFILIATION (which links a child to the line of descent generally) and see especially COMPLEMENTARY FILIATION, the process by which children form emotional ties to what might be thought less significant relatives.

film. See VISUAL ANTHROPOLOGY.

Finnegan, Ruth H. (1933–). See ORAL LITERATURE, POETICS.

First World. A term used from the 1960s onward to describe the industrialized, developed capitalist countries of western Europe, North America, Australia and New Zealand, and Japan. Compare SECOND WORLD, THIRD WORLD.

First Nations. A Canadian term for GOVERNMENT-recognized tribes of native peoples.

Firth, Raymond (1901–2002). Social anthropologist associated with the Pacific area and early ECONOMIC ANTHROPOLOGY. Firth was born in Auckland, New Zealand and studied at the London School of Economics

(LSE) from 1924, under SELIGMAN and MALINOWSKI. After taking a Ph.D. in 1927, he undertook fieldwork in Tikopia, Solomon Islands, which he was to visit several times (he later did further fieldwork in Kelantan, Malaya; his wife Rosemary wrote a monograph on the region). He returned to the LSE where he held the Chair of Anthropology from 1945 to 1968, and was life president of the ASSOCIATION OF SOCIAL ANTHROPOLOGISTS from 1975. His many works include *We, the Tikopia* (1936; 2nd ed. 1957), *Human types* (1938; rev. ed. 1956), *Primitive Polynesian economy* (1939), *Man and culture* (ed., 1957), *Essays on social organization and values* (1964), and *Themes in economic anthropology* (ed., 1967). See also AMBILINEAL, POLYNESIA, RAMAGE.

Further reading: Freedman (1967).

fishing. Killing or capture of fish, shellfish, or sea mammals, usually for FOOD. Sometimes regarded as a form of foraging or hunter-gathering, fishing is a human activity that dates back to very early times and takes many forms (such as seasonal, year-round, or industrial-scale) in a variety of settings—rivers, lakes, on the shore, and at sea. Anthropologists have studied the over-EXPLOITATION of these resources, and considered the way of life of fishing communities. See also MARITIME, WHALING.

Further reading: Barnes (1996); van Ginkel (2007).

flagellation. The practice of whipping. Sometimes associated with sexual activities, but RITUAL beating or self-flagellation is connected to the expression of religious beliefs (e.g. showing penitence for sins) and the whip may be used in punishment by the STATE (for instance in the MIDDLE EAST).

folk classification. The TAXONOMY devised by particular groups to name PLANTS (see also ETHNOBOTANY), ANIMALS (see also ETHNOZOOLOGY), and so on, and place them within a CLASSIFICATION system. Investigated by Brent Berlin, among others.

Further reading: Berlin (1992).

folk–urban continuum. A term associated with the work of REDFIELD (though Pitirim Sorokin first spoke of a "rural–urban continuum"), who placed various types of COMMUNITY on a scale showing DEVELOPMENT. At one end is the TRADITIONAL SOCIETY of the VILLAGE; at the other the (so-called) MODERN urban setting. Between these two extremes are intermediate locales that share features of both. Traditional societies are "low-tech" and have high internal cohesion; modern societies have advanced TECHNOLOGY and greater personal autonomy.

Further reading: Redfield (1941).

folklore. Beliefs, TRADITIONS, and CUSTOMS passed on, usually orally, within a CULTURE. Folklore may be expressed in various ways, for example as proverbs, tales, songs, and rhymes. The term was coined by William J. Thoms in 1846.

The study of folklore—from literary and historical perspectives—developed in early-nineteenth-century northern Europe (e.g. Germany, Finland, Britain) and overlaps with the history of anthropology in such areas as popular MYTH-making (for instance as regards NATIONALISM and supposed NATIONAL CHARACTER). In the twentieth century, folklore particularly appealed to linguistic scholars, such as Propp (see CODE). Modern theorists of folklore include Alan Dundes. See also EVIL EYE.

Further reading: Dundes (2005).

folkways. NORMS regarding manners in a particular SOCIETY; ways of ensuring appropriate behavior at a less consequential level than that of MORES. Distinguished by W. G. Sumner in the early twentieth century.

Further reading: Sumner (1979).

food. Many aspects of food PRODUCTION, distribution, and CONSUMPTION are of anthropological interest. These include the methods and TECHNOLOGY of AGRICULTURE and other methods of gaining food; changing labor relations (including issues of GENDER) and land use (e.g. for CASH CROPS); regional and global POWER movements and their effects; FAMINE and food shortage (see HUNGER), including DEVELOPMENT issues; the requirements of nutrition and cultural expectations regarding diet (e.g. FOOD TABOOS, OBESITY); and food as SYMBOL and as GIFT. See also BIOTECHNOLOGY, COOKING, NUTRITIONAL ANTHROPOLOGY.

Further reading: Harris (1985); MacClancy (1992).

food system. The entire chain of FOOD procurement, treatment, distribution, and CONSUMPTION, including food rules. Anthropologists have produced many studies of how larger systems interact and have an impact on communities, for instance in cases of food shortages and when MARKETS operate to alter availability.

Further reading: Richards (1995); Wilk (2006).

food taboo. A TABOO by which things that could be safely eaten are avoided. Many of these, such as the Jewish and Muslim avoidance of pork, are well-known, but many cultures have FOOD taboos, sometimes for special categories of people at specific times. Theorists have suggested that notional links to totems (see TOTEMISM) may be behind such prohibitions; to Mary DOUGLAS, ANIMALS classed as "unclean"/inedible are often held to be *anomalous*, possessing uncharacteristic qualities for their kind and thus "dangerous."

Further reading: Douglas (2002).

forager. See HUNTER-GATHERER.

forced migration. A form of MIGRATION involving people who are displaced from necessity or coercion. As with general migration, this can be either internal to a region or transnational; causes may include WAR, political force (as within APARTHEID-era South Africa), DEVELOPMENT projects (for instance, the siting of dams), DISASTERS, and FAMINE. See also REFUGEE—a person who seeks shelter away from their home. A useful resource is the Forced Migration Online site: http://www.forcedmigration.org.

Further reading: Betts (2009).

forces of production. In MARXIST theory, the MEANS OF PRODUCTION plus the technological knowledge and other human input (e.g. labor) required for their use. Compare MODE OF PRODUCTION, RELATIONS OF PRODUCTION.

Forde, Daryll (1902–73). British anthropologist, born and educated in London. He held professorships at University College, Wales and University College, London; his fieldwork took place in the south-west United States and Nigeria. Forde was director of the INTERNATIONAL AFRICAN INSTITUTE from 1945 to 1973; he edited *Africa* and other publications. Apart from his considerable reputation as an Africanist, he is notable for showing an early interest in cultural aspects of the ENVIRONMENT. His works include *Habitat, economy and society* (1934, several later editions), *African systems of kinship and marriage* (edited with RADCLIFFE-BROWN, 1950) and *African worlds* (ed., 1954).

forensic anthropology. The application of techniques drawn from physical or BIOLOGICAL ANTHROPOLOGY, such as osteology (analysis of the human skeleton), to problems concerning legal cases ("forensic" derives from Latin, "*forum*," where legal assemblies were held). A forensic anthropologist may be requested to examine human corpses (often decomposed or mutilated) where death is suspicious, and be a witness at any subsequent proceedings. Noted practitioners in this specialized field include the anthropologist and novelist Kathy Reichs. See the website of the American Board of Forensic Anthropology: http://www.theabfa.org.

Further reading: Byers (2011).

forestry. The cultivation and management of forests, including the use of timber and oversight of other natural resources. Many peoples studied by anthropologists have close ties to forest regions. See also LOGGING, RAINFOREST.

formalist/substantivist debate. An argument in ECONOMIC ANTHRO-POLOGY that emerged in the 1960s: a debate between those who said that standard, "rational" concepts taken from theories of western CAPITALISM could be applied to SIMPLE SOCIETIES (formalists) and those who held that non-western EXCHANGE operated on different principles (substantivists). Karl POLANYI was a leading proponent of the second view. See also DISEMBEDDED.

Further reading: LeClair & Schneider (1968).

Fortes, Meyer (1906–83). South-African-born anthropologist (with an influential background in psychology) who taught at the London School of Economics and Oxford; he was professor of social anthropology at Cambridge from 1950 to 1973. Fortes undertook fieldwork in the Gold Coast (later Ghana) and Nigeria. A key exponent of DESCENT THEORY, he published numerous works including *African political systems* (ed. with EVANS-PRITCHARD, 1940), *Oedipus and Job in West African religion* (1959, reissued 1983), and *Time and social structure* (1970).

Fortune, Reo (1903–79). See MEAD [M.].

Foster, George M. (1913–2006). See LIMITED GOOD.

fostering. See ADOPTION.

Foucault, Michel (1926–84). French philosopher and intellectual, influenced by Nietzsche. His theories relating to the use of knowledge to extend POWER have greatly influenced SOCIOLOGY, and his writings covered a wide array of historical and cultural topics, often from a critical standpoint. His ouput includes *Folie et déraison* (1961; *Madness and civilization: a history of insanity in the Age of Reason*, 1967), *Surveiller et punir* (1975; *Discipline and punish: the birth of the prison*, 1977), and *Histoire de la sexualité* (1976–84; *History of sexuality*, 1978–86). See also ARCHAEOLOGY OF KNOWLEDGE, BIOPOLITICS, BODY, DISCOURSE, EPISTEME, PHILOSOPHICAL ANTHROPOLOGY, RESISTANCE, SOCIAL CONTROL.

Further reading: Rabinow (1984).

four fields. In American universities, anthropology is traditionally divided into four areas: SOCIAL ANTHROPOLOGY and/or CULTURAL ANTHROPOLOGY; BIOLOGICAL ANTHROPOLOGY or PHYSICAL ANTHROPOLOGY; ANTHROPO-LOGICAL LINGUISTICS; and ARCHAEOLOGY. While particular practitioners may be expert in one specific field, effective study of social questions some-times involves a mix of these four. British universities often treat the four fields as discrete disciplines.

Fourth World. A term for INDIGENOUS groups (Native Americans, Amazonian peoples, and others) who live as ethnic minorities in nations where non-native groups are dominant. In SOCIAL SCIENCES it may simply designate countries of the THIRD WORLD that are particularly poor and lacking DEVELOPMENT.

Fox, James J. (1940–). See SOUTHEAST ASIA.

francophone. French-speaking (from Latin, "French" and Greek, "voice").

Frankfurt School. See CRITICAL ANTHROPOLOGY, HABERMAS.

fratricide. Killing of one's own brother, or one who does this.

Frazer, J. G. (1854–1941). Scottish classicist and anthropologist, born Glasgow. He was educated at Glasgow and at Cambridge, at the latter of which he remained a fellow for life. His highly popular twelve-volume *The golden bough*, investigating the origins of RELIGION, exerted a major influence over several literary figures (e.g. T. S. Eliot) but was too theoretical and evolutionist to survive the rise of MALINOWSKI-style, FIELDWORK-based ethnography with its credibility intact. He was the first professor of social anthropology at Liverpool in 1908. However, his career may have suffered as a result of his aversion to public life. See also SORORATE, SYMPATHETIC MAGIC.

Freedman, Maurice (1920–75). See CHINESE ANTHROPOLOGY.

Freeman, Derek (1916–2001). See MEAD [M.], POLYNESIA, UTROLATERAL.

French anthropology. The first stirrings of a French anthropological TRADITION can be traced as far back as the sixteenth century and MONTAIGNE. In 1799 the *Société des observateurs de l'homme* was founded; the philosophical background of its members was to remain common to many later French anthropologists. An arguably more colonialist slant emerged in the nineteenth century, and the focus on *ethnologie* was replaced by one on *anthropologie générale*, which was broader in approach, drawing in elements of PHYSICAL ANTHROPOLOGY and HUMAN GEOGRAPHY. In the twentieth century, the *ANNÉE SOCIOLOGIQUE* group around DURKHEIM and MAUSS made great strides in a sociological direction; there was significant work by ethnographers such as Maurice Leenhardt in MELANESIA and several Africanists (among them the surrealist Michel Leiris and the film-maker Jean ROUCH). After a period in America under the influence of JAKOBSON, LÉVI-STRAUSS developed the structuralist approach; STRUCTURALISM itself influenced a number of fields, including psychology and literature.

Modern French anthropology is dominated by a number of large organizations (e.g. CNRS, EHESS) with GOVERNMENT funding, rather than being university-based. Anthropologists reach a wider public than is usual in the US or UK. In addition to such figures as BOURDIEU, wider-ranging intellectuals such as FOUCAULT and Jean BAUDRILLARD have been influential both at home and abroad.

Further reading: *L'homme* [journal]; Rogers (1999).

French Revolution (1789–99). See CONDORCET, HUMAN RIGHTS, ROUSSEAU, SOCIALISM, TERRORISM.

Freud, Sigmund (1856–1939). The founder of psychoanalysis, whose influence on twentieth-century thought in general has been considerable, including altering the development of fields such as ART and literary criticism and the understanding of RELIGION, anthropology, and medicine. Freud was born in Moravia, in what is now the Czech Republic. His seminal works include *Totem und Tabu* (1913; *Totem and taboo: resemblances between the psychic lives of savages and neurotics*, 1919), in which he discussed INCEST, and *Die Traumdeutung* (1900; *The interpretation of dreams*, third, rev. ed., 1932). In general, Freudian approaches to psychology have fallen from favor somewhat in recent years. See also MANIFEST AND LATENT.

Fried, Morton H. (1923–86). See RANK SOCIETY.

Friedman, Milton (1912–2006). See CHICAGO SCHOOL, NEOLIBERALISM.

frontier. The edge of an inhabited region, as distinct from its political boundary (BORDER), though the terms may be used interchangably. Frontiers tend to be sparsely populated and less amenable to STATE control; they may be subject to various kinds of disorder and disputes, and may change over time.

f.s. Female speaking (in KINSHIP accounts).

function word. In GRAMMAR, a word (such as an article—e.g. "the" or "a"—or auxiliary verb) that has little or no meaning apart from the grammatical sense it expresses. Sometimes called a "functor," or similar term. See also PARTICLE.

functionalism. The study and theory of functional interactions and adaptation of elements within a framework (see SYSTEM). Functionalism operates from several varying perspectives within the SOCIAL SCIENCES, but anthropologically is associated with the work of twentieth-century British-based practitioners such as MALINOWSKI, RADCLIFFE-BROWN, and EVANS-PRITCHARD (see also STRUCTURAL-FUNCTIONALISM) and a SYNCHRONIC approach to SOCIAL ORGANIZATION. These writers themselves, however, had reservations about the term or its definition. Many of its assumptions have, nevertheless, been absorbed into contemporary anthropology. See also MANIFEST AND LATENT.

Further reading: Stocking (1984).

fundamentalism. In RELIGION, any movement prioritizing an essential requirement of belief, especially in the literal truth (rather than allegorical meaning, for instance) of the Bible in CHRISTIANITY and of the Koran in ISLAM.

Although the term was first linked with Protestant Christians in post-World War I America, and is sometimes applied to adherence to Creationism—the view that God created the Universe, as opposed to the

Figure 11   **Funeral rites**. Shah Nasr Ed-Din's funeral, in what was then Persia, 1896. Photo: A. Sevrugin (?), National Anthropological Archives, Smithsonian Institution, DOE Mid East: Iran NM 53942 04049200.

theory of EVOLUTION—and similar beliefs, it is more widely used in the analysis of Islamist politics in the MIDDLE EAST, in the context of unrest, TERRORISM, and so on.

Further reading: Antoun (2008).

funeral rites. The ways in which different cultures observe the RITE OF PAS-SAGE (in this case, of *separation*) appropriate to DEATH. Famously studied by HERTZ and since shown by a number of studies to involve a wide spectrum of responses, from celebration and elaborate and/or expensive stages of RITUAL (including reburial or preservation of the corpse, SATI, feasting, and drinking) and MOURNING, to (apparent) near-indifference.

Further reading: Hertz (1960), van Gennep (1960), Bloch & Parry (1982), Metcalf & Huntingdon (1991); Kammen (2010).

Fur. A large ethnic group of western Sudan, after whom the DARFUR region is named.

Fürer-Haimendorf, Christoph von (1909–95). See INDIAN ANTHROPOLOGY.

Furnivall, J. S. (1878–1960). See PLURAL SOCIETY.

Furst, Peter T. (1922–). See PEYOTE.

G

g. A KINSHIP abbreviation for GENERATION; see KINSHIP DIAGRAM.

Galbraith, John Kenneth (1908–2006). See ORIGINAL AFFLUENT SOCIETY.

Galla. See OROMO.

Gallie, W. B. (1912–98). See ESSENTIALLY CONTESTED CONCEPTS.

Galton, Francis (1822–1911). See EUGENICS, GALTON'S PROBLEM.

Galton's problem. An issue raised by Francis Galton in response to a paper by TYLOR in 1888. CROSS-CULTURAL comparison of CUSTOMS involves determining to what extent the CULTURES involved have a common HISTORY—in other words, whether their customs are genuinely independent of each other or derive from common sources. Several attempts have since been made to "solve" the problem.

Further reading: [Galton, F.] (1889).

Galtung, Johan (1930–). See STRUCTURAL VIOLENCE.

game theory. The study of the structure and strategy of games and game-like human behavior. First developed by von Neumann and Morgenstern; later taken further in several SOCIAL SCIENCES. A well-known example of game theory is the "prisoner's dilemma," turning on altruistic versus selfish choices. See ALTRUISM, UTILITARIANISM.

Further reading: von Neumann & Morgenstern (2004).

games. See PLAY, SPORT.

Concise Dictionary of Social and Cultural Anthropology, First Edition. Mike Morris.
© 2012 Michael Ashley Morris. Published 2012 by Blackwell Publishing Ltd.

Gandhi, Mahatma (1869–1948). See ASHRAM, DALIT.

garden. A piece of land usually near a home and used for small-scale growing of crops and/or flowers. In NON-WESTERN societies (especially), home gardens may be used to provide saleable produce, as well as the means of domestic subsistence. See HORTICULTURE, and compare the larger-scale AGRICULTURE.

Garfinkel, Harold (1917–). See ETHNOMETHODOLOGY.

gay and lesbian anthropology. The study of gay life (see HOMOSEXUALITY) from a broadly cultural, arguably sympathetic viewpoint. Some anthropologists in this emerging field self-identify as lesbians or gay men, and the field's domain also includes TRANSGENDER and other "non-NORMATIVE" sexual practices. The Society of Lesbian and Gay Anthropologists (SOLGA) is a section of the AMERICAN ANTHROPOLOGICAL ASSOCIATION. See also QUEER THEORY.

Further reading: Lewin & Leap (2009).

Geertz, Clifford (1926–2006). Eminent (though much-debated) US anthropologist, born in San Francisco. Educated at Harvard under PARSONS, Geertz was also influenced by WEBER. His first wife, Hildred Geertz, is also an anthropologist. He conducted his fieldwork in Java, Bali, and Morocco. After attachment to the University of Chicago from 1960, he joined the Institute for Advanced Study, Princeton in 1970. His many works include *Agricultural involution* (1963), *Islam observed* (1968), *The interpretation of cultures* (2000 [1973]), and *Local knowledge* (1983; 3rd ed. 2000). He developed an influential view of CULTURE that regards it as a web of meaning, a SYSTEM, to be interpreted using THICK DESCRIPTION. See also HERMENEUTICS, INTERPRETIVE ANTHROPOLOGY, SYMBOLIC ANTHROPOLOGY.

Further reading: Ortner (1999); Geertz (2010).

geisha. A female entertainer in Japanese tea-houses. Now diminishing in number and often associated with tourist venues. The term also implied PROSTITUTION at one time, though it may have originated as a distinction from it.

Gellner, David N. See BUDDHISM, GELLNER [E.].

Gellner, Ernest (1925–95). An anthropologist with interests in philosophy and social theory, born in Paris to Czech Jewish parents, raised in Prague and England, and educated at Oxford and London. Gellner taught at the London School of Economics and was professor of social anthropology at Cambridge from 1984 to 1993; he returned to Prague as first director of the Centre for the Study of Nationalism, Central European University. His many publications include *Words and things* (1959, rev. ed. 1979), *Saints of the Atlas* (1969), *Soviet and western anthropology* (1980), *Nations and nationalism* (1983, 2nd ed. 2006). His son David is also an anthropologist. See NATIONALISM.

Gemeinschaft and *Gesellschaft*. Sociological terms first coined by Ferdinand Tönnies in his eponymous book (*Community and society*) to describe two kinds of social organization—that built around affection, relationships, and community (*Gemeinschaft*) and that built on duty and competition (*Gesellschaft*). The former is regarded as "real," the latter "artificial."

Further reading: Tönnies (1955).

gender. Usually used in SOCIAL SCIENCES to refer to human sexual IDENTITY, particularly as a cultural construct as distinct from biological facts (see SEX). Studied increasingly, particularly in the context of FEMINIST ANTHRO-POLOGY, since the 1980s. See also BIRTH, CLOTHING, DISCRIMINATION, EXPLOITATION, INEQUALITY, MISOGYNY, POWER, PROSTITUTION, REPRODUCTIVE TECHNOLOGIES, SEX ROLE, TRANGENDER, WITCHCRAFT, WOMEN, WORK.

Further reading: Ortner & Whitehead (1981); Moore (2007).

gene. A basic unit of hereditary material, which affects particular character-istics in an INDIVIDUAL. See also GENETICS.

genealogy. The study of family HISTORY, or a diagram representing family relationships; also used to describe the study of the evolution of PLANTS and ANIMALS. The "genealogical method," based on gathering family information from field INFORMANTS, was developed by RIVERS during the TORRES STRAITS EXPEDITION, since when it has been a central tool in the study of KINSHIP.

Further reading: Rivers (1968).

generalized exchange or indirect exchange. A form of MARRIAGE rule associated with ELEMENTARY STRUCTURES in which wives are exchanged in only one direction; rather than passing directly between two groups (see DIRECT EXCHANGE), women of the first group marry into the second, the second into the third, and so on, in a way that may well also be circular (e.g. women of group A marry into group B; those of group B marry into group C; those of group C may marry into group D *or* group A). A man may not marry into the group that his female relatives marry into. Generalized exchange is asymmetrical (see ASYMMETRICAL ALLIANCE) whereas direct exchange is symmetrical (see SYMMETRICAL ALLIANCE).

generation. In RELATIONSHIP TERMINOLOGY, a group of people who occupy the same level in a GENEALOGY (the key factor being a roughly common age, not a particular relationship). In wider SOCIAL STUDIES, a COHORT of those born around the same time (e.g. "the pre-war generation"). Consideration of *generational* differences—in attitudes and expectations—may be a way of understanding cultural change. See also G.

generative anthropology. A THEORY developed by Eric Gans (*The origin of language*, 1981, and several subsequent works) that postulates an "originary" incident in which members of an early group surround a desired object but no INDIVIDUAL takes it; the object thus becomes "sacred" and remembered thereafter as a SYMBOL, thus creating the seeds of RELIGION and LANGUAGE. Gans himself drew on the work of the French critic and thinker René Girard.

generative grammar. See TRANSFORMATIONAL-GENERATIVE GRAMMAR.

Genesis (Bible). See COSMOGONY, LEACH, SEMITIC.

genetics. The term coined by William Bateson (1907) to describe the study of biological HEREDITY through GENE transmission. Genetics was first practiced by Gregor Mendel (1822–84). See also BIOLOGICAL ANTHROPOLOGY, BIOTECHNOLOGY, HUMAN GENETICS, MEME.

genetrix or **genitrix.** The biological mother of a child, as opposed to the socially recognized mother (MATER).

Genghis Khan (1162–1227). See KHAN.

genie. See JINN.

genitor. The biological father of a child, as opposed to the socially recognized father (PATER).

Gennep. See VAN GENNEP.

genocide. The deliberate and systematic killing of a specific ethnic or national group by the authorities. The term was coined by the lawyer Raphael Lemkin in 1944 to describe Nazi atrocities against the Jews and other groups, and the practice was banned formally by the UN in 1951. Other acts of genocide have occurred throughout HISTORY, including the Turkish slaughter of Armenians in the early twentieth century; it has been argued that the current situation in DARFUR is comparable. Derived from Greek and Latin, "race-killing." See also ETHNIC CLEANSING.

Further reading: Hinton & O'Neill (2009).

genotype. In biology, the genetic make-up of a particular organism. From Greek, "race character." Compare PHENOTYPE (observable characteristics of an organism).

genre de vie. A concept in HUMAN GEOGRAPHY associated with Vidal de La Blache (see POSSIBILISM), who placed the study of human communities firmly in local regions and specific cultures and livelihoods, or, in French, "way[s] of living."

gens. Originally the Roman term for (an aristocratic) CLAN; adopted for anthropological use by L. H. MORGAN and occasionally thereafter by other American writers. "Gens" is the singular form; "gentes" is the plural. In some cases *gens* may specify a group where DESCENT is traced by the male line (where *clan* would specify the female equivalent).

geographical determinism. The belief that GEOGRAPHY determines such human traits as character and CULTURE. Found in ancient Greek thought, and in the nineteenth century associated with such theories as Ratzel's notion of *lebensraum* (living space), which was taken up in a later form by the Nazi regime (see GERMAN ANTHROPOLOGY). It was rejected by BOAS and others. See also DETERMINISM.

geographical information system. See GIS.

geography. The academic discipline that deals with the earth's form, physical features, climate, resources, and so on. It may be subdivided into *physical* geography (which covers land forms and climatology) and HUMAN GEOGRAPHY (those aspects concerning people). From Greek, "earth writing."

German anthropology. German-speaking anthropology encompasses the TRADITIONS not only of Germany and Austria but also of the German-speaking part of Switzerland. It began to develop in the ENLIGHTENMENT: one of its earliest notable exponents was Alexander von Humboldt, writing on South America around the turn of the nineteenth century. Initially much interest centered on *Volkskunde*—German folk studies—rather than, as later, VÖLKERKUNDE—anthropology of non-European peoples. German anthropologists tended to favor MUSEUM-centered studies (in common with others of this period). Major figures of the late nineteenth to early twentieth centuries were Adolf Bastian, Richard Thurnwald, and, in particular, the émigré Franz BOAS. Many of Boas' central beliefs, which greatly influenced the course of American CULTURAL ANTHROPOLOGY, can be traced back to his German roots.

  Also important in the nineteenth century were the diffusionist views propagated by Friedrich Ratzel (see also ANTHROPOGEOGRAPHY, DIFFU-SIONISM), Leo Frobenius, and, later, Fritz Graebner (see KULTURKREIS, VIENNA SCHOOL OF ETHNOLOGY).

  The *Volkskunde* end of German social science, which had always shaded into NATIONALISM, was tarnished by association with the Nazi regime in the 1930s. After World War II (see WAR), German influence was diminished for a considerable period. Today major German organizations include the Deutsche

Gesellschaft für Völkerkunde (German Anthropological Association) and the Max-Planck-Institut für Ethnologische Forschung, Halle.

Further reading: *Zeitschrift für Ethnologie* [journal]; *Anthropos* [journal]; Stocking (1996), Gingrich (2005).

gerontocracy. Rule by older people, or a STATE that is run this way. See also ELDER.

Gesellschaft. See GEMEINSCHAFT AND GESELLSCHAFT.

Gestalt theory. A psychological approach stressing the importance of the whole (*"Gestalt,"* in German), rather than the parts—as an aid to treatment, and in understanding how people perceive the world. An influence on the CULTURE AND PERSONALITY school. See also HOLISM.

gestational mother. A woman carrying a fetus for another, and not generally intending to be the socially recognized mother (MATER). See SURROGACY.

gesture. A form of SIGN or SYMBOL conveyed through bodily movement. A kind of NON-VERBAL COMMUNICATION, the scope of which may be taken to include non-linguistic sounds. Particular gestures (e.g. raising a hand, nodding the head) may carry different meanings in different CULTURES; their study is included in KINESICS. SIGNING is a particular kind of LANGUAGE developed for use by and with deaf people.

ghost dance. A North American Indian RITUAL intended to contact the dead and associated with a desire for the way of life that existed before contact with European settlers. Instituted by the Paiute prophet Wovoka in 1888; most fervently adopted by the Sioux, until the Wounded Knee Massacre of 1890. The ghost dance is an example of a millenarian practice (see MILLENARIANISM).

ghost marriage. An African institution by which a dead man is "provided" with heirs by a wife chosen by his brother, who then fathers children in his name. Practiced among the NUER, for example. Compare LEVIRATE, by which a man marries a dead brother's wife.

Giddens, Anthony (1938–). See PRACTICE THEORY.

gift. A form of EXCHANGE famously studied by MAUSS, who drew on comparative data to discuss the social ties and obligations created and maintained by gift-giving.

Gift exchange may be seen as more important for confirming bonds of RECIPROCITY between the parties involved than for any economic value attached to the items given (contrast the more impersonal COMMODITY relationship). Mauss' work was followed up by LÉVI-STRAUSS, amongst others; Mauss' essay remains a core text in the study of EXCHANGE.

See also KULA, PRESTATION, POTLATCH. Gift exchange is sometimes called "ceremonial exchange."

Further reading: Mauss (1954); Sykes (2005).

Gillen, F. J. (1856–1912). See ABORIGINAL, AUSTRALIAN ANTHROPOLOGY, GROUP MARRIAGE.

Girard, René (1923–). See GENERATIVE ANTHROPOLOGY.

GIS. Geographical information systems use computer TECHNOLOGY to process spatial data, thus allowing accurate assessment and manipulation of potentially difficult research material. They have been used since the late twentieth century and are of interest not only to anthropologists and archaeologists but also those involved in FORESTRY and DEMOGRAPHY. See also REMOTE SENSING.

Glaser, Barney G. (1930–). See GROUNDED THEORY.

globalization. The growth of a single global system, and what is implied politically, economically, and culturally by it. Associated with the rise of multinational corporations, international agencies, improved communications technologies, and wide-scale MIGRATION. All these areas have been investigated by anthropologists extensively. Compare TRANSNATIONALISM, WORLD-SYSTEM.

Further reading: Inda & Rosaldo (2008).

glocalization. A compound word describing an idea originally taken from Japanese and contracting "global localization"—a hybrid approach or attitude arising from GLOBALIZATION and balancing both local and global matters. Given currency by sociologists such as Roland Robertson in the 1990s.

glottochronology. A form of LEXICOSTATISTICS attempting to analyze COGNATES in the VOCABULARY of two apparently related languages with the intention of calculating the time at which they split from a common source. As with lexicostatistics, the procedure rests on contentious grounds. See also COMPARATIVE LINGUISTICS, HISTORICAL LINGUISTICS.

Gluckman, Max (1911–75). South African anthropologist; born in Johannesburg and based in Britain. Educated at the University of Witwatersrand and Oxford. Gluckman did fieldwork in Zululand.

Gluckman was director of the Rhodes-Livingstone Institute from 1942 to 1947; he then lectured at Oxford. As first professor of social anthropology at Manchester (1949–71), he led the MANCHESTER SCHOOL and was an authority on SOCIAL CHANGE and LAW, especially in South Africa. See also LAND TENURE, RITUAL OF REBELLION. His works include *Custom and conflict in Africa* (1955) and *Order and rebellion in tribal Africa* (1963).

GM crops. See BIOTECHNOLOGY.

Gobineau, Joseph Arthur (1816–82). French writer and diplomat whose *The inequality of human races* (French 1853–5) supplied the Nazi regime with a pretext for ethnic persecution in twentieth-century Germany.

Godelier, Maurice (1934–). See MODE OF PRODUCTION.

godparent. A RITUAL relation of a child undergoing Christian baptism. The godfather or godmother, who may be unrelated by blood or MARRIAGE, accepts responsibility for the child's spiritual EDUCATION and welfare. See also COMPADRAZGO, FICTIVE KINSHIP, PADRINAZGO, RITUAL KINSHIP, SPIRITUAL KINSHIP.

Goffman, Erving (1922–82). See ROLE, STIGMA.

Goldenweiser, Alexander (1880–1940). See TOTEMISM.

Goody, Jack (1919–). Prolific British social anthropologist. Educated at Cambridge and Oxford, Goody served in World War II and later did fieldwork in the Gold Coast (Ghana). He was professor of social anthropology at Cambridge from 1973 to 1984. Associated especially with outstanding work on LITERACY and KINSHIP, Goody has latterly written on many areas of interest including comparisons of western and eastern cultures. His books include *The developmental cycle in domestic groups* (ed., 1958), *Death, property and the ancestors* (1962), *Literacy in traditional societies* (ed., 1968), *Comparative studies in kinship* (1969), *The domestication of the savage mind* (1977), *The oriental, the ancient and the primitive* (1990), and *The expansive moment* (1995).

Further reading: Goody (1991); Goody (1996).

gossip. Commonly thought of as "idle talk," gossip has been investigated for its deeper meanings from a number of perspectives. It may be argued to reinforce group morality, or be seen as a way for the individual to advance a personal agenda in a way that avoids overt CONFLICT. Gossip is also a way of discussing social boundaries. It may sometimes be linked to rumors of WITCHCRAFT, and can be studied as a product of HUMAN EVOLUTION.

Further reading: Dunbar (1996).

government. The exercise of POWER, AUTHORITY, or control, and the formal body that does this. More generally, the rules by which governing is done (from the Latin and Greek, "to steer").

Early writers such as MAINE tended to conceive of a dichotomy between "civilized" governmental institutions and PRIMITIVE polities that lacked such government. In the twentieth century, ethnographers such as EVANS-PRITCHARD and FORTES began to distinguish different kinds of African government, some of which were centralized and linked to sharp social divisions, others of which were not. MAIR later argued that the crucial distinction was between the STATE, with its familiar (to westerners) apparatus, and the SMALL-SCALE SOCIETY, in which aspects of "government"—the redress of wrongs, the appointment of leaders—also exist, but in rather different forms.

Modern POLITICAL ANTHROPOLOGY has addressed issues arising from the various *forms* of government, for instance the collapse of state SOCIALISM in Eastern Europe; there is also a keen interest in governmental relations to VIOLENCE, and questions of HUMAN RIGHTS.

Further reading: Mair (1977).

Graebner, Fritz (1877–1934). See CULTURE COMPLEX, GERMAN ANTHRO-POLOGY, *KULTURKREIS*.

graffiti. From Italian, *graffiare* ("to scratch"): words or drawings scratched on a rock, or (more usually now) painted or drawn on public spaces such as walls, often illegally. "Graffito" is an ART technique involving scratching off layers.

grammar. In LINGUISTICS, the study of word forms and relationships in a sentence, encompassing MORPHOLOGY, SYNTAX, SEMANTICS, and PHONETICS. Grammar may concern itself with both "proper" use and the way people actually speak. See also TRANSFORMATIONAL-GENERATIVE GRAMMAR.

Gramsci, Antonio (1891–1937). Italian journalist and MARXIST theoretician; he argued that the economic POWER of the ruling CLASS was backed up by the unwitting complicity of the workers. Gramsci popularized the use of the term HEGEMONY. A founding member of the Italian Communist Party, he wrote the *Quaderni del carcere* (1947; *Prison notebooks*, 1971) while serving a ten-year sentence under Mussolini's regime.

grapheme. In LINGUISTICS, a written representation of a single PHONEME.

great divide. A term occasionally used to describe the (now outdated) contrast between PRIMITIVE ways and thought, and more MODERN attitudes (as advanced in the work of theorists such as LÉVY-BRUHL).

great tradition. REDFIELD drew a distinction between "great" and "little" TRADITIONS in the mid twentieth century. Great traditions represent a formalized, complex set of values (e.g. orthodox, mainstream religions) with historical appeal. Little traditions are local, often peasant-based, oral, and informal. The distinction is similar to that in language between LANGUE AND PAROLE. Since Redfield, other anthropologists (e.g. McKim Marriott) have extended and widened his distinctions, or disputed them.

Further reading: Redfield (1989).

green movement. The general name for INDIVIDUALS and organizations involved in activities aiming to protect and enhance the ENVIRONMENT. The roots of modern Green thinking may be traced back as far as Malthus' *An essay on the principle of population...* (1798), and several broadly "environmental" organizations (e.g. the National Trust, UK, 1893) were founded well before such contemporary groups as the Friends of the Earth (UK, 1971), Greenpeace (Canada, 1971), and the Green Party (originally Germany, 1980).

green revolution. The dramatic increase in crop PRODUCTION in THIRD WORLD countries of Asia consequent on the introduction of new methods of cultivation, for instance of wheat and RICE, from the mid twentieth century onward. It was controversial inasmuch as its success depended on factors such as heavy fertilizer use, which raised issues of sustainability and affordability.

griot. An itinerant traditional poet, musician, and story-teller of North and West Africa. Griots' functions include reciting HISTORY and praise-singing.

grounded theory. A sociological method with applications in many fields, devised by Glaser and Strauss in reaction to excessive abstract theory. Grounded theory prioritizes real-life observation and an open-minded approach to forming research questions (as opposed to starting from a rigid hypothesis to which data must be fitted). The two authors eventually differed over details of the theory. One objection to grounded theory is that, to be meaningful, all sociological research must inevitably balance theory and reality.

Further reading: Glaser & Strauss (1968); Bryant & Charmaz (2007).

group marriage. Nineteenth-century theorists such as Spencer and Gillen (discussing Australia) and MORGAN hypothesized a PRIMITIVE form of MARRIAGE by which a group of men wed a group of WOMEN to form a single FAMILY unit. Morgan suggested CLASSIFICATORY KINSHIP systems arose from such "communal families." This idea was later discredited.

Further reading: Morgan (1997).

growth. See AUXOLOGY, BIOLOGICAL ANTHROPOLOGY.

Guattari, Félix (1930–92). See DELEUZE.

guerrilla or **guerilla.** One engaged in small-scale acts of WAR, usually against STATE forces. From Spanish, "little war." Compare TERRORISM.

Guha, Ranajit (1922–). See SUBALTERN.

gumsa and *gumlao*. Two opposing poles of politics among the Kachin people of Burma, according to LEACH. *Gumsa* is similar to the feudal hierarchical approach of the neighboring Shan, and *gumlao* is anarchistic and egalitarian. In PRACTICE, the Kachin are said to oscillate between these types.

Further reading: Leach (2004).

guru. In BUDDHISM, HINDUISM, and SIKHISM, a spiritual guide or teacher. From Sanskrit, "weighty."

Guru Nanak. See SIKHISM.

gypsy or **gipsy.** A member of people called by themselves *Rom* (or other names), characterized by a traveling lifestyle, probably of South Asian descent and historically subject to persecution by some host communities. The name derives from "Egyptian." The majority of gypsies live in Europe, but they are also found in the Americas and Africa.

Further reading: Okely (1983).

H

H or Hu. In RELATIONSHIP TERMINOLOGY, the abbreviation for "husband."

Habermas, Jürgen (1929–). German philosopher, born Düsseldorf and principally associated with the Frankfurt School (see CRITICAL ANTHROPOLOGY), whose work he continued (he was ADORNO's assistant for a time). A critic of RATIONALISM and POSITIVISM, he has produced a number of works on SOCIOLOGY and social COMMUNICATION, including *Theorie und Praxis* (1962; *Theory and practice*, 1974) and *Theorie des kommunikativen Handelns* (1981; *The theory of communicative action*, 1984).

habitus. A set of received beliefs enabling structured social improvisation. The habitus allows people to create ways of achieving their aims within an existing context. The term was adapted from Latin by BOURDIEU. See DISPOSITION, PRACTICE THEORY, TASTE.

Further reading: Jenkins (2002).

Haddon, A. C. (1855–1940). British zoologist and anthropologist, leader of the TORRES STRAITS EXPEDITION, which was seminal to the development of anthropology in Britain. Haddon was professor of zoology at Dublin from 1880 and visited the Torres Strait to study coral; becoming interested in the people he encountered, he returned with a group of other scientists to study them. Following this famous expedition of 1898, Haddon became reader in ethnology at Cambridge (1909–26) and wrote a number of monographs, including *Evolution in art: as illustrated by the life-histories of designs* (1895), *The races of man and their distribution* (1909; new ed. 1924), and *History of anthropology* (1910; 2nd ed. 1934).

Concise Dictionary of Social and Cultural Anthropology, First Edition. Mike Morris.
© 2012 Michael Ashley Morris. Published 2012 by Blackwell Publishing Ltd.

Haeckel, Ernst (1834–1919). See ECOLOGY, ONTOGENESIS, PHYLOGENESIS, PHYLUM.

Haiti. See VOODOO.

Hall, Edward T. (1914–2009). See PROXEMICS.

hallucinogen. A substance that, when ingested, acts on the central nervous system to alter PERCEPTIONS or thoughts, for instance by causing hallucinations. Hallucinogens, though often illegal in western societies, may be used to accompany RITUAL in some CULTURES. The best-known hallucinogens include PLANTS such as PEYOTE and synthetic substances such as LSD. See also DRUGS, SHAMAN.

Hamilton, W. D. (1936–2000). See INCLUSIVE FITNESS, KIN SELECTION ALTRUISM.

Hannerz, Ulf (1942–). Swedish social anthropologist, long associated with Stockholm University, where he is professor emeritus. He has done fieldwork in the US, West Africa, and the Caribbean and engaged in URBAN ANTHROPOLOGY and studies of the MEDIA and GLOBALIZATION. His books include *Soulside: inquiries into ghetto culture and community* (1969; reprint with new afterword, 2004), *Exploring the city: inquiries toward an urban anthropology* (1980), *Transnational connections: culture, people, places* (1996), and *Foreign news: exploring the world of foreign correspondents* (2004).

hapax or **hapax legomenon.** In LINGUISTICS, a word or form that occurs only once in a body of writing or work of an author. From Greek, "thing said once."

happiness. See WELL-BEING.

haptics. The study of touch and the sensations derived from it. A haptic person or creature is more oriented toward touch than the other SENSES.

harijan. A synonym for DALIT.

harmonic. According to LÉVI-STRAUSS, a KINSHIP system in which DESCENT recognition accords with residence rules (so that, for example, those who hold recognized rights from a relationship with the father's side of a family live with the husband's relatives) is a harmonic regime. It is linked with GENERALIZED EXCHANGE.

A *disharmonic* regime entails oppositions: patrilineal descent/uxorilocal residence (i.e. rights via father/living with wife's relatives), or matrilineal descent/virilocal residence (rights via mother/living with husband's relatives). It also involves EXOGAMY. See MATRILINEALITY, PATRILINEALITY, UXORILOCALITY, VIRILOCALITY.

Further reading: Lévi-Strauss (1969[b]).

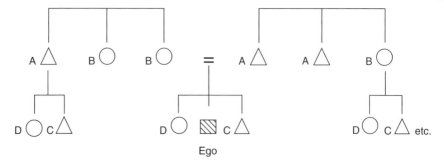

Figure 12   Hawaiian terminology.

Harris, Marvin (1927–2001). American anthropologist, born Brooklyn, New York. He obtained his doctorate from Columbia (1953), where he taught before becoming a professor at the University of Florida (1981–2000). He did fieldwork in Brazil. Best known as the prime mover of CULTURAL MATERIALISM. His many works include *The rise of anthropological theory* (1968, updated 2001), *Cultural materialism* (1979, updated 2001), and *Good to eat* (1985).

Hart, Keith (1943–). See INFORMAL ECONOMY.

Hawaiian terminology. A RELATIONSHIP TERMINOLOGY in which EGO's relatives are called by the same term if they are of the same GENERATION and SEX: so, male COUSINS are equivalent to brothers, female cousins to sisters; mother and mother's sister (M and MZ) are equivalent, as are father and father's brother (F=FB); and (for example) father's sister and Ego's mother (FZ=M).

One of several systems identified by G. P. MURDOCK (see ESKIMO TERMINOLOGY and Murdock reference there), common in POLYNESIA.

headman. A locally recognized leader in various cultures; the headman may have sole charge of a small group such as a BAND, or be subordinate in his turn within a larger group, to a CHIEF.

headhunter. A member of a people who collect the severed heads of enemies; there are a number of explanations for the PRACTICE, some disputed.

healing. See DISEASE, MEDICAL ANTHROPOLOGY, SHAMAN.

Hegel, G. W. F. (1770–1831). See CULTURAL MATERIALISM, DIALECTICAL MATERIALISM, VOLKSGEIST.

hegemony. In general use, a term for leadership or dominance, especially by one corporate entity over another (from Greek, "leader"). In the thought of GRAMSCI, the process by which the dominant CLASS or ELITE retains its position by obtaining the unreflecting consent of those below it. The ELITE uses cultural means to normalize a state of affairs advantageous to it, and thus does not require force alone to maintain it.

heliocentrism. In astronomy, a system that places the sun at the centre. In anthropology, may refer to G. Elliot SMITH and others' belief in the importance of (sun-worshipping) Egypt to the development of world CULTURE.

herder. See NOMAD.

Herder, J. G. (1744–1803). See CULTURE, VOLKSGEIST.

Herdt, Gilbert (1949–). See HOMOSEXUALITY, MASCULINITY.

heredity. In GENETICS, the transmission of particular characteristics from one generation of an organism to the next. In a similar way, heredity is synonymous with legal principles of INHERITANCE.

heritability. The quality of being capable of being inherited.

hermaphrodite. A person (or ANIMAL or plant) in whom anatomical characteristics of both sexes appear to exist.

hermeneutics. The PRACTICE of interpretation: originally of religious TEXTS, later of social situations, focusing on the meanings those involved ascribe to an event. In anthropology, associated with GEERTZ and, later, the authors of *WRITING CULTURE*: in short, ethnography as an act of interpretation. See INTERPRETIVE ANTHROPOLOGY, THICK DESCRIPTION.

Herodotus (c. 484–425 BCE). Greek historian, noted for the relative rigor of his work, who was also interested in people and places. He left early ethnographic descriptions of the Greeks' "barbarian" neighbors.

Herskovits, Melville J. (1895–1963). American cultural anthropologist, born Ohio. One of BOAS' students at Columbia, Herskovits went on to teach at Northwestern University and is principally known for his many contributions toward advancing African studies, such as establishing the first US university program on this subject in 1951. His numerous publications, often in collaboration with his wife, Frances, include *The American Negro* (1928), *Man and his works* (1948), and *The human factor in changing Africa* (1962). He also coined the terms CATTLE COMPLEX and ENCULTURATION.

Hertz, Robert (1881–1915). French sociologist. A student of DURKHEIM whose career was cut short in World War I. Made more familiar to English readers by a 1960 translation of two essays, *Death* and *The right hand*.

Further reading: Parkin (1996).

hetaerism. An occasional synonym for PRIMITIVE PROMISCUITY.

heterarchy. A form of social organization involving equality among members, as opposed to their being ranked in a HIERARCHY. The term is mainly of interest to students of PREHISTORY.

heteroglossia. A term from the work of BAKHTIN to describe multiple "VOICES" in literature and, by extension, other arenas.

Further reading: Smith (2004).

heuristics. The study or application of heuristic methods. A heuristic method is one that involves starting with an approach that offers a good chance of finding an answer to a given problem; if this approach is unsuccessful, the next most reasonable approach is tried, and a solution may eventually be found. A heuristic approach in education encourages the student to discover solutions for themselves. From Greek, *heuriskein*, "to find"; "heuristic" was first used by the poet Coleridge.

hierarchy. A system within which INDIVIDUALS, CLASSES, or groups are ranked from greatest to least. Such a CLASSIFICATION is widely used in natural sciences; it is also studied in such contexts as CASTE and other social STRATIFICATION. Louis DUMONT famously characterized India as the land of "*Homo hierarchicus.*"

Further reading: Rio & Smedal (2009).

hieroglyph. A SYMBOL used in some WRITING SYSTEMS, most famously ancient Egyptian, to represent a concept, syllable, or sound, usually through the representation of a concrete object (e.g. an ANIMAL or tree). A kind of PICTOGRAM. The name means "sacred carving" in Greek and reflects a belief that the Egyptian system had mystical properties. Compare CUNEIFORM.

highland/lowland. One of the many binary divisions that can be made in anthropological theory: between cultures and modes of life that are held to be distinguishable according to geographical factors. The distinction particularly crops up in South American ETHNOGRAPHY (Andean societies, with their long—recoverable—history, versus Amazonian ones), in Southeast Asian AGRICULTURE and politics, as well as in the description of many other places with upland communities (e.g. Scotland).

Hinduism. An externally invented term (a "Hindu" in Persian and Urdu being simply an Indian) for the diverse interconnected religious TRADITIONS of South Asia, apart from ISLAM. Although there are a vast number of local variations, Hindus often recognize the importance of three major deities—Brahma, Vishnu, and Siva—as well as many goddesses and lesser gods. As with BUDDHISM, there is a belief in the operation of KARMA and REINCARNATION, with the aim of achieving NIRVANA (also called *moksa*). Hinduism is also associated with the development of the CASTE system. Among the many TEXTS developed over its 3000-year history are the *Vedas* (see VEDA), the epic *Ramayana* and *Mahabharata* (the latter of which includes the *Bhagavadgita*) and others. The term "sacred cow" derives from Hindu beliefs that cattle are sacred and should not be killed.

Further reading: Gellner (2001); Fuller (2004).

historical linguistics. The branch of LINGUISTICS dealing with LANGUAGE change over time, also called "diachronic linguistics." Language change is inevitable and complex, and its study encompasses several social factors. Contrast DESCRIPTIVE LINGUISTICS and see also COMPARATIVE LINGUISTICS, GLOTTOCHRONOLOGY, LEXICOSTATISTICS.

historical particularism. An outlook espoused by BOAS and his followers that stressed the uniqueness of each INDIVIDUAL CULTURE and rejected the idea that general social laws could be extrapolated from comparative studies. This was influential in supplanting evolutionary and diffusionist approaches in anthropology.

Further reading: Boas (1994).

historicism. In HISTORY, a form of RELATIVISM that emphasizes the importance of historical context to our understanding of earlier events (rather than viewing them through the standards of our own time). In SOCIAL SCIENCES, a belief that general laws can be discerned about the shape of history, and future events thereby predicted. Anthropologists may use the term to refer to any broadly DIACHRONIC approach.

historiography. The study of the writing of HISTORY, its principles, methodology, criticism, and its own history.

history. The discipline that records and interprets past events; as such it is related to anthropology, not least through common forebears such as HERODOTUS and MONTESQUIEU. The first "real" anthropologists of the nineteenth century were concerned to establish their own evolutionist theories of human development (see EVOLUTIONISM) and tended to use whatever data would fit these conceptions, regardless of historical method. As a reaction to such approaches, and to DIFFUSIONISM, later writers such as MALINOWSKI and RADCLIFFE-BROWN concentrated more on a SYNCHRONIC viewpoint, ignoring the historical perspective. In the US, BOAS and his disciples focused on the histories of particular CULTURES rather than the wider view. In the latter half of the twentieth century, interest among historians themselves began to move toward recounting events from the point of view of the marginalized and "inferior," as in the work of authors such as E. P. Thompson, and from the viewpoint of subject peoples rather than their administrators. At the same time, radical anthropologists began to deconstruct or question the classical anthropological stance (see e.g. REFLEXIVITY). Latterly, anthropology and history have worked much more closely together.

history of anthropology. Although earlier surveys had been made, a serious broadly historical view of anthropology itself became more feasible as the subject matured. Some authors, such as EVANS-PRITCHARD and HARRIS, chose to reinterpret the past in particular ways to bolster their own viewpoints. More recently, George W. Stocking has written or edited a large number of works on various aspects of anthropology's beginnings. As anthropology has increasingly become its own subject in some quarters (compare HISTORY), journals such as *Critique of anthropology* have brought a critical distance to bear on it. The amount of source material accessible for such work has grown with the availability of online and physical archives, ethnographers' autobiographies and diaries (most notoriously, MALINOWSKI's), and so on.

Further reading: Stocking & Handler (1983–2010); Kuper (1996).

history of ideas. The general study of concepts from a historical perspective, without necessarily confining them to one particular discipline. Also known as "intellectual history." Compare ARCHAEOLOGY OF KNOWLEDGE.

HIV. See AIDS.

Hobbes, Thomas (1588–1679). See SOCIAL CONTRACT, VIOLENCE.

Hocart, A. M. (1883–1939). British anthropologist and archaeologist, born near Brussels. He was educated on Guernsey and at Oxford (1902–6), and later at Berlin University. Hocart did fieldwork under RIVERS on Melanesia (1908) and then in Fiji. He held the Chair of Sociology (succeeding EVANS-PRITCHARD) at King Fuad I University, Cairo, from 1934 to 1939. Although he was out of step with the development of social anthropology by the time he died, Hocart was to influence Oxford figures such as NEEDHAM in the mid-century. His books include *Kingship* (1927), *Kings and councillors* (1936), and *The life-giving myth* (ed. Raglan, 1970).

Further reading: Hocart (1970); Hocart (1954); Needham (1967).

Hodder, Ian (1948–). See PROCESSUAL.

Hoijer, Harry (1904–76). See WHORFIAN HYPOTHESIS.

holism. The term coined by General J. C. Smuts in 1926 to describe the tendency of nature to produce wholes from units. Generally, "holistic" describes any system or theoretical approach that emphasizes the whole over its parts (as opposed to ATOMISM). In anthropology, FUNCTIONALISM would be an example of a holistic approach. See also GESTALT THEORY.

Further reading: Parkin & Ulijaszek (2007); Otto & Bubandt (2010).

homeopathic magic. One of the forms of SYMPATHETIC MAGIC.

homeopathy. See ALLOPATHY.

Homer (c. eighth century BCE). See ORAL LITERATURE.

homicide. The killing of another human being. Social attitudes to homicide may depend on context—to what degree it is to be avoided, and whether it is permissible during WAR, for punishment, or in self-defense. Permission to kill may be restricted to certain individuals (e.g. soldiers, executioners). The motive of the killer is usually important; in "everyday" homicide, many legal systems distinguish between MURDER and lesser CRIMES such as manslaughter. In small-scale polities, homicide may be rife at certain times and associated with phenomena such as feuding (see FEUD).

homme total. A phrase from MAUSS advocating the primacy of the "total man": that is, that social or psychological phenomena need to be investigated holistically (see HOLISM) as both mental *and* physical events, not one or the other in isolation.

Further reading: Mauss (1979: 27–9).

homo duplex. A shorthand term for DURKHEIM's delineation (in *The elementary forms of religious life*) of the mutually antagonistic double nature of the individual, torn between egotistical drives on the one hand and the greater good of wider SOCIETY on the other. Latin for "two-fold man." Compare DUALISM.

homo economicus. See ECONOMIC MAN.

homo faber. The term coined by the philosopher Henri Bergson (first appearing in English in 1911) for "man the creator": humankind considered as TOOL-users, workers (see WORK), or craftsmen. Compare *HOMO LUDENS*. See also TECHNOLOGY.

homo ludens. In the work of Johan Huizinga, a Latin phrase meaning "man the player." Huizinga considered PLAY (in various manifestations, from art to WAR and LAW) to be a central theme of human experience. Compare *HOMO FABER*.

Further reading: Huizinga (1949).

homo oeconomicus. See ECONOMIC MAN.

homonym. In LINGUISTICS, one of two or more words having the same pronunciation (and sometimes spelling) but different meanings (words that are spelled differently but sound the same are "homophones"). In English, "light" meaning "illumination" and "light" meaning "not heavy" are homonyms.

homosexuality. Sexual preference for one's own SEX. Various theories have been advanced as to how homosexuality develops, though biological and social factors both have been seen as important. In western societies homosexual people have been historically ostracized and (more recently) judged to be "ill," but more liberal attitudes developed in the twentieth century. In some societies, homosexual practices are the NORM for certain groups or at certain stages of (for example) adolescence. See also GAY AND LESBIAN ANTHROPOLOGY, QUEER THEORY.

Further reading: Herdt (1994); Robertson (2005).

honor. Respect, social esteem. Particularly studied by anthropologists of the MEDITERRANEAN region, but important in several other areas. Honor is usually bracketed analytically with the concept of *shame*: a cultural GENDER division assigns the interconnected cultivation of honor to men and a "proper" sense of shame (sexual discretion, modesty) to the women of a HOUSEHOLD. See also STATUS.

Further reading: Peristiany (1966).

horticulture. The cultivation of fruit and vegetables in a GARDEN (compare larger-scale AGRICULTURE). Horticulturalist societies may be small-scale, may combine their activities with other methods of gaining a living, and may be at risk from outside encroachment on their land.

hot and cold societies. A BINARY OPPOSITION drawn by LÉVI-STRAUSS: "hot" societies are geared toward change and social differentiation, with a focus on HISTORY; "cold" societies aim for stasis and lack of differentiation, and focus on MYTH. Each kind of society may be considered successful by its own criteria.

Further reading: Charbonnier (1969).

house. See ARCHITECTURE.

household. A group of people living together (although it is possible to have a one-person household), for instance a FAMILY of some form, possibly including servants. Historically the term has particular connotations in the west that may not be helpful in considering the arrangements of other CULTURES, and so needs to be used carefully and with an awareness that many societies are organized in different ways, or according to different conventions, from those classically found in (for example) European cultures.

Howes, David (1957–). See SENSES.

Hu. See H.

Huizinga, Johan (1872–1945). See *HOMO LUDENS*.

human ecology. The study of human populations and their interaction with their ENVIRONMENT. The term is used in several disciplines (such as anthropology, biology, GEOGRAPHY), with differing emphases at different times. To anthropologists it is a division of BIOLOGICAL ANTHROPOLOGY.

Further reading: Vayda (2009).

human evolution. The study of the development of modern humans (*Homo sapiens*) from their hominid ANCESTORS. A specialism within BIOLOGICAL ANTHROPOLOGY, using data from PALEOANTHROPOLOGY and the study of PREHISTORY.

Further reading: Tattersall (2009).

human genetics. A specialism of BIOLOGICAL ANTHROPOLOGY that generally investigates such areas as HEREDITY and the role of GENETICS in DISEASE.

human geography. The study of GEOGRAPHY as it affects, and is affected by, human activities. Human geographers are interested in a number of areas that match anthropological concerns—the way people occupy PLACES, their economic activities, and so on. Compare the earlier form of ANTHROPOGE-OGRAPHY. See also *GENRE DE VIE*.

Human Relations Area Files (HRAF). A large (by 2010, over one million pages covering 400 groups) ethnographic database founded by G. P. MURDOCK and associated with Yale University since the 1930s. Its records can be used for cross-cultural comparisons. The electronic version of the "world cultures" set can be found at http://www.yale.edu/hraf.

human rights. Rights assumed to be held by all people, regardless of ETHNICITY, SEX, or other factors. Derived from the belief in "natural" laws popularized by thinkers such as John Locke from the late seventeenth century onward; argued for by Robespierre at the time of the French Revolution (*Declaration of the rights of man and the citizen*, 1789). What are commonly envisaged as "human rights" in contemporary SOCIETY—the right to life, freedom from SLAVERY and torture—were largely enshrined by the United Nations' *Universal declaration of human rights* in 1948. States that are held to violate these expectations are routinely monitored by organizations such Amnesty International.

Issues raised include the scope and degree of such "rights" and the impact of cultural variations encountered in their application. Anthropologists have been wary of appearing partisan in this area but some have become more overt in their interest in recent years (see APPLIED ANTHROPOLOGY).

Further reading: Goodale (2009).

human science(s). A general term covering those studies dealing with humankind and its activities in an empirical (see EMPIRICISM), scientifically rigorous fashion (originally as opposed to the *natural* sciences: those dealing with the physical world). Associated early on with the work of the German philosopher Wilhelm Dilthey. An academic course in human sciences might include elements not only of anthropology but also biology, psychology, and SOCIOLOGY.

humanism. An intellectual movement beginning during the European Renaissance and centered on the achievements of humankind alone, as opposed to viewing people mainly in relation to God. Associated with the rediscovery of classical Greek and Roman literature, and with authors such as Erasmus and Petrarch. Initially these writers espoused "Christian humanism," but the movement led to greater scientific and artistic accomplishments, and became associated with the defense of such developments as DARWINISM, which undermined religious certainties. William James and other twentieth-century writers advocated a "scientific humanism" based on EMPIRICISM. Humanism came to be associated with ATHEISM.

In anthropology, humanism has been an element of thought in such writers as SAPIR and his disciples. There is an American Society for Humanist Anthropology (SHA, founded 1974) and a dedicated journal, *Anthropology and humanism*. Humanist anthropologists tend to focus on the INDIVIDUAL's response to their ENVIRONMENT. Some of their theoretical assumptions have been challenged in recent years by, for instance, advocates of REFLEXIVITY.

Humboldt, Alexander von (1769–1859). See GERMAN ANTHROPOLOGY.

Hume, David (1711–1776). See ENLIGHTENMENT, PHILOSOPHICAL ANTHROPOLOGY.

humor. Humor may be thought of as a universal feature of human society, although what is found humorous obviously varies from CULTURE to culture. Anthropologists have considered humor in relation to story-telling, use of irony, and subversion; as a tool of political oppression or resistance; and in its ritualistic aspects (see JOKING RELATIONSHIP).

hunger. Anthropologists studying FOOD SYSTEMS have considered the several causes of hunger in the world: these are often linked not just to unusual events such as natural DISASTERS but also to unequal distribution of otherwise adequate resources, which can be caused by political or cultural factors. See also ENTITLEMENT THEORY, FAMINE, and NUTRITIONAL ANTHROPOLOGY.

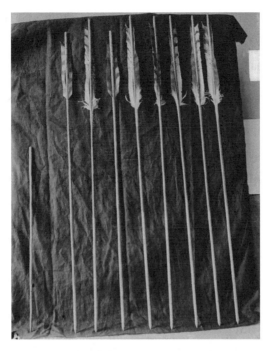

Figure 13 Hunting. Arrows from the Pima Reservation, Arizona, 1902. Photo: D. L. W. Gill; National Anthropological Archives, Smithsonian Institution, negative 2678A.

Hunger may also have significance as a volitional enterprise ("fasting"), for religious or other reasons; a particular area of study in affluent societies is the investigation of conditions such as anorexia.

Further reading: Drèze et al. (1995).

hunter-gatherer. A person or type of CULTURE subsisting by means of HUNTING, FISHING, or foraging rather than by growing crops or tending livestock. Hunting and gathering was once regarded as originally universal, with the assumption that it was replaced by AGRICULTURE in most societies. This belief has recently come under question, for instance in its view that hunter-gatherers had no other means of SUBSISTENCE. Modern hunter-gatherers include the SAN.

Further reading: Lee & DeVore (1968); Barnard (2004).

Hunter, Monica. See WILSON [M. H.].

hunting. The pursuit, capture, and/or killing of ANIMALS for FOOD SUBSISTENCE, to obtain other resources from them (skins, ivory, and so on), or for SPORT. Hunting or HUNTER-GATHERER methods may have once been universal means of survival (hence their significance to the archaeological record); even today, hunting makes a significant contribution in many societies, even parts of western nations. Particular ways of hunting, and the TOOLS (weapons, snares, and also other animals, such as trained dogs) used for it, may vary from place to place. The vast majority of societies regard hunting as a GENDER-based activity linked to MASCULINITY. Recreational hunting in Europe is sometimes viewed as CLASS-related. See also FISHING.

Further reading: MacKenzie (1988).

Husserl, Edmund (1859–1938). See INTENTIONALITY, PHENOMENOLOGY.

hydraulic society. An alternative term for ORIENTAL DESPOTISM.

Hymes, Dell H. (1927–2009). See ANTHROPOLOGICAL LINGUISTICS, ETHNOGRAPHY OF COMMUNICATION, ETHNOGRAPHY OF SPEAKING, ETHNOPOETICS, SPEECH ACT, SPEECH COMMUNITY, TRANSLATION.

hypergamy. The CUSTOM of "marrying up," by which a woman (originally) must take a spouse from an equal or higher social group. First used in the context of nineteenth-century CASTE, the term is now more generally applied. It is associated with ASYMMETRICAL ALLIANCE.

hypogamy. "Marrying down"; the (less familiar) opposite of HYPERGAMY. See also ASYMMETRICAL ALLIANCE.

I

icon. In philosophy and SEMIOTICS, a SIGN that shares some characteristic of the thing that it represents. From Greek, "likeness."

iconicity. The quality of being an ICON; intentional signification as a concept.

ideal type. Max WEBER's term for a MODEL of a phenomenon drawn from some features of its reality and intended as an aid to measurement and analysis of actual situations (e.g. "the spirit of capitalism").

identity. The combination of characteristics that collectively demarcate an INDIVIDUAL or group, both to themselves and others. Anthropologists are interested not only in the features that people may feel give them a valid identity as INDIVIDUALS but also in the collective identities—of FAMILY, ethnicity, and nation—to which they subscribe. See also SELF.

Further reading: Campbell & Rew (1999).

ideology. A system of ideas, sometimes held to justify a particular social or political program. Thus, one might examine, for instance, the ideology behind the actions of a particular STATE or belief. Ideology is often historically associated with MARXIST approaches to capitalist society, within which it is seen as a tool of the dominant CLASS that aims to make that class' advantages seem "natural," but debate has latterly moved on to how intentional the expression of an ideology can actually be.

ideophone. A word or phrase that is a phonetic representation of what it signifies; for instance, by including an onomatopoeic element ("bow-wow" for dog barking). An imitative word or phrase. Much studied in African languages but found everywhere, ideophones may operate by separate rules from standard speech.

Concise Dictionary of Social and Cultural Anthropology, First Edition. Mike Morris.
© 2012 Michael Ashley Morris. Published 2012 by Blackwell Publishing Ltd.

Ifá. A RELIGION of the Yoruba people of Nigeria, characterized by DIVINATION and also found in Cuba.

IK. An abbreviation for INDIGENOUS KNOWLEDGE.

illness. The personal or social PERCEPTION that one is "not right"—unwell, or, sometimes, in some other way abnormal. Social scientists contrast illness in this sense with the more objective term, DISEASE.

illocution. In philosophy, a SPEECH ACT that amounts to its own performance: for example, "I apologize," "I order you to…," and so on. See also PERFORMATIVE.

Further reading: Austin (1975).

immediate-return. Opposite of DELAYED-RETURN.

imperialism. Strictly speaking, GOVERNMENT by an emperor; more generally, a policy of acting in the interests of an empire or STATE, for example by exercising political POWER over foreign colonies (see COLONIALISM). MARXIST critics have argued that imperialism is necessary for the growth of CAPITALISM. See also RAJ.

improvisation. The art of giving a performance (of MUSIC, SONG, story, or DANCE) without a script, or using such a script as a basis for one's own invention. Anthropologists have studied numerous types of improvisation in this general sense, and also talk of the *improvised* ways in which people respond to the need for new social interaction.

Further reading: Hallam & Ingold (2007).

Inca. See AYLLU.

incest. Prohibited sexual activity between people whose relationship precludes MARRIAGE. Once believed to be a universal TABOO, though some societies do not proscribe it, on the assumption that it will be avoided as a matter of course. The incest taboo confers certain biological and social advantages, and may predate the development of modern humans. Nevertheless, there are historical examples of it being tolerated among certain groups and cultures.

Further reading: Arens (1986).

inclusive fitness. In SOCIOBIOLOGY, a THEORY advanced by W. D. Hamilton in the 1960s that attempted to explain reproductive fitness in terms of the ability of an organism *and* its relatives to produce offspring. Associated with DARWINISM and debates over ALTRUISM.

Further reading: Hamilton (1964).

incorporation. Literally, placing within one BODY (from Latin, *corpus*, "body"). It may refer to the process whereby, according to MARXIST thought, workers are coerced by HEGEMONY into accepting the established order of INDUSTRIAL SOCIETY rather than fighting it. It may also refer to a more general absorption of people into a group.

independent invention. An explanation for the occurrence, in different CULTURES, of similar traits or phenomena. An alternative theory to DIFFUSIONISM.

indexicality. The word "index" and its derivatives have meanings in several fields, all related to their root sense of "SIGN, indicator." Linguistically, indexical words are those that derive sense only from their context: "he/she," for example (compare DEIXIS). In SOCIAL SCIENCES we can speak of social contexts as also containing indexical elements: those that must be *interpreted* by participant or observer.

Indian. In popular writing, a term not only describing inhabitants and ARTEFACTS of South Asia but also the INDIGENOUS peoples and products of North America and the "West Indies." The term arose from confusion among early European navigators as to where their expeditions had landed, and is not used in mainstream anthropology in this sense any longer. Nevertheless, AMERICAN INDIAN may be acceptable in some contexts.

Indian anthropology. With its close ties to Britain in the colonial era of the RAJ and its enormous variety of peoples and cultures, it is hardly surprising that India and the wider region of South Asia have attracted considerable outside attention since the earliest beginnings of anthropology. The linguist Sir William Jones founded the Asiatic Society in 1784 and was followed in time by leading twentieth-century figures such as DUMONT, who outlined a theory of CASTE and co-founded *Contributions to Indian sociology* (1957–); the historian Bernard S. Cohn; and writers on tribal peoples such as Verrier Elwin and Christoph von Fürer-Haimendorf.

Equally significantly, India itself has embraced an often sociological strain of anthropology, with home-trained graduates coming from the University of Calcutta (now Kolkata) from the early 1920s and a host of notable authors such as S. C. Roy, L. K. Iyer, N. K. Bose, M. N. Srinivas, and, latterly, S. J. Tambiah, Gananath Obeyesekere, André Béteille, Veena DAS, and Arjun APPADURAI.

A major project of the Indian government that provides data on its peoples is the Anthropological Survey of India (http://www.ansi.gov.in).

See also VILLAGE studies, a notable subfield.

Further reading: Das (2003); Uberoi et al. (2008).

indigenism. A social or political movement prioritizing the concerns of INDIGENOUS peoples (for instance those of South America).

indigenous. Native (person, ANIMAL, plant, belief) to a particular place. The term is frequently used of original inhabitant peoples, as opposed to colonists, for instance in disputes regarding INTELLECTUAL PROPERTY.

indigenous knowledge. The ideas, wisdom, practical skills, and so on accumulated over time by an INDIGENOUS people in order to thrive within a particular ENVIRONMENT. The domain of ETHNOSCIENCE. Study of IK is complicated by the fact that western models of scientific understanding do not automatically equate to indigenous perceptions. Much debate in recent years has concerned the EXPLOITATION of NON-WESTERN indigenous knowledge by western interests and the violation of INTELLECTUAL PROPERTY rights (often communal rather than individual) involved. Sometimes also called "traditional knowledge" (TK), "indigenous technical knowledge" (ITK), or LOCAL KNOWLEDGE.

Further reading: Ellen et al. (2000); Posey (2004).

indirect exchange. See GENERALIZED EXCHANGE.

indirect rule. A method of GOVERNMENT in colonial societies (see COLONIALISM): the ruler is a selected member of the subject people rather than one of the colonizing ethnic group (the opposite case is termed DIRECT RULE).

individual. A particular person, ANIMAL, or similar entity, as distinct from a larger group or CLASS. While it is in the nature of human existence that people possess individuality (distinct consciousness and AGENCY), the concept of *individualism* is more problematic, and revolves around the value of the individual considered separately from his/her purely social role (see PERSON, SELF). Discussion in this area tends to refer back to the work of DURKHEIM and MAUSS. Ethnographers have suggested examples of societies in which consideration of the autonomous individual's personality or needs is absent, or very lightly considered.

Further reading: Mauss (1979: part III); Carrithers et al. (1985); Morris (1994); Celtel (2005); Miller (2009).

individualizing. See DESCRIPTIVE KINSHIP.

Indo-European. A term applied to a large language family of Europe and parts of Asia, including (for example) English, Greek, Sanskrit, and Spanish. Earlier known as "Indo-German" or "Aryan." The languages in this group are believed to derive from a common ANCESTOR, "proto-Indo-European" (see also PROTOLANGUAGE).

Industrial Revolution. See INDUSTRIAL SOCIETY, MODERNIZATION THEORY, SAINT-SIMON, SOCIAL CHANGE.

industrial society. A SOCIETY characterized by certain economic and other features, notably large-scale manufacture of goods based on factories and machine power, the DIVISION OF LABOR, and URBANIZATION of the working population (and declining rural AGRICULTURE). In such a system, TIME becomes organized and monitored, as processes may depend on maintaining sequences of WORK. Industrial society was studied notably by SAINT-SIMON in the early nineteenth century, and later by DURKHEIM, MARX, and others. Marx identified it with CAPITALISM but others have regarded it as quite feasible in socialist STATES. Latterly, as industrialization has spread around the world, many social scientists have come to regard the west as being in a *post-industrial* phase based around service industries, information TECHNOLOGY, and so on, rather than on classical PRODUCTION.

inequality. Although it has been argued (especially by early theorists) that totally egalitarian societies (see EGALITARIANISM) have existed, pretty much every SOCIETY can be seen to tolerate inequalities in its PRACTICE. While modern democracies often subscribe to equality—of treatment, opportunity, and so on—they can be seen to fall short in numerous areas, as evidenced by the experience of those treated as inferior on grounds of GENDER, ETHNICITY, sexual preference, or age (see DISCRIMINATION). Anthropologists have even studied societies they regarded as predisposed to inequality, such as India in the work of DUMONT. See also NOBLE SAVAGE, POWER, RACE, URBAN ANTHROPOLOGY.

Further reading: Dumont (1980).

INESOR. See RHODES-LIVINGSTONE INSTITUTE.

infanticide. The killing of children, strictly speaking those under twelve months old, although the definition varies. In modern western SOCIETY generally regarded as a rare and frightening ACT, but the PRACTICE may well be acceptable in other places in certain circumstances. A mother may be unable to provide for herself and any existing offspring if the new child survives; the child may suffer a disability, or be of unacceptable paternity. In societies such as India and China a strong cultural preference for sons may tip the balance toward some male children surviving and female ones being killed after birth or aborted. See also TWINS.

Further reading: Hausfater & Hrdy (2008).

inference. The drawing of conclusions from statements by exercising one's judgment and prior experience to analyze their context. Beyond stating a surface meaning, a speaker or writer may *imply* things that may be *inferred* by the hearer or reader.

Further reading: Sperber & Wilson (1995).

infibulation. A form of female CIRCUMCISION involving the removal of the vaginal labia and possibly sewing of the vaginal opening. Practiced mainly in some African and Muslim societies, particularly in Northeast Africa. Infibulation is an example of an issue that causes ethical problems for western anthropologists dealing with local practices (and for some of those expected to undergo the practice).

informal economy. Also known as "black economy." The PRODUCTION and distribution of legal goods, or provision of permitted services, outside normal GOVERNMENT regulation. Informal WORK is distinct from criminal activity as such, and from work done in the HOUSEHOLD or voluntarily. The "informal sector" was originally identified by Keith Hart in 1973. Being outside formal controls, informal workers avoid taxation and immigration checks but do not receive the benefits and protections of conventional workers. In THIRD WORLD countries they may be the majority of the workforce, but informal workers are found everywhere, and interaction often exists between the formal and informal economy.

Further reading: Hart (1973).

informant. In the context of anthropology, an informant is any member of a group who gives information freely about that group to an ethnographer. They may have a complex and shifting relationship with the ethnographer, and the ETHICS of this kind of involvement have been discussed widely.

Further reading: Metcalf (2002).

infrastructure. The facilities that enable a SOCIETY to function—assets such as roads, schools, and military installations. In MARXIST theory, sometimes used as an alternative to "base" (see BASE AND SUPERSTRUCTURE).

inheritance. In GENETICS, the acquisition of characteristics from one's forebears. Anthropologists have also studied how members of new generations inherit PROPERTY, political office (see SUCCESSION), and social relationships.

initiation. Formal introduction, usually by a ceremony, into a particular group. The initiate may be required to wear special CLOTHING and undertake a physical and/or psychological ordeal of some kind. In anthropology the term usually refers to the RITE OF PASSAGE by which those at PUBERTY enter adulthood.

Further reading: La Fontaine (1985).

insider/outsider. A common way of conceptualizing perspectives in SOCIAL SCIENCES: the anthropologist doing FIELDWORK, for instance, may be an "outsider" to a particular society who is trying to live as an "insider." See also EMIC, MARGINALITY.

institution. In SOCIOLOGY, "institution"refers to the large-scale structures societies use to fulfill basic needs, such as the FAMILY, the STATE, and RELIGION. In FUNCTIONALISM, the term designated smaller components of social SYSTEMS—BRIDEWEALTH, MARRIAGE, and so on. It is also, of course, often used more loosely.

intellectual history. Synonym for HISTORY OF IDEAS.

intellectual property (IP). IP can be summarized as any imagined or invented non-tangible product. It includes copyright material, trademarks, and patents; the intention legally speaking is also to protect creative works such as songs, literature, and particular expressions of ideas.

The intellectual rights of INDIGENOUS peoples have become a subject of great interest in recent anthropology (see INDIGENOUS KNOWLEDGE), with a number of academics (and the peoples themselves) involved in disputes with, for example, foreign commercial interests over who "owns" such property.

intensification. The ACT of making something greater or stronger. Intensification is most commonly discussed in relation to AGRICULTURE, where it involves more of some kind of resource (such as WATER—e.g. by IRRIGATION—or human labor) being applied to a particular area to increase yields. Forms of intensification can occur in FISHING and other contexts. See also RITE OF INTENSIFICATION, a means of restoring balance to a group.

intentionality. A philosophical concept particularly linked to the work of Edmund Husserl (early twentieth century): the capacity of people to direct their MINDs to a particular object. The concept is relevant to PHENOMENOLOGY and ETHNOMETHODOLOGY.

intermediate technology. A term popularized by E. F. Schumacher in the 1960s for TECHNOLOGY that represents a transitional phase of DEVELOPMENT between "low-tech" INDIGENOUS crafts and complex western TECHNOLOGY. Thus, it is similar to APPROPRIATE TECHNOLOGY.

internal colonialism. Political relations reproducing the dynamics of COLONIALISM *within* a particular STATE: typically, a metropolitan ELITE enjoying unequal shares of resources at the expense of an exploited (often MINORITY) group. Associated early on with MARXIST theory (Lenin, GRAMSCI) but also applied more generally, particularly to areas such as ethnic relations.

Further reading: Hechter (1999).

International African Institute (IAI). British organization (http://www. internationalafricaninstitute.org/index.html), founded as the International Institute of African Languages and Cultures in 1926. A major publisher of African anthropology; it also produces the journal *Africa*.

International Monetary Fund. See STRUCTURAL ADJUSTMENT.

interpretation. In general, the explication of something ("My interpretation of this story would be..."). In LINGUISTICS, a synonym for TRANSLATION, sometimes with an implication that interpreters usually deal with *oral* translation—typically, relaying the words of a foreign-language speaker to another hearer.

interpretive or **interpretative anthropology.** A school of thought associated with GEERTZ and others and originating in the 1960s (see also SYMBOLIC ANTHROPOLOGY, with which it intersects). The focus is on the EMIC ("insider") account of a group: the anthropologist's task is to translate the actors' own explanations into terms accessible to an outsider as accurately as possible, as well as to be aware of the questions raised by these explanations. A key element is THICK DESCRIPTION, the accurate rendering of the complex data available.

Further reading: Geertz (2000 [1973]); Panourgiá & Marcus (2008).

intersubjectivity. In philosophy and SOCIOLOGY, the quality that exists between people and permits them to share an understanding of the world. This need not correspond to objective reality.

intertextuality. In literary criticism, the range of ways in which one TEXT draws on another, either deliberately or not. Deliberate means would include similar or contrasting themes and quotation. The THEORY derives from DECONSTRUCTIONISM.

interview. A direct meeting between a person gathering information (the interviewer) and one or more subjects (interviewee(s)). Much used in the SOCIAL SCIENCES to gather quantitative or qualitative data (see QUALITATIVE/ QUANTITATIVE). The interview may be structured using a questionnaire or be less formal, with the interviewer reacting to the answers received. Issues in interviewing include bias that may be brought in by the nature of the questions or the personal interaction involved, and the truthfulness of the responses.

Further reading: Bernard (2006).

involution. In general use, turning in, or enveloping. Used by Clifford GEERTZ to describe a process whereby RICE farmers in Java responded to population growth by over-elaborating existing methods of cultivation rather than innovating.

Further reading: Geertz (1963).

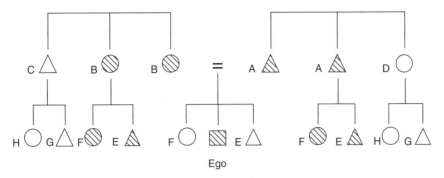

Figure 14 Iroquois terminology.

Iroquois. See IROQUOIS TERMINOLOGY, LAFITAU, LONGHOUSE, MORGAN.

Iroquois terminology. A type of RELATIONSHIP TERMINOLOGY using *bifur-cate merging* (bracketing of same-sex relations—see BIFURCATION) in which EGO's parents' same-SEX SIBLINGS are called by the same term (i.e. mother's sister is equivalent to mother, or MZ=M; father's brother is equivalent to father, or FB=F), and also PARALLEL COUSINS (those related via a same-sex sibling of the parent) are called by the term for siblings of that sex (so mother's sister's daughter is equivalent to sister, or MZD=Z; father's brother's son is equivalent to brother, or FBS=B) but CROSS-COUS-INS are called by a separate term. One of several types identified by Spier and MURDOCK.

Further reading: Spier (1925); Murdock (1949).

irredentism. A political policy of seeking the return of territories held by other STATES to a country that regards them as part of itself. From an Italian group that from 1878 onward claimed the areas called *Italia irredenta* ("unredeemed Italy").

irrigation. Artificial watering of land for crop PRODUCTION, for instance by channeling WATER from streams or lakes. In countries with hot climates (Egypt, parts of Asia, China) irrigation has been used for thousands of years; it can also be used in milder climates in, for instance, HORTICULTURE. Irrigation may require a good deal of technical skill and social cooperation, especially where it is on a large scale.

A secondary meaning of the term refers to washing the BODY in medical procedures.

Ishi (c.1861–1916). The "last wild INDIAN," apparently the sole survivor of the otherwise annihilated Yahi people. Born near Mt. Lassen, California, he was discovered in poor health in 1911 and eventually settled at what is now the University of California, San Francisco. There he collaborated with A. L. KROEBER and T. H. Waterman.

Further reading: Sackman (2010).

Islam. A world RELIGION centered around the teachings of the Prophet Muhammad (died equivalent to 632 CE) as expounded in the SHARI'A. Islam spread quickly around the MIDDLE EAST, North Africa, and eventually parts of Europe and South-East Asia. Today nearly a billion people follow some form of Islam (see SHIA, SUFISM, SUNNI, UMMA) in a wide range of cultural contexts. A major concern from the point of view of western secular STATES is the unity of thought by which Islam regards religious beliefs as inseparable from social life. This may be viewed as a challenge to liberal secularism. Against this, anthropologists have done much to further understanding of a complex and diverse phenomenon. Islamic societies have, arguably, been historically disadvantaged in western writings by the processes of ORIENTALISM.

Further reading: Gilsenan (2000); Ahmed (2007); Rosen (2008).

isogamy. Generally used in biology to refer to the union of equal gametes; in anthropology, isogamy refers to MARRIAGE between partners of equal STATUS. Compare ANISOGAMY.

isomorphism. The condition of having the same or similar forms; a term used in several areas, including LINGUISTICS.

Israel. See DIASPORA, JUDAISM, KIBBUTZ, MIDDLE EAST.

ITK. Abbreviation for "indigenous technical knowledge." See INDIGENOUS KNOWLEDGE.

J

Jainism. See NIRVANA.

jajmani. See CASTE.

Jakobson, Roman (1896–1982). Moscow-born American linguist. He worked in Czechoslovakia until World War II, was one of the founders of the Prague Linguistic Circle (see PRAGUE SCHOOL), and was highly influential in linguistic STRUCTURALISM (see STRUCTURAL LINGUISTICS). Jakobson later taught at the Massachusetts Institute of Technology. Soon after coming to New York, he met and greatly influenced LÉVI-STRAUSS. Key works include *Fundamentals of language* (with M. Halle, 1956) and *Language in literature* (1987).

Janjaweed. See DARFUR.

James, William (1842–1910). See HUMANISM.

jati. See CASTE.

Jesus Christ. See CHRISTIANITY.

jihad or **jahad** (etc). The "holy war" of ISLAM against those who do not follow its tenets, including whole states such as Israel. Sometimes regarded as a Koranic obligation. The term may also be applied to the individual believer's struggle, and comes from the Arabic for "conflict."

jinn (spelling varies). In the Muslim world, malevolent SPIRITS. From the Arabic for "demons." The singular is "jinnee."

Concise Dictionary of Social and Cultural Anthropology, First Edition. Mike Morris.
© 2012 Michael Ashley Morris. Published 2012 by Blackwell Publishing Ltd.

John Frum (or Frumm) movement. A CARGO CULT on Tanna Island, Vanuatu, MELANESIA, centered on a mythical US serviceman (possibly "John frum America"). Its adherents espouse INDIGENOUS TRADITIONS ("kastom").

joint family. A form of EXTENDED FAMILY in which the families of SIBLINGS share a HOUSEHOLD.

joking relationship. Permitted use of (quite rough) HUMOR between specific KINSHIP relations. The term describes behavior that would be regarded as insulting between people outside this relationship. Widely discussed in the early part of the twentieth century, it was analyzed in particular—with regard to, for instance mother's brother (MB) and his sister's son (ZS)—by RADCLIFFE-BROWN. It is said to lower or defuse tension within families; in this it is analogous to the AVOIDANCE RELATIONSHIP.

Further reading: Radcliffe-Brown (1952: chapters 1, 4, & 5).

Josselin de Jong, J. P. B. de (1886–1964) and **P. E. de** (1922–99). Cultural anthropologists at the University of Leiden. Major figures in DUTCH ANTHROPOLOGY and the ethnology of SOUTHEAST ASIA. They were both influenced by LÉVI-STRAUSS and were among a group of writers who popularized a distinctive strain of STRUCTURALISM in Holland. P. E. was J. P. B.'s nephew and edited *Structural anthropology in the Netherlands* (2nd ed. 1983).

Judaism. The Jewish RELIGION and its CULTURE. Jewish people worship a single god (see MONOTHEISM) and may be categorized along a spectrum from non-observance through reform Judaism to ultra-orthodoxy. Their sacred work, the Talmud, comprises the Mishnah and its commentaries, the Gemara.

The Jews, originally the people of Judaea, underwent major DIASPORAS under Babylonian and Roman rule, culminating in being dispersed around the MIDDLE EAST, North Africa, and Europe in the second century CE. Eventually settling in many countries, they became the objects of persecution (see SEMITIC), the best-known of recent times being the mass extermination by the Nazis in the years leading into World War II. Following the establishment of a new STATE of Israel in 1948, many diasporic Jews immigrated to their Biblical homeland.

Jewish culture has been much studied by social theorists and writers on MIGRATION. Israel's troubled relationship with its Arab (specifically Palestinian) neighbors has been a key element of the recent politics of the Middle East.

Jung, Carl (1875–1961). See ARCHETYPE, RADIN.

jural level. An aspect of (usually) KINSHIP dealing with cultural *rules* of conduct—what actions are prescribed—as opposed to what people *actually* do (BEHAVIORAL LEVEL). Compare the CATEGORICAL LEVEL, which covers cultural preferences. See also PRESCRIPTIVE MARRIAGE.

ju-ju or juju. A FETISH object in West Africa said to have SUPERNATURAL POWER, or the power itself. The term may be from Hausa or French and occurs mostly in older writing.

K

Kabyle. A BERBER people (or their DIALECT) resident in Algeria and Tunisia. Extensively studied by BOURDIEU.

Kachin. See *GUMSA* AND *GUMLAO*, LEACH.

kampung. A VILLAGE in Malaysia (and adjacent regions). Variant spellings include "campong" and "kampong."

Kant, Immanuel (1724–1804). See AESTHETICS, CATEGORY, ENLIGHTENMENT, PHILOSOPHICAL ANTHROPOLOGY, SCHEMA.

Kapferer, Bruce (1940–). Australian social anthropologist, born Sydney and educated at Manchester University. He spent some years at the RHODES-LIVINGSTONE INSTITUTE before holding professorships at Adelaide and University College, London. He joined the University of Bergen in 1999. Kapferer has undertaken fieldwork in Zambia, Sri Lanka, Australia, and India, and made major contributions to the study of RITUAL, NATIONALISM, VIOLENCE, and the STATE. His many works include *Transaction and meaning* (ed., 1976), *A celebration of demons* (2nd ed. 1991), and *Legends of people, myths of state* (1988); he also edits the journal *Social analysis*.

karma. In BUDDHISM, HINDUISM, and other South Asian religions, a force generated by actions during a particular lifetime that determines one's destiny thereafter. Positive actions result in good karma and an improved condition in the next life; negative actions result in the opposite. From Sanskrit, "action."

Kastom. See JOHN FRUM MOVEMENT.

Concise Dictionary of Social and Cultural Anthropology, First Edition. Mike Morris.
© 2012 Michael Ashley Morris. Published 2012 by Blackwell Publishing Ltd.

Keesing, Roger (1935–93). See MANA.

Kenyatta, Jomo (1889–1978). See MAU MAU.

khalif. Variant spelling of CALIPH.

khan. The title ("lord") originally given to successors of the Mongol ruler Genghis Khan (1162–1227); later used more generally in Asia.

khat (or **qat**, or similar). A shrub (*Catha edulis*) native to East Asia and the southwest Arabian peninsula and cultivated for its leaves, which have NARCOTIC properties and can be chewed or made into a DRINK. Also used in parts of Africa.

Further reading: Anderson (2007).

kibbutz. An Israeli collective SETTLEMENT, characteristically (from the early twentieth century onward) based on a farm with rotating labor, self-sufficiency in FOOD production, and group responsibility for childcare. Kibbutzim are sometimes analyzed as a form of Utopian SOCIETY (see UTOPIANISM). From modern Hebrew, "gathering."

Kikuyu. See MAU MAU.

kin. A general term for people who are related. See KINSHIP.

kin group. A group of people socially recognized as being related, either by blood or MARRIAGE.

kin selection altruism. A THEORY of ANIMAL behavior that suggests that apparent ALTRUISM is linked to nearness of relationship. Associated especially with W. D. Hamilton.

kin terms. See RELATIONSHIP TERMINOLOGY.

kin type. The KINSHIP designation for an individual, specific relative. Note that in RELATIONSHIP TERMINOLOGY "kin terms" may be ambiguous in a *given* culture (for instance "nephew") whereas "kin types" describe a precise genealogical position in *any* culture (e.g. brother's son (BS), sister's son (ZS)).

kindred. A general term for everyone in a particular set of KINSHIP relations. Kindred (or particular "kindreds") are usually reckoned from the point of view of EGO, tracing BILATERAL DESCENT (i.e. taking account of both the mother's and father's sides of the family).

kinesics. BODY movements, posture, and GESTURE considered as NONVERBAL COMMUNICATION. From Greek, "movement."

kingship. In many cultures the monarch is a figure apart from ordinary people (see DIVINE KINGSHIP for the best-known example) and wields symbolic or RITUAL power on a different plane from politics. Anthropologists have studied notable examples of kingship in Africa and Polynesia. See also SOVEREIGNTY.

Further reading: Quigley (2005).

kinship. A common method of SOCIAL ORGANIZATION based on recognized ties of relatedness (sometimes held to be one of the few UNIVERSALS, although kinship systems take such varied forms that this is very debatable).

Early anthropologists often assumed social configurations arose from the logic of the European FAMILY unit, but in various CULTURES different elements of relationships are emphasized in dealing with KIN—for instance, PATRILINEALITY and MATRILINEALITY: the recognition of rights and obligations based on one's membership of the father's or mother's side of the family. Kinship tends to exert more influence in the SMALL-SCALE SOCIETY. See RELATIONSHIP TERMINOLOGY for caveats concerning the term "kinship."

Kinship is a central concern in the history of anthropology, and the large amount of written material available to the student reflects this, even though kinship's current standing within the discipline has been questioned in many quarters over the last few years; accordingly this dictionary lists many terms that may occasionally require explanation. See (for types of relationships) ADOPTION, AFFINITY, ATOM OF KINSHIP, AVOIDANCE RELATIONSHIP, AVUNCULATE, CLAN, CLASSIFICATORY KINSHIP, COLLATERAL, CONSANGUINITY, DESCENT, DESCRIPTIVE KINSHIP, DRAVIDIAN KINSHIP, FAMILY, FICTIVE KINSHIP, GODPARENT, JOKING RELATIONSHIP, MARRIAGE, RITUAL KINSHIP, UNIVERSAL KINSHIP. See also BIFURCATION, ELEMENTARY STRUCTURES, REPRODUCTIVE TECHNOLOGIES.

kinship diagram. A representation of KINSHIP that conveys pictorially a set of genealogical relations (ideal, hypothesized, or actual), using certain conventions. The main symbols include:

Triangle (Δ) for male
Circle (O) for female
Rectangle (□) for an INDIVIDUAL regardless of sex
Slash (/) through one of the above indicates that the person is dead
Equals sign (=) for married (or other equivalence; e.g. of terms used in same way)
Slash through equals sign (≠) for divorced (or non-equivalence)
Horizontal line (—) for sexual relationship
Vertical line (|) for DESCENT relationship (e.g. parent/child)
Shading (e.g. ■) to highlight EGO
Half-circle (⌒) where lines connecting unrelated symbols intersect
G+1, G–1 (etc) to indicate the GENERATION (above or below Ego, though this varies)

Kiriwina. See TROBRIAND ISLANDS.

KITLV (Koninklijk Instituut voor Taal-, Land- en Volkenkunde). A leading Dutch anthropological/social science organization (http://www.kitlv.nl), founded in 1851 in Leiden, with a dominant interest in SOUTHEAST ASIA and the Caribbean. It publishes *Bijdragen tot de taal-, land- en volkenkunde* and a large number of monographs. See also DUTCH ANTHROPOLOGY.

Kleinman, Arthur (1941–). American medical anthropologist, born New York City and educated at Stanford and Harvard. He holds professorships in both psychiatry and anthropology at Harvard and has advised a number of public health bodies. His fieldwork in Taiwan and China led to much work on the region, particularly concerning depression and SOMATIZATION, VIOLENCE, and SUFFERING. He has made important contributions to the understanding of cultural elements in the treatment of ILLNESS (see MEDICAL ANTHROPOLOGY). The co-founder of the journal *Culture, medicine and psychiatry* (1977–), Kleinman has also produced *Patients and healers in the context of culture* (1980), *The illness narratives: suffering, healing and the human condition* (1988), *Social suffering* (ed. with DAS and M. Lock, 1997), and *What really matters: living a moral life amidst uncertainty and danger* (2006).

Klu Klux Klan. See SECRET SOCIETY.

knowledge. See INDIGENOUS KNOWLEDGE.

Koninklijk Instituut voor Taal-, Land- en Volkenkunde. See KITLV.

Koran. See FUNDAMENTALISM, SHARI'A.

Kroeber, A. L. (1876–1960). American cultural anthropologist, born Hoboken, New Jersey. One of BOAS' students at Columbia (where he gained a Ph.D. in 1901), he helped to develop the anthropology department at the University of California, serving as professor from 1919 to 1946. He did extensive fieldwork among NATIVE AMERICANS (see ISHI) and collected ARTEFACTS. His publications include *Anthropology* (1923, rev. ed. 1948), *Handbook of the Indians of California* (1925), and *The nature of culture* (1952). Among his contributions was work on the CULTURE AREA.

Kuhn, Thomas S. (1922–96). See PARADIGM.

kula. An EXCHANGE system in MELANESIA (especially the TROBRIAND ISLANDS) by which shell products (necklaces, armbands) circulate among communities (hence "kula ring"). First significantly described by MALINOWSKI and compared to other practices by MAUSS in *The gift*, it is bound up with personal STATUS and has been further analyzed by a number of anthropologists.

Further reading: Leach & Leach (1983); Malinowski (2002).

kulturkreis. German for "CULTURE circle." A THEORY within GERMAN ANTHROPOLOGY developed by Fritz Graebner and, later, Father Wilhelm Schmidt (early twentieth century) concerning the supposed diffusion of CULTURE TRAITS from a few centers to create particular cultural groupings. Compare CULTURE AREA and CULTURE COMPLEX in English-speaking anthropology. See also DIFFUSIONISM, VIENNA SCHOOL OF ETHNOLOGY.

Kunst, Jaap (1891–1960). See ETHNOMUSICOLOGY.

Kwakiutl. See BOAS, POTLATCH.

L

Labov, William (1927–). See SPEECH COMMUNITY, VARIATION.

Lacan, Jacques (1901–1981). French psychoanalyst who reinterpreted FREUD in the light of STRUCTURALISM. In his view, linguistic models best describe the unconscious. Key works include *Écrits* (French ed. 1966, English eds. 1977 onward).

lacustrine. Related to lakes; usually used of PLANTS, ANIMALS, or SETTLEMENTS on shores, but occasionally also of societies.

Lafitau, Joseph-François (1681–1746). French MISSIONARY to Canada who studied the Iroquois and produced an influential example of early anthropology: *Moeurs des sauvages amériquains* (1724; *Customs of the American Indians*).

laissez-faire (economics). See SOCIAL DARWINISM, SPENCER [H.].

lama. A Buddhist teacher, usually a priest, of Mongolia and Tibet; the Dalai Lama—the figurehead of the order—is regarded as a *bodhisattva*, a person near final enlightenment.

Lamarck, J. B. (Jean Baptiste de Monet, Chevalier de Lamarck, 1744–1829). French naturalist who developed an early THEORY of EVOLUTION (LAMARCK-IANISM) in such works as *Philosophie zoologique* (1809): in his view, ANIMALS altered during their lifetime and passed new characteristics onto their offspring. Lamarck was an early adopter of the term "biology."

Concise Dictionary of Social and Cultural Anthropology, First Edition. Mike Morris.
© 2012 Michael Ashley Morris. Published 2012 by Blackwell Publishing Ltd.

Lamarckianism or Lamarckism. An early (pre-DARWIN) THEORY of EVOLUTION advanced by LAMARCK; later modified by those who disagreed with DARWIN ("neo-Lamarckians").

land tenure. Land tenure concerns how people relate to land they use; in anthropology the dichotomy of public or private ownership breaks down in the face of a wide variety of customary rights and obligations. These concern not simply the land itself but also access to grazing or WATER. The ways in which such resources are made available may reveal underlying social hierarchies and structures. Changing conditions such as a new form of GOVERNMENT or increased competition may bring tensions to a head. Anthropologists such as GLUCKMAN have done work on INDIGENOUS understandings of these issues in Africa.

In recent years, land tenure and resource rights have been debated in cases involving Australian ABORIGINAL peoples, South American groups, and others. In some cases anthropologists have attempted to advise or arbitrate (see ADVOCACY). See also SHARECROPPING.

Further reading: Gluckman (1972); Wilmsen (1989).

Lang, Andrew (1844–1912). Scottish classicist, poet, and writer on FOLKLORE (born Selkirk; educated in Scotland and at Oxford) whose interests led to disputes with a number of writers on MYTH and RELIGION, such as FRAZER and Max Müller. His many and varied works include *Custom and myth* (1884), *The making of religion* (1898), and *The secret of the totem* (1905).

language. Any kind of symbolic system of communication, frequently understood as strictly meaning human speech and writing in particular but also encompassing SIGN language, codes such as Morse or semaphore, and arguably ANIMAL communication behavior. By analogy it extends to such areas as computer coding.

Language is a fertile area for anthropologists, even at the most basic level (it is necessary for an ethnographer doing FIELDWORK to be able to speak the language of the CULTURE studied). See also ANTHROPOLOGICAL LINGUISTICS.

Further reading: Jourdan & Tuite (2006).

language acquisition. The study of language acquisition touches on all elements that new speakers—notably, small children—must learn: SYNTAX, VOCABULARY, and usage conventions. To acquire a LANGUAGE the learner must have access to others who use it and sufficient motivation (e.g. necessity, prestige) to want to learn. In addition to the core data of what words are used and how, the learner picks up contextual information—when and how to take TURNS, appropriate REGISTER, and other elements that vary in importance according to the particular language and CULTURE. Some languages are easier to learn than others, but it has been observed that children especially seem to be predisposed to certain kinds of acquisition.

language classification. Traditionally languages have often been classified by *family*—those languages assumed to share a common PROTOLANGUAGE are grouped together (thus, proto-Indo-European is the ANCESTOR of INDO-EUROPEAN, which encompasses English, Greek, and a number of other tongues). This kind of *genetic* classification is the domain of COMPARATIVE LINGUISTICS.

Languages may also be grouped by shared features, which might be explained as the outcome of CULTURE CONTACT in a region or analyzed by language type (those that follow particular grammatical rules, for instance).

Further reading: Campbell & Poser (2008).

language death. The point at which a LANGUAGE becomes completely disused or disappears, for instance because speakers adopt an incoming language instead. Extinct or dying languages may be those of minorities, and may be of great interest to linguists and anthropologists.

language games. The notion, associated with the later writings of WITTGENSTEIN, that the use of LANGUAGE should be regarded as similar to a group of games, each with its own rules and context. There are FAMILY RESEMBLANCES between languages, but these are not sufficient to make generalizations about all language use. What is important is how languages are used or modified in PRACTICE.

Further reading: Wittgenstein (2009).

langue and parole. A linguistic distinction made by SAUSSURE: langue, or "language," is the structured set of rules and conventions established communally. Parole, or "speech," is the LANGUAGE as it is actually used by an INDIVIDUAL speaker. Saussure characterizes this as the difference between the "essential" and the "accessory."

Further reading: Saussure (1983).

latent. See MANIFEST and LATENT.

Latin America. The area of Southern America (including Mexico and the Caribbean) characterized by cultures in which there is a legacy of COLONIALISM. Such cultures commonly have Spanish or Portuguese as the dominant LANGUAGE and have a mixed heritage of INDIGENOUS "INDIAN" roots and European influences ("Latin" originally refered to the origins of western European languages). Among the anthropologists who have investigated diverse aspects of Latin American societies such as INEQUALITY, POWER, POVERTY, RURAL and urban ways of life, SEX ROLES, and VIOLENCE are Eric Wolf, Robert Redfield, and Oscar Lewis. See also CATHOLICISM, MESTIZO.

law. In a narrow sense, the rules governing a community, whether derived from AUTHORITY or CUSTOM. The anthropological study of law builds on foundations laid by such figures as MAINE (who made important comments on CONTRACT and STATUS) and ethnographic descriptions from MALINOWSKI of local rules. Other distinguished early work was done by GLUCKMAN and, later, Llewellyn and Hoebel. Around the mid twentieth century there was debate about the difference between measures intended to strengthen cultural institutions and less codified forms of social control or SANCTION, and whether this was all "law" or only some of it was. With fresh awareness of what became known as LEGAL PLURALISM in the colonial era, anthropologists began also to study the *variety* of legal conventions people obey. Other newer forms of legal anthropology consider CONFLICT resolution, RESISTANCE to law and POWER, and law and TERRORISM.

Further reading: Maine (2006); Malinowski (1926); Llewellyn & Hoebel (1941); Mundy (2002).

Leach, Edmund (1910–89). British anthropologist, originally an engineer. Captured in Burma during World War II, he worked among the peoples of the Kachin region. At the London School of Economics (at which he was reader from 1947 to 1953) and under the influence of MALINOWSKI and FIRTH, he gravitated toward LÉVI-STRAUSS and STRUCTURALISM. He became professor of social anthropology at Cambridge (1972–8). His key work is *Political systems of Highland Burma* (2004 [1954])—in which he discusses the contrasting political approaches of GUMSA AND GUMLAO—but others include *Rethinking anthropology* (1961) and *Genesis as myth* (1969).

Lee, Richard B. (1937–). See ETHOLOGY, HUNTER-GATHERER.

Leenhardt, Maurice (1878–1954). See FRENCH ANTHROPOLOGY.

left. See RIGHT AND LEFT.

legal anthropology. See LAW.

legal pluralism. A concept in anthropology of law: what people do in settling matters of justice is governed not just by the formal court system (or its equivalent) that nominally regulates them but also by customary PRACTICE. Thus the LAW has two (or more) potentially conflicting strands. Legal PLURALISM can also refer to the situation in areas in which there are two or more *formal* legal systems.

legend. See MYTH.

Leibniz, G. W. (1646–1716). See THEODICY.

Leiris, Michel (1901–90). See FRENCH ANTHROPOLOGY.

Lemkin, Raphael (1900–59). See GENOCIDE.

leopard-skin chief or **priest.** Among the NUER, an INDIVIDUAL who mediates between parties in a dispute, as described by EVANS-PRITCHARD. The original term (*kuaar muon*) can be translated as "earth-master" or "chief of the earth."

Le Play, Frédéric (1806–1882). See STEM FAMILY.

Lévi-Strauss, Claude (1908–2009). Belgian-born (in Brussels) French anthropologist, widely admired outside the discipline and the central figure in STRUCTURALISM as applied to anthropology. While teaching at the University of São Paulo (from 1935), he pursued amateur fieldwork among Brazilian Indians; on returning to France he encountered antisemitism during the wartime OCCUPATION. Fleeing in 1941 to New York, he taught at the New School for Social Research and met JAKOBSON, whose influence precipitated his development of structuralist THEORY.

His seminal work, *The elementary structures of kinship*, first appeared in 1949 (rev. English ed. 1969). From 1950 to 1974 he directed anthropology at the École pratique des hautes etudes, and held a chair at the Collège de France from 1959. His other major publications include *Tristes tropiques*

Figure 15   Lévi-Strauss. A photograph inscribed by Lévi-Strauss to Oxford colleagues, 1964. Used by permission of Oxford University, School of Anthropology.

(aka *World on the wane*, 1955; English ed. 1961), the two-volume *Anthropologie structurale* (1958–73; *Structural anthropology*, 1963–76), *Le totémisme aujourd'hui* (1962; *Totemism*, 1964), *La pensée sauvage* (1962; *The savage mind*, 1966), and the four-volume *Mythologiques* (1964–71). He also co-edited the journal *L'Homme*.

See also ALLIANCE, ATOM OF KINSHIP, BRICOLAGE, COOKING, DISTINCTIVE FEATURE, ELEMENTARY STRUCTURES, HARMONIC, HOT AND COLD SOCIETIES, MECHANICAL MODEL, MYTHEME, STRUCTURAL LINGUISTICS, STRUCTURALISM.

Further reading: Wiseman (2009).

levirate. A MARRIAGE CUSTOM by which a man marries his dead brother's wife or wives; children of this union will be regarded as those of the dead brother. Familiar to Bible scholars from Old Testament Jewish PRACTICE; current in several parts of Africa and elsewhere. Compare SORORATE (the practice of a man marrying his dead wife's sister), GHOST MARRIAGE, WIDOW INHERITANCE.

Lévy-Bruhl, Lucien (1857–1939). French philosopher who taught at the Sorbonne in Paris. His book *La mentalité primitive* (1922; *Primitive mentality*, 1923) outlined the now-abandoned dichotomy between mystically minded "primitive" peoples and "rational" westerners—a popular view in its in time but one countered by anthropologists such as EVANS-PRITCHARD.

Lewis, Oscar (1914–70). See CULTURE OF POVERTY, LATIN AMERICA, POVERTY.

lexicon. A word-list (originally a dictionary in Latin covering Greek, Hebrew, Syriac, or Arabic). In LINGUISTICS, a compilation of words and forms in a particular LANGUAGE or area.

lexicostatistics. A method of analyzing the VOCABULARY of apparently related languages, by checking COGNATES. Sometimes used interchangeably as a term with GLOTTOCHRONOLOGY, with which it shares contestable assumptions.

Lienhardt, R. Godfrey (1921–93). British anthropologist of Africa, born in Bradford. Educated at Cambridge and at Oxford, where he taught alongside EVANS-PRITCHARD. His works include *Divinity and experience* (1961) and *Social anthropology* (2nd ed. 1966). His brother Peter (1928–86) was an anthropologist of the MIDDLE EAST.

lifecycle. In biology, the successive stages of an organism's development; similarly, in SOCIAL SCIENCES, the progress of a person through CHILDHOOD, YOUTH, maturity, old age, and DEATH. The term may also apply analogously to comparable phases in the life of a HOUSEHOLD. More recently the term "life-course" has been adopted to better describe these changes as experienced in new forms of household (e.g. after DIVORCE) and to acknowledge that real life is generally less rigid than the original image implies.

life expectancy. The age to which a person may reasonably expect to live given health, social, and age factors. In western countries, for example, both men and women would normally anticipate survival into their seventies.

life history. The NARRATIVE of a person's life as usually related by themselves to an anthropologist. While a life HISTORY cannot be taken as objective truth, any more than any INTERVIEW, it may be a useful way of understanding the nature of INDIVIDUAL experience within a particular CULTURE. See also AUTOETHNOGRAPHY.

life sciences. The scientific study of living organisms. Life sciences include traditional fields such as biology and medicine, along with newer specialisms such as biophysics, GENETICS, SOCIOBIOLOGY, and particularly ECOLOGY.

liminality. From Latin, "threshold": the condition of an INDIVIDUAL or group passing through a STATUS boundary (and concomitant psychological changes), for instance during a RITE OF PASSAGE or PILGRIMAGE; a stage thought to be ambiguous and powerful. It has been studied notably by VAN GENNEP and Victor TURNER.

Further reading: Turner (1974).

limited good. A THEORY advanced by George M. Foster (originally in 1965) that suggested PEASANT societies believed good things to be finite and insufficient for everyone, so advantage to one person meant others lost out. It was criticized and subsequently modified by Foster. Compare AMORAL FAMILISM.

Further reading: Foster (1972).

Linnaean taxonomy. The binomial ("two names") CLASSIFICATION system of Carl von Linné (1707–78), known as Linnaeus, that covers PLANTS and ANIMALS (and, originally, minerals).

Linnaeus (Carl von Linné, 1707–78). See LINNAEAN TAXONOMY, TAXONOMY.

line. In KINSHIP, a series of people in chronological order, as can be seen in the vertical axis of a KINSHIP DIAGRAM, showing one's ancestry ("he has a long line of forebears").

lineage. The KINSHIP term for a UNILINEAL DESCENT group (one recognizing rights through membership of the mother's *or* father's side of the family) with a traceable common ANCESTOR. A lineage tends to be better-defined than a CLAN.

lineal (noun or adjective). A KINSHIP term for a blood relative (see CONSANGUINITY) in the *direct* line of DESCENT. For example, grandfather, father, and son (in RELATIONSHIP TERMINOLOGY: FF–F–S) have a lineal relationship. EGO's SIBLINGS (brothers and sisters) are usually also reckoned as lineal relatives. Contrast COLLATERAL, the term for a close relative who is not directly in line.

linguistic determinism. The strongest form of LINGUISTIC RELATIVISM, holding (hypothetically) that LANGUAGE actually determines available thought. A more moderate (and generally accepted) version would regard language as a major influence on thought. See also DETERMINISM.

linguistic reconstruction. See RECONSTRUCTION.

linguistic relativism or **relativity.** A concept that suggests different LANGUAGES formulate different ways to think about the world, such that speakers of one language have ideas that do not translate completely to another. This concept has applications in PSYCHOLINGUISTICS; compare LINGUISTIC DETERMINISM, RELATIVISM, TRANSLATION. The best-known statement of linguistic relativism is the WHORFIAN HYPOTHESIS.

Further reading: Whorf (1956); Lucy (1992).

linguistic variation. See VARIATION.

linguistics. Knowledge and study of LANGUAGES. Most notably associated with the work of SAUSSURE, who changed the focus of linguistics from DIACHRONIC to SYNCHRONIC, and more recently with Noam CHOMSKY. See ANTHROPOLOGICAL LINGUISTICS.

Linnean taxonomy. See LINNAEAN TAXONOMY.

Linton, Ralph (1893–1953). See NATIVISM, ROLE, STATUS.

literacy. Use of a written LANGUAGE; ability in reading and/or writing (see WRITING SYSTEMS). In western societies, literacy rates grew (usually after restriction to an educated ELITE) with the greater availability of printed books and an increasing expectation (by the nineteenth century) that most people should be literate. Many peoples of interest to anthropology were once labeled PRELITERATE or NON-LITERATE, but the importance of ORAL LITERATURE was later recognized, along with a growing understanding of the complex range of possibilities for communication that different cultures offered. Compare ORALITY: preference for speech.

Further reading: Street (1993).

literary anthropology. A term claimed by Fernando Poyatos (*Literary anthropology*, 1988) to cover the study of CULTURES as revealed through national literatures; more generally associated with the group of post-modern anthropologists (see POST-MODERNISM) around George Marcus who contributed to WRITING CULTURE. In this sense, literary anthropology approaches cultures as varieties of TEXTS to be interpreted, and is influenced by then-recent developments in literary criticism and HERMENEUTICS, as well as the earlier work of Clifford GEERTZ (compare INTERPRETIVE ANTHROPOLOGY). It has been criticized for, among other things, being overly skeptical of scientific perspectives.

lithic. Relating to stone; in ARCHAEOLOGY, the lithic period is the "Stone Age," characterized by development of stone TOOLS and divided into the Paleolithic, Mesolithic, and Neolithic eras.

little tradition. See GREAT TRADITION.

Livingstone, David (1813–73). See SCHAPERA.

loan word. A word adopted by one LANGUAGE from another, possibly with modification. "Naïve" is a French loan word in English.

local knowledge. A phrase popularized by GEERTZ as his version of INDIGENOUS KNOWLEDGE: it emphasizes the importance of remembering that different cultures have different data available to them, and different ways of understanding them.

Further reading: Geertz (2000 [1983]).

Locke, John (1632–1704). See ASSOCIATION, HUMAN RIGHTS, PERSON, TABULA RASA.

locution. Meaningful speech; the "saying" part of speaking. So named by J. L. Austin. Compare (for example) ILLOCUTION.

Further reading: Austin (1975).

logging. An aspect of FORESTRY: the action of cutting down trees for logs. Conservation and other social issues may be involved. Logging is significantly practiced in Indonesia, Scandinavia, the Americas, and other areas.

longhouse. A dwelling used by the Iroquois and other native North Americans, and found in parts of Southeast Asia (some also survive in Europe). The one-storey structure provides integrated spaces for individual households together with communal areas.

Lorenz, Konrad (1903–89). See AGGRESSION.

Lounsbury, Floyd G. (1914–98). See TRANSFORMATIONAL ANALYSIS.

love. Love affects in various ways our understanding of RELIGION, COMMUNITY, FAMILY, SEX, and GENDER (including issues of HOMOSEXUALITY). The western attachment to romantic ideals of overwhelming personal affection color a huge range of literature and MEDIA, and have done for centuries (from chaste courtly love to *Romeo and Juliet* and on to "romcoms"). Nevertheless, "love" may be partly a meeting of individual preferences and wider social expectations about "suitable" partners—a blending of biology, psychology, and CULTURE. NON-WESTERN societies may not share the cultural assumptions of the west, but anthropologists have found a wide range of COURTSHIP patterns, poetic TRADITIONS, and so on.

Further reading: Goody (2009); Overing & Passes (2000).

Lowie, Robert H. (1883–1957). Austrian-born American ethnographer; one of BOAS' first students. Born in Vienna, he gained a Ph.D. from Columbia in 1908. He did several spells of fieldwork among NATIVE AMERICAN peoples, especially the Crow. After being attached to the American Museum of Natural History, he settled at the University of California from 1921 to 1950. His works include *Primitive society* (1920), *Primitive religion* (1924), and *The Crow Indians* (1935).

lowland. See HIGHLAND/LOWLAND.

lusophone. Portuguese-speaking (from "Lusitania," the ancient name for the province roughly equivalent to Portugal, and the Greek for "voice").

Lyotard, Jean-François (1924–98). See METANARRATIVE.

M

M or Mo or m. In RELATIONSHIP TERMINOLOGY, the abbreviation for "mother."

machismo. In Latin American cultures, the quality of being "macho"—that is, manly, typically virile. It may imply SEXISM. From Mexican Spanish, "manliness."

Madge, Charles (1912–96). See EIDOS.

madrasa (Spellings vary). An Islamic (usually religious) school or place of higher learning. Sometimes allegedly connected with TERRORISM, though the reality is more complex.

magic. Professedly SUPERNATURAL PRACTICES believed to influence people or events and usually involving secret knowledge.

Early anthropologists such as FRAZER and TYLOR started from the assumption that PRIMITIVE peoples were "irrational" in ascribing POWER to magic since they were empirically wrong. As theory developed, ethnographers such as EVANS-PRITCHARD (among the ZANDE) and MALINOWSKI presented belief in magic more sympathetically, suggesting it was not inimical to, for example, an understanding of causality, but still "explained" wider issues for its adherents or relieved their anxieties.

Modern anthropologists tend to examine magic on its own terms, and have shifted the focus in some cases to practitioners in western "rationalist" settings.

See also CANNIBALISM, EVIL EYE, SORCERY, SUPERSTITION, SYMPATHETIC MAGIC, WITCHCRAFT.

Further reading: Evans-Pritchard (1937); Luhrmann (1989).

Concise Dictionary of Social and Cultural Anthropology, First Edition. Mike Morris.
© 2012 Michael Ashley Morris. Published 2012 by Blackwell Publishing Ltd.

Mahabharata. See HINDUISM.

Mahayana Buddhism. See BUDDHISM.

Maine, Sir Henry (1822–88). British legal historian who is most famous for his work on the posited shift from STATUS to CONTRACT in early societies. As a result of this he exerted considerable influence on anthropological thought. His key work is *Ancient law: its connection with the early history of society and its relation to modern ideas* (2006 [1861]).

Mair, Lucy (1901–86). British social anthropologist; born in Surrey. She was educated in classics at Cambridge; later she lectured at the London School of Economics and attended MALINOWSKI's seminars. After fieldwork in Buganda she received a Ph.D. in 1932. Mair was a professor at the London School of Economics from 1963 to 1968; her books include *An African people in the twentieth century* (1934), *Studies in applied anthropology* (1957), *Introduction to social anthropology* (1965; 2nd ed. 1972), and *Anthropology and social change* (1969).

Further reading: Davis (1984).

Malinowski, Bronislaw (1884–1942). Polish anthropologist; a major proponent of the centrality of FIELDWORK and of the theory of FUNCTIONALISM. Born in Kraków and educated at Jagiellonian University (1902–6), he gained a doctorate with honors in philosophy and physics before attending Leipzig University and the London School of Economics. HADDON, RIVERS, and SELIGMAN were among the anthropologists already at the LSE. After the publication of *The family among the Australian aborigines* in 1913, Malinowski did fieldwork in Southern Papua. He took a second doctorate at London University in 1916. His fieldwork in Kiriwina (TROBRIAND ISLANDS) of 1915–18 involved two visits.

Argonauts of the Western Pacific, published in 1922, marks a methodological shift from speculation based on THEORY (compare e.g. FRAZER) to close analysis drawn from fieldwork; this was a major influence on later anthropologists. Malinowski returned to the LSE, becoming first professor of social anthropology, in 1927. Later books include *Crime and custom in savage society* (1926), *Sex and repression in savage society* (1927), *The sexual life of savages* (1929), and *Coral gardens and their magic* (1935). Malinowski visited several American universities and undertook fieldwork in Mexico in his final years. See also ARGONAUT, FIELDNOTES, MYTHICAL CHARTER.

Further reading: Malinowski (1948); Malinowski (1989); Firth (1957[a]); Ellen et al. (1988); Young (2004).

Malthusian. Characteristic of the views of the English economist T. R. Malthus (1766–1834), author of *An essay on the principle of population*, who advocated sexual restraint in order to prevent (in his view) population growth exceeding sustainable levels. Compare CARRYING CAPACITY. Malthus' essay is an early classic of DEMOGRAPHY. See also GREEN MOVEMENT.

mana. Originally defined by anthropologists of OCEANIA as an elemental, impersonal force believed to confer POWER on a divine being, INDIVIDUAL, or object (from MAORI, "AUTHORITY") and posited as a very early focus of RELIGION, preceding ANIMISM. This definition has been challenged by Roger Keesing.

Further reading: Keesing (1984); Tomlinson (2006).

Manchester School. An influential group of British anthropologists connected with Manchester University in the mid twentieth century. The head of the department was Max GLUCKMAN; other members included Victor TURNER and J. Clyde Mitchell. Several of them also worked at the RHODES-LIVINGSTONE INSTITUTE in what is now Zambia. The Manchester School worked in an empirical fashion (see EMPIRICISM), mostly on Central Africa; they are notable for a sharp focus on the CASE STUDY approach, an interest in the dynamics of SOCIAL NETWORKS (rather than in constructing static models of SOCIAL STRUCTURE), and a concern with CONFLICT resolution.

Not to be confused with the nineteenth-century group of free-trade economists.

Further reading: Evens & Handelman (2006).

Mandarin (dialect). See TONE.

manifest and latent. In the SOCIOLOGY of Robert Merton, a distinction between the overt, recognized (manifest) function of a practice (see FUNCTIONALISM) and its unintended or hidden (latent) consequences. For instance, a RITUAL might fail in its stated purpose but still promote SOLIDARITY. The terms were borrowed from an earlier analytical use by FREUD.

Further reading: Merton (1968).

manioc. The root of the cassava plant (*Manihot*), cultivated in many tropical regions, with several FOOD and DRINK uses. The term derives from the Tupi language of Brazil.

Maori. The dominant pre-European inhabitants of New Zealand, and their LANGUAGE. After British colonization in the mid nineteenth century the Maori declined, but they have enjoyed greater political POWER in the latter part of the twentieth century and early twenty-first century, and have reclaimed some of the lands previously appropriated by the settlers amid renewed external interest in their activities, such as wood-carving and making TATTOOS. They have been studied by Raymond FIRTH and others.

Further reading: Makereti (1986).

Marcus, George E. (1946–). See LITERARY ANTHROPOLOGY, MULTI-SITED ETHNOGRAPHY, *WRITING CULTURE*.

Marett, R. R. (1866–1943). Anthropologist and philosopher; born on Jersey, educated at Oxford (in classics) and Berlin. He was reader in social anthropology at Oxford from 1910 to 1936, and acting (first) professor of social anthropology at Oxford from 1936 to 1937. His works include *The Threshold of religion* (1909), *Anthropology* (1912), and *Psychology and folklore* (1920).

Further reading: Buxton (1936); Marett (1941).

marginality. The state of being partly inside and partly outside the dominant CULTURE, as in the case of ethnic minorities and those stigmatized by others (see STIGMA). Explored in the SOCIOLOGY of writers such as Robert Park (early twentieth century, US). Compare INSIDER/OUTSIDER.

mariticide. Killing of one's own husband, or one who does this. Very rarely used. See also UXORICIDE.

maritime. Connected with the sea, shipping, TRADE by sea, or similar activities. See FISHING, WHALING.

marker. In linguistics, a word or part of one (a PREFIX or SUFFIX) that shows a particular distinguishing feature. For instance, the SUFFIX "-ed" often "marks" the use of the past tense in English. Similar in meaning to a component in COMPONENTIAL ANALYSIS.

market. A place in which TRADE takes place, usually involving MONEY rather than BARTER or GIFT EXCHANGE. Markets are a key topic of ECONOMIC ANTHROPOLOGY, whether as literal gatherings for selling goods in an open space or in the more abstract sense of large-scale movements of commodities between enterprises. It is important to hold in mind the distinction between the former (characteristic of small PEASANT societies) and the latter (characteristic of CAPITALISM).

Further reading: Dilley (1992).

marriage. A socially sanctioned (see SANCTION) union of two (or more) people (usually, but not always, of the opposite SEX), often with the expectation that they will cohabit and raise children. The western (recent) expectation of a match founded on romantic LOVE between a young man and woman is challenged by HISTORY, and by PRACTICE in many cultures: anthropologists working in ALLIANCE theory (and others) have highlighted aspects that are closely bound up with EXCHANGE—such as BRIDEWEALTH or DOWRY. The parties to a union may also be of the same sex—not only in modern western societies but in institutions such as WOMAN MARRIAGE. In some cases, one

Figure 16 Market. St George's Market Hall, Belfast, Northern Ireland, 2007. Photo: Mike Morris.

party may not even be alive (GHOST MARRIAGE, LEVIRATE, SORORATE). There may be many partners (POLYGAMY). In recent years advances in medicine have allowed yet further variation of the child-rearing element—see REPRO- DUCTIVE TECHNOLOGIES. In all, marriage is a classic example of an apparently straightforward phenomenon rendered complex by ethnological reality.

See also AFFINITY, ARRANGED MARRIAGE, BIGAMY, CONCUBINAGE, DIVORCE, ENDOGAMY, EXOGAMY, INCEST, NUCLEAR FAMILY, POST-MARITAL RESIDENCE, SISTER EXCHANGE, STEP-RELATIONS.

Further reading: Needham (2004); Comaroff (1980).

marriage exchange. See under specific forms: CROSS-COUSIN, DIRECT EXCHANGE, GENERALIZED EXCHANGE, SISTER EXCHANGE, SISTER'S DAUGH- TER'S MARRIAGE, SYMMETRICAL ALLIANCE.

marriage payment. See under the separate forms: BRIDEWEALTH (which is given for a bride), DOWRY (which is brought with a bride).

marriage system. A label for a particular kind of MARRIAGE as practiced in a given CULTURE or circumstance—for instance, MONOGAMY, POLYGYNY, CROSS-COUSIN marriage. An important area in ALLIANCE theory, especially.

Marriott, McKim (1924–). See GREAT TRADITION.

Mars, Louis (1906–). See ETHNOPSYCHIATRY.

Marx, Karl (1818–83). Revolutionary philosopher and political writer; a crucial influence on twentieth-century politics, as well as on the SOCIAL SCIENCES. Born in Trier, Prussia, Marx was educated in Bonn and Berlin (in law and philosophy). He received his doctorate from Jena in 1841. He lived in exile in London from 1849. His major works include the *Manifest der Kommunistischen Partei* (with F. ENGELS, 1848; "Manifesto of the German communists," 1850); *Das Kapital* (1867; *Capital: a critical analysis of capitalist production*, ed. Engels, 1887); *Achtzehnte Brumaire des Louis Bonaparte* (1852; *The eighteenth Brumaire of Louis Bonaparte*, 1869).

Further reading: Bloch (2004 [1975]); Marx & Engels (1975–2004); Donham (1999); Patterson (2009).

Marxist. An adherent of an IDEOLOGY derived from the economic and political writings of Karl MARX. Marx and his collaborator ENGELS drew partly on the work of MORGAN, and Engels' *The origin of the family* became well-known to anthropologists. Early Marxist thought promulgated its own "EVOLUTIONARY STAGES"—humanity was theorized to progress from PRIMITIVE economics through FEUDALISM and CAPITALISM to COMMUNISM.

While Marxist academic thought was the (enforced) norm in twentieth-century Soviet Russia and China (see CHINESE ANTHROPOLOGY, RUSSIAN ANTHROPOLOGY), it was not until the 1960s that western universities liberalized to the point of accepting avowedly Marxist anthropology. Emerging primarily from France in the 1960s, the branch called STRUC-TURAL MARXISM was supplemented by a wider interest in the west in left-wing perspectives, which fed into areas such as CULTURAL STUDIES.

Even after the collapse of Soviet Marxism, a concern with certain concepts associated with Marx—among them BASE AND SUPERSTRUCTURE, the MODE OF PRODUCTION, CLASS, POWER and INEQUALITY, and COMMODITY FETISHISM—continues to influence a number of anthropologists. See also CENTER AND PERIPHERY, CULTURAL MATERIALISM, DIALECTICAL MATERIALISM, GRAMSCI, IDEOLOGY, POLITICAL ANTHROPOLOGY, REIFICATION.

Further reading: Engels (2001[1884]); Bloch (2004 [1983]); Lem & Leach (2002).

masculinity. The study of maleness in a social context has gained greater impetus in the later twentieth century with the emergence of feminism in academia and wider society (see FEMINIST ANTHROPOLOGY). Ethnographers have shown that beyond stereotypes of how "real men" behave (see for example MACHISMO) there is a considerable variety of PRACTICE in the construction of GENDER-based activities. In some cases, as Gilbert Herdt has shown, HOMOSEXUALITY may be socially expected. Masculinity has often been linked to acts of VIOLENCE and WAR.

Further reading: Gilmore (1990).

mater. The socially recognized mother of a child, as opposed to the biological mother (GENETRIX).

material culture. The ARTEFACTS—TOOLS, HOUSEHOLD items, CLOTHING, through to ART, religious objects, and ARCHITECTURE—considered as evidence of the CULTURE that produced them. A major shaper of early anthropological thought thanks to MUSEUM collections, material culture became associated with outmoded typologies during the early twentieth century. It has enjoyed a revival latterly thanks to greater interest in the symbolism of artefacts and the history of PRODUCTION. In addition, material culture has always been a major source of evidence to ARCHAEOLOGY. See also TECHNOLOGY.

Further reading: Edwards et al. (2006); Tilley et al. (2006).

materialism. An approach that emphasizes the objective physical world over that of the subjective MIND or spirit. In philosophy it dates back to the ancient Greeks (c. fifth century BCE); in SOCIOLOGY it is associated with MARX and ENGELS' views concerning historical or DIALECTICAL MATERIALISM (in which physical reality determines one's WORLDVIEW, not vice versa) and subsequent variations such as the anthropologist Marvin HARRIS' CULTURAL MATERIALISM.

matriarchy. A SOCIETY in which WOMEN rule. Formerly believed by some to be the earliest stage of cultural EVOLUTION, before PATRIARCHY (see MOTHER-RIGHT), and to be the origin of MATRILINEALITY (the tracing of rights through membership of the mother's side of a family). Although no evidence for an outright matriarchy has ever been found, some societies have accorded female groups and INDIVIDUALS considerable POWER.

matricide. Killing of one's own mother, or one who does this.

matrifocality. Matrifocal FAMILY life or relationships are those organized around the mother, sometimes with the father absent. The father may be absent temporarily (for WORK or other reasons) or permanently, by choice—as in a "single-mother family." Matrifocality is often found in the Caribbean and some MEDITERRANEAN cultures.

matrilaterality. In KINSHIP, matrilateral relations are *all* those on the mother's side, whether they are traced by male or female KIN. Contrast PATRILAT-ERALITY, which is the masculine equivalent.

Matrilaterality should not be confused with MATRILINEALITY, which is connected to DESCENT. Matrilateral kin only have rights and obligations where so recognized by *matrilineal* cultures.

matrilineal dilemma. A CONFLICT arising for a man who is subject to matrilineal convention and finds himself obliged to support his sister's children as well as his own.

matrilineality. In KINSHIP, matrilineal societies trace a person's DESCENT— and thus reckon their rights and obligations—solely through their mother's side of the family (their "matrilineage"; note that for descent purposes their own GENDER is irrelevant). This form of UNILINEAL descent contrasts with PATRILINEALITY. Note also the difference between matrilineality and MATRI-LATERALITY.

matrilocality. A synonym for UXORILOCALITY.

Mau Mau. A SECRET SOCIETY drawn from the Kikuyu and other ethnic groups and formed to violently oppose British rule in Kenya in the 1950s. Jomo Kenyatta, independent Kenya's first president, had served prison time for involvement with the Mau Mau following a controversial trial. See also TERRORISM.

Mauss, Marcel (1872–1950). French sociologist and anthropologist, born Épinal; the nephew of DURKHEIM. Mauss studied at Bordeaux, and from 1901 was professor of primitive religion at the École pratique des hautes etudes. He co-founded the Institute of Ethnology, Paris, lectured there from 1926, and was attached to the Collège de France from 1931 to 1939.

Although he wrote numerous influential essays, he did not publish a monograph in his lifetime. His outstanding work, *Essai sur le don* (1925; *The gift*, 1954) has been extremely influential in the understanding of EXCHANGE. Nevertheless, he is almost equally important for his efforts to promote the work of colleagues in the ANNÉE SOCIOLOGIQUE circle. See also BODY, GIFT, HOMME TOTAL, INDIVIDUAL, PRESTATION, RECIPROCITY, SACRIFICE, TIME.

Further reading: James & Allen (1998); Fournier (2006).

Maya. A people of southern Mexico and Central America who created a major early civilization from the second millennium BCE. Among other features, they were early exponents of advanced WRITING SYSTEMS and practiced SACRIFICE. The Maya were in decline by the time of the Spanish Conquest of the sixteenth century, but their modern counterparts are still studied.

Further reading: Wainwright (2008); Tedlock (2010).

Maybury-Lewis, David (1929–2007). See AMAZONIA.

maxim. A pithy statement expressing a general truth (e.g. "more haste, less speed"). In LINGUISTICS, associated with the work on conversation principles of Paul Grice (twentieth century). Compare PROVERB.

Mead, George H. (1863–1931). See ROLE, SELF, SYMBOLIC INTERACTIONISM.

Mead, Margaret (1901–78). American cultural anthropologist, author of popular works and associated with the NATURE AND NURTURE debate. Born in Philadelphia, Mead was educated at Columbia under BOAS, gaining a Ph.D. in 1929. With her contemporaries she developed the CULTURE AND PERSONALITY school. She was three times married to other anthropologists— Luther S. Cressman, Reo Fortune, and Gregory Bateson. Her best-known work, *Coming of age in Samoa* (1928), found American anxieties around adolescence lacking in her fieldwork site (see YOUTH). Her many other books include *Growing up in New Guinea* (1930), *Sex and temperament in three primitive societies* (1935; 1963 with new preface), *Balinese character* (with Bateson, 1942), and *Male and female* (1949). Notoriously, she was the subject of a series of attacks by Derek Freeman (e.g. *Margaret Mead and Samoa*, 1983). See also AMERICAN MUSEUM OF NATURAL HISTORY, SOCIALIZATION.

Further reading: Mead (1972); Shankman (2009).

means of production. A central concept in MARXIST thought: the machinery and materials required by processes of PRODUCTION. Ownership of these differentiates capitalists from workers. Compare MODE OF PRODUCTION.

Mecca (Saudi Arabia). See BURCKHARDT, PILGRIMAGE.

mechanical model. In LÉVI-STRAUSS' theory, a MODEL of social activity that is "on the same scale" as that which it describes. For example, a specific form of MARRIAGE that people generally conform to in a given group may be such that one can draw up a local model showing what people are likely to do. Social phenomena whose forms are more complex and variable in practice are comprehensible only on the *larger* scale, requiring a STATISTICAL MODEL—so, for instance, where marriage options are more open to personal preference, one must analyze statistics of what people actually do to plot more and less likely choices, without the aid of a simple model.

Further reading: Lévi-Strauss (1963: 283–9).

mechanical solidarity. According to DURKHEIM, the type of social cohesion found in "simpler," more traditional societies. Their members perform similar tasks and share similar values; in practical terms they are interchangeable. There is a strong COLLECTIVE CONSCIENCE. Contrast with ORGANIC SOLIDARITY, the opposite form.

Further reading: Durkheim (1933).

mechanistic analogy. The opposing view to the ORGANIC ANALOGY: SOCIETY is constructed by INDIVIDUALS, like a kind of machine, and is amenable, for instance, to social engineering. Similar ideas occur in fields outside SOCIOLOGY, for example economics.

media. The various means by which COMMUNICATION is achieved, usually on a large scale ("mass media"). ("Media" is technically the plural of "medium" but is often used as a singular.) In contemporary societies, older media such as public speaking and print publications (books, newspapers, pamphlets) have increasingly been supplemented by cinema, TV, radio, and "electronic media." Issues arising include questions of REPRESENTATION (of stories, ethnic groups, places, and so on), the relationship between the CULTURE of the audience and that of the producers (especially where these diverge in expectations and TABOOS), control and censorship, and so on.

Further reading: Armbrust (2000); Kottak (2009).

mediation. In general use, mediation simply describes the process of "being in the middle" of two parties—for instance, mediating in a labor dispute. A separate meaning refers to the process of passing reality through the MEDIA, with consequent questions as to how much the raw data presented have been modified by the process, intentionally or otherwise.

medical anthropology. A growing subdivision of anthropology that places health and healing in its diverse social contexts, studying local PRACTICE and accounts of DISEASE or ILLNESS.

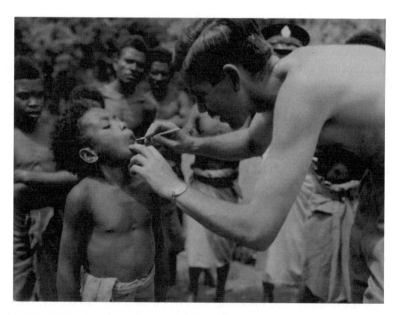

Figure 17   Medical anthropology. David Cameron, a dentist, examines a Papuan boy, 1947. Photo: J. Fitzpatrick; National Anthropological Archives, Smithsonian Institution, DOE Oceania: Massim: Trobriands, Australian Dept., 05032100.

Although an interest in "PRIMITIVE medicine" already existed (compare ETHNOMEDICINE), it was not until the later twentieth century that anthropologists began to think of western BIOMEDICINE as a MEDICAL SYSTEM similar to any other (one not intrinsically superior to INDIGENOUS healing). As such, it might be investigated anthropologically, or clinicians might be assisted to treat patients from different cultures ("clinically applied anthropology"). Arthur KLEINMAN pointed out the significance of "explanatory models"—the way patient and healer understand a condition. In contrast to some of their colleagues, advocates of CRITICAL MEDICAL ANTHROPOLOGY preferred to maintain a greater distance from clinicians. As with other aspects of cultural pluralism, MEDICAL PLURALISM also became an area for study.

Major specialisms within medical anthropology also include ETHNOPSYCHIATRY, which has its own substantial background. See also AIDS, ALLOPATHY, ANIMAL, BIRTH, BODY, CULTURE-BOUND SYNDROME, DRUGS, ETHNOBOTANY, RISK, SEX, TOBACCO.

Further reading: Kleinman (1980); Singer & Baer (2007); Good et al. (2010); Singer & Erickson (2011).

medical pluralism. The idea that different varieties of healing (western BIOMEDICINE and local PRACTICE, or non-biomedical approaches) are simultaneously available to certain groups.

medical system. The total social system by which a particular CULTURE deals with health. Ayurvedic medicine (see AYURVEDA) is an example of a system specific to a particular culture, with its own notions of ILLNESS and cure.

Other issues include patient/doctor relations (or their cultural equivalent) and the way medical care is organized. The "scientific" approach of BIOMEDICINE is, of course, one approach among many, some of them overlapping (compare MEDICAL PLURALISM).

medicine man. A healer or SHAMAN of certain tribal societies, such as North American Indians. The term is probably derived from its Ojibwa equivalent, *mashkikiiwinini*. Occasionally also "medicine woman." Compare WITCH DOCTOR.

Mediterranean. The large sea and surrounding lands of southern Europe, the western MIDDLE EAST, and north Africa. Associated with the study of HONOR; see also AMORAL FAMILISM, DAVIS, EVIL EYE, MATRIFOCALITY, PATRON–CLIENT RELATIONSHIP, PITT-RIVERS.

Melanesia. A group of islands in the southwest Pacific Ocean, including Papua New Guinea, Vanuatu, Fiji, and others, forming one part of OCEANIA. Of great historical importance to the development of anthropological thought, from the TORRES STRAITS EXPEDITION to MALINOWSKI's groundbreaking FIELDWORK in the TROBRIAND ISLANDS. Much subsequent interest has turned on themes in Malinowski's writings, for instance on EXCHANGE practices (see KULA). Others who have worked on Melanesia include Andrew Strathern and Marilyn STRATHERN. See also BIG MAN, MEN'S HOUSE.

Further reading: Malinowski (2002); Robbins & Wardlow (2005).

meme. A term from GENETICS coined by Richard Dawkins (*The selfish gene*, 1976) to describe a single cultural element that is transmitted by imitation in the same way that GENEs are transmitted by biological INHERITANCE. The unit involved may be an idea, a belief, a phrase, a fashion, a way of designing an ARTEFACT, or a skill, for example.

men. See MASCULINITY.

menarche. First MENSTRUATION.

Mendel, Gregor (1822–1884). See GENETICS.

men's house. A building in which men only may sleep and fraternize; found for example in MELANESIA and other parts of Asia, as well as South America.

menstruation. Periodic discharge of blood and mucous membrane from the uterus in WOMEN and some female PRIMATES, approximately monthly from MENARCHE to menopause except during pregnancy and lactation. The "meaning" of menstruation varies greatly from CULTURE to culture; menstrual blood is often held to be potent or dangerous, and numerous TABOOS attach to it, such as the prohibition on sexual activity during the period (see also PURITY). Sometimes menstruation is construed differently (as positive or negative) by WOMEN and men of the same CULTURE.

Further reading: Buckley & Gottlieb (1988); Knight (1991).

mentality. The intellectual disposition of a particular INDIVIDUAL or social group. See also PRIMITIVE MENTALITY (though the term does not automatically imply this perspective).

merging. See BIFURCATION, and compare SKEWING.

Merina. See ORATORY.

Merton, Robert K. (1910–2003). See MANIFEST AND LATENT.

Mescaline. See PEYOTE.

Mesoamerica. Another name for Central America, sometimes including Mexico. Often used in regional history and ARCHAEOLOGY.

Mesopotamia. See CUNEIFORM, WRITING SYSTEMS.

Mestizo. A person of mixed European and non-European DESCENT (originally: having a Spanish father and NATIVE AMERICAN mother) in South and Central American regions that were once Spanish colonies.

meta-. A PREFIX found in many scientific words and that can have several meanings. In the original Greek it meant "with," "after," or "between" but it can be used to denote a change (e.g. in the word METAPHOR) or a position behind or beyond ("metatarsal"). In many modern uses it means "about" or "higher-level" (as in METALINGUISTICS), dealing with the nature of the sub-ject itself. In biology it can mean a later, more developed form ("metazoan").

metaculture. Defined by Greg Urban as "culture that is about culture": forms such as film reviews or "news" items about TV shows. Metaculture helps disseminate CULTURE.

Further reading: Urban (2001).

metalinguistics. The branch of LINGUISTICS dealing with the relation of LANGUAGE to CULTURE generally.

metanarrative. A "story about a story": either concerned with storytelling itself or a wider NARRATIVE (or schema) held to explain experience. Associated with the philosopher Jean-François Lyotard, who regarded metanarratives (or "grand narratives") as inimical to POST-MODERNISM.

metaphor. In LINGUISTICS, using a word or phrase to refer to something to which it applies by analogy rather than literally. Anthropologists have exam-ined how the use of metaphors in particular CULTURES may provide insights into those cultures. Contrast METONYMY.

Further reading: Lakoff & Johnson (2003).

meter. In the linguistic sense, a measure used in two ways. In MUSIC, meter is shown by the number of beats in a bar and their values, as indicated by the "time signature" written at the start—for example, a waltz in 3/4 meter. In POETRY, meter covers all the formal features that distinguish a poem from speech or prose: particular patterns of stress (for instance, the trochee meter) analogous to musical beats, but also rhyming, for instance. Linguistic anthropologists often take note of the use of meter in both contexts.

methodological individualism. The sociological belief that phenomena must be explained by reference to INDIVIDUALS rather than social groups; as against the alternative view proposed by DURKHEIM and his followers.

Further reading: Lukes (1977); Just (2004).

metonymy. In LINGUISTICS, the ACT of referring to something by the name of a thing associated with it—so, "the turf" would be a metonym for horse racing. Contrast METAPHOR.

Mexico. See BORDER, CULTURE OF POVERTY, LATIN AMERICA, MALINOWSKI, MAYA, MESOAMERICA, NEW SPAIN, TYLOR, WHITE.

Micronesia. An island group in the western Pacific, north of MELANESIA; it includes the Caroline Islands (except—politically—Palau), Kiribati (formerly the Gilbert Islands), and others. See also OCEANIA.

Middle East. An imprecise label for the countries around the Eastern MEDITERRANEAN region, many predominantly Arab-speaking and MUSLIM. The term gained currency in the US and Britain in the late nineteenth century and originally referred to India and its neighbors; latterly it became a kind of shorthand for Western Asia and parts of North Africa, conflating ethnically diverse countries such as Israel and Iran. It was sometimes distinguished from the Near East, which included the Balkan countries and Turkey.

The term "Middle East" may be particularly problematic because it reflects a view of the world that puts Western Europe in the centre; it also homogenizes a region of enormous cultural variety (critics of ORIENTALISM such as Said pointedly avoid using it). It should therefore be handled with caution.

Further reading: Eickelman (2002).

middleman minorities. Ethnic groups drawn to a country in anticipation of favorable conditions and who come to occupy an intermediate place in the host CULTURE. They may encounter DISCRIMINATION and persecution (e.g. Chinese people in early-twentieth-century America, Jews in Nazi Europe, South Asians in Uganda during the 1970s). There is debate over whether such groups can ever achieve successful ASSIMILATION or whether they always relocate again. Compare MINORITY.

migration. The movement of people from one place to another, usually with the intention of settling. This move may be voluntary, for example to advance economic prospects, or it may be classed as FORCED MIGRATION (displacement through WAR, DISASTER, FAMINE, etc—see also REFUGEE). Migration may be temporary—as in seasonal movements by NOMADS—or permanent (termed EMIGRATION). At least two more divisions are clear: those between RURAL dwellers moving *internally* to cities, and movement crossing international borders. Such *transnational* movements have been seen to cause friction in the MEDIA and host populations of "developed" countries, where a perception may arise that purely economic motives are involved (compare ASYLUM SEEKER). See also DIASPORA, GLOBALIZATION.

Further reading: Vertovec & Cohen (1999); Koser (2007).

Mill, John Stuart (1806–73). See UTILITARIANISM.

millenarianism. Belief in a future golden age; associated with oppressed groups responding to social change, and with movements such as the CARGO CULT. The term is used by extension from such beliefs among Christian sects (ultimately based on the Bible, Revelation 20), although non-Christian groups have behaved in ways consistent with analogous beliefs—for example, the Xhosa of South Africa during the cattle-killing crisis of 1856–7, and the Plains Indians with the GHOST DANCE.

Further reading: Cohn (1970).

mimesis. From Greek, "imitation": the imitation of action or speech, originally as discussed by Plato and Aristotle. Much debated in critical THEORY (given its centrality to many styles of works of ART) and latterly by anthropologists concerned with the nature of REPRESENTATION.

mind. The notional seat of mental processes (see MENTALITY, PRIMITIVE MENTALITY), encompassing thoughts, feelings, will-power, and unconscious phenomena. The exact nature of the mind and its relation to the BODY (or its differences from the BRAIN) have been debated in many fields (see e.g. DUALISM). The mind is a central concern of COGNITIVE ANTHROPOLOGY.

Further reading: Reyna (2002); Erneling & Johnson (2005).

mining. The industry of extracting minerals (coal, copper and tin ore, silver, gold, and diamonds) from beneath the land (or sea). As many natural resources become depleted, the plight of mining communities has attracted attention in several regions (e.g. the north of England and Wales, once heavily linked to coal mining); environmental, health, and political concerns have also centered on mining operations in South America, Africa, and elsewhere. See also COPPERBELT.

Further reading: Nash (1993).

minority. The smaller part of any group, for example subsets within a larger CULTURE having different ethnic origins or sexual preferences; mostly used in SOCIAL SCIENCES in the context of HUMAN RIGHTS and political POWER as minorities often suffer DISCRIMINATION. Agencies such as the UK-based Minority Rights Group research and publish findings on the world's numerous minority cultures. See also MIDDLEMAN MINORITIES.

misogyny. Hatred of WOMEN, a manifestation of (for example) SEXISM.

missionary. One sent by a religious order (usually to foreign countries) to spread their teaching and do good works. Associated particularly with CHRISTIANITY (and missions to Africa). Many early ethnographers were associated with missionary WORK, for example Father Wilhelm Schmidt, though anthropologists did not always agree with the work of missions. Later social scientists have investigated the issues raised by the missionary process (such as cultural RESISTANCE to it). See also CATHOLICISM, CONVERSION.

Further reading: Comaroff & Comaroff (1991–7); *Missionaries, anthropologists, and human rights* (1996).

Mitchell, J. Clyde (1918–95). See MANCHESTER SCHOOL.

mo. See M.

mode of production. The way in which a particular CULTURE arranges the supply of goods, services, and so on. In MARXIST theory, a mode of production can be analyzed as the interplay of FORCES OF PRODUCTION (the materials, equipment, TOOLS, and techniques required) and RELATIONS OF PRODUCTION (the more intangible relationships between people and these things, and people to each other, for example as employers and employees). Key examples of different modes of PRODUCTION include FEUDALISM, CAPITALISM, the slave mode (see SLAVERY), and the ASIATIC MODE OF PRODUCTION. A number of French anthropologists, in particular, such as Maurice Godelier and Emmanuel Terray, have drawn on MARX's theory; compare also Marshall SAHLINS' use of the term DOMESTIC MODE OF PRODUCTION. See also MEANS OF PRODUCTION, STRUCTURAL MARXISM.

model. In the SOCIAL SCIENCES, a simplified or idealized way of describing a situation or process; a REPRESENTATION that aids understanding and hypothetical thought. All anthropologists try to create models of reality, and have spent much time in debating the issues around them (notably in KINSHIP studies). See also IDEAL TYPE.

modern. Forward-thinking, not bound to the past. In anthropological terms, "modern" may be contentious where it implies an opposition with TRADITION: in the stereotyped view, a TRADITIONAL SOCIETY is homogenous and conservative in its WORLDVIEW, while modern (industrialized, usually western) society is diverse, innovative. While this works as shorthand, it has overtones of EVOLUTIONISM that may mislead the student. Anthropologists in recent years have often been skeptical in their ethnographies of organizations associated with "modernity." Compare PRIMITIVE. See also POST-MODERNISM.

Further reading: Latour (1993).

modernization theory. A belief in mid-twentieth-century SOCIOLOGY that THIRD WORLD societies would develop along the same lines as did Europe and North America following the Industrial Revolution, with concomitant changes in their CULTURES—broadly, away from "traditional" (see TRADITION) social organization and toward complex, democratic, and urban institutions (see INDUSTRIAL SOCIETY). It was criticized from the left for failing to allow for inequities in DEVELOPMENT and not reflecting the reality of social change. See also the opposed view of DEPENDENCY THEORY.

moiety. One of two social divisions of a SOCIETY (each equaling half of its CLANS) for purposes of RITUAL and/or MARRIAGE exchange. Studied anthropologically in the Americas and Australia. Moieties are usually patrilineal or matrilineal.

monarchy. See KINGSHIP.

money. Objects commonly accepted as representing value symbolically, for purposes of TRADE or EXCHANGE. As well as coins and paper money, or their electronic surrogates, money can take the form in particular places of precious metals, shells (see COWRIE), beads, and so on. It can index an individual or corporate body's worth and be used as capital (see CAPITALISM). It avoids the need to BARTER though bartering may co-exist alongside a money economy.

Anthropologists are aware that money (and its socially endorsed value) can be a slippery concept, and that social conventions and TABOOS moderate its use. For instance, usury—making interest from money-lending—is forbidden in Islamic law and was historically barred to early Christians.

Further reading: Simmel (2004); Parry & Bloch (1989).

monism. A system of thought or philosophical view recognizing *one* force or principle, as opposed to DUALISM, PLURALISM.

mono-. PREFIX denoting something "single, alone."

monoculture. In AGRICULTURE, the raising of a single crop. Also sometimes used to denote a region characterized by the dominance of one ethnic, social, or religious group, or by one cultural phenomenon.

monogamy. MARRIAGE (or fidelity) to a single spouse, as opposed to (for example) POLYGAMY. The most common form of marriage in most places; other forms may be illegal or unacceptable.

monogenism. The belief that humans evolved from one set of ANCESTORS ("monogenesis") rather than several. A mainstream assumption in the mid nineteenth century. A similar meaning applies for monogenesis in biology. Contrast POLYGENISM, which posits several sets of ancestors.

monolingualism. Ability to communicate in only one LANGUAGE (compare BILINGUALISM, MULTILINGUALISM).

monotheism. Belief in a single god. Contrast POLYTHEISM, belief in many gods. A common view among early anthropologists was that monotheism developed from polytheism, but this was later disproved. Even monotheistic belief systems sometimes encompass notions of lesser or opposed divine beings (e.g. angels, SAINTS, demons).

Montaigne, Michel de (1533–92). French humanist writer; inventor of the essay form. He was mayor of Bordeaux from 1581 to 1585. Some of his writings anticipate anthropological themes.

Montesquieu (Charles-Louis de Secondat, baron de Montesquieu, 1689–1755). French satirist and legal philosopher, a major figure in the ENLIGHTENMENT.

Born near Bordeaux, he was educated in Bordeaux and Paris. Montesquieu was president of the local Parlement from 1716 to 1721. His major work, *l'Ésprit des lois* (*The spirit of the laws*), sets comparative analysis of legal systems within a cultural and environmental context, thus anticipating the concerns of anthropology. See also VOLKSGEIST.

moral economy. An economic way of life in which ideals of social justice prevail over a drive for personal gain. First mentioned in the nineteenth century, and discussed by historians such as E. P. Thompson and political scientists such as James C. Scott.

Further reading: Scott (1976).

morality. See ETHICS.

morbidity. The state of being diseased, associated with DISEASE. Of particular interest in historical and MEDICAL ANTHROPOLOGY.

More, Sir Thomas (saint, 1478–1535). See UTOPIANISM.

mores. The NORMS of a particular SOCIETY; the CUSTOMS that reveal its moral standards. Named by W. G. Sumner around 1900; distinct from less consequential FOLKWAYS.

Morgan, Lewis Henry (1818–81). American ethnographer and pioneer of KINSHIP studies. Born in Aurora, New York, he was educated at Union College, Schenectady. Morgan initially worked for rail and MINING interests while collecting data on the Iroquois. He published *League of the Ho-dé-no-sau-nee, or Iroquois* in 1851.

Systems of consanguinity and affinity of the human family (1870; new ed. 1997) was a landmark work that began to develop a sophisticated, comparative approach to RELATIONSHIP TERMINOLOGY, even though some of Morgan's views were later discredited. *Ancient society* (1877) developed the materialist approach to social EVOLUTION, which caught the attention of MARX and ENGELS (who wrote *The origin of the family, private property, and the state* in response). It also made famous the nineteenth-century model of cultural progression as running from SAVAGERY through BARBARISM to CIVILIZATION.

Further reading: Trautmann (2008).

Morin, Edgar (1921–). See ROUCH.

morpheme. In linguistics, a basic morphological (see MORPHOLOGY) unit that will not subdivide any further (loosely corresponding to syllables of a word, for instance).

morphology. The study of forms. In biology, the shape and structure of organisms, originally for CLASSIFICATION. In LINGUISTICS, of the internal structure of words (via MORPHEMES, their constituent units).

Morphy, Howard (1947–). See ABORIGINAL, AUSTRALIAN ANTHROPOLOGY, YOLNGU.

mortuary rites. See FUNERAL RITES.

Mosca, Gaetano (1858–1941). See ELITE.

mother-right. The THEORY that MATRIARCHY was an early stage of cultural EVOLUTION, conferring POWER through a mother's LINE. First espoused by J. J. Bachofen in *Das Mutterrecht* (1861).

mourning. Expressions of grief at DEATH are subject to cultural expectations, just as are FUNERAL RITES. Many western readers will be familiar with traditions involving black CLOTHING, veils, or armbands; equally familiar to students of the MIDDLE EAST are organized displays of lamentation. Mourning may also involve deliberate POLLUTION by the mourner, or other markers.

m.s. Male speaking, or man speaking (in KINSHIP accounts).

Muhammad. Founder and prophet of Islam. See CALIPH, ISLAM, SHARI'A, SHIA, SUNNI.

Müller, Max (1823–1900). See LANG.

multilineality. Infrequently in KINSHIP, recognition of relationship or rights in a system in which membership of a mother's *or* father's line may be equally valid for some purposes, as opposed to strictly UNILINEAL recognition. See also DOUBLE DESCENT.

multilinear evolutionism. See EVOLUTIONISM.

multilingualism. Ability to communicate in more than two LANGUAGES. Of interest in the study of LANGUAGE ACQUISITION.

multiplex. Having many forms, parts, or facets. The term is used is several ways in medicine and communications, and more metaphorically of social phenomena.

multi-sited ethnography. A term coined by George Marcus in the 1990s. Instead of ethnography centered on one static fieldwork locale, Marcus advocates research into cultures that are "in circulation," in different places, so acknowledging the interconnectedness of real lives.

Further reading: Marcus (1998); Faubion & Marcus (2009).

murder. Unlawful HOMICIDE, the definition of which varies according to CULTURE and period. In the US and Britain, intention and context play a part in determining guilt.

Murdock, George P. (1897–1985). American cultural anthropologist; a pioneer of CROSS-CULTURAL surveys and writer on RELATIONSHIP TERMI-NOLOGY. Born in Meriden, Connecticut, he was educated at Yale and taught there (1928–60) and at Pittsburgh (1960–71). He was associated especially with the HUMAN RELATIONS AREA FILES and also founded the journal *Ethnology*. His books include *Social structure* (1949) and numerous editions of the co-written *Outline of cultural materials* (several eds. from 1938).

Murngin. An earlier name for the YOLNGU.

museum. Generally thought of as an institution dedicated to conserving and displaying ART, technical and cultural ARTEFACTS, the museum has evolved from a classical-era place of study to wealthy individuals' collections of travelers' curios (frequently brought back to Europe from sea voyages) to a variety of scholarly and popular collections with differing purposes. Many countries have long-established public museums, sometimes with a specific ethnographic background (hence "museum anthropology"). Examples such as the SMITHSONIAN INSTITUTION group in the US and the British Museum and the Pitt Rivers in England (see PITT-RIVERS) spring readily to mind.

Such organizations have come under intense scrutiny over the last few decades, as the nature of the relationship of the collector to the collected has been destabilized. Where once colonial administrators (see COLONIALISM) and merchants might appropriate artefacts without consideration of their INDIGENOUS context, a greater sensitivity to ETHNOCENTRISM now prevails and legal attention is paid to those peoples (e.g. NATIVE AMERICANS, Australian ABORIGINALS) who wish to recover objects or human remains associated with their traditions. The long-running argument between Greece and the UK over the "Elgin marbles" is just one example of such issues.

Further reading: Edwards et al. (2006); Karp et al. (2006); Macdonald (2006).

Muslim. A follower of ISLAM, or a concept associated with it.

music. Commonly understood as a meaningful grouping of sound, especially vocal and/or instrumental, producing its effects through control of pitch, timbre, and so forth. This definition may be extended to include ANIMAL SONG and mechanically generated noises. Music has many uses culturally, not only for entertainment but as part of RITUAL, in rites of passage (see RITE OF PASSAGE), and so on. It is often performed with DANCE. Its study is the province of ETHNOMUSICOLOGY. It is important, as with all ART, to remember that the western concept of music as a discrete phenomenon with a particular meaning may well not apply in every CULTURE, and that apparently equivalent terms may have different connotations. See also GRIOT, IMPROVISATION, METER, SONG, SUFISM, TRANCE.

Further reading: Blacking (1973).

Mutterrecht. See MOTHER-RIGHT.

myth. A story that has usually developed orally over a long time, and that is used by a SOCIETY to explain certain phenomena or aspects of its IDENTITY. It may describe SUPERNATURAL events. Myth has some similarities to legends (stories regarded as historical though not amenable to proof). Studied anthropologically by LÉVI-STRAUSS, among others. Compare FOLKLORE and see MYTHICAL CHARTER.

Further reading: Lévi-Strauss (1987).

mythical charter. A notion in MALINOWSKI's writings that MYTHS encode cultural information and support social NORMS.

Further reading: Malinowski (1948: 101).

mytheme. In the same way as LANGUAGE is sometimes discussed in terms of the particular use of MORPHEMES and PHONEMES, LÉVI-STRAUSS proposes that MYTHS can be broken down into similar component parts, albeit more complex than those of language (see STRUCTURALISM). These he terms mythemes, by analogy. See also DISTINCTIVE FEATURE.

Further reading: Lévi-Strauss (1963: chapter 11).

N

name. The names by which people, things, and places are known are revealing of their cultural contexts. Some widely observed features include PRACTICES concerned with naming infants or new members of a group (e.g. giving newborns a temporary name) and the POWER accorded to a name in some societies, leading to care about its use. People often voluntarily adopt new names, for a variety of reasons. See also TEKNONYMY (identification using offspring's name).

nanotechnology. Extremely-small-scale TECHNOLOGY, dealing with the manipulation of atoms and molecules. The term was first used by Norio Taniguchi in 1974 (from Latin and Greek, "dwarf-craft").

narcotic. A drug the effect of which is to depress BRAIN activity and thus relieve pain or promote drowsiness (from Greek, "benumb"). Although it mainly covers opiates such as morphine, codeine, and heroin, the label can be applied more generally to DRUGS with similar effects (see NICOTINE). While narcotics are sometimes used for medicinal purposes, they are frequently linked with recreational drug abuse and addiction problems.

Further reading: Dikötter et al. (2004).

narrative. Recounting events in a way that connects them meaningfully; in a literary TEXT, the "story" element. As well as in speech and writing, narrative can be conveyed in numerous other ways, for instance DANCE and SONG, and narrative elements appear in activities such as RITUAL.

Although narrative shares common elements in many CULTURES, it can adopt a great number of different forms and viewpoints, and elicit different responses from its audience. As anthropology has lost certainty in its own

Concise Dictionary of Social and Cultural Anthropology, First Edition. Mike Morris.
© 2012 Michael Ashley Morris. Published 2012 by Blackwell Publishing Ltd.

objectivity (see REFLEXIVITY) there has been a greater tendency to recount INFORMANTS' original narratives in a less mediated way, allowing readers closer access to ethnographic source material. See also ARCHETYPE, CODE, METANARRATIVE.

Further reading: Atkinson & Delamont (2006).

natal group. The group into which one is born; sometimes used in discussions of ANIMAL families.

national character. A concept developed by the CULTURE AND PERSONALITY school, within which attempts were made to identify the personality types most likely to be found in particular national societies. Prominent in the mid twentieth century, and associated with such works as Ruth BENEDICT's monograph on Japan. Although it has been criticized as simplistic, the notion of national character has influenced later areas such as social psychology.

Further reading: Benedict (1946).

nationalism. Support for the interests of one's own nation, particularly against others; often associated with the struggle for political POWER or self-determination. Famously studied by GELLNER, who suggested that its core demand was the congruence of political and national unit—that is, those

Figure 18   **Nationalism.** Republican (Catholic) murals on the Falls Road, Belfast, Northern Ireland, 2007. Photo: Mike Morris.

born outside the nation should not control it. Tension arises when different self-identified national groups (defined by, for example, ETHNICITY) are bound together within a common STATE. Anthropologists have frequently argued that both state and nation are competing *constructions* rather than real entities, and that they reflect an outmoded view that people can be separated into batches for study or administration. See also FOLKLORE.

Further reading: Anderson (2006); Gellner (2006).

Native American. The current preferred term among most speakers for INDIGENOUS people of the Americas. Compare AMERICAN INDIAN, INDIAN.

nativism. In philosophy, nativism refers to the belief that some ideas are innate rather than absorbed from outside; the term can also refer historically to anti-immigration movements such as the Native American Party of the US (1850s).

The term's primary meaning in anthropology is the phenomenon described by Ralph Linton of INDIGENOUS groups reasserting their own TRADITIONS in response to contact with other CULTURES—a phenomenon also known as REVITALIZATION, under which name it has been examined by Anthony F. C. Wallace. Compare MILLENARIANISM.

Further reading: Linton (1943).

natural disaster. See DISASTER.

Figure 19   Native American. Wa-kma-he-za, a Lakota Oglala, 1910. Photo: D. L. W. Gill, National Anthropological Archives, Smithsonian Institution, BAE GN 3302A.

natural sciences. See HUMAN SCIENCE(S).

nature and culture. An opposition common in twentieth-century anthropology between humankind's biological, ANIMAL qualities and its learned, socially programmed behavior. Associated with the work of BOAS in CULTURAL ANTHROPOLOGY and later LÈVI-STRAUSS, in particular.

nature and nurture. A shorthand phrase for a debate in philosophy, psychology, and biology as to the relative influence of biological INHERITANCE as against environmental and social influences in the formation of offspring. The idea gathered momentum in the nineteenth century. See also MEAD [M.], TABULA RASA.

Naturvölker. The term for "natural" (NON-WESTERN) peoples in early GERMAN ANTHROPOLOGY, from J. G. Herder (eighteenth century).

Nazi regime (Germany). See EUGENICS, GENOCIDE, GEOGRAPHICAL DETERMINISM, GERMAN ANTHROPOLOGY, GOBINEAU, JUDAISM, MIDDLEMAN MINORITIES.

Ndembu. See DIVINATION, ROLE, TURNER.

Near East. See MIDDLE EAST.

necrophagy. The eating of dead bodies. See also CANNIBALISM.

Needham, Rodney (R. P. N. Green: legally changed in 1947; 1923–2006). British social anthropologist, born in Kent and educated in London and Oxford. A leading critic of LÉVI-STRAUSS, he generated interest in French and Dutch STRUCTURALISM and produced significant work on classification (see e.g. POLYTHETIC CLASSIFICATION). Needham did fieldwork in Sarawak. He was professor of social anthropology at Oxford from 1976 to 1990 (in absentia from 1978). His numerous works include *Structure and sentiment* (1962), *Rethinking kinship and marriage* (ed., 1971), and *Belief, language, and experience* (1972).

Negrito. One of a number of PYGMY peoples of Eastern Asia and Africa, among them the Andamanese and the Semang of Malaysia. From Spanish, "little black person."

negritude. A movement associated with African and Caribbean intellectuals in Paris in the 1930s. Coined by Aimé Césaire, a leading exponent along with Léopold Senghor. Negritude emphasized consciousness of black CULTURE and BLACK themes in writing. It was also supported by some European thinkers in the post-war years.

Negro. An ethnic CLASSIFICATION for people of non-"white" parentage, from Spanish and Portuguese ("black person"). The standard term from the sixteenth to the early twentieth century, sometimes among BLACK writers themselves; gradually displaced by COLORED and then (from the 1960s) the sometimes politically charged "black."

neo-. PREFIX usually meaning "new" (from Greek); it often designates revived or adapted forms of an idea.

neoclassical economics. The dominant MODEL of western economic thought for much of the modern age: broadly, the idea that a free MARKET operating on laws of supply and demand offers the rational consumer a choice of goods from competing businesses who also provide employment to INDIVIDUALS. Most STATES accept that the market cannot operate completely without restraint. The model, developed in the nineteenth century from the work of earlier theorists such as Adam Smith, is obviously flawed (e.g. in its assumption of fair competition), and has been criticized especially from the left.

neocolonialism. The perpetuation of the kind of POWER relations experienced under COLONIALISM, after a colonized SOCIETY's independence: the former colonial power continues to influence the "free" STATE. Many writers would cite American foreign policy in the twentieth century; western corporations may be seen to dominate global TRADE in a similar fashion.

neo-Darwinism. See EVOLUTIONISM.

neoevolutionism. See EVOLUTIONISM.

neoliberalism. A political and economic doctrine that espouses free market CAPITALISM and downplays STATE intervention and the ROLE of the public sector, trusting instead in the ability of entrepreneurs, suppliers, and consumers to safeguard their own interests in deregulated environments. While associated with right-wing figures such as Margaret Thatcher in Britain ("there is no such thing as SOCIETY," 1987 interview), Ronald Reagan in America, and the CHICAGO SCHOOL theorist Milton Friedman, it can also be used to describe more general policies intended to create INDIVIDUAL autonomy. In practice, classically neoliberal methods have often been applied (e.g. in post-communist Russia) with mixed results, leading to a perception in some quarters that it is a failed IDEOLOGY.

Further reading: Harvey (2005).

neolocal. Of POST-MARITAL RESIDENCE, describing a HOUSEHOLD that a new couple establish in a location *separate* from the husband's and wife's relatives. Contrast AMBILOCALITY, UXORILOCALITY, VIRILOCALITY.

network analysis. The study of SOCIAL NETWORKS—not just mapping a single person's ties to others ("egocentric" networks) but also the interconnections between organizations, MARKETS, and so on. While social networks are much studied in SOCIOLOGY, which has elaborated at length on the types of connection possible, and their functions, they are less intensively covered by anthropologists. (There are other technical meanings of this phrase in, for example, mathematics and computing.)

neuroanthropology. The study of neuroscience (investigating the nervous system) from an anthropological standpoint (see also BRAIN). Areas of specialization include comparative studies of human and ANIMAL brain EVOLUTION and CROSS-CULTURAL studies of humans.

new archaeology. See PROCESSUAL.

new ethnography. See ETHNOSCIENCE.

new reproductive technologies. See REPRODUCTIVE TECHNOLOGIES.

New Spain. A viceroyalty established by Spain in the early sixteenth century (*Nueva España*) including what are now parts of the southern United States, Mexico, and Central America. Independence was achieved in the early nineteenth century.

NGO. Abbreviation for non-governmental (see GOVERNMENT) organization: that is, one that operates in several countries for purposes other than commerce, for example charity. Examples include units of the United Nations and Oxfam.

nicotine. The active ingredient in TOBACCO, derived from a plant (*Nicotiana*). See also DRUGS, NARCOTIC.

nirvana. Ultimate freedom from SUFFERING, in several South Asian religions (BUDDHISM, HINDUISM, Jainism). The adherent seeks to overcome the limits of physical desires and release themselves from the cycle of mortal existence. From Sanskrit, "extinction." See also REINCARNATION.

noble savage. A romantic ideal developed by ROUSSEAU in *Discours sur l'origine & les fondements de l'inequalité parmi les hommes* (1775) that regards "PRIMITIVE" man as enjoying a carefree, "natural" existence that is morally superior to that lived within "civilized" constraints, and that is free from INEQUALITY. See also PRIMITIVISM, SAVAGERY.

nomad. A member of an itinerant people who regularly move around to obtain pasture, FOOD, and WORK, or for political expedience: for example, herders, HUNTER-GATHERERS, and pastoralists (see PASTORALISM). Nomads usually live in areas where conditions require such movement. Compare BAND, SEDENTARISM.

Further reading: Beck (1991).

non-literate. Not using a written LANGUAGE. See LITERACY.

non-verbal communication. The whole range of communication that does not use LANGUAGE or SYMBOLS: principally BODY language—GESTURES, facial expressions, and posture (see KINESICS). The use of body SPACE may be relevant (see PROXEMICS). Such signals may be conscious or unconscious, and reinforce or contradict any linguistic message delivered with them. See also HAPTICS, the study of touch.

non-violence. See PEACE.

non-western. An adjective that covers areas of the world considered as distinct culturally or economically (for example) from western SOCIETY. It supersedes earlier terms that now hold negative or judgmental overtones (such as PRIMITIVE, TRADITIONAL SOCIETY) but is itself becoming outdated as GLOBALIZATION and TRANSNATIONALISM erode old boundaries.

norm. The accepted standard of behavior within a group; a person following norms acts in accordance with the implicit guidelines for what is expected from the rest of their SOCIETY. See also DEVIANCE, MORES.

normative. Implying or prescribing a NORM.

Notes and queries on anthropology. A book series published by the ROYAL ANTHROPOLOGICAL INSTITUTE to encourage information-sharing: it began with the intention of helping field-workers collect data such as anthropometrical measurements. There were six editions between 1874 and 1951. Early contributors included TYLOR.

NRTs. See REPRODUCTIVE TECHNOLOGIES.

nuclear family. A basic heterosexual-parented family group of father, mother, and children; compare EXTENDED FAMILY. It may sometimes be found with extra members (e.g. widowed parent, SIBLING of one spouse). Once believed to be universal, though that is challenged by the wide variety of family forms now found even in western societies. May also be referred to as the "conjugal family" or the "elementary family."

Nuer. An African people (or their LANGUAGE) of southeast Sudan and Ethiopia, known to themselves as "Naath." The name "Nuer" is the DINKA form. Famously studied by EVANS-PRITCHARD. See also GHOST MARRIAGE, LEOPARD-SKIN CHIEF, WOMAN MARRIAGE.

Further reading: Evans-Pritchard (1940).

numbers. Mathematical SYMBOLS that aid counting and (in many cultures) abstract calculation. It has been argued that basic arithmetical concepts are UNIVERSALS, though how they are applied may vary greatly from culture to culture.

Further reading: Crump (1990).

Figure 20   Nutritional anthropology. Onions and rice on a market stall, Eastern Tanzania. Photo copyright: N. Beckmann.

nutritional anthropology. A specialism developed from the later twentieth century onward, in which purely biological aspects of FOOD are set in the cultural contexts of its use, questions of DIET, social conventions, and expectations. See also OBESITY.

Further reading: Ulijaszek & Strickland (1993).

Nyakyusa. See WILSON [M. H.].

O

obesity. A condition of being seriously overweight, allowing for height, GENDER, and age; linked to excessive CONSUMPTION of FOOD and DRINK. Obesity is often seen as a disorder of affluent CULTURES, but is of growing concern in many places. It seems increasingly to afflict children and young people. Some people may be genetically predisposed to obesity or become obese through DISEASE; usually environmental or cultural factors are held to be more significant, and adjusted DIET and less sedentary lifestyles (see SEDENTARISM) are recommended for its alleviation.

A large number of researchers are currently working on obesity, including the Unit for Biocultural Variation and Obesity (http://www.oxfordobesity.org).

Further reading: Kulick & Meneley (2005); Brewis (2011).

Obeyesekere, Gananath (1930–). See INDIAN ANTHROPOLOGY, POLYNESIA.

objectification. The action of treating ideas as if they were concrete things; also the same process applied to people or groups ("the use of pornography objectifies women"). Compare REIFICATION.

objectivism. An approach that regards certain "truths" as existing independently of human apprehension. Objectivists (e.g. DURKHEIM and COMTE) incline to POSITIVISM and a "scientific" outlook. Compare SUBJECTIVISM.

occidentalism. An equivalent term to ORIENTALISM appropriated to describe over-simplified conceptions of how "westerners" behave or think. There has been debate over whether it can be used as a label for "Oriental" images of the west only, or whether it also describes western self-images.

Further reading: Carrier (1995).

Concise Dictionary of Social and Cultural Anthropology, First Edition. Mike Morris.
© 2012 Michael Ashley Morris. Published 2012 by Blackwell Publishing Ltd.

occupation. An occupation is a type of job, pursuit, or similar activity that absorbs a person's TIME; occupation in a more spatial sense may refer to where people live ("they have occupied the farm house for several centuries"), or, on a political level, to military invasion followed by the relevant army remaining in place to control the conquered SPACE (as in "the invasion of Iraq by coalition forces"). As with terms such as TERRORISM, the label itself is emotionally freighted—as in the "Occupied Territories" of Palestine.

Oceania. Collectively, the islands of the Pacific Ocean region, including MELANESIA, MICRONESIA, and POLYNESIA. Sometimes held to include AUSTRALASIA and the Malaysian archipelago.

Further reading: *Oceania* [journal]; Thomas (1997).

Ogoni. See OIL.

oil. A liquid (usually) substance characterized by viscosity and smoothness; often flammable, and insoluble in WATER. Socially significant in several forms—as a mineral, it can be a valuable fossil fuel (e.g. petroleum) and the focus of sometimes controversial industries (e.g. in the Ogoni regions of Nigeria). Countries with deposits of crude oil beneath their land or waters (for instance in the MIDDLE EAST) may have greater economic and political POWER as a result.

Separately, vegetable oil can be used with or as FOOD and to make products such as soap. For animal oils see WHALING.

oligarchy. GOVERNMENT by a small group of people, usually in their own interest. First defined by Aristotle.

Omaha terminology. A RELATIONSHIP TERMINOLOGY identified by MURDOCK that is like an inverse CROW TERMINOLOGY.

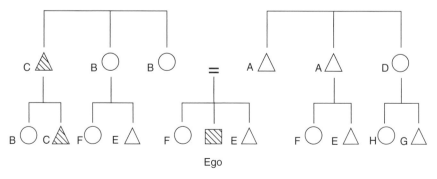

Figure 21   Omaha terminology.

EGO's parents' same-sex SIBLINGS and PARALLEL COUSINS are treated as in IROQUOIS TERMINOLOGY: so, for instance, father's brother and father share a term (FB=F), while GENERATIONS merge such that Ego's mother's brother and mother's brother's son share a term (MB=MBS). Associated with PATRILINEALITY; see also CROW-OMAHA.

Further reading: Murdock (1949); Barnes (2005).

ontogenesis or ontogeny. In biology, the development of a single living organism to maturity. From a Greek root (originally coined by Ernst Haeckel in the German form, 1866), "being-PRODUCTION." Contrast PHYLOGENESIS, development of a group.

ontology. A term from metaphysics: the science of the nature of being.

open system. See CLOSED SYSTEM/OPEN SYSTEM.

opiate. See NARCOTIC.

oracle. A person, place, or procedure through which the gods communicate. Historically associated with ancient Greece, for instance the oracle at Delphi. In contemporary societies the most famous study is that by EVANS-PRITCHARD on the ZANDE. Compare AUGURY, DIVINATION.

Further reading: Evans-Pritchard (1937).

oral literature. Stories that have been passed down by PERFORMANCE or recitation in cultures that do not depend on WRITING SYSTEMS. Several world classics (e.g. the works ascribed to Homer) are believed to have been composed orally. Oral literature has been notably studied by anthropologists such as Jack GOODY. See also TEXT.

Further reading: Goody (1968); Finnegan (1988).

orality. The quality of being concerned with the oral, which has several meanings; for example, sexual connotations in psychology, and to do with sound PRODUCTION in PHONETICS. In anthropology it is mostly understood as referring to speech, as opposed to writing, as the vehicle for knowledge transmission (hence the opposition of "LITERACY and orality"). Debate has turned on whether orality is inferior to literacy or whether it is a valid alternative, with particular uses.

oratory. Public speaking, within cultural conventions. In the west, famous orators date back to classical times (e.g. Cicero in Rome) and have influenced a TRADITION that persists into modern politics. Oratory is found in most places (assuming special importance in oral cultures), and uses a variety of tones and strategies, though certain features are common. Effective public speakers may often be skilled performers with a flair for the dramatic and strong verbal abilities (employing a restricted VOCABULARY, for instance). Oratory may reinforce the social order or challenge it.

Anthropologists who have studied oratory include Maurice BLOCH, among the Merina of Madagascar.

Further reading: Bloch (1975); Brenneis & Myers (1991).

organic analogy. A sociological viewpoint that sees SOCIETY as a kind of organism, separate from its INDIVIDUAL members. The various parts of society are interdependent. An idea associated with FUNCTIONALISM and writers such as COMTE, Herbert SPENCER, DURKHEIM (compare ORGANIC SOLIDARITY), and RADCLIFFE-BROWN. The organic analogy—sometimes called the biological analogy—fails to account for conflicting societal interests; its opposite is the MECHANISTIC ANALOGY.

organic solidarity. According to DURKHEIM, the type of cohesion found in "advanced," complex societies. INDIVIDUALS perform diverse, complementary tasks through the DIVISION OF LABOR, and may have varying interests and outlooks. COLLECTIVE CONSCIENCE is less powerful than appeals to INDIVIDUAL judgment. Compare the opposing notion of MECHANICAL SOLIDARITY.

Further reading: Durkheim (1933).

oriental despotism. An idea associated with Karl Wittfogel, refining previous notions of despotism (MARX associated the ASIATIC MODE OF PRODUCTION with it). Wittfogel identified a number of STATES in which central control over WATER led to citizens being tightly organized and commanded (he offered the alternative label "hydraulic SOCIETY"). The idea was contentious.

Further reading: Wittfogel (1957).

Orientalism. Defined by Edward Said as the style adopted by western writers to impose a dominating and distorted view of Eastern CULTURES. It is associated with colonial assumptions and simplistic oppositions—broadly constructing western travelers and colonists as dynamic and rational and the eastern other as exotic but lazy and morally suspect, and hence in need of firm control. See also OCCIDENTALISM.

Further reading: Said (1995).

original affluent society. In ECONOMIC ANTHROPOLOGY, a term coined by Marshall SAHLINS, after the economist J. K. Galbraith's title *The affluent society* (1958). Where Galbraith anatomized western consumerism, Sahlins attempted to reverse the stereotype of HUNTER-GATHERER societies as materially underachieving by claiming that they could easily supply all their own needs and did not desire unending increase. Therefore they were "affluent" despite what appeared to be a poor standard of living. Sahlins' view became popular, but was later undermined by, for instance, the argument that poorer health was not conducive to WELL-BEING. See also SCARCITY.

Further reading: Rowley-Conwy (2001); Sahlins (2004: chapter 1).

Oromo. African people of Southern Ethiopia and western Kenya, making up the dominant ethnic group in Ethiopia. The Oromo are mainly Muslims, with some Christians and, in the south, traditional religion being upheld. These people were formerly called Galla, a name now considered pejorative.

Further reading: Baxter et al. (1996).

ostalgia (German: *ostalgie*). Punning term for nostalgia regarding supposedly better times under COMMUNISM in East Germany (*Ostdeutschland*), prior to reunification with the west at the end of the twentieth century.

ostracism. Originally a means of temporary banishment for over-influential citizens of early Greek city-STATES (they were nominated on an *ostrakon*, a piece of pottery). More generally, the SANCTION of withdrawing communal support from an individual, whether informally (such as avoiding a friend who has offended one) or formally (expulsion from a group or organization, up to exile from a STATE). Similar behavior has been observed in PRIMATES.

other. A term with applications in several fields. In anthropology, literature, and philosophy, it refers to those outside a particular group, sometimes emphasizing the exclusion of the other's viewpoint. See also ALTER, ORIENTALISM.

Oxfam (charity). See NGO.

P

P or Pa. In RELATIONSHIP TERMINOLOGY, an abbreviation for "parent."

padrinazgo. The relationship of godfatherhood.

pain. See SUFFERING.

paleoanthropology or palaeoanthropology. The anthropological study of hominid fossils from which information about physical development and human origins may be deduced. The term was coined by Paul Topinard (in its French form) in 1885. See also HUMAN EVOLUTION.

paleontology or palaeontology. The general study of fossils left by all forms of ancient life, including PLANTS and ANIMALS (hominids are included, and are the particular concern of PALEOANTHROPOLOGY).

Palestinians. See JUDAISM, OCCUPATION.

pandemic. Similar to an EPIDEMIC but on a greater scale: a DISEASE outbreak that has spread very widely with high rates of infection. Examples include the Spanish influenza pandemic of 1918–19 and, more recently, HIV/AIDS. From Greek, "all the people."

paradigm. Originally from Greek, "example," and used in this sense generally. Developed by Thomas Kuhn (*The structure of scientific revolutions*, 1962) to describe a working theoretical MODEL that is based on past scientific achievements but that remains capable of revision. A major change in outlook arising from this method is thus a "paradigm shift." Kuhn later accepted criticisms of the concept as he defined it.

Concise Dictionary of Social and Cultural Anthropology, First Edition. Mike Morris.
© 2012 Michael Ashley Morris. Published 2012 by Blackwell Publishing Ltd.

Linguists also use "paradigm" in a separate sense, to do with the placing of words or sounds (see SYNTAGM). In GRAMMAR a paradigm is a table showing possible forms of (for example) a verb.

Further reading: Kuhn (2000).

paralinguistics. Elements of LINGUISTICS beyond the merely verbal: that is, TONE, pace of speaking, non-verbal noises, pauses, and so on. May be held to include GESTURES (see also KINESICS).

parallel cousin. A cousin (of either SEX) linked through parents of the same sex (e.g. father's brother's son, or FBS). Often classified in the same relationship terms as SIBLINGS. Compare CROSS-COUSIN.

parallel descent. In RELATIONSHIP TERMINOLOGY, a parallel DESCENT system is one in which males have rights and obligations through their membership of the father's side of the family and females have them through their mother's side. Contrast DOUBLE DESCENT. Parallel descent is rarely recorded, one disputed case being among the Apinayé of Brazil.

Further reading: Maybury-Lewis (1960).

Pareto, Vilfredo (1848–1923). Italian economist and engineer (born in Paris). He devised Pareto's law, which states that eighty percent of a country's income benefits twenty percent of its people.

Park, Robert E. (1864–1944). See CHICAGO SCHOOL, MARGINALITY, REDFIELD, URBANISM.

parole. See LANGUE AND PAROLE.

parricide. Killing of one's own parents, or one who does this. See also MATRICIDE, PATRICIDE.

Parsee. See ZOROASTRIANISM.

Parsons, Talcott (1902–79). American sociologist whose work drew on WEBER, DURKHEIM, and PARETO and whose theories combined FUNCTIONAL-ISM with insight into the importance of CULTURE. Born in Colorado, Parsons was educated at Amherst, the London School of Economics, and Heidelberg; he taught at Harvard from 1927 and was professor of sociology there from 1944 to 1973. His TRANSLATION of Weber's *Protestant spirit* was influential in increasing awareness of Weber; Parsons himself wrote *The structure of social action* (1937), *The social system* (1951), and *Social structure and personality* (1964). See also EVOLUTIONISM, PATTERN VARIABLES, SOCIETY, SYSTEMS THEORY.

Further reading: Parsons (1999).

participant observation. A central element of anthropological FIELDWORK (and other SOCIAL SCIENCES) in which the researcher lives with their subjects and adopts their lifestyle for several months or even years. Always supplemented by more formal research, such as INTERVIEWS. Much discussion concerns ethical problems raised by this process, and the impossibility of producing verifiable results from subjective experience (see QUALITATIVE/QUANTITATIVE).

participation. In a general sense, the active involvement of people in matters that usually concern them directly ("we hope for increased participation in this election"). In LINGUISTICS, the interaction between speaker and hearer— for example, the various (verbal and non-verbal) adjustments a speaker makes to retain a hearer's attention.

particle. In GRAMMAR, a FUNCTION WORD, PREFIX, SUFFIX, or a word used similarly in a phrasal verb ("he worked *up* a thirst").

pastoralism. A mode of economic life involving the tending of sheep, cattle, or other herd ANIMALS, usually in a mix of species (which will vary with locale—e.g. also camels, reindeer, etc). Pastoral societies are often associated with nomadic (see NOMAD) movement. Pastoralists do not operate independently of settled populations, and may be constrained by encroaching SEDENTARISM.

Further reading: Galaty & Johnson (1990).

pater. The socially recognized father of a child, as opposed to the biological father (GENITOR).

patriarchy. A SOCIETY in which men rule, especially fathers. Compare MATRIARCHY. Patriarchy is associated with, but is not a precondition of, PATRILINEALITY. Patriarchy is not a "pure" state; even within it certain WOMEN have some POWER. The term is also used in wider SOCIAL SCIENCE to criticize male social dominance.

patricide. Killing of one's own father, or one who does this.

patrifocal. Of a family, centered on the father (contrast MATRIFOCALITY). Rarely used.

patrilaterality. The male equivalent of MATRILATERALITY: concerned with all KINSHIP relations on the father's side. Rights are only recognized through PATRILINEALITY.

patrilineality. Recognition of relationship, rights, or obligations based on membership of the father's side of a family or DESCENT on the male side. Compare MATRILINEALITY, and note the "lineal/lateral" distinction in MATRILATERALITY.

patrilocality. A synonym for VIRILOCALITY.

patron–client relationship. A social and political convention in which a weaker party depends on a stronger one for protection or access (e.g. to the means of livelihood) and offers reciprocal favors or GIFTS. Typically this is an arrangement between INDIVIDUALS (such as PEASANTS and landlords) though it may operate on larger scales. It is often found in TRADITIONAL SOCIETY, for instance in the MEDITERRANEAN and in LATIN AMERICA. Anthropologists have debated how such relationships relate to wider politics, CLASS, HONOR, and POWER. Compare BROKER.

Further reading: Gellner & Waterbury (1977).

pattern variables. A set of five pairs of alternative strategies for dealing with social situations identified by PARSONS; one of the best-known is ACHIEVEMENT/ASCRIPTION.

Further reading: Parsons & Shils (1951).

peace. Peace is often regarded as the absence of WAR (or, "nonviolence"). It can be viewed more positively, its study incorporating not only the avoidance of direct VIOLENCE or unrest but also the reduction of indirect or STRUCTURAL VIOLENCE—the deployment of RACISM, SEXISM, and so on. Some theorists have challenged the view that war is "natural" and have argued that peaceful human relations (e.g. among small-scale, egalitarian societies) are actually "normal."

Further reading: Howell & Willis (1989); Fry (2007).

peasant. A member of a RURAL agricultural CLASS, usually though not always poor, geared to HOUSEHOLD SUBSISTENCE and self-sufficiency within a context of wider economic demands (e.g. for "rent" of various kinds). Peasants have been studied by REDFIELD, Chaianov (see CHAYANOV SLOPE), and a number of economists and political theorists. Peasant forms of RESISTANCE to POWER have been discussed in some ethnographic works. See also LIMITED GOOD, PETTY COMMODITY PRODUCTION.

Further reading: Scott (1985); Chaianov (1986); Redfield (1989).

Peirce, Charles S. (1839–1914). See SEMIOTICS, SIGN.

perception. The process by which one becomes aware of stimuli, through the SENSES, and interprets them. The exact nature of perception has been disputed by philosophers. The cultural dimensions of perception are among the concerns of COGNITIVE ANTHROPOLOGY. See also AESTHETICS.

Further reading: Merleau-Ponty (2002).

performance. In LINGUISTICS, a speaker/hearer's actual—potentially imperfect—use of a LANGUAGE, as opposed to their COMPETENCE (linguistic understanding). Introduced by CHOMSKY. Also note the more general meaning, as used in POETICS and DRAMA.

performative (noun and adjective). In LINGUISTICS and philosophy, an utterance by which the speaker performs an action—usually that in the verb itself (e.g. "I apologize"). See also ILLOCUTION. From J. L. Austin, though the idea originated earlier.

perinatal. In medicine, relating to the final months before the BIRTH of a child and the period immediately after.

perlocution. In LINGUISTICS and philosophy, speech or writing intended to bring about a response, for example persuasion. A perlocutionary ACT may be assumed to affect its audience. Compare ILLOCUTION.

Further reading: Austin (1975).

Perry, W. J. (1868–1949). See DIFFUSIONISM.

person. A way of categorizing the INDIVIDUAL that has special resonance for followers of MAUSS, whose essay "A category of the human mind" (1938) argues for the social construction of the "person" as a moral agent, irrespective of the SELF behind it. There are similar notions in the philosophy of Locke, for example. The idea does not hold equal importance for all cultures.

Further reading: Carrithers et al. (1985).

Petra (Jordan). See BURCKHARDT.

Petrarch (Francesco Petrarca, 1304–74). See HUMANISM.

petty commodity production. In MARXIST economic THEORY, PRODUCTION for the MARKET on a small scale, by those who own their MEANS OF PRODUCTION and do not require extra labor. Also called "simple commodity production." Associated with PEASANTS.

peyote. A cactus (*Lophophora willamsii*) containing mescaline, a HALLUCI-NOGEN. Used in RITUAL by indigenous groups of Mexico and the Southwest US, and discussed by anthropologists such as Peter Furst.

phatic communion. In LINGUISTICS, utterances that do not primarily convey or elicit information but simply establish or reaffirm social relations—for example, remarks about the weather, formulaic sayings, and pleasantries. So named by MALINOWSKI in 1923.

Further reading: Malinowski (1946: 315).

phenomenology. A concern with the nature of subjective experience rather than abstract THEORY or preconceptions. Associated with Edmund Husserl (early twentieth century) in philosophy, and later with Alfred Schutz and Peter L. Berger in SOCIOLOGY. Also associated with GESTALT THEORY in psychology. While it has been criticized by anthropologists, phenomenology has affinities with modern anthropological method (in which one aims to eradicate ETHNOCENTRISM) and in particular with ETHNOMETHODOLOGY.

Further reading: Jackson (1996); Merleau-Ponty (2002).

phenotype. In biology, the observable characteristics of an organism; that is, of the combination of genetic make-up (GENOTYPE) and environmental (see ENVIRONMENT) factors. From Greek, "apparent character."

philology. An earlier term for what is now called LINGUISTICS, dating back to the first attempts to study written LANGUAGEs technically and critically. "Comparative philology" developed in the same era as anthropology—the nineteenth century—and specialized in tracing affinities across languages.

philosophical anthropology. Given that philosophy is concerned with the human understanding of existence, it is closely tied in some ways to anthropology. A number of philosophers have been drawn to anthropological themes, including David Hume, Immanuel Kant, MARX, and FOUCAULT. The phrase "philosophical anthropology" also marks a particular strain of philosophy in Germany from the 1920s associated with Max Scheler and Helmuth Plessner, as well as Ernst Cassirer. Man is regarded as a combination of biological and social being with a unique capacity for self-definition. See also CRITICAL ANTHROPOLOGY.

Further reading: Wisnewski (2008).

phone. From Greek, "voice." In LINGUISTICS, the smallest sound unit of speech that may be distinguished (e.g. those represented by single letters in English).

phoneme. From Greek, "sound." In LINGUISTICS, the smallest sound unit of a given LANGUAGE that can *also* distinguish different meanings in a word; for example, the "b" and "p" in "bin" and "pin," respectively (compare PHONE).

phonemics. The study of the speech sounds, or PHONEMES, of a *particular* LANGUAGE. Contrast PHONETICS.

phonetics. The study of speech sounds *as such*, regardless of their use in particular languages (PHONEMICS). See also PHONE.

phonology. In LINGUISTICS, the study of how speech sounds are organized in a *system* by a particular LANGUAGE or in languages generally; or, such a system itself. Originally "phonology" was nearer in meaning to what is now PHONEMICS.

photography. Photographs have been extensively made, used, and collected by anthropologists from the earliest days of the medium. They have been found particularly helpful in recording movement, processes, and spatial relations. With the rise of REFLEXIVITY, attention has been paid to the attitudes and POWER relations implied in photographs, both those made by ethnographers and those intended for wider audiences (compare TOURISM).

Further reading: Comaroff et al. (2007); Morton & Edwards (2009).

phratry. In KINSHIP: originally an ancient Greek group of families claiming a common ANCESTOR. Used by anthropologists from the late nineteenth century to designate a similar group of CLANS, especially among NATIVE AMERICANS.

phylogenesis or **phylogeny**. In biology, the evolutionary development of a group of organisms or a species, as opposed to ONTOGENESIS (development of a single organism). Coined by Haeckel ("TRIBE-production").

phylum. In biology and related fields, a category for a large related group of organisms (thus the class "mammal" belongs within the phylum "Chordata," vertebrates). As with ONTOGENESIS, coined by Haeckel in the nineteenth century (from the Greek, "TRIBE"). "Phylum" can be used in LINGUISTICS to group together (conjectural) families of LANGUAGES.

physical anthropology. An alternative term, in older British works and currently in the US, for all or part of the field of BIOLOGICAL ANTHROPOLOGY.

physical geography. See GEOGRAPHY.

pictogram or **pictograph**. A SYMBOL or SIGN that may be one of three things: a representation of a word or phrase pictorially, as in ancient WRITING SYSTEMS; the same kind of symbol used on a map, in a guidebook, or similar; or a diagram using pictures. From Latin and Greek, "painted writing." See also HIEROGLYPH.

pidgin. A language with simplified GRAMMAR and VOCABULARY usually developed during TRADE between peoples with no common LANGUAGE, typically mixing English, French, or another (usually) European tongue with languages found in colonies in the Americas, Africa, and so on. The term "Pidgin English" originally represented a "Chinese" pronunciation of the phrase "business English." Pidgin languages are by definition non-natural; once adopted as first languages by new speakers they are reclassified as CREOLES.

pigmy. See PYGMY.

pilgrimage. A journey undertaken to a SACRED site. Different TRADITIONS stress different PLACES (e.g. Jerusalem, Mecca) but have enough in common to attract significant attention from anthropologists, including Victor TURNER (see also LIMINALITY). The requirements of pilgrimage vary and the study of it may now encompass similar acts of homage to secular places.

Further reading: Turner & Turner (1978); Coleman & Eade (2004).

pirogue. A dug-out canoe, originally made from a hollowed tree-trunk, in the Caribbean and South America. Sometimes spelled "piragua."

Pitt-Rivers, Augustus (Augustus Henry Lane-Fox, 1827–1900). British soldier, archaeologist, and MUEUM pioneer. Born in Hope Hall, Yorkshire, Lane-Fox was a lieutenant-general in the Crimean War of 1853–6 and succeeded to the Rivers estate, and name, in 1880; on his land in Dorset he did research in stratigraphy (study of the strata of soil) and opened a small related museum in Blandford. His personal collection of ethnological artefacts eventually grew large enough for public exhibition and he showed it in London from 1873 before moving it to the large museum bearing his name (but without the hyphen) in Oxford in 1884. His publications include *The evolution of culture and other essays* (1906).

   The general's many descendants include his grandson George Pitt-Rivers (1890–1966), a controversial figure whose writings include *The clash of culture and the contact of races* (1927) and George's son Julian Pitt-Rivers (1919–2001), a distinguished ethnographer of MEDITERRANEAN societies who held professorships at Chicago and the London School of Economics. His works include *The people of the Sierra* (2nd ed. 1971) and *The fate of Shechem: or, The politics of sex* (1977).

See also TECHNOLOGY.

Further reading: Bowden (1991).

Pitt Rivers Museum. See BALFOUR, MUSEUM.

place. Places and people's relation to them have been of great interest to geographers and sociologists (e.g. Louis Wirth, mid twentieth century) and latterly have become of greater concern to anthropologists. Areas of interest include the moral dimensions assigned by groups to key sites of spiritual importance (for instance Uluru or "Ayers Rock" to ABORIGINAL peoples, and Stonehenge in Britain), the emotional ties generated by historically significant places, and contested meanings of places. Anyone who has studied a map of Africa from the nineteenth century will also be aware that place NAMES are potentially contentious, and may indicate balances of POWER (as in "Rhodesia"). See also PROXEMICS, TERRITORIALITY.

Further reading: Low & Lawrence-Zúñiga (2003); Walkowitz & Knauer (2009).

plants. As with ANIMALS, plants and the way people use them feature heavily in some areas of anthropology. Plants are the special concern of ETHNOBOTANY and may be studied as medicinal (ETHNOPHARMACOLOGY) or agricultural entities (see MANIOC, RICE, SHIFTING CULTIVATION), as resources for recreation (in ALCOHOL; see also AYAHUASCA, DRUGS, HALLUCINOGEN, PEYOTE, TOBACCO), and as the objects of TAXONOMY (FOLK CLASSIFICATION, LINNAEAN TAXONOMY).

Plato (c. 428–347 BCE). See EIDOS, EUGENICS, MIMESIS, SOUL.

play. An activity often characterized by culturally developed conventions, at least among older players (see e.g. SPORT). Children may use improvised games to explore serious social contact in a "safe" way: by play-fighting, for example. These issues have been discussed by Gregory Bateson.

Play is also the subject of Huizinga's *HOMO LUDENS* and has been studied by GEERTZ (see DEEP PLAY). See also WITTGENSTEIN's discussion of games with FAMILY RESEMBLANCES.

Further reading: Caillois (1961); Bateson (2000).

plural marriage. A synonym for POLYGAMY.

plural society. The term coined by Furnivall in 1939 to describe colonial societies in Asia and SOUTHEAST ASIA in which diverse ethnic groups coexisted economically and politically but lived otherwise separate lives. The ruling group would be an ethnic MINORITY (e.g. the British in India). Later writers expanded the concept to cover post-colonial situations in Africa, the Caribbean, and elsewhere. Theorists such as M. G. Smith and Pierre L. van den Berghe adapted the notion, and an interest emerged not just in producing a static MODEL of a "plural society" (most current societies are inevitably multiethnic to some extent) but also in studying how interdependence plays out between groups, and questions of coercion and asymmetrical POWER. See also CULTURAL PLURALISM, PLURALISM.

Further reading: Furnivall (1948); Smith (1965).

pluralism. Essentially, a preference for many things, but pluralism has different connotations in different fields. Philosophical pluralism holds that there are more than two basic kinds of substance (as opposed to "monism" or "dualism"). Political pluralism advocates a variety of competing interests rather than a central AUTHORITY. In a similar way, CULTURAL PLURALISM accepts a diversity of ethnicities and social groups within wider SOCIETY. Studies of MEDICAL PLURALISM and LEGAL PLURALISM investigate competing systems for healing and justice. Anthropological studies of cultural pluralism have evolved from delineations of plural societies (see PLURAL SOCIETY) to examinations of the processes involved in them, and to something nearer APPLIED ANTHROPOLOGY in regard to INDIGENOUS peoples.

poetics. The study of forms and features of verbal and literary ART. While anthropologists can use poetics to analyze DRAMA, POETRY, MYTH, and FOLKLORE, they have particularly been interested recently in the interplay between spoken TEXTS and PERFORMANCE, a DIALOGICAL approach giving weight to context championed by such writers as Dennis Tedlock. Others working in this area include Ruth Finnegan and Steven C. Caton. This has also become known as ETHNOPOETICS. A separate branch of poetics deals with ETHNOGRAPHY itself reflexively, taking up the notion that the ethnographic TEXT, rather than being a repository of scientific truth, is itself a cultural product requiring analysis of its assumptions and stylistic tricks.

poetry. A literary composition (written or oral), usually regarded in the western TRADITION as being in heightened LANGUAGE and marked as separate by its form (use of rhyme, rhythm, and line spacing). The study of poetry in its various manifestations is known as POETICS.

Polanyi, Karl (1886–1964). Austrian-born economic historian who worked in Britain and at Columbia University (1947–58). His works include *The great transformation* (1944) and *Trade and market in the early empires* (ed. with Arensberg and Pearson, 1957). See CAPITALISM, DISEMBEDDED, ECONOMIC ANTHROPOLOGY, FORMALIST/SUBSTANTIVIST DEBATE, RECIPROCITY.

Further reading: Hann & Hart (2009).

political anthropology. Anthropological study of politics encompasses not just western but also more particularly NON-WESTERN forms of dealing with POWER and CONFLICT. Following some of the interests of MORGAN and MAINE (see LAW), a distinct political anthropology emerged with FORTES and EVANS-PRITCHARD's seminal *African political systems*. GLUCKMAN and the MANCHESTER SCHOOL extended this work and Edmund LEACH and others investigated AGENCY. As the era of COLONIALISM passed there was a focus on ELITE groups in new STATES; later anthropologists were sometimes influenced by MARXIST critiques of established GOVERNMENT as a means of perpetuating CLASS oppression.

Recently, anthropologists have discussed politics as it relates to WAR and VIOLENCE, including violence used by the state itself (and RESISTANCE to it); much of this work derives from the influence of extra-disciplinary figures, such as BOURDIEU, FOUCAULT, and SAID. Other key themes are GENDER, post-socialism, GLOBALIZATION, and NEOLIBERALISM. The study of TERRORISM has taken on a new edge post-2001.

See also APARTHEID, AUTHORITY, BIOPOLITICS, CAPITALISM, CHIEF, CIVIL SOCIETY, COMMUNISM, DEVELOPMENT, ECOLOGY, EGALITARIANISM, FEUDAL-ISM, HUNGER, IMPERIALISM, INTERNAL COLONIALISM, KINGSHIP, MINORITY,

NATIONALISM, OCCUPATION, PATRON–CLIENT RELATIONSHIP, SOCIALISM, SUCCESSION, TRIBE.

Further reading: Fortes & Evans-Pritchard (1940); Nugent & Vincent (2004); Graeber (2009).

polity. The STATE considered as a political organization, or the specific form of a people's politics.

pollution. Corruption by harmful substances: used generally to describe environmental degradation, but in earlier uses relating to moral or spiritual conditions. An important theme anthropologically; see PURITY.

poly-. A PREFIX meaning "many," from Greek.

polyandry. The MARRIAGE of a woman to more than one man (nearly always a group of brothers—ADELPHIC POLYANDRY). Compare POLYGAMY.

Further reading: Levine (1988).

polygamy. MARRIAGE to more than one spouse (usually POLYGYNY, though contrast POLYANDRY). It may also refer to sexual relations generally.

polygenism. The belief that humans evolved from several sets of ANCESTORS ("polygenesis") rather than one. Popular in the early nineteenth century. Compare MONOGENISM, belief in one set of ancestors.

polygyny. MARRIAGE of a man to more than one woman. See also POLYGAMY.

Polynesia. The largest part of the islands of OCEANIA, usually defined as the area east of MELANESIA and MICRONESIA. The term covers Hawaii, New Zealand, Samoa, Tahiti, and other islands. Long a focus for European exploration (e.g. by Captain Cook in the late eighteenth century) and colonization, Polynesia has yielded numerous anthropological studies such as those by Margaret MEAD and the works of Raymond FIRTH on Tikopia. In the post-colonial era critics such as Derek Freeman and Gananath Obeyesekere have adopted a more skeptical stance toward some of these readings.

Further reading: Mead (2001); Obeyesekere (1997).

polysemy. In LINGUISTICS, the condition of a TEXT or word having multiple meanings.

polytheism. Belief in many gods (contrast MONOTHEISM, belief in one god). Even in polytheistic belief systems there may be a "supreme divinity" above the others. Major religions such as BUDDHISM and HINDUISM incorporate elements of polytheism.

polythetic classification. CLASSIFICATION based not on one guiding principle ("monothetic") but many: NEEDHAM claimed it was often found outside anthropology and that it more accurately reflected people's real-life TAXONOMY. Compare FAMILY RESEMBLANCES.

Further reading: Needham (1975).

portage. The act of carrying (from French, "porter")—supplies, resources, or even boats between stretches of WATER.

positivism. A philosophy developed by Auguste COMTE from around 1830 that rejected metaphysical enquiry and concentrated on observable empirical phenomena (see EMPIRICISM); more generally, any such viewpoint, especially one requiring scientific proof of propositions.

Early positivists argued for SOCIOLOGY as a form of physical science (compare HUMAN SCIENCE(S)) rather than a subject for abstract speculation: what people did in society could be quantified and studied in a detached way. Following the work of influential figures such as DURKHEIM, positivism became a prism through which a number of fields were viewed.

Latterly it has been criticized for some of its assumptions—for example, that there are unbiased observers who are able to judge phenomena dispassionately, without cultural, sexual, or similar prejudices.

possession. A state in which a person is said to be controlled by a SPIRIT. The possessed person may no longer be held responsible for their words or deeds, and it has been argued that some groups use possession to express social tensions. Instances of possession are found in many cultures and the notion has affinities with TRANCE and shamanism (see SHAMAN). See also EXORCISM, VOODOO, ZĀR.

Further reading: Crapanzano (1980); Lambek (1993).

possibilism. Roughly the opposite belief to GEOGRAPHICAL DETERMINISM: according to possibilism, human potential is *not* especially constrained by natural conditions. Associated with the French theorists Vidal de La Blache and Febvre (early twentieth century) and several authors in the US and Britain. Also framed as "environmental possibilism" later on. Not to be confused with Bernard Shaw's term for moderate political reform.

post-. A PREFIX meaning "after."

post-colonialism. An area of study concerning places that have formerly experienced COLONIALISM. Students of post-colonialism are concerned with issues such as relations between the former dominant POWER and the ex-colony (in terms, for instance, of economics or CULTURE). Drawing on literary criticism and authors such as Edward Said (see ORIENTALISM), anthropologists and sociologists have extended the analysis of post-colonialism. It is also associated with POST-STRUCTURALISM; see also NEOCOLONIALISM.

post-marital residence. Where spouses live after MARRIAGE. See, for example, UXORILOCALITY, VIRILOCALITY.

post-modernism. A term used in art, literature, and so on to indicate rejection of early twentieth-century century *modernist* style in favor of a plurality of values and methods. It may involve references to previous styles, pastiche, quotation, or borrowing from another CULTURE. Sometimes abbreviated to "po-mo." Post-modernist concerns in anthropology include the study of new social pressures arising from global technological and ideological change, and a drive to create new forms of ETHNOGRAPHY more adequate to the description of changing social configurations and competing DISCOURSES (see AUTOETHNOGRAPHY, DISCOURSE, *WRITING CULTURE*; compare METANARRATIVE).

Further reading: Marcus & Fischer (1999); Clifford & Marcus (2011).

post-nuptial residence. Synonym for POST-MARITAL RESIDENCE.

post-processual. See PROCESSUAL.

post-structuralism. The critical extension of STRUCTURALISM from around the 1970s in which unitary textual meanings are rejected in favor of multiple meanings and a view that TEXTS are not fixed. Associated with such writers as LACAN and Derrida, and methods such as DECONSTRUCTIONISM.

potlatch. An EXCHANGE ceremony among (for example) northwest NATIVE AMERICANS (the word means "to give" in Nootka and Chinook) at which possessions are given away or destroyed as a means of enhancing the donor's standing. Rivals are then expected to reciprocate. The PRACTICE was legally banned for a time in the twentieth century. Described by BOAS among the Kwakiutl, potlatch is also found in other parts of the world.

Further reading: Rosman & Rubel (1971).

poverty. Definition of the concept of poverty can be difficult. We can distinguish between *absolute* poverty, in which people are unable to obtain necessities to sustain life, and *relative* poverty, in which they fall below the normal standards their own CULTURE would regard as comfortable. In western societies, welfare expenditure is a significant issue for any GOVERNMENT. Arguments similar to Lewis' theory of a CULTURE OF POVERTY are frequently rehearsed, as are counterarguments about the INEQUALITY inherent in MARKET economies, which affects both the "micro" level—wives may get uneven shares of HOUSEHOLD income—and the "macro": NON-WESTERN countries may be seen as starved of resources by the west. Anthropologists frequently write about the human face of poverty—those people at the sharp end, for instance, of economic policy decisions around the world.

One view suggests that some "poor" cultures do not perceive themselves as such: SAHLINS termed such groups the ORIGINAL AFFLUENT SOCIETY. Nevertheless, most people living in poverty suffer higher child mortality, poorer health, and lower LIFE EXPECTANCY. See also EXPLOITATION.

Further reading: Day et al. (1999).

power. Power is manifested in the ability to achieve ends or affect events. It has a wide range of meanings; social scientists have been particularly concerned with how INDIVIDUALS or groups wield various forms of political power. Early writers on the mechanisms deployed included MARX, DURKHEIM, and WEBER. In the twentieth century, anthropologists identified several alternatives to the western template of centralized STATE power, some of which avoid concentration in a HIERARCHY (see also ELITE). Theorists such as BOURDIEU and FOUCAULT have advanced ideas about the social *relations* through which power operates, seeing power not as an attribute of individuals or systems but as the product of a DISCOURSE in which the powerless are persuaded to accept their position (compare HEGEMONY). Anthropologists themselves may be complicit in such a discourse—and through its historical ties to COLONIALISM the discipline may already be regarded as rooted in INEQUALITY. Power relations may also be viewed through the prisms of ETHNICITY, GENDER, LANGUAGE conventions, medicine, resource allocation (e.g. ENTITLEMENT), transnational CAPITALISM, and GLOBALIZATION. See also BIOPOLITICS, CONFLICT, SYMBOLIC POWER, VIOLENCE, WAR.

Further reading: Dirks et al. (1994); Foucault (2000).

practice. How something is applied by people, as opposed to THEORY. It can also refer to specific actions or CUSTOMS, as in "the practice of POLYGAMY." Compare PRACTICE THEORY, PRAXIS.

practice theory. A THEORY associated with BOURDIEU that is concerned with the gap between what people are expected to do (e.g. according to DOXA) and what they do in reality (see HABITUS). The idea has parallels in "structuration," a sociological theory proposed by Anthony Giddens.

Further reading: Bourdieu (1990).

practicing anthropologist. See APPLIED ANTHROPOLOGY.

pragmatics. One of the three divisions of SEMIOTICS: the study of how LANGUAGE is actually used, rather than its superficial meaning. Pragmatics focuses on the assumptions and context that inform the understanding of words. See for example SPEECH ACT theory.

Further reading: Levinson (1983).

Prague School. A group of LINGUISTICS scholars active in Prague around 1930 including Roman JAKOBSON and N. S. Trubetskoi. Their attempts to understand the way LANGUAGE functions had a lasting general influence in several areas of linguistic theory, particularly PHONOLOGY. Jakobson went on to influence LÉVI-STRAUSS in key areas of his thought.

praxis. From Latin and Greek, "action": used in similar ways in several fields, most notably by MARX, for whom it denoted the fusing of philosophical THEORY with practical activity to produce change. The term was used slightly earlier by August von Cieszkowski (1838).

prayer. Spoken or internalized address to God or a god, or a similar SUPERNATURAL being or object of veneration. Prayer is central to many belief systems and may be conducted privately, by an individual, or corporately, such as at a religious gathering or on a STATE occasion. People may pray to solicit health, WELL-BEING, protection, or military superiority, or to give praise or thanks; they may adopt a variety of tones. Prayer often involves formulaic LANGUAGE and may be linked to RITUAL.

preferential marriage. In ALLIANCE theory, MARRIAGE to certain categories of people may be preferred or prescribed (see PRESCRIPTIVE MARRIAGE) in a particular CULTURE. In PRACTICE, the penalty for violating preferences may be heavy or light. There has been a certain amount of debate over the validity of such distinctions, which are associated with the work of LÉVI-STRAUSS and NEEDHAM.

prefix. In GRAMMAR, an element placed at the beginning of a word or stem that modifies its meaning or acts as an inflection (e.g. in English "un-," "pre-," and similar forms). Compare SUFFIX.

prehistory. The HISTORY of the era before written records, the particular domain of ARCHAEOLOGY. The standard divisions of prehistory are the the Stone Age, Bronze Age, and Iron Age. See also LITHIC.

preliterate. Not yet using a written LANGUAGE. The term carries certain assumptions: see LITERACY.

prescription/proscription. Although prescription has several meanings in medicine and law, anthropologists sometimes focus on one particular use, in opposition to proscription. Behaviors *pre*scribed by a society are expected to be enacted; *pro*scribed behaviors must be avoided.

prescriptive marriage. According to ALLIANCE theory, certain conventions categorize the types of people one may marry (for instance, particular cousins) in a given CULTURE. As with PREFERENTIAL MARRIAGE, there has been some debate over how strong such "rules" are in reality, and how the concept appears in the work of LÉVI-STRAUSS and NEEDHAM. Some writers treat such prescriptions as a form of CLASSIFICATION.

presentism. The interpretation of HISTORY with a bias toward current attitudes ("people in the nineteenth century were sexist and racist").

prestation. Payment, GIFT, or service rendered in accordance with TRADITION. Used by MAUSS in *The gift* to describe an (effectively) obligatory system of inter-group EXCHANGE.

prestige. See HONOR, STATUS.

primate. In zoology, the order of mammals encompassing humans, apes, and monkeys (collectively, "anthropoids") as well as lemurs, bush-babies, lorises, and similar creatures (collectively, "prosimians"). Primates are characterized by forward-directed eyes, gripping hands, and opposable thumbs. They are of particularly interest in BIOLOGICAL ANTHROPOLOGY. The study of primates is known as "primatology."

Further reading: Haraway (1989).

primitive. In an early stage of development: when used of people, the term implies a now-discredited nineteenth-century view of social EVOLUTION (toward written LANGUAGE, industrialization, and a COMPLEX SOCIETY) that is bound up with ETHNOCENTRISM, though it was not always used pejoratively. Compare SAVAGERY, SIMPLE SOCIETY.

primitive economic man. See ECONOMIC MAN.

primitivism. Idealization of supposedly PRIMITIVE cultures; for instance, the NOBLE SAVAGE stereotype and elements of the ART of Gaugin and Picasso.

primitive communism. A view—associated with MORGAN and later MARX and ENGELS, and appealing to some twentieth-century anthropologists— that certain (past or current) societies naturally hold goods and resources in common and do not acknowledge private PROPERTY; thus they are classless (see CLASS).

Further reading: Lee (1992); Engels (2001).

primitive mentality. The simplistic THEORY that so-called PRIMITIVE peoples had a pre-logical, mystical view of the world, as opposed to the rational approach of western, MODERN cultures. Advanced by LÉVY-BRUHL in *La mentalité primitive* (1922).

primitive promiscuity. The belief that early mankind was naturally promiscuous prior to the development of FAMILY life, as found in the work of MORGAN and others. It was rejected by Edward WESTERMARCK.

primogeniture. The condition of being first-born, often specifically the first son. In many societies, such as modern northern Europe, primogeniture has carried the right to inherit PROPERTY and titles. Compare ULTIMOGENITURE, the condition of being latest-born.

prisoner's dilemma. See GAME THEORY.

processual. Concerned with process rather than with separate events. *Processual archaeology* (or "new archaeology") arose in the 1960s and aimed to infer chronological developments in the people it studied using physical evidence and ETHNOGRAPHIC ANALOGY. It was countered by *post-processual archaeology*, which lays greater emphasis on CULTURE and is associated with Ian Hodder especially.

production. A key concept (along with distribution and CONSUMPTION) in economics. Production is usually thought of as a process by which raw materials are converted to saleable goods, though the term can also cover any similar activity (e.g. thought or social processes, as in "the production of space"). Widely discussed in MARXIST theory: see, for example, ASIATIC MODE OF PRODUCTION, MEANS OF PRODUCTION, MODE OF PRODUCTION.

profane. Generally understood to mean offensive to the SACRED, but literally only meaning secular (from Latin, "outside the temple"). Described by DURKHEIM as one contrasted sphere of experience: the profane is quotidian, capable of being understood; the sacred is awe-inspiring, mysterious and restricted, requiring the mediation of RELIGION. While this dichotomy has been disputed, it has also been influential, especially in external views of Australian ABORIGINAL peoples.

Further reading: Eliade (1987); Durkheim (1995).

property. The things that are accepted as attached to a particular person or entity (FAMILY, HOUSEHOLD, corporate body, STATE), comprising not only material possessions, land holdings, housing, and ANIMALS but also intangibles such as INTELLECTUAL PROPERTY and even other people (see SLAVERY). A concept that crosses disciplines, being of great interest to theorists of LAW, economists, and politicians. Widely associated with the work of MARX, property is of great concern to students of INEQUALITY and the workings of INHERITANCE.

Further reading: Hann (1998); Engels (2001); Widlok & Tadesse (2005).

prophecy. Revelation of the will of God (or a god) by an INDIVIDUAL, known as a prophet; or, the prediction of future events. WEBER distinguished the charismatic figure of the prophet from the priest, whose influence derived from holding office.

Further reading: Weber (2009).

proscription. See PRESCRIPTION/PROSCRIPTION.

prostitution. The performance of sexual acts in return for payment. The cliché of the prostitute as a woman of a particular CLASS walking the street is not matched by the reality of the modern SEX industry. Not only are male and TRANSGENDER sex workers also active, but attitudes to prostitution vary, as do legal approaches. Scholarly focus has shifted over the twentieth century from a moralistic view toward the ameloriation of ills arising from the sex TRADE such as infections and TRAFFICKING, and toward the POWER and GENDER issues raised, particularly from a feminist perspective.

protectorate. A territory over which an external STATE exercises control without having formally annexed it. The term's most common use in anthropology is with regard to regions under the influence of European states in the nineteenth and early twentieth centuries. Botswana, for instance, was once the Bechuanaland protectorate.

protestant (work) ethic. A notion that, according to WEBER, developed from Christian asceticism to become a guiding spirit of post-Reformation CAPITALISM. In this view one had a moral obligation toward self-denial in order to build up resources through hard WORK, saving, and so on.

Further reading: Weber (2009).

proto-. A PREFIX from Latin, meaning "early, original."

Proto-Indo-European. See INDO-EUROPEAN, LANGUAGE CLASSIFICATION, PROTOLANGUAGE.

protolanguage. A hypothetical LANGUAGE that is assumed to be an ANCESTOR of other languages or DIALECTs, as suggested by comparing them. An example would be Proto-Indo-European (see INDO-EUROPEAN). First known by the German term *Ursprache* ("PRIMITIVE language"). See COMPARATIVE LINGUISTICS.

prototype theory. A view of CLASSIFICATION in several areas that holds that people form categories around examples that best typify category members—prototypes—rather than starting with hard-and-fast boundaries into which everything must slot. Compare FAMILY RESEMBLANCES.

proverb. A short, memorable saying, similar to a MAXIM. Proverbs are quoted in many CULTUREs, often with the implication that they convey widely accepted truths.

provisioning. See ECONOMIC ANTHROPOLOGY.

proxemics. Study of the social use of SPACE, for example between people, and of what this reveals about cultural standards. Associated with the work of Edward T. Hall in the 1960s.

pseudo-kinship. A term that covers KINSHIP-like relationships between unrelated people, such as FICTIVE KINSHIP and RITUAL KINSHIP.

psychic unity (of mankind/humankind). The contention that all peoples share the same basic mental structure. Associated with a number of nineteenth-century anthropologists (such as TYLOR and Adolf Bastian) but influential across the subject.

psycholinguistics. The branch of LINGUISTICS dealing with psychological processes underlying LANGUAGE ACQUISITION, comprehension, and use. Areas studied include the question of whether such understanding is innate and to what degree, and language and memory.

Further reading: Aitchison (2008).

psychological anthropology. Early anthropologists such as BOAS were drawn to insights from psychology to try to trace common human features (compare PSYCHIC UNITY). Psychological anthropology, as it was later named, went on to inform the work of the CULTURE AND PERSONALITY school. Numerous other writers have studied the field, among them Melford Spiro. More recently debate has focused on the applicability of western conceptions of the MIND to other CULTURES, the domain of ETHNOPSYCHOLOGY.

Further reading: LeVine (2010).

psychotropic. Applied to DRUGS: altering the MIND of the user (alternatively, "psychoactive"). Opium and ALCOHOL are two examples.

puberty. The period at which a person reaches sexual maturity, is capable of reproducing, and attains secondary sexual characteristics such as BODY hair. This transition is often held to be of social significance and marked by rites of passage (see RITE OF PASSAGE). See also INITIATION, YOUTH.

Pueblo. See WHITE.

purdah. From Persian, "curtain": a MUSLIM or upper-CLASS Hindu CUSTOM of secluding WOMEN from the gaze of males and outsiders behind a screen.

purity. A state considered free from POLLUTION. In addition to the way a layman would understand this term (medically, environmentally, of FOOD quality, and so on) anthropologists have long opined that the distinction between pure and polluted is present in, for example, all of the great world RELIGIONS and arguably every CULTURE (it is often regarded as one of the few UNIVERSALS) on a metaphorical or symbolic level. Early writers including DURKHEIM investigated such ideas, but the key works may be those by Mary DOUGLAS, with their examination of the concept that purity reinforces social boundaries and secures one from RISK, while pollution—by things, actions, or people specified by a CULTURE—creates uncertainty and disorder. One example of polluting material is one's own discarded BODY matter—for instance, menstrual blood. DUMONT applied the opposition of pollution/

Figure 22   **Purity.** An outside bathroom in Eastern Tanzania, with pit latrines (right) and shower area (left). Photo copyright: N. Beckmann.

purity to SOCIAL STRUCTURE in India, viewing CASTE as founded on gradations of purity, with the "untouchable" (DALIT) at the bottom. Later writers challenged this as too reliant on BINARY OPPOSITION. See also TABOO, the means of enforcing purity.

Further reading: Dumont (1980); Douglas (2002).

Purum. A South Asian people whose relationship system was notably studied by NEEDHAM.

pygmy. A member of one of several peoples characterized by small stature (less than one and a half meters); found in parts of Africa and Southeast Asia. The term has derogatory associations in modern use. See also NEGRITO.

Q

qat. See KHAT.

qualitative/quantitative. Qualitative methods are those based on verbal descriptions of a situation: they tend to be interpretive, impressionistic, and context-dependent—for instance, the understanding of a particular CULTURE developed by PARTICIPANT OBSERVATION, or anecdotal INTERVIEW material. Quantitative methods are numerical at base and non-context-dependent, and aim at precise analysis through data collection, SAMPLING, and so on. A variety of statistical methods (see STATISTICS) have developed, many of which have been used by anthropologists.

Further reading: Bernard (2006).

quaternary. In ARCHAEOLOGY, relating to the most recent period of geological TIME, from about two million years ago to the present.

queer theory. A term for research that aims to challenge NORMATIVE heterosexual assumptions about SEX and GENDER. Though contentious, it has influenced many areas in recent years, including GAY AND LESBIAN ANTHROPOLOGY.

questionnaire. See INTERVIEW, SAMPLING.

R

Rabinow, Paul (1944–). American anthropologist who pioneered work on REFLEXIVITY, latterly examining the place of BIOTECHNOLOGY in society; he is also an expert commentator on FOUCAULT. Rabinow gained a doctorate from Chicago in 1970 after studying at EHESS; since 1978 he has taught at the University of California. His key works include *Reflections on fieldwork in Morocco* (30th anniversary ed. 2007), *Making PCR: a story of biotechnology* (1996), and *French DNA: trouble in purgatory* (1999). He also edited *The Foucault reader* (1984).

race. A group of people held to be descended from a common ANCESTOR and believed to share certain physical and/or psychological characteristics. In anthropology much effort has gone into showing "race" to be a social concept with no real basis in biology: for example, a racial group's STATUS in any nation is contested politically, and changes over time. Historically, categorizations based on assumed characteristics of "races" have been associated with INEQUALITY and pseudo-scientific prejudices (e.g. that white civilization was inherently superior to BLACK CULTURE; see also ANTHROPOMETRY, SCIENTIFIC RACISM). The concept of ETHNICITY supplanted "race" in the later twentieth century, though it too has problematic aspects.

Further reading: Sanjek (1998).

racism. A belief in the superiority or inferiority of peoples based on their presumed ethnic characteristics (RACE). Racists often extrapolate from superficial factors such as skin color to generalize about group behavior. Racism can be characterized as a product of European IMPERIALISM and as

Concise Dictionary of Social and Cultural Anthropology, First Edition. Mike Morris.
© 2012 Michael Ashley Morris. Published 2012 by Blackwell Publishing Ltd.

Figure 23   Radcliffe-Brown. "R-B" (center front) with his class of 1945–6 at Oxford. Fortes sits at his left. Photo: Gillman & Soame, used by permission of Oxford University, School of Anthropology.

such may be linked to the history of western anthropology, including its early evolutionary schema. While later anthropologists argued that ETHNICITY was paramount, racism remains a force strongly linked to DISCRIMINATION, INEQUALITY, POWER, and STATUS.

Further reading: Frankenberg (1997).

Radcliffe-Brown, A. R. (1881–1955). British social anthropologist, associated particularly with STRUCTURAL-FUNCTIONALISM. Born near Birmingham and educated at Cambridge (1902–6) under HADDON and RIVERS. He did fieldwork in the Andaman Islands (1906–8) and Western Australia (1910–12), and taught school and directed an education department (in Tonga) before holding professorships at Cape Town (1921–5), Sydney, Chicago, Alexandria, and Oxford (1937–46), teaching finally at Rhodes University.

His publications include *The Andaman islanders* (1922), *The social organization of Australian tribes* (1931), *African systems of kinship and marriage* (ed. with D. FORDE, 1950), *Structure and function in primitive society* (1952, probably his essential work), and *The social anthropology of Radcliffe-Brown* (ed. A. Kuper, 1977). See also JOKING RELATIONSHIP.

Further reading: Fortes (1949).

Radin, Paul (1883–1959). American cultural anthropologist (born in Lódz, Poland). One of BOAS' many noted students, he obtained a Ph.D. from Columbia in 1911 and undertook fieldwork with a number of NATIVE AMERICAN groups. He taught in several universities, concluding his career at Brandeis. Radin produced a number of studies of the Winnebago people; his work touched on elements of RELIGION, mythology, and psychology, and he was an accomplished linguist. His publications include *The Winnebago tribe* (1923), *Primitive man as philosopher* (1927), *Primitive religion* (1937), and *The trickster* (1956, with a commentary by Carl Jung).

RAI. See ROYAL ANTHROPOLOGICAL INSTITUTE.

rainbow serpent. A mythical snake common to a number of ABORIGINAL popular beliefs. Linked to WATER, fertility, and creation stories.

rainforest. A dense equatorial forest characterized by heavy rainfall and heat; notably found in Central and South America (e.g. AMAZONIA), Africa, and SOUTHEAST ASIA. Rainforests account for very significant amounts of plant and animal life; their continued destruction is a major environmental issue. Anthropologists often study peoples living in such settings, recording their INDIGENOUS KNOWLEDGE.

raj. A Hindi word meaning STATE or GOVERNMENT. Commonly used of the British Raj: the period (1858–1947) during which Britain ruled directly in India. See also SATI.

ramage. In (mainly) Polynesian societies, a hierarchical, COGNATIC, DESCENT GROUP, or system of ranked descent groups, characterized by SAHLINS as non-exogamous (see EXOGAMY), internally stratified (see STRATIFICATION), and UNILINEAL. The term was coined by FIRTH in 1936. Compare DEME.

Further reading: Firth (1957[b]); Sahlins (1958).

Ramayana. See HINDUISM.

rank society. A rank society, according to Morton Fried, is one in which valued positions are limited so that not everyone who has the potential will occupy one. There may or may not be STRATIFICATION. Fried's views were later challenged, for instance on the question of the privileges that might be involved.

Further reading: Fried (1967).

Rappaport, Roy A. (1926–97). See ECOLOGICAL ANTHROPOLOGY.

rational choice theory. See UTILITARIANISM.

rationalism. A TRADITION of thought deriving from seventeenth-century philosophers such as Descartes that asserted that reason alone should provide knowledge of the world (rather than sense data—see EMPIRICISM—or divine revelation). Rationalism has affinities with POSITIVISM and STRUCTURALISM. Anthropologists' work has tended to disprove the opposition of "rational" westerners against "irrational" INDIGENOUS peoples (compare PRIMITIVE MENTALITY).

Ratzel, Friedrich (1844–1904). See ANTHROPOGEOGRAPHY, GEOGRAPHICAL DETERMINISM, GERMAN ANTHROPOLOGY.

Reagan, Ronald (1911–2004). See NEOLIBERALISM.

reciprocal altruism. ALTRUISM connected to an expectation that the "giving" party will later benefit from altruistic behavior in return. It can be studied in humans and other animals, and is often considered to contribute to reproductive advantage. Compare GAME THEORY, KIN SELECTION ALTRUISM.

reciprocity. The element of EXCHANGE usually implying *mutual* interaction of goods or benefits between parties. Of great concern to economic anthropologists, and notably studied by MAUSS, Karl POLANYI, and Marshall SAHLINS, who extended the definitions involved (*generalized* reciprocity: giving without overt requirement of any return; *balanced* reciprocity: giving where the return is of equivalent value and timely; *negative* reciprocity: attempting to get "something for nothing," or near to it; associated respectively with diminishing ties of closeness between the exchanging parties).

Further reading: Polanyi et al. (1957); Sahlins (2004).

reconstruction. In LINGUISTICS, a facet of several methods for tracing similarities in disparate LANGUAGES (or the EVOLUTION of one particular language), involving making hypotheses about the nature of a PROTO-LANGUAGE that no longer survives.

recursiveness. Recursive elements, in mathematics, computing, and logic, refer back to earlier elements of a series; the idea is used analogously to describe aspects of SOCIAL ORGANIZATION. CHOMSKY and other linguists also used the term in a similar fashion.

Redfield, Robert (1897–1958). American anthropologist, associated with his native Chicago, where he worked; he was the son-in-law of sociologist Robert E. Park. Starting with *Tepoztlan, a Mexican village* (1930), he made numerous contributions to the understanding of PEASANT cultures and SOCIAL CHANGE; his other works include *A village that chose progress* (1950) and *The little community* (1955). See also FOLK–URBAN CONTINUUM, GREAT TRADITION.

redistribution. Distributing resources again, sometimes to promote fairness. The idea is common to many economies. Generally some form of AUTHORITY will collect FOOD, goods, money, or other resources, process and/or partly use some for itself, and then share out the remainder to its subjects or citizens.

Further reading: Polanyi et al. (1957).

reductionism. The intellectual attempt to explain complex phenomena in terms of phenomena that are simpler. For example, SOCIAL STRUCTURE in a country might be presented as purely a result of economic factors rather than several factors interacting. The label "reductionist" on a THEORY can be regarded as pejorative. Compare ESSENTIALISM.

reference terms. Relationship terms used to describe their subject indirectly, to talk *about* them. These may be used more strictly than ADDRESS TERMS (terms used to speak *to* their subjects) and specify the precise connection involved.

referent. In LINGUISTICS (the meaning is slightly different in philosophy), the thing or person referred to by a word or phrase.

reflexivity. In a general sense, the process of turning in on oneself; a key feature of INTERPRETIVE ANTHROPOLOGY. Reflexive thought is apparent both in the SOCIETY observed by the ethnographer—in terms of the meanings participants ascribe to their actions—and in modern ethnographic writing itself, which normally takes account of the cultural preconceptions an anthropologist brings to the field (see e.g. AUTOETHNOGRAPHY).

Further reading: Rabinow (2007); Davies (2008)

refugee. A person displaced by persecution, WAR, disaster, or adverse economic conditions at home who seeks shelter elsewhere, either within their own country or in another. Refugees may live in a variety of locations, such as semi-permanent camps or within existing urban areas. See also ASYLUM SEEKER, FORCED MIGRATION, MIGRATION.

regicide. Killing of a king or queen, or one who does this. See also DIVINE KINGSHIP.

register. While "register" has several meanings, it refers in LINGUISTICS to a style of speech or writing adopted in order to convey appropriate social messages: a speaker using a specific register will expect his/her audience to receive his/her words in a certain way, and to respond accordingly. Choice of register may be determined by a combination of the context, the social STATUS of those involved, and the degree of formality expected culturally.

Reichs, Kathy (1950–). See FORENSIC ANTHROPOLOGY.

reification. Consideration of a person or concept as if they/it were a thing; by extension, dehumanization of workers in MARXIST theory. See COMMODITY FETISHISM, and compare ESSENTIALISM, OBJECTIFICATION.

reincarnation. A process by which the SOUL or individual consciousness is believed to leave the BODY at DEATH and return in a different embodiment.

Although reincarnation is sometimes associated particularly with HINDUISM and BUDDHISM, many RELIGIONS and philosophies espouse it, though details vary. The returning form may be said to inhabit a new human being, or an ANIMAL. Similarly, there may or may not be a link between behavior in one's life and the nature of one's reincarnation. Compare NIRVANA, attainment of which breaks the cycle of reincarnation.

relations of production. The human relationships involved within a MODE OF PRODUCTION. In classic MARXIST theory they are usually conceived of as bound up with ownership and CLASS tensions: the key relationship is that of the capitalist factory owner (for example) and his workers, who do not themselves own a MEANS OF PRODUCTION. However, the term covers all kinds of economic relations.

relations of relations. Relations between ASSOCIATIONS. The term has other meanings in several areas.

relationship terminology. The particular terms that people use to classify relatives in a given CULTURE. While these may also be called "kin terminology" or "KINSHIP terminology," such labels may be used to cover blood relations (CONSANGUINITY) only; "relationship terminology" has the virtue of including affines and those connected by such conventions as FICTIVE KINSHIP; its looser meaning acknowledges the variety of real practice. Note that a particular *term* may encompass more than one KIN TYPE: an Englishman may use the ambiguous term "uncle" to describe his father's brother, his mother's brother, or the husbands of his parents' sisters—four discrete *types*. See also ADDRESS TERMS, MORGAN, REFERENCE TERMS.

In addition to abbreviations or symbols (F for father and so on), anthropologists use various compound terms to designate less immediate relations. To avoid the ambiguous connotations of western terms such as "uncle" or "aunt" they will usually follow INDIGENOUS practice and be specific: MZ (for mother's sister), FB (father's brother), and so on (see also DESCRIPTIVE KINSHIP). These terms can be extended as necessary (e.g. MMBS=mother's mother's brother's son).

relativism. Relativism argues that truth and moral standards are not fixed and absolute for everyone but vary according to TIME, PLACE, and context. This is of greatest interest to anthropology in the form of CULTURAL RELATIVISM, but other variants include LINGUISTIC RELATIVISM and HISTORICISM. See also SCIENCE AND TECHNOLOGY STUDIES.

religion. Belief in a higher POWER than humankind, and attitudes and actions following from this; a system of such beliefs, frequently the basis of ETHICS.

Figure 24   **Religion.** A room in the American Legation, formerly a Chinese temple, 1904. National Anthropological Archives, Smithsonian Institution DOE Asia: China: Beijing (Peking), NM 90351 04491400.

Definitions based around INDIVIDUAL religions can be vague or fluid, and it is difficult to be too prescriptive about what constitutes a religion (in some cases, for example, the worship of a god or gods is not required).

Nineteenth-century theorists in SOCIAL SCIENCES differed over whether religions (in general) were attempts to explain the natural world or simply symbolic systems reflecting the order of SOCIETY. Later, anthropologists tended to focus more narrowly on the so-called PRIMITIVE religions they encountered; of late their gaze has broadened to include all kinds of belief. Major religions include BUDDHISM, CHRISTIANITY, CONFUCIANISM, DAO-ISM, HINDUISM, ISLAM, JUDAISM, and SIKHISM. In addition, many local religions have attracted study—for example, CANDOMBLÉ, IFÁ, SANTERIA, SHINTO, VOODOO, and ZOROASTRIANISM. See also ANIMISM, ATHEISM, CONVERSION, CULT, EVIL, EXORCISM, FRAZER, LOVE, POLYTHEISM, PRAYER, PURITY, REINCARNATION, RITUAL, SACRED, SECT, SUFFERING, SYNCRETISM, WEBER.

Further reading: Evans-Pritchard (1965); Segal (2006).

remote sensing. Acquisition of geographical data from a distance, usually photographs or other representations of the Earth's surface taken from a plane or satellite.

Renaissance. See HUMANISM.

repetition. Repeated forms occur in all spheres of human activity. Among many examples, RITUAL often involves the repetition of specific actions, and may be viewed as fitting within a framework in which TIME itself is partly comprehended through the regular repetitions required by daily life, seasonal variations, and so on. Repetition is also a central component in LANGUAGE: from the mimicry of accomplished speakers, which aids LANGUAGE ACQUISITION, to its use for RHETORIC or poetic effect. Along with literature, much pictorial ART and MUSIC derives force from repetition.

representation. Representation involves the substitution of one thing or person for another, and is a concept with several applications. The most relevant to anthropology derive from philosophy and LINGUISTICS, as well as politics and the arts: the philosophical viewpoint that perceived objects can represent others beyond our immediate understanding preceded the work of SAUSSURE et al., which denied the "objectivity" of linguistic representations of experience. In an analogous way, anthropologists in the later twentieth century began to question the ethnographer's ability to accurately represent the CULTURE they studied—thus treating the anthropological TEXT as a kind of artwork, a representation similar to a group portrait, and open to the same sort of criticisms (see also MIMESIS, REFLEXIVITY).

reproduction. The biological process by which organisms create new beings, either sexually or asexually. Cultural processes and attitudes around human reproduction have been of great interest in BIOLOGICAL ANTHROPOLOGY and MEDICAL ANTHROPOLOGY, with a number of recent studies adopting a critical attitude to BIOMEDICINE and a feminist reading of the GENDER issues involved, for instance regarding REPRODUCTIVE TECHNOLOGIES.

A separate meaning covers the replication of social processes and structures ("social reproduction") or the handing on of cultural beliefs and values—BOURDIEU is among those who have discussed "cultural reproduction."

Further reading: Bourdieu & Passeron (1990); Martin (2001).

reproductive technologies. The various technical means by which conception and pregnancy can be averted, managed, or stimulated.

While there is some anthropological interest in social aspects of CONTRACEPTION, much research has centered on the methods and people involved in encouraging conception. The technologies involved encompass FERTILITY DRUGS, in vitro ("test tube") fertilization, SURROGACY, and so on. While these are sometimes called "new reproductive technologies" (NRTs), they may include established practices. As scientific advances have occurred, much discussion has revolved around ETHICS (see also BIOETHICS) and the GENDER issues raised (including men's "rights"). Within anthropology specifically, questions for KINSHIP studies arise from new relationships and forms of FAMILY.

Further reading: Inhorn (2007).

residence rules. The social conventions according to which married couples choose a particular PLACE to live (in other words, their POST-MARITAL RESIDENCE). See NEOLOCAL, UXORILOCALITY, VIRILOCALITY.

resistance. Opposition to oppression, domination, or military OCCUPATION (as in "the French Resistance"). Following a strand of thought associated with writers on the political left, and in the works of FOUCAULT and others, a number of anthropologists have seen resistance as a cultural theme informing many relationships. Resistance may be overt or covert, from open defiance to strategies to subvert AUTHORITY.

Further reading: Comaroff (1985); Scott (1985).

restricted exchange. A synonym for DIRECT EXCHANGE.

Revelation (Bible). See MILLENARIANISM.

revitalization. Revitalization movements constitute a form of MILLENARIANISM associated with cultural and religious retrenchment in the face of contact with other CULTURES. Compare also NATIVISM. Revitalization was extensively discussed in its manifestation among the Seneca of the northeastern US by Anthony Wallace.

Further reading: Wallace (1956, 1970).

rheme. In LINGUISTICS, that part of a sentence adding new information about the theme.

rhetoric. The art of using LANGUAGE or argument to persuade in speech or writing. Rhetoric is a skill highly valued in the western classical literary TRADITION, and more generally is a notable part of much social interaction. It may be linked to IDEOLOGY.

rhizome. See DELEUZE.

Rhodes-Livingstone Institute. An anthropological research unit, originally headed by Godfrey Wilson from 1938. Later directors included Max GLUCKMAN, under whom the Institute attracted several members of the MANCHESTER SCHOOL. Its publications included the *Rhodes-Livingstone papers* as well as monographs. Originally based at Livingstone, Northern Rhodesia (now Zambia), it moved to Lusaka in 1951 and in 1965 adopted the first of several new names. Since 1996 it has been known as INESOR (Institute for Social and Economic Research), University of Zambia.

Further reading: Schumaker (2001).

rice. A cereal grain, usually *Oryza sativa*, of great importance for FOOD and cultivated in large amounts across Asia and elsewhere. The characteristic flooded "paddy field" gets its name from the Malay word *padi* ("rice"). See also INVOLUTION.

Richards, Audrey I. (1899–1984). See ARDENER, WORK.

right and left. In many cultures the right side or hand is associated with goodness or fortune and the left with EVIL or bad luck (consider, for example, the contrasting etymologies of the words "dexterous" and "sinister"). Right and left may also symbolize other (e.g. GENDER) oppositions. The pioneering work on this field was done by Robert HERTZ. See also DUAL CLASSIFICATION.

Further reading: Hertz (1960); Needham (1973).

risk. The chance of incurring loss (of money or other resources), injury, or damage. A major concern of economics, risk is also of interest to sociologists and anthropologists—for instance, as an issue in MEDICAL ANTHROPOLOGY, where sexual behavior carries the risk of infection with HIV/AIDS. Mary DOUGLAS also investigated risk several times in her work (compare PURITY).

Further reading: Douglas (1992).

rite of intensification. A type of RITUAL identified by Chapple and Coon in contradistinction from a RITE OF PASSAGE. They held that, whereas rites of passage address a crisis concerning the INDIVIDUAL, rites of intensification aim at restoring balance to the group as a whole.

Further reading: Chapple & Coon (1942).

rite of passage. A term coined by VAN GENNEP in the title of his seminal work on the subject. A ceremony marking the transition of an INDIVIDUAL or group through key moments of their life cycle (such as BIRTH, PUBERTY, MARRIAGE, DEATH) or marking major temporal events. Typically the former involves stages of separation, LIMINALITY (marginalization), and reincorporation. Van Gennep's work was taken up by Victor TURNER.

Further reading: Van Gennep (1960).

ritual. A formal, often religious, set of practices characterized by themes of celebration, renewal, or affirmation. Actions performed in ritual often have symbolic meaning. Theorists such as DURKHEIM have discussed the social purposes of ritual, a question taken up in various ways by GLUCKMAN (see RITUAL OF REBELLION), TURNER, BLOCH, and many others.

Ritual can be seen as strengthening the status quo, enforcing the notion that everyday concerns must yield to transcendent ones (or the requirements of their representatives); it can alternatively be read as a site of debate and dissent, with different participants viewing the ritual in different ways (compare CARNIVAL).

Possible elements of ritual include CLOTHING, DANCE, DRINK, DRUGS, and MUSIC. RITUAL PRACTICES include CANNIBALISM, CARGO CULT, EXORCISM, FUNERAL RITES, GHOST DANCE, PRAYER, SACRIFICE, SECRET SOCIETY, and SUBINCISION. See also KINGSHIP, SYMBOLIC ANTHROPOLOGY, VIOLENCE.

Further reading: Metcalf & Huntingdon (1991); Turner (1995).

ritual kinship. A type of FICTIVE KINSHIP created ritually to forge bonds between people who are not literally related. An example is the institution of COMPADRAZGO, or GODPARENTS in general. See also SPIRITUAL KINSHIP.

ritual of rebellion. A RITUAL that permits an inversion of, or apparent challenge to, the social order, but that can be argued to actually reinforce it. Studied by Max GLUCKMAN in relation to the Swazi. Compare CARNIVAL.

Further reading: Gluckman (1963).

Rivers, W. H. R. (1864–1922). British psychiatrist and anthropologist, born Chatham, Kent. A participant in the TORRES STRAITS EXPEDITION, where he devised the "genealogical method" (see GENEALOGY). A key influence on British anthropology through his connections with MALINOWSKI and RADCLIFFE-BROWN, he is also well known for his work during World War I, which included treating Siegfried Sassoon. His publications include *The Todas* (1906), *Kinship and social organization* (1914), and *History and ethnology* (1922).

Further reading: Slobodin (1997).

Robespierre, Maximilien (1758–94). See HUMAN RIGHTS.

role. Originally a term for the part an actor plays on stage, "role" was taken up by the sociologist G. H. Mead in the early twentieth century and developed by Ralph Linton, Erving Goffman, and others to refer to the analogous "part" an individual plays in social life. One's STATUS in a certain situation carries expectations of what is appropriate to the role one plays: a father, for instance, is assumed to relate to his child in ways a stranger does not. When there is a CONFLICT between the various requirements of a role, stress ensues. Anthropologists such as TURNER (among the Ndembu of Zambia) and Bruce KAPFERER have produced notable work on roles.

Further reading: Mead (1934).

romantic love. See LOVE.

Rouch, Jean (1917–2004). French anthropological film-maker, born Paris, one of the leading directors of the *cinema vérité* movement, which in turn influenced wider trends such as the French new wave.

Having studied under MAUSS, Rouch adopted lightweight equipment for his early work in West Africa and was said to have begun using a hand-held camera as a result of dropping his tripod in the Niger river. He coined the term "ethnofiction" for work mixing documentary and fiction. His many films include *Les mâitres fous* (1954, *Mad masters*); *Moi, un noir* (1958, *Me, a black*), and the Parisian collaboration with Edgar Morin, *Chronique d'un été* (1960, *Chronicle of a summer*).

Further reading: Rouch (2003); Henley (2009).

Rousseau, Jean-Jacques (1712–78). French Enlightenment philosopher (born Geneva). Rousseau developed the ideal of the NOBLE SAVAGE and influenced the Romantic writers and French revolutionaries. He is best known for *Du contrat social* (1762, *The* SOCIAL CONTRACT).

routinization. According to WEBER, the process by which a charismatic leader (see CHARISMA) is given stable AUTHORITY: the leader, from being an anomaly, is integrated into traditional leadership structures. Routinization can also refer generally to actions becoming habitual.

Further reading: Weber (1964).

Royal Anthropological Iinstitute (RAI). A British and Irish ASSOCIATION (www.therai.org.uk) formed by the merger of earlier groups as the Anthropological Institute in 1871. The oldest anthropological association in the world, its publications include the journals *Anthropology today* and *Journal of the Royal Anthropological Institute*.

rural. Relating to the countryside (contrast URBAN ANTHROPOLOGY). Issues in the anthropology of rural communities include aspects of AGRICULTURE, ECOLOGY, and ENVIRONMENT, and patterns of MIGRATION. See also FOLK–URBAN CONTINUUM, PEASANT, VILLAGE.

Russell, Bertrand (1872–1970). See WITTGENSTEIN.

Russian anthropology. Early Russian anthropology tended to focus on INDIGENOUS groups of Central Asia. The Imperial Russian Geographical Society was established in 1845, and included an ethnology division.

The Soviet regime after 1917 encouraged work on ETHNICITY but severely restricted intellectual inquiry, hindering scholars such as BAKHTIN; Chaianov (see CHAYANOV SLOPE) was one of many who were executed in this period.

As in CHINESE ANTHROPOLOGY, Soviet anthropologists were necessarily constrained in their choice of field sites, concentrating on internal areas such as Siberia. Iulian Bromlei (Yu. Bromley) was among the leading figures of the later period.

Since the fall of COMMUNISM, MARXIST approaches have been challenged by other perspectives, and areas such as Russian NATIONALISM have become fertile topics.

Further reading: Gellner (1988).

Ryle, Gilbert (1900–1976). See THICK DESCRIPTION.

S

S or **So** or **s.** In RELATIONSHIP TERMINOLOGY, the abbreviation for "son"; if a less common notation is used, "S" or "s" may mean "sister" (in these cases, "s" or "S" means "son," respectively). For "sister" see also Z.

sacred. That which is set apart from ordinary experience, by its association with religious or spiritual meanings. Contrast PROFANE, the realm of the everyday.

sacrifice. The RITUAL preparation and killing of an ANIMAL, or occasionally a human being, as an offering to a deity. The offering may then be eaten by the sacrificing party as a kind of "communion" with the SUPERNATURAL (compare COMMENSALITY). In some cases other FOOD or DRINK is offered. Different communities place different emphases on the elements of sacrifice; anthropologists have failed to find a sufficiently elastic definition of sacrifice to cover every instance. Historically they have also been hampered by too close an attachment to the definitions of sacrifice accepted in the Christian TRADITION. One of the key theorists in this regard was W. Robertson SMITH.

Further reading: Hubert & Mauss (1964); de Heusch (1985).

Sahara desert. See TUAREG.

Sahlins, Marshall D. (1930–). American cultural anthropologist, born Chicago. Educated at Michigan and Columbia University, he taught at Michigan and Chicago (until 1997). A major figure in ECONOMIC ANTHROPOLOGY, culture theory, and the study of OCEANIA, Sahlins has published, among other titles, *Stone age economics* (1972, new preface 2004), *Culture and practical reason* (1976), *The use and abuse of biology*

Concise Dictionary of Social and Cultural Anthropology, First Edition. Mike Morris.
© 2012 Michael Ashley Morris. Published 2012 by Blackwell Publishing Ltd.

(1976), and *How "natives" think: about Captain Cook, for example* (1995). See also CHAYANOV SLOPE, DOMESTIC MODE OF PRODUCTION, ORIGINAL AFFLUENT SOCIETY, RECIPROCITY.

Said, Edward W. (1935–2003). See MIDDLE EAST, ORIENTALISM, POST-COLONIALISM.

saint. A person recognized by a RELIGION as especially holy. Most commonly thought of as a phenomenon of Catholic CHRISTIANITY, saints are also revered in BUDDHISM and ISLAM. See also CARGO SYSTEM, *FIESTA*, SHEIKH.

Saint-Simon (Claude-Henri de Rouvroy, comte de Saint-Simon, 1760–1825). French social reformer, born Paris. Influenced by CONDORCET, he collaborated with COMTE and advanced enlightened, positivist plans to improve society. His thinking anticipated developments arising from the Industrial Revolution (see INDUSTRIAL SOCIETY) and influenced socialists and other later theorists. His works include *De la réorganisation de la société européenne* (1814, *On the reorganization of European society*).

salvage ethnography. The study of a CULTURE or phenomenon that is likely to disappear rapidly, for instance owing to ASSIMILATION. In the same way, "salvage ARCHAEOLOGY" is found on *sites* that are at risk.

sampling. The process of selecting INDIVIDUAL people, things, or sections of things from a larger group or entity in order to derive information representative of the whole. News MEDIA frequently report the results of surveys that have been administered to sample groups. Methodologically, samples should be truly representative—for instance, selection criteria should be applied randomly, and unintentional selection biases eliminated. See also STATISTICS.

San. An ABORIGINAL, HUNTER-GATHERER group of peoples of Southern Africa, formerly called "Bushmen" by Dutch colonists.

sanction. A method of enforcing social rules by which praise or (often) blame and punishment is meted out in response to certain actions. Sanctions may be formal, for example by LAW enforcement, or informal, for example by one's peers (as in GOSSIP). See also OSTRACISM, VIOLENCE, WITCHCRAFT.

Santeria. A RELIGION found in Cuba and (to a lesser extent) the US, involving the worship of Yoruba gods. The Yoruba are a people of West Africa (Benin and Nigeria).

Further reading: Wirtz (2007).

Sapir, Edward (1884–1939). American linguist and anthropologist. Born in Lauenburg, Germany, Sapir migrated to New York at the age of five. He obtained a Ph.D. at Columbia as one of BOAS' students. Sapir worked at the University of Chicago (1925–31) and Yale (1931–9). A pioneer of ANTHROPOLOGICAL LINGUISTICS, he did much fieldwork among NATIVE AMERICAN groups, co-founded the CULTURE AND PERSONALITY school, and is best known for the "Sapir-Whorf" or WHORFIAN HYPOTHESIS. His publications include *Language* (1921) and *Selected writings of Edward Sapir in language, culture and personality* (ed. Mandelbaum, 1949). See also HUMANISM, PSYCHOLOGICAL ANTHROPOLOGY.

Sapir-Whorf hypothesis. Synonym for the WHORFIAN HYPOTHESIS.

Sassoon, Siegfried (1886–1967). See RIVERS.

sati or **suttee.** The Indian funeral rite (or person performing it) of self-immolation by a widow, usually on the husband's pyre. Made illegal by British rulers in 1829 but not completely eradicated. From Sanskrit, "good wife." See also FUNERAL RITES.

Saud family, Saudi Arabia. See WAHHABI.

Saussure, Ferdinand de (1857–1913). Swiss academic, educated in Leipzig, who taught at the University of Geneva and is usually regarded as the father of modern linguistic THEORY, especially as applied to STRUCTURAL LINGUISTICS. His *Cours de linguistique générale* (1916) was posthumously assembled from lecture notes. Concepts associated with Saussure include LANGUE AND PAROLE, SYNCHRONIC and DIACHRONIC, SYNTAGM and PARADIGM, SIGNIFIER and signified. See also REPRESENTATION, SEMIOTICS.

savagery. In early proto-anthropological thought, associated with such ideas as ROUSSEAU's NOBLE SAVAGE. In the nineteenth century, SAVAGERY was held to be the lowest level of human existence, from which peoples might evolve (see EVOLUTIONISM) to BARBARISM and finally CIVILIZATION (as outlined in the subtitle to Morgan, below). "Savagery" fell into disuse as social evolutionism became discredited as a theoretical framework. The word comes from Latin, *silvaticus*, meaning "belonging to woodland." Compare PRIMITIVE.

Further reading: Morgan (2000); Kuklick (1991).

Sb. In RELATIONSHIP TERMINOLOGY, an abbreviation for SIBLING. An alternative is G.

scarcity. Insufficiency of resources relative to demand; though the resources may be materials, commodities, or intangible assets such as TIME, scarcity is a major issue in studies of FOOD distribution, FAMINE areas, and so on. Much work here focuses on African societies (e.g. Zimbabwe).

scarification. Marking of the BODY with small scars; in the anthropological sense usually connected with RITUAL.

Schapera, Isaac (1905–2003). South African social anthropologist, born Garies (northwestern Cape), best known for his studies of South Africa and Bechuanaland (now Botswana). Originally a law student at Cape Town, Schapera was drawn to anthropology by RADCLIFFE-BROWN's lectures and went on to study under MALINOWSKI and C. G. SELIGMAN at the London School of Economics. He became a professor at Cape Town before returning to the LSE from 1950 to 1969. His numerous works include *The Khoisan peoples of South Africa: Bushmen and Hottentots* (1930), *A handbook of Tswana law and custom* (1938; 2nd ed. 1955), and *Married life in an African tribe* (1940). He also edited the papers of the explorer David Livingstone.

Further reading: Comaroff et al. (2007).

scheduled caste. See DALIT.

schema. Schema (plural: schemata; from Greek, "form") has several meanings going back to the philosophy of Kant. In anthropology it usually describes a cognitive MODEL (see COGNITIVE ANTHROPOLOGY) through which the INDIVIDUAL understands experience.

schismogenesis. According to Gregory Bateson, a social process by which two people become polarized through their interactions with each other— for example, an aggressive person provokes a passive person into greater passivity, and vice versa. The term can be extended to cover groups.

Further reading: Bateson (1935, 1958).

Schmidt, Wilhelm (1868–1954). See KULTURKREIS, MISSIONARY, VIENNA SCHOOL OF ETHNOLOGY.

Schumacher, E. F. (1911–77). See INTERMEDIATE TECHNOLOGY.

science and technology studies (STS). An interdisciplinary field chiefly influenced by SOCIOLOGY (especially sociology of scientific knowledge, or SSK) that investigates the ways in which scientific research is done, how it is moderated by social and cultural factors, and, in turn, how society is affected by science. STS can be regarded as relativist and radical in outlook, questioning the privileged position of scientific knowledge. Its tributaries include ACTOR/NETWORK THEORY and social construction of TECHNOLOGY (SCOT), which specifically rejects TECHNOLOGICAL DETERMINISM.

The European Association for the Study of Science and Technology has a useful site at http://www.easst.net/index.shtml.

Further reading: *Social studies of science* [journal]; Bauchspies et al. (2006).

scientific racism. A label for nineteenth-century evolutionary theories that asserted that RACE determined cultural outcomes. Associated with early writers such as GOBINEAU, it bolstered white NATIONALISM and

IMPERIALISM, and was opposed by later anthropologists such as BOAS and BENEDICT. See RACISM.

scientism. An excessive belief in the POWER of science to solve human problems, or a tendency to apply methods associated with physical sciences to less predictable human areas such as SOCIAL STUDIES. In this pejorative way (as opposed to simply describing a scientific outlook) first used by Bernard Shaw in 1921. Compare POSITIVISM.

Scott, James C. (1936–). See MORAL ECONOMY, PEASANT.

scrimshaw. The practice among sailors of making carvings on bone, shell, ivory, or similar materials, for example during WHALING voyages.

Second World. Developed and industrialized countries in the communist bloc of the late twentieth century. Compare FIRST WORLD, THIRD WORLD.

secret society. An organization characterized by clandestine RITUALS and activities and the exclusion of certain groups (especially WOMEN). Betrayal of the group's secrets may incur harsh punishment. Certain European and North American organizations (e.g. the Ku Klux Klan) meet these criteria and anthropologists have studied many others, for example in Africa (for instance the MAU MAU) and China.

sect. A group of believers holding views opposed in some way to the orthodoxy of their RELIGION (or political movement). Compare CULT.

section systems. In KINSHIP theory, a way of dividing groups up into sections or classes from which given individuals select a spouse. Associated early on with Australian ABORIGINAL peoples; also observed elsewhere.

sedentarism. In general use, having a way of life or OCCUPATION characterized by sitting (from Latin, "to sit"). It can also be used to describe a community that does not move around, as opposed to one that is nomadic (see NOMAD). See also OBESITY.

segmentary lineage system or **society.** A form of social organization in which opposed LINEAGES determine obligations—new members inherit a place within a pyramidal network of relations branching down from an APICAL ANCESTOR. The possible involvement of entire lineages becomes a key factor in disputes between individual members of different lineages. Notably used by EVANS-PRITCHARD with the NUER, this MODEL has been criticized as not corresponding closely with reality, but has also been developed cautiously in other sites with success.

Further reading: Holy (1979).

self. The INDIVIDUAL considered as separate from their social context in the work of G. H. Mead, MAUSS, and their followers (see e.g. SYMBOLIC

INTERACTIONISM). In this view it is particularly clear that the self will sometimes be at odds with SOCIETY. Compare PERSON.

Further reading: Mead (1934); Carrithers et al. (1985); LeVine (2010).

Seligman, C. G. (Charles Gabriel, 1873–1940). British physician and social anthropologist, born London. Originally a doctor at St. Thomas' Hospital, Seligman joined the TORRES STRAITS EXPEDITION of 1898 and later undertook fieldwork in New Guinea, Ceylon (Sri Lanka), and the Sudan. He taught at the London School of Economics from 1910 to 1934, obtaining the first Chair of Ethnology there in 1913. His interest in psychology influenced his students, among them MALINOWSKI, SCHAPERA, and EVANS-PRITCHARD. His publications, several written in collaboration with his wife, Brenda Z. Seligman (1882–1965), include *The Veddas* (1911), *Races of Africa* (1930; 4th ed. 1966), and *Pagan tribes of the Nilotic Sudan* (1932).

Semang. See NEGRITO.

semantics. A term used in LINGUISTICS, philosophy, and anthropology to describe the study of meanings; in particular, referential meanings (loosely, the relationship between words and the things they describe; see REFERENT). A branch of SEMIOTICS.

semeiosis. See semiosis.

semi-complex structures. Synonymous with CROW-OMAHA systems.

semiology. See SEMIOTICS.

semiosis. The process studied by SEMIOTICS: the way a SIGN functions, involving the interplay of sign, object (that which the sign represents), and interpreter.

semiotics. A term originally from philosophy and LINGUISTICS, developed in differing ways by the philosopher C. S. Peirce and SAUSSURE (as "semiology") to describe the study of signs or SYMBOLS. The three branches of semiotics are syntactics (study of GRAMMAR), SEMANTICS, and PRAGMATICS (study of actual use). Noteworthy semioticians include BARTHES.

Semitic. Semites are people supposedly descended from Shem, the son of Noah (Bible, Genesis 10). They include Jews and Arabs, though the term is often used to specify the former, hence "anti-semitism": prejudice against Jewish people. Semitic LANGUAGES historically included not just Hebrew and Arabic but also, for example, Aramaic and Ethiopic.

Sen, Amartya (1933–). See ENTITLEMENT.

Seneca. See REVITALIZATION.

Senghor, Léopold (1906–2001). See NEGRITUDE.

senses. Interest has developed lately in cultural aspects of the senses considered together, as in the work of David Howes; see also HAPTICS, PERCEPTION, SIGNING, TASTE, VISUAL ANTHROPOLOGY, VOICE.

Further reading: Howes (2005).

seriation. The condition of being in series order; in ARCHAEOLOGY, the placing of ARTEFACTS in a putative (usually date) order.

Service, Elman (1915–96). See BAND.

settlement. A group of people living together. The term often implies recent establishment of living areas, as in a new colony or region, rather than permanence. It occurs in the study of NOMADS, REFUGEES, COLONIALISM, and so on. See also CENTRAL PLACE THEORY.

sex. Sexes are the divisions into which humans and many other creatures are divided for purposes of REPRODUCTION ("sex" comes from Latin, "secare": to cut); "sex" is also an activity arising from these divisions.

"Sex" is usually understood now to refer to biology and GENDER to CULTURE. Anthropologists have revealed a broad spectrum of attitudes to sexual behavior, from extreme prohibition to extreme permissiveness. Some concerns appear to be widespread—notions of SEX ROLES, perceptions of the differing drives of men and WOMEN, and views of what is desirable in a mate. There is often a gulf between ideal and actual behavior. Sex is often "dangerous"—quite literally, from the point of view of MEDICAL ANTHROPOLOGY in the time of AIDS—and has thorny relationships with LOVE and MARRIAGE.

In recent years anthropologists have explored with far greater openness issues of HOMOSEXUALITY (see also GAY AND LESBIAN ANTHROPOLOGY, QUEER THEORY). Sex, like gender, is partly bound up with POWER, and feminist anthropologists in particular have anatomized cultural aspects of PROSTITUTION ("SEX WORK"), TRAFFICKING, and the preference for male children.

Further reading: Donnan & Magowan (2009, 2010).

sex role. The behavior or attitudes a particular CULTURE holds to be appropriate to each SEX. See also ROLE.

sexism. Belief in the superiority or inferiority of people based on SEX, usually the superiority of male over female. Compare MISOGYNY.

'S Gravenhage. The Dutch name for The Hague, the seat of the Netherlands GOVERNMENT. Also known as Den Haag.

shaman. A traditional healer in Asia and other areas (e.g. the Americas) characterized by the ability to enter a TRANCE and mediate with the SPIRIT world and with ANIMALS. Shamans may use HALLUCINOGENS. A number of anthropologists and religious scholars have investigated shamanic practices, among them LÉVI-STRAUSS. One modern school of thought is more skeptical, regarding the label as covering diverse phenomena.

The word comes from the Evenki (Tungus) people of Siberia. See also CZAPLICKA.

Further reading: Harvey (2003); Eliade (2004); DuBois (2009).

shame. See HONOR.

sharecropping. A form of LAND TENURE in which a farmer agrees to work a landowner's holdings and share produce with the owner rather than pay rent. Commonly thought of as an outdated, exploitative system; associated with the late-nineteenth-century southern US, though anthropologists have studied sharecroppers in numerous settings including Italy and Africa.

Further reading: Robertson (1987).

shari'a. The traditional (see TRADITION) law of ISLAM, drawn from the Koran and the Hadith (traditions concerning Muhammad).

Shaw, (George) Bernard (1856–1950). See POSSIBILISM, SCIENTISM.

sheikh. An Arabic term that can be transcribed in a number of ways (e.g. also "shaykh," "shaikh") and that has two distinct meanings: the leader or CHIEF of a given family, TRIBE, region, or STATE; or, a distinguished MUSLIM teacher or (particularly) SAINT. From Arabic, "old man."

Shia or Shi'ism. One of the two major branches of ISLAM (compare SUNNI): Shi'ites are mainly found in Iran and Southern Iraq. They follow the AUTHORITY of the Prophet Muhammad's son-in-law, Ali. From Arabic, "sect."

shifting cultivation. An agricultural system also known as "swidden cultivation" or "slash and burn" ("swidden" is Old Norse for "to be singed"). It involves clearing the land, burning existing PLANTS to transfer nutrients into the soil, a short time of crop growing, and then a lengthy fallow period while the process is repeated elsewhere. Extensively practiced in tropical regions.

Further reading: Dove (1985).

Shilluk. See DIVINE KINGSHIP.

Shinto or Shintoism. A traditional Japanese RELIGION in which the Emperor was believed to be the descendant of the sun-goddess Amaterasu. Characterized by reverence for nature and nature SPIRITS, it was disestablished as the STATE religion after Japan's defeat in World War II.

Shternberg, Lev (1861–1927). See RUSSIAN ANTHROPOLOGY.

Si. In RELATIONSHIP TERMINOLOGY, an abbreviation for "sister"; see also Z.

sib. In general use, a near relation, especially a brother or sister (= SIBLING). In anthropology, a CLAN or number of clans, though the term is no longer current. See GENS for usage.

sibling. Any of two or more children of the same set of parents.

sign. The field of study of SEMIOTICS: basically, anything that stands as a representation of anything else, abstract or concrete. According to C. S. Peirce, signs are divisible into ICONS, indexes (see INDEXICALITY), and SYMBOLS. SAUSSURE divided them as outlined in SIGNIFIER. A group of signs forms a CODE.

signifier. According to SAUSSURE, a SIGN can be understood as having two parts: the *signifier* (the sounds or written image of the sign itself, which are essentially arbitrary) and the *signified* (the underlying concept expressed).

signing. In LINGUISTICS, the use of a LANGUAGE based not on spoken words but on hand GESTURES, reinforced by facial expression and posture. Deaf people use American or British Sign Language, or regional equivalents, to communicate. The academic study of sign languages was pioneered by such writers as William C. Stokoe.

Sikhism. A major RELIGION developed in the Punjab, India by GURU Nanak (1469–1539), the first of ten gurus who defined the faith. Sikhs rejected the CASTE HIERARCHY of HINDUISM and established their own communities, such as the holy city of Amritsar. Following MIGRATION to western countries they have often been distinguished by customary dress, such as the turban. "Sikh" derives from Sanskrit, "disciple."

Silverman, Sydel (1933–). See WOLF.

Simmel, Georg (1858–1918). German sociologist whose writings include *Philosophie des Geldes* (1900; *The philosophy of money*, 1990) and *Soziologie* (1908; partly translated as *Conflict* and *The web of group-affiliations*, 1955). His influence was noted in the CHICAGO SCHOOL and in certain economic anthropologists. See also DYAD, TRIAD.

simple society. A small-scale, family-oriented SOCIETY without significant STRATIFICATION (compare COMPLEX SOCIETY). The term goes back to the SOCIOLOGY of Herbert SPENCER and has connotations of an evolutionary view, as with "PRIMITIVE society." It must be remembered that even "simple" cultures contain elements of complexity. See also SMALL-SCALE SOCIETY, SOCIAL SOLIDARITY.

Sioux. See GHOST DANCE.

sister exchange. A MARRIAGE EXCHANGE convention by which sisters (or those classed using the same relationship terms as sisters) are exchanged between groups as wives. Its meaning has been discussed by LÉVI-STRAUSS.

Further reading: James (1975).

sister's daughter's marriage. An EXCHANGE convention by which a man gives his sister in MARRIAGE and himself marries a daughter of this union. Such an arrangement can persist over GENERATIONS as a form of CLASSIFICATORY CROSS-COUSIN marriage. Notably studied in South America, it is also known as "ZD marriage."

skewing. In RELATIONSHIP TERMINOLOGY, the bracketing under one term of INDIVIDUALS of different GENERATIONS (so EGO's father's sister's daughter (FZD) is called by the same term as Ego's father's sister (FZ), for example). The individuals bracketed thus usually are of the same LINEAGE. See CROW TERMINOLOGY, OMAHA TERMINOLOGY, TRANSFORMATIONAL ANALYSIS. Compare BIFURCATION, especially bifurcate merging.

slash and burn. See SWIDDEN.

slavery. A slave is a person deprived of what most cultures would regard as their rights, to the extent of being owned by somebody else. Widespread at several points in HISTORY, for instance in the United States and Europe, slavery is now technically illegal everywhere but persists in some areas (compare TRAFFICKING).

Further reading: Meillassoux (1991).

small-scale society. A SOCIETY operating simply with few members, as a BAND does, as opposed to a large-scale COMPLEX SOCIETY. See also SIMPLE SOCIETY.

Smith, Adam (1723–90). See DIVISION OF LABOR, NEOCLASSICAL ECONOMICS.

Smith, G. Elliot (1871–1937). Anatomist and anthropologist; a leading advocate of DIFFUSIONISM. Born in Grafton, New South Wales, he was educated at the University of Sydney (becoming a doctor of medicine in 1895). A fellow of Cambridge University from 1899, Smith was made the first professor of anatomy at Government Medical School, Cairo, in 1900 and later held the same post at Manchester University. He collaborated with RIVERS during World War I and held the Chair of Anatomy, University College, London, from 1919 to 1936. His works include *The ancient Egyptians* (1911), *The migrations of early culture* (1915), *The evolution of man* (1924), and *The diffusion of culture* (1933). See also HELIOCENTRISM.

Further reading: Dawson (1938); Slobodin (1997).

Smith, M. G. (1921–93). See PLURAL SOCIETY.

Smith, W. Robertson (1846–94). Scottish religious scholar, born in Keig, Aberdeenshire. His career at the Free College, Aberdeen (1870–81) ended in controversy. He co-edited the *Encyclopaedia Britannica* (9th ed., 1875–89) and became professor of Arabic at Cambridge from 1883. His theory that religious practice *preceded* belief influenced DURKHEIM and others. His writings include *Kinship and marriage in early Arabia* (1885) and *Lectures on the religion of the Semites* (1889; rev. ed. 1894). See also SACRIFICE.

Smithsonian Institution. The world's largest MUSEUM complex (http://www.si.edu), founded in Washington, D. C. in 1846. It includes the National Museum of Natural History (see BUREAU OF AMERICAN ETHNOLOGY), the American Indian Museum, and the African Art Museum. It publishes *Smithsonian contributions to anthropology.*

So. In RELATIONSHIP TERMINOLOGY, an abbreviation for "son." See also S.

social anthropology. The twentieth-century British anthropological TRADITION (as opposed to American CULTURAL ANTHROPOLOGY) in which the focus tended to be on the ethnographic description of a group (usually a SMALL-SCALE SOCIETY and NON-WESTERN) through its social relations and PRACTICES. The distinction between "social" and "cultural" approaches has become less marked recently. See BRITISH ANTHROPOLOGY.

social change. The modification of the character of a social system, either from within or without. In the wake of widespread upheaval during the Industrial Revolution in western Europe (eighteenth and nineteenth centuries), sociological interest grew in constructing theories to account for social change (work was done by COMTE, DURKHEIM, Herbert SPENCER, and others). MARX was a major influence, suggesting that change came by *revolution* as much as EVOLUTION. Anthropologists, working in NON-WESTERN, small-scale groups, were constrained in their views by EVOLUTIONISM and, later, STRUCTURAL-FUNCTIONALISM, which constructed static MODELS of CULTURES. Gradually, grand THEORY—compare METANARRATIVE—has given way to an understanding that social change can be investigated on the micro-level of particular CULTURES, that social change is inherent in all societies, that the TRADITIONAL SOCIETY can adapt aspects of modern TECHNOLOGY, and so on (as seen in the work of GEERTZ), and that phenomena such as GLOBALIZATION are agents of change.

social contract. A notional agreement by which INDIVIDUALS give up certain freedoms to an AUTHORITY in exchange for protection and a code of ETHICS. Associated primarily with ROUSSEAU and earlier philosophers such as Thomas Hobbes.

Further reading: Rousseau (2004).

social control. In SOCIAL STUDIES, the ability of a SOCIETY to regulate itself and thus maintain order and values, for example through INSTITUTIONS. Often linked to the study of DEVIANCE. Social control is a theme in the work of FOUCAULT.

social Darwinism. A THEORY that extended DARWINISM in the nineteenth century to suggest that social groups operate in ways analogous to the natural world, with competition, "survival of the fittest," and so on; used to justify right-wing policies such as *laissez-faire* economics, and what would now be seen as RACISM. Social Darwinism was opposed by DARWIN himself, and is nearer to the ideas of Herbert SPENCER. Compare EUGENICS.

social exchange. The phenomenon of EXCHANGE regarded as a way of making relationships between INDIVIDUALS or groups. Social exchange theory developed from strands in the work of several early theorists (as well as e.g. MAUSS) in the later twentieth century. See also EXCHANGE THEORY.

social fact. A social phenomenon existing independently of INDIVIDUAL psychology but still influencing individual behavior. The idea comes from DURKHEIM ("*fait social*"), who argued that such "real" facts could be analyzed in relation to (for example) law and suicide.

Further reading: Durkheim (1938); Durkheim (1952).

social formation. A MARXIST alternative term for SOCIETY, considered as a specific instance of CLASS relations and tensions and popularized by ALTHUSSER and his followers. Compare SOCIAL ORGANIZATION.

social network. The system of relationships—between KIN, friends, acquaintances, and neighbors—that tie individuals together. Such relationships may vary in the intensity and proximity of those involved, and act as an aid to, and constraint on, the INDIVIDUAL. Increasingly the term is used generally to refer to "social networking" websites that reproduce such relations (e.g. Facebook). See also NETWORK ANALYSIS.

Further reading: *Social networks* (1978–).

social organization. Depending on the background of the writer (for instance, sociological or anthropological) and the time they are writing, "social organization" may imply slightly different things. Early anthropologists such as L. H. MORGAN tied it directly to KINSHIP networks. Writers such as RADCLIFFE-BROWN regarded it as the "doing" part of SOCIAL STRUCTURE—how individuals function within a social framework. For LÉVI-STRAUSS, "social structure" is itself sometimes used to cover these activities. MARXIST theorists later preferred the term SOCIAL FORMATION. In recent years such labels have been used more vaguely.

social science(s). The collective term for all the disciplines studying social phenomena in a systematic way, principally SOCIOLOGY, economics, political science, psychology, and anthropology, with others such as HISTORY and geography overlapping. The claim to be "scientific" rests rather on the use of particular research methods (data collection, mathematical MODELS, etc) than on any claim to produce "laws" of human behavior. The term has nevertheless been challenged by writers such as the philosopher Peter Winch. SOCIAL STUDIES may be employed as a broader label.

social solidarity. The type of social cohesion found in a particular SOCIETY. In DURKHEIM's view, the basic alternatives were MECHANICAL SOLIDARITY (associated with the SIMPLE SOCIETY, whose members shared common values and tasks and a strong COLLECTIVE CONSCIENCE) and ORGANIC SOLIDARITY (found in the COMPLEX SOCIETY, where values and tasks might both be highly divergent and the collective conscience expressed less forcefully, or indirectly). Compare SOLIDARITY.

Further reading: Durkheim (1933).

social stratification. See STRATIFICATION.

social structure. Generally, the system of relationships that binds a SOCIETY together. Sometimes used interchangeably with SOCIAL ORGANIZATION though possible distinctions have been debated by anthropologists such as RADCLIFFE-BROWN.

social studies. A synonymous term for SOCIAL SCIENCES. Its use may indicate a difference in emphasis.

socialism. A political and economic THEORY or system centered around ideals such as common ownership of the MEANS OF PRODUCTION and subsuming INDIVIDUAL desires to universal benefits. Elements of such ideas have existed since the ancient world, and can be traced in (for example) early CHRISTIANITY. Following the emergence of an urban working CLASS in Europe (late eighteenth century onward) and events such as the French Revolution, socialist theories developed more formally, reaching an apogee in the tenets of COMMUNISM proposed by MARX and ENGELS (Marx regarded socialism as an intermediate stage before full communism). While "socialism" is sometimes used as a synonym for the style of communism practiced in STATE economies such as Soviet Russia in the twentieth century, its broader sense is of milder policies intended to soften the human consequences of free-MARKET CAPITALISM.

Further reading: Verdery (1996); West & Raman (2009).

sociality. The desire of people (or ANIMALS) to form social groups, interact, and live together. Originally used in the seventeenth century, sometimes preferred by anthropologists to describe the INDIVIDUAL's relation to SOCIETY.

socialization. The process by which INDIVIDUALS are integrated into a SOCIETY, adopting its CULTURE through behavior and values. Although Margaret MEAD distinguished between ENCULTURATION (the process of learning a particular culture) and socialization (which takes in the more general "species-wide requirements" of human society), the terms are interchangeable.

Further reading: Mead (1963).

society. The total of organized human interaction, both in general and within specific groups (e.g. "Alur society"). Different societies were historically thought of as bounded by political STATES in the west, though this is less applicable in some societies studied by anthropologists, and less true anywhere with greater MIGRATION, GLOBALIZATION, and TRANS-NATIONALISM. Debates have centered on whether it is valid to see "society" as more than the sum of its components (as DURKHEIM thought) and on whether it makes sense even to talk of discrete societies within a global community.

KROEBER and PARSONS drew an influential distinction between society (or "social system") and CULTURE, saying that the former should specify relations between members of *cultures*. Confusion often arises because "society" and "culture" are often used in overlapping ways, or as if they were equivalent.

Further reading: Kroeber & Parsons (1958).

sociobiology. The study of biology as the basis for social behavior, usually from a Darwinian (see DARWIN), evolutionary (see EVOLUTION) perspective drawing parallels between ANIMAL and human characteristics. Popularized by Edward O. Wilson in the 1970s.

Further reading: Wilson (1975); Alcock (2001).

sociolinguistics. The study of LANGUAGE in SOCIETY, a field drawing on SOCIOLOGY, LINGUISTICS, and social psychology, from the mid twentieth century on. Sociolinguists may have a particular interest in areas such as the politics underlying language use in multilingual societies, DIALECT versus language, language and GENDER, or language and CLASS.

Further reading: Llamas et al. (2007).

sociology. The study of human SOCIETY, its organization and INSTITUTIONS, and social life and behavior. The term comes from COMTE. To some extent sociology shares the concerns of SOCIAL ANTHROPOLOGY, although its purview was originally western rather than NON-WESTERN; sociologists such as DURKHEIM and WEBER influenced nascent anthropological thought significantly and have been followed in this by PARSONS, DUMONT, BOURDIEU, and FOUCAULT. Nevertheless the two disciplines have developed differently in focus and methodology.

For sociological (or cross-disciplinary) terms see CHARISMA, COHORT, CULTURE, DEVIANCE, DYSFUNCTION, MARGINALITY, MATERIALISM, MODERNIZATION THEORY, SIMPLE SOCIETY.

Further reading: Bruce (1999).

Socrates (469–399 BCE). See ETHICS.

sodality. A group of people drawn together by shared interests; a fellowship (especially in the Catholic church).

solidarity. A feeling of cohesion or unity within a group. Regarding SOCIAL SOLIDARITY, DURKHEIM distinguished between MECHANICAL SOLIDARITY and ORGANIC SOLIDARITY; in wider use the term is associated particularly with the rhetoric of labor unions (as in the name of the Polish union, Solidarność). Feelings of solidarity may also be based on shared ETHNICITY or KINSHIP, particular objectives and interests, and so on.

somatic anthropology. An occasional synonym for PHYSICAL ANTHROPOLOGY.

somatization. The manifestation of mental or emotional disorder through physical symptoms. Sometimes linked to depression. "Soma" is Greek for BODY. Somatization has been studied by KLEINMAN, among other anthropologists.

song. MUSIC performed vocally, often accompanied by instruments. Anthropologists have found much valuable material in folk songs, for instance looking at how they reflect social or political events.

sorcery. The conscious use of MAGIC; an ability to apparently manipulate occult forces that is sought by the sorcerer (contrast WITCHCRAFT). Anthropologists have sometimes taken sorcery on its own terms, as in the work of Paul Stoller.

Further reading: Stoller & Olkes (1987).

sororate. A MARRIAGE CUSTOM by which a man marries his dead wife's sister or sisters. This may apply especially where BRIDEPRICE was paid and where the deceased has left no children. It may also be acceptable when the first wife is still alive but unable to bear offspring. "Sororate" has also been used as a term for general sororal POLYGYNY, a preference for the wife's sisters as co-wives (see CO-WIFE). Compare LEVIRATE, the practice of a man marrying his dead brother's wife. Coined by J. G. FRAZER.

sororicide. Killing of one's own sister, or one who does this.

souk. A MARKET in an Arab country.

soul. The immaterial seat of morality, will, and emotions in INDIVIDUALS, which can be viewed as guiding the BODY. Notions such as the immortality of one's soul go back to Plato in western thought. In some CULTURES souls are held to be capable of moving out of the body, for example in TRANCE states. See also SPIRIT.

Southeast Asia. The region of mainland Asia bordered by India, China, and the Pacific or Indian Oceans and the Andaman Sea, together with a number of islands. Southeast Asia includes Burma, Cambodia, Indonesia, Malaysia, Thailand, Vietnam, and other countries.

Southeast Asia is a large area with a diverse population in terms of AGRICULTURE (e.g. lowland RICE production), ETHNICITY, LANGUAGE, and RELIGION, and a history of colonization by the Dutch, Portuguese, and other Europeans. It has been a focus of much work on KINSHIP (see e.g. CIRCULATING CONNUBIUM) and is associated with authors such as GEERTZ (see INVOLUTION), NEEDHAM, S. J. Tambiah, James J. Fox, and many others.

Further reading: Barnes (1974); King (2008).

sovereignty. The final source of AUTHORITY, whether vested in a monarch, GOVERNMENT, STATE, "the people," or another entity. Sovereignty has been investigated in numerous cultures, and is a theme in the work of the philosopher Giorgio Agamben.

Soviet anthropology. See RUSSIAN ANTHROPOLOGY.

Sp or E. In RELATIONSHIP TERMINOLOGY, the abbreviation for "spouse."

space. Spatial relations have been understood as social constructions at least since the time of DURKHEIM. Anthropologists have discovered a wide range of understandings about space, such as differentiations between types of area, and buildings that reflect a particular COSMOLOGY. The study of space is often linked to that of TIME. See also PROXEMICS.

Further reading: Coleman & Collins (2006).

speech act. In LINGUISTICS, an utterance by which one accomplishes a social ACT. Speech act THEORY is associated with the work of J. L. Austin and (for example) Dell Hymes in anthropology. Kinds of speech act include ILLOCU-TION, LOCUTION, PERFORMATIVE, and PERLOCUTION; see also PRAGMATICS.

Further reading: Austin (1975).

speech community. A group of people who share a particular LANGUAGE, DIALECT, or speech style. Anthropologists such as Dell Hymes and William Labov have investigated speech communities. COMPETENCE in a particular form of speech may no longer be restricted to those born in a particular area, as global COMMUNICATION increases.

Spencer, Baldwin (1860–1929). See ABORIGINAL, AUSTRALIAN ANTHRO-POLOGY, GROUP MARRIAGE.

Spencer, Herbert (1820–1903). English sociologist; a major figure in nineteenth-century thought. Born in Derby, Spencer was originally a railway engineer. He eschewed academic life but wrote copiously, espousing a *laissez-faire* approach and adapting evolutionary theory to social life. SOCIAL DARWINISM, as this became known, was a key strand of the late-Victorian outlook. Spencer's publications include *The principles of biology* (1864)— which includes the phrase "survival of the fittest"—and the multi-volume *Descriptive sociology* (1873 onward). Although his vision was rejected by later writers, Spencer remains a formative influence on the SOCIAL SCIENCES. See also SIMPLE SOCIETY, SUPERORGANIC.

spheres of exchange. Discrete arenas for EXCHANGE identified by Paul Bohannan among the Tiv of Nigeria in the 1950s.

Further reading: Hornborg (2007).

Spier, L. (1893–1961). See CROW TERMINOLOGY, ESKIMO TERMINOLOGY, IROQUOIS TERMINOLOGY.

spirit. A nebulous term sometimes regarded as synonymous with SOUL, though as with many English words it may not cover all the implications of equivalent terms in other CULTURES. Often heard in the context of spirit POSSESSION. "Spirit" also occurs metaphorically in many phrases, for example "spirit of the age" and VOLKSGEIST. From Latin, *spirare* ("to breathe"). See also EXORCISM, JINN, SHINTO, VOODOO.

spiritual kinship. A kind of RITUAL KINSHIP often involving religious (specifically Christian) endorsement. The term may be applied in the case of GODPARENTS.

Spiro, Melford E. (1920–). See PSYCHOLOGICAL ANTHROPOLOGY.

Spivak, Gyatri C. (1942–). See VOICE.

sport. Recreational pursuits usually involving physical exertion and agreed rules or conventions. In the western world, often played professionally and enjoyed by spectators. Examples of such sports are baseball, boxing, horse racing, soccer, and swimming. Anthropological interest in sport often turns on the behavior and attitudes of supporters of teams or individuals involved in contests, political contexts, and so on, touching for instance on questions of NATIONALISM and VIOLENCE. Compare ANIMALS, GAME THEORY, HUNTING, PLAY.

Srinivas, M. N. (1916–99). See INDIAN ANTHROPOLOGY.

state. A highly developed form of GOVERNMENT often found in COMPLEX SOCIETY. A state will usually manage a large and diverse population, be accepted as the source of AUTHORITY and POWER, and have its SOVEREIGNTY recognized by other states.

Much early work in what became POLITICAL ANTHROPOLOGY concerned the processes of STATE FORMATION; latterly many writers have turned their attention to the relations between state and SOCIETY, sometimes from a critical perspective. See also ACEPHALOUS, ALTHUSSER, ASIATIC MODE OF PRODUCTION, BORDER, CAPITALISM, CIVIL SOCIETY, GERONTOCRACY, HEGEMONY, HUMAN RIGHTS, IDEOLOGY, IMPERIALISM, INSTITUTION, NATIONALISM, NEOLIBERALISM, ORIENTAL DESPOTISM, SOCIALISM.

Further reading: Sharma & Gupta (2006).

state formation. The process by which a STATE evolves out of earlier groups. An area of debate among theorists; while some have attempted to isolate specific precipitants of state formation (e.g. the need to organize IRRIGATION), later anthropologists have suggested it is a more complex process involving several factors.

Further reading: Engels (2001); Krohn-Hansen & Nustad (2005).

statistical model. For LÉVI-STRAUSS, a MODEL of social activity that covers phenomena too complex or variable to be represented accurately by a simpler MECHANICAL MODEL. For example, if one studies a society in which marriage partners are selected by personal choice (rather than by conforming to cultural PRESCRIPTION/PROSCRIPTION), one can use STATISTICS to collate and analyze the partner choices that have already been made in that society in order to determine what choices of partner would be more or less likely in a given case.

Further reading: Lévi-Strauss (1963: 283–9).

statistics. Statisticians gather and interpret numerical data, using methods such as SAMPLING a given "population" and deploying highly developed techniques to adjust results and to validate what they infer. Statistical methods are widely applied in the SOCIAL SCIENCES. See also QUALITATIVE/ QUANTITATIVE.

status. Status describes a position in a system, such as that of the INDIVIDUAL in a SOCIETY, and it implies separately the prestige or HONOR derived therefrom.

MAINE contrasted status with CONTRACT; perhaps more importantly for anthropologists, Ralph Linton distinguished status from ROLE: status is a kind of office occupied by people who then fulfill the appropriate role (one person has numerous statuses: employer, husband, consumer, and so on).

The major theorist of the "prestige" sense of status is WEBER, who drew a distinction from POWER and CLASS (the poor and weak can still have high status). Weber's work has been followed up by BOURDIEU and others, who have investigated (broadly) status as a socially negotiated value.

Further reading: Linton (1936).

stem family. The most compact form of EXTENDED FAMILY: a household containing two GENERATIONS, usually an older NUCLEAR FAMILY and their eldest son's family. First identified in Europe by Frédéric Le Play in the nineteenth century; debated since then.

step-relations. The PREFIX "step-" denotes a relation who is linked to EGO through a MARRIAGE to one of Ego's parents. If Ego's father dies or divorces and Ego's mother remarries, the new husband is Ego's stepfather; if the stepfather has a daughter she becomes Ego's stepsister. The term has its roots in the Old English for "bereaved" (although it has lost its associations with DEATH).

Steward, Julian (1902–72). US cultural anthropologist; a key figure in the development of cultural ecology or ECOLOGICAL ANTHROPOLOGY and the study of ADAPTATION. Born in Washington, D. C., he was educated at Cornell and the University of California. After fieldwork among the Shoshoni, Steward taught in several places, latterly Columbia (1946–52) and Illinois (1952–70). He also headed the Institute of Social Anthropology at the SMITHSONIAN INSTITUTION from 1943 to 1946. His works include *Theory of culture change* (1955) and the seven-volume *Handbook of South American Indians* (ed., 1946–59). See also CULTURAL CORE, EVOLUTIONISM.

stigma. Originally a physical sign (from Greek, "mark of a brand"); later also an abstract quality ascribed to a person who is made to feel blemished or devalued in their CULTURE. Stigma can attach to one's appearance (e.g. disfigurement) or any behavior linked to DEVIANCE: non-mainstream sexual ETHICS, some kinds of ILLNESS, connections with CRIME, and so on.

Further reading: Goffman (1990).

stochastic. In mathemathics and STATISTICS: random, not easily predictable.

Stokoe, William C. (1919–2000). See SIGNING.

Stoller, Paul (1947–). See SORCERY.

Stonehenge (England). See PLACE.

story-telling. See NARRATIVE.

Strathern, Andrew (1939–). See MELANESIA, STRATHERN [M.].

Strathern, Marilyn (1941–). British social anthropologist noted for her important work on KINSHIP, GENDER, and PROPERTY, often challenging conventional scholarly wisdom. Following education at Cambridge she undertook fieldwork in New Guinea (1964–5 and 1967), producing *Self-decoration in Mount Hagen* (with Andrew Strathern, to whom she was then married) in 1971. She held professorships at Manchester (1985–93) and Cambridge (1993–2008); her later publications include *The gender of the gift* (1988), *Reproducing the future* (1992), and *Kinship, law and the unexpected* (2005). See also MELANESIA.

stratification. Stratification is the deposit or formation of layers. Social stratification is the emergence of different social levels based on occupational, economic, political, ethnic, or other groupings of INDIVIDUALS. This can be viewed positively or negatively (by linking the strata, for example to POWER or INEQUALITY). Manifestations of social stratification include CASTE, CLASS, and other kinds of HIERARCHY.

Further reading: Sahlins (1958); Béteille (1996); Nutini & Isaac (2009).

Strauss, Anselm L. (1916–96). See GROUNDED THEORY.

structural adjustment. In DEVELOPMENT, a group of economic policies endorsed by the International Monetary Fund and the World Bank from the 1980s on, under which failing THIRD WORLD countries were encouraged to reduce STATE expenditure on welfare and to deregulate their MARKETS (following the tenets of NEOLIBERALISM).

structural anthropology. See STRUCTURALISM.

structural form. A term used by RADCLIFFE-BROWN to describe the conventional social relations that obtain in a particular SOCIETY. While precise details of these relationships would change relatively quickly, the *kind* of relations involved would not.

Further reading: Radcliffe-Brown (1952: chapter 10).

structural-functionalism. A potentially confusing phrase that has several meanings. It is used in political science and SOCIOLOGY, with different implications (in sociology it refers to a method of PARSONS). In anthropology it denotes the form of FUNCTIONALISM (arguably) espoused by RADCLIFFE-BROWN, who, like other early leaders of British SOCIAL ANTHROPOLOGY, was influenced by DURKHEIM in his thought. He viewed SOCIAL STRUCTURES as the framework within which SOCIETY is able to *function*, as if it were a living organism. This viewpoint held sway in much of British anthropology in the mid twentieth century.

Further reading: Radcliffe-Brown (1952).

structural linguistics. An approach to LINGUISTICS derived from SAUSSURE and given weight in anthropology by JAKOBSON's influence on LÉVI-STRAUSS. Structural linguistics looks beyond surface features to the (unconscious) rules by which linguistic components (such as PHONEMES) are combined in order to produce meaning. The method fed into wider STRUCTURALISM.

structural Marxism. A strain of MARXIST theory associated with ALTHUSSER and incorporating elements of STRUCTURALISM. Some major issues in 1970s anthropology were the nature of "pre-capitalist" economies and the varieties of the MODE OF PRODUCTION. French anthropologists such as Claude Meillasoux wrote on such areas.

structural violence. A similar idea to BOURDIEU's theory of SYMBOLIC VIOLENCE; the term is used by peace theorist Johan Galtung to label systemic, indirect oppression of certain groups.

Further reading: Galtung (1969).

structuralism. An influential approach in several fields, particularly LINGUISTICS, in which the focus is not the surface "meaning" of phenomena but the elements underlying them, which are understood in *relation* to each other.

"Structural anthropology," in the work of LÉVI-STRAUSS, developed the method of SAUSSURE and JAKOBSON in what became known as STRUCTURAL LINGUISTICS to posit a "GRAMMAR" of human mental activity and communication based on the combination of PHONEME-like symbols or elements; things are less meaningful in themselves than they are in relationships (particularly relationships of BINARY OPPOSITION). Such theories had common ground with CYBERNETICS.

Lévi-Strauss went on from the mid twentieth century to apply the structuralist method in studies of KINSHIP, TOTEMISM, and the MIND; he produced much work on MYTH (see MYTHEME), which he again argued worked by the relationship *between* myths.

Although structuralism became fashionable widely (in literature and the arts, as well as academia), it remained controversial. Nevertheless, it was very influential in anthropological thought, and led to STRUCTURAL MARXISM, POST-STRUCTURALISM, and DECONSTRUCTIONISM. See also DUTCH ANTHROPOLOGY, JOSSELIN DE JONG.

Further reading: Lévi-Strauss (1963, 1977[b]); Deliège (2004).

structuration. See PRACTICE THEORY.

structure. In SOCIOLOGY, the broad social context (institutions, conventions, rules) within which AGENCY operates. Compare STRUCTURALISM.

STS. See SCIENCE AND TECHNOLOGY STUDIES.

style. In LANGUAGE, the expressive features of a writer or speaker, or of a literary group or era, that give them a particular character. The style of an eighteenth-century British poet will differ from that of a modern Mexican folk singer, even if they are describing the same subject.

subaltern. In general, relating to an inferior, for example a junior army officer; in SOCIAL SCIENCES, connected with the "Subaltern studies" produced by Ranajit Guha and others in the 1980s, which presented an alternative view of HISTORY focusing on those who had previously been marginalized by mainstream DISCOURSE and its IDEOLOGY. See also VOICE.

Further reading: Guha (1997).

subculture. A small and usually not powerful (see POWER) group within a larger CULTURE that may be differentiated by unorthodox attitudes and life-style. Such groups may share a particular ETHNICITY and/or CLASS, and in the west are often associated with YOUTH movements and marked by fash-ion and choice of MUSIC (e.g. punks, Rastafarians, skinheads, Teddy boys).

Further reading: Hebdige (2003); Hall & Jefferson (2006).

subincision. An INITIATION RITUAL among Australian ABORIGINAL peoples involving cutting along the underside of the penis. Compare CIRCUMCISION.

Further reading: Cawte (1968).

subjectivism. A philosophical standpoint holding that all knowledge is subjective and that there are no "objective" truths. In social THEORY, an approach foregrounding the AGENCY of INDIVIDUALS—subjects—rather than the quantification of things (objects). Compare EMPIRICISM, INTERSUBJECTIVITY, OBJECTIVISM, POSITIVISM.

subsistence. From Latin, "be adequate to": the minimum required for basic needs (e.g. for FOOD, shelter, CLOTHING). Subsistence AGRICULTURE involves the PRODUCTION of food for a group's immediate needs, rather than for example CASH CROPS. Subsistence agriculture is frequently mixed with a degree of production for sale or EXCHANGE.

Further reading: Gudeman (2004).

substantivism. See FORMALIST/SUBSTANTIVIST DEBATE.

succession. The process whereby things or INDIVIDUALS follow one another, most often used to mean the transfer of an office or title, frequently from an older to a younger person, typically when the first holder dies. Compare INHERITANCE (an individual may succeed *by* inheritance).

Further reading: Goody (1966).

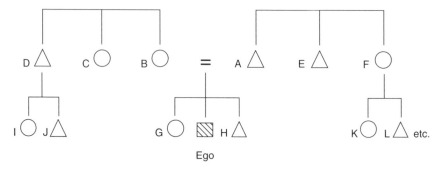

Figure 25   Sudanese terminology.

Sudanese terminology. A RELATIONSHIP TERMINOLOGY labeled by G. P. MURDOCK that uses fully DESCRIPTIVE KINSHIP: that is, it distinguishes between all first COUSINS and siblings, parents' siblings, and so on. Usually found in patrilineal societies of North-East Africa.

Further reading: Murdock (1949).

suffering. The experience of physical pain—as caused by DISEASE or ILLNESS, injury, and disability—and/or mental distress associated with POVERTY, VIOLENCE, WAR, and INEQUALITY.

The notion of suffering covers a wide range of human (and ANIMAL) concerns. In its physical sense it is a major concern of MEDICAL ANTHROPOLOGY, and the more general aspects are of interest to all kinds of sociologists and anthropologists, who may be concerned with political or POWER issues, economics, and/or ETHICS (including the ROLE of the observer). Suffering is also a core concept in a number of RELIGIONS, for instance BUDDHISM and CHRISTIANITY. Compare EVIL and see THEODICY.

Further reading: Kleinman et al. (1997); Mattingly (2010).

suffix. In GRAMMAR, an element placed at the end of a word or form that makes a new word (e.g. in English "-ness") or acts in an inflectional way (e.g. "-en") or creates derivatives (e.g. "-ly"). Compare PREFIX.

Sufism. An ascetic strand within ISLAM that developed from the eighth century onward. Sufis are named after the rough woolen garments they originally wore (*suf* is Arabic for wool) and historically encountered difficulties for what were viewed as contentious beliefs. Sufi leaders are called SHEIKHs and there are numerous Sufi brotherhoods. They are associated with poetry and MUSIC, chanting, and a commitment to an intense personal understanding of God.

Sumerian (language). See CUNEIFORM, WRITING SYSTEMS.

Sumner, William G. (1840–1910). See ETHNOCENTRISM, FOLKWAYS, MORES.

Sunni. An adherent of one of the two main branches of ISLAM (compare SHIA). The Sunni comprise the mainstream of Islam; they are literally followers of the Sunna, the body of Islamic CUSTOM ("path") derived from the Prophet Muhammad. They acknowledge the AUTHORITY of the first four CALIPHS.

supernatural. The realm above or beyond ordinary human experience and knowledge—religious or WITCHCRAFT phenomena, MAGIC, or SORCERY. Used with caution by contemporary anthropologists.

Further reading: White (2003).

superorganic. The elements of CULTURE transcending the INDIVIDUAL. An evolutionary analogy applying to humans and other social ANIMALS, introduced by Herbert SPENCER in 1862, and popularized in anthropology by KROEBER.

Further reading: Kroeber (1952).

superstition. An irrational belief or PRACTICE, associated with the unknown or RELIGION, or perhaps fear of particular things (a western example would be not walking under ladders). The origins of particular superstitions may have been lost over time. Since the judgment implied by the term is subjective, anthropologists normally only use it in the context of the people in question's own perceptions. Compare EVIL EYE, MAGIC.

superstructure. See BASE AND SUPERSTRUCTURE.

surface structure. See DEEP STRUCTURE.

surplus. In economics, that which is produced beyond basic requirements. MARXIST theory talks of "surplus value"—the value of what remains after PRODUCTION costs have been met. This surplus may be taken by the owner of the MEANS OF PRODUCTION.

surrogacy. A surrogate is a substitute for another; thus, a surrogate mother (or GESTATIONAL MOTHER) is a woman who agrees to bear a child for another with the intention that the other party will assume responsibility for the child at birth. Much debate has taken place over the legal and ethical issues involved, which include the possibility of the surrogate wishing to keep the child and the question of payments that may be demanded (illegally, in some countries).

sustainable development. A refinement of DEVELOPMENT theory that emphasizes meeting current needs without depleting resources available to future generations, and conserving the ENVIRONMENT. It has been particularly significant in politics since the World Commission on Environment and Development in the 1980s and the 1992 "Earth Summit" (UN Conference on Environment and Development). Offshoots include "sustainable TOURISM." Sustainable development has been attacked both by critics who want its scope increased and by those who want it diminished (in favor of free MARKET economics). Many GOVERNMENTS have been criticized for their track record on sustainability.

suttee. See SATI.

Swazi. See RITUAL OF REBELLION.

swidden. See SHIFTING CULTIVATION.

switching. See CODE-SWITCHING.

symbol. A word or object representing another abstract or concrete entity, as in SIGNS (e.g. ICONS), PICTOGRAMS, and so on. Objects with symbolic meanings might include flags, Christian crosses, or royal crowns. The domain of SYMBOLIC ANTHROPOLOGY. Symbols are of great importance in SEMIOTICS and the study of RELIGION, RITUAL, CLOTHING, DANCE, GESTURE, LANGUAGE in general, and MONEY. From Greek, "token."

Further reading: Womack (2005).

symbolic anthropology. An approach particularly associated with the work of later twentieth century writers such as TURNER and GEERTZ, in which a CULTURE is regarded as a kind of symbolic system to be evaluated by analysis of RITUAL and MYTH, as well as of dress, games, art, and other elements. Partly influenced by STRUCTURALISM, it yielded several anthropological classics. See also HERMENEUTICS, INTERPRETIVE ANTHROPOLOGY.

Further reading: Turner (1967); Sperber (1975); Dolgin et al. (1977).

symbolic capital. An INDIVIDUAL's social prestige regarded as a commodity that might be exchanged for recognition or tangible benefits. Associated with the work of Pierre BOURDIEU. Compare CULTURAL CAPITAL.

Further reading: Bourdieu (1977: 171–83).

symbolic interactionism. A social THEORY associated with the work of G. H. Mead and Herbert Blumer that stressed dynamic relations between the individual and their social context, based on the notion that the social actors involved in COMMUNICATION share a common understanding of meanings. This contrasts with the approach of BEHAVIORISM; compare TRANSACTIONALISM.

Further reading: Blumer (1986).

symbolic violence. A notion in the work of BOURDIEU that groups that are dominated are led to unconsciously accept their domination, thus obviating the need for actual VIOLENCE to oppress them. Compare HEGEMONY and STRUCTURAL VIOLENCE. Bourdieu also spoke similarly of the force of "symbolic power."

symmetrical alliance or **exchange.** MARRIAGE exchange in which DIRECT EXCHANGE takes place—that is, equally between two groups—as opposed to GENERALIZED EXCHANGE. See also ALLIANCE.

sympathetic magic. The attempt to produce a desired MAGIC outcome at one remove. FRAZER categorizes it into "homeopathic/imitative" (involving the principle of like actions producing like; for instance, the practice of sticking pins into dolls) and "contagious magic" (the belief that items once connected to others can still affect them; for example, use of human hair or fingernails, or personal possessions, in charms).

Further reading: Frazer (1911).

synchronic. A term derived from the linguistic work of SAUSSURE that indicates a concern with a situation at a particular time; contrast DIACHRONIC. "Social anthropologists generally study synchronic problems while historians study diachronic problems" (see Evans-Pritchard 1951: 60f).

synchronic linguistics. A synonym for DESCRIPTIVE LINGUISTICS.

syncretism. In RELIGION, the adoption of elements of one religion into the fabric of another; used by anthropologists to refer to analogous cultural processes, sometimes in preference to ACCULTURATION.

syntagm or **syntagma.** In LINGUISTICS, following SAUSSURE, an arrangement of two or more words in sequence. The units of the syntagm derive meaning from their context. From Greek, "arrange together." Compare PARADIGM, which in the linguistic sense refers to what Saussure called "associative relations": that is, a number of conceptually related units that might replace any *single* unit of a sentence. See also SYNTAX.

Further reading: Saussure (1983).

syntax. The aspect of GRAMMAR that is concerned with the relationships of words in a sentence and the rules governing such relationships. See also SYNTAGM.

system. A group of elements that are interconnected and may often be held to have a particular function (see FUNCTIONALISM). In STRUCTURAL-FUNCTIONALISM, the SOCIETY as a whole can be seen as a system; such a system can be subdivided into smaller INSTITUTIONS.

systems theory. A perspective emphasizing the interrelatedness (SYSTEM) of social or ecological phenomena (as in CYBERNETICS). In SOCIOLOGY it is associated in particular with Talcott PARSONS; in anthropology it was influenced by writers on ecology (and compare SYSTEM) and largely superseded by COMPLEXITY THEORY.

T

taboo. A PRACTICE, person, or thing that is forbidden. From Tongan "*tabu*," first recorded in print by Captain Cook in 1777. Taboos are widespread regarding certain activities (e.g. INCEST, MENSTRUATION) and can be regarded as a means of maintaining social order. See also FOOD TABOO, PURITY.

Further reading: Steiner (1956); Leach (1964).

tabula rasa. From Latin, "scraped tablet"(a writing surface that has been cleaned). The THEORY that the MIND begins life with no innate ideas or behavior and that we learn these things socially. Its key advocate was the philosopher John Locke in the seventeenth century. The "tabula rasa" theory argues for the "nurture" side of the NATURE AND NURTURE debate.

Further reading: Pinker (2002).

Talmud. See JUDAISM.

Tambiah, Stanley J. (1929–). See INDIAN ANTHROPOLOGY, SOUTHEAST ASIA.

Taniguchi, Norio (1912–99). See NANOTECHNOLOGY.

Taoism. See DAOISM.

taste. The sense centered on the taste buds, and the abstract ability to make valid judgments in ART and AESTHETICS (studied sociologically by BOURDIEU).

Further reading: Bourdieu (1999).

tattoo. A design made on the BODY using pigment applied by a needle, knife, bone, or similar TOOL. Tattooing is an ancient and widespread ART, used to signify membership of groups or as adornment, though it has also been used

Concise Dictionary of Social and Cultural Anthropology, First Edition. Mike Morris.
© 2012 Michael Ashley Morris. Published 2012 by Blackwell Publishing Ltd.

to mark criminals, for example. First used as an English term by Captain Cook. See also MAORI.

Tax, Sol (1907–95). American anthropologist, born in Chicago and educated in Wisconsin and Chicago; later professor at Chicago (from 1948). Following fieldwork with groups of NATIVE AMERICANS, he became involved in ACTION ANTHROPOLOGY. The founder of the journal *Current anthropology*, he edited *Evolution after Darwin* (1960) and *The people vs. the system* (1968).

taxonomy. The science of CLASSIFICATION and naming, particularly of living organisms; or such a classification. First developed in botany by Carl von Linné ("Linnaeus") in the mid eighteenth century.

technological determinism. The view that social phenomena are determined by the prevailing level of TECHNOLOGY and changes therein. Questioned by some sociologists (see SCIENCE AND TECHNOLOGY STUDIES). See also DETER-MINISM, WHITE.

technology. The ways in which people interact with materials found in their ENVIRONMENT, including the TOOLS and material required to perform tasks, make things, or provide goods and services, and the skills and knowledge required for their use. All technology involves the use of objects to modify existing matter. Technology has been of interest to anthropologists since the subject's early days; writers such as Augustus PITT-RIVERS and MORGAN regarded technological sophistication as an indicator of level of EVOLUTION. Beyond those features explained by practical expedience, technological ARTEFACTS were recognized as embodying cultural values in their design and decoration, and even in the question of which tools and technologies were of concern to a given SOCIETY. Recent approaches to the field tend to synthesize the practical and the cultural. Technology is of course central to the more sociological field of SCIENCE AND TECHNOLOGY STUDIES. See also APPROPRIATE TECHNOLOGY, INTERMEDIATE TECHNOLOGY, ITK.

Further reading: Schiffer (2001).

Tedlock, Dennis (1939–). See DIALOGIC, ETHNOPOETICS, POETICS, TRANSLATION.

teknonymy. The PRACTICE of identifying a parent by reference to their offspring ("father of James"). Widespread in Southeast Asia.

teleology. The doctrine of final causes, especially as seen in nature: in other words, that things have developed as they have in order to serve the purpose they serve. See also HISTORICISM.

Terray, Emmanuel (1935–). See MODE OF PRODUCTION.

territoriality. Preference for a particular PLACE, and the behavior associated with marking such territory and defending it against others. The concept is of particular interest in ARCHAEOLOGY, the study of HUNTER-GATHERERS, and ANIMAL behavior studies.

terrorism. Intimidation through acts of VIOLENCE, such as bombing, hijacking, assassination, or kidnapping, usually for political ends. The term was originally coined at the time of the French Revolution (late eighteenth century) but describes an activity that has existed for millennia. As with many political terms, use of this label may be emotional and subjective as often as it is scientific and objective. In the twentieth century famous "terror" groups included the Irish Republican Army (IRA), ETA (Euskadi Ta Askatasuna) in the Basque region of Spain, and Sendero Luminoso ("Shining Path") in Peru. The African National Congress (ANC) in South Africa is one example of a "terror" group that later achieved recognized POWER. For Americans the "WAR on Terror" followed the destruction of the World Trade Center by Al-Qaida in 2001. In the modern era a good deal of such "counter-terrorism" has involved western GOVERNMENTS operating in the MIDDLE EAST.

Further reading: Strathern et al. (2006); Asad (2007).

text. Commonly, the body of a written work, sometimes in the sense of a particular version ("the text of Shakespeare's play is corrupted"). Anthropologists have broadened this meaning to include not just film, DANCE, and other cultural productions but ORAL LITERATURE too. The process of transcribing a text for study is called "entextualization." See also LITERARY ANTHROPOLOGY, NARRATIVE.

Further reading: Barber (2007).

textiles. Fabrics that have been woven, knitted, or bonded for use as CLOTHING, carpets, or other materials. These include natural fibers such as silk and wool, and various types of synthetic (artificially formed) textiles such as rayon and polyester. Cultural traditions and other facets of textile production have been studied in many places by anthropologists; they are also important to historians and economists.

Further reading: Weiner & Schneider (1989).

Thatcher, Margaret (1925–). See NEOLIBERALISM.

theatre. See DRAMA.

theodicy. The attempt to justify God's ways to humankind, given the philosophical problems raised by his apparent tolerance of EVIL. It may be argued, for instance, that some bad things are necessary for the achievement of good ends. The term was coined by the philosopher G. W. Leibniz in 1710 (originally in French, from Greek "God" and "justice"). Theodicy has been examined by WEBER, among others.

theology. The study of God and his relation to man, for example through the examination of religious teachings. Often understood as limited to CHRISTIANITY, but it is possible, for instance, to speak of "Muslim theology." Subdivisions in modern thought include "liberation theology."

theory. An idea or set of ideas that advances a view of how the world works or should work; often opposed to what actually people do (PRACTICE). Compare PARADIGM.

Theravada Buddhism. See BUDDHISM.

thick description. A term popularized by GEERTZ for a style of ETHNOGRAPHY in which data are carefully accumulated, seen as embedded in a web of cultural meanings, and shown in context. The anthropologist's task is to interpret this complex of information (see HERMENEUTICS, INTERPRETIVE ANTHROPOLOGY). The phrase originally comes from the philosopher Gilbert Ryle.

Further reading: Geertz (2000 [1973]: chapter 1).

Third World. Countries outside the western and communist blocs of the late twentieth century, usually impoverished: mostly in South America, Asia, and Africa. Compare FIRST WORLD, SECOND WORLD. The term is not universally accepted.

Thompson, E. P. (1924–1993). See HISTORY, MORAL ECONOMY.

Thurnwald, Richard (1869–1954). See GERMAN ANTHROPOLOGY.

Tikopia. See FIRTH, POLYNESIA.

time. As with SPACE, time is often regarded as socially constructed—this was, for instance, the view of DURKHEIM. Early studies include MAUSS' essay on the *Seasonal variations of the Eskimo* and, later, EVANS-PRITCHARD's work on the NUER. "E-P" pointed out that peoples with differing interests judged time in different ways.

A stereotype places TRADITIONAL SOCIETY, with a supposedly simple, repetitive sense of time based on daily activities and recurrent festivals, in opposition to western CULTURE, with its requirement for precisely measured time units (see INDUSTRIAL SOCIETY). Some have challenged this dichotomy, denying that traditional rhythms preclude understanding time as, for example, linear and irreversible.

Further reading: Thompson (1967); James & Mills (2005).

tobacco. The product of the plant *Nicotiana*, whose leaves are smoked in pipes, cigars, or cigarettes, or chewed or inhaled as snuff. First cultivated by NATIVE AMERICANS and later disseminated to European colonists and overseas (by the early sixteenth century). Its principle constituent, NICOTINE, is a NARCOTIC. During the twentieth century links were established between tobacco use and cancer. Much interest now turns on sociomedical issues: attempts to restrict or abolish tobacco use, the strategies of tobacco producers and their advocates, and major MARKETS for tobacco such as China. See also DRUGS.

tone. In general use, tone refers to sound quality or character (e.g. loud/soft, harsh/smooth). In PHONETICS, it refers to an accent or inflexion placed on a syllable in the words of some languages to distinguish separate sounds, thus clarifying pronunciation and meaning, for instance of HOMONYMS. "Tone languages" use tones to mark discrete meanings of the same word (as in Mandarin Chinese) or for other purposes, such as tense indicators.

Tönnies, Ferdinand (1855–1936). See COMMUNITY, *GEMEINSCHAFT* AND *GESELLSCHAFT*.

tool. An implement used in TECHNOLOGY, such as a hammer or ax. As well as their anthropological interest (regarding comparative sophistication, decoration, and so on), tools may be studied by archaeologists and primatologists (see PRIMATE).

Topinard, Paul (1830–1911). See PALEOANTHROPOLOGY.

Torres Straits expedition. A seminal moment in BRITISH ANTHROPOLOGY: the Cambridge anthropological expedition to Torres Straits of 1898 brought a number of British ethnologists and others, including HADDON, SELIGMAN, and RIVERS, to the Torres Strait (as it is now called), between Australia and what is now Papua New Guinea. Apart from its pioneering importance in testing ideas through FIELDWORK, the expedition became celebrated for RIVERS' development of the genealogical method (see GENEALOGY).

Further reading: Haddon et al. (1901–35); Herle & Rouse (1998).

torture. See HUMAN RIGHTS.

total man. See *HOMME TOTAL*.

totemism. A totem is the emblem of a TRIBE, CLAN, or similar group of NATIVE AMERICANS or Australian ABORIGINALS, usually an ANIMAL or plant. The group will consider themselves in a special relationship to the totemic entity, and may view their own welfare as bound up with its wellbeing. Totemism has been famously considered by DURKHEIM, A. A. Goldenweiser, FREUD (*Totem and taboo*), and LÉVI-STRAUSS. As with several other areas, it has been argued that notions of totemism are as much projections of "civilized" illusions as they are real INDIGENOUS practices. See also ETHNOZOOLOGY, FOOD TABOO.

Further reading: Lévi-Strauss (1991); Knight (1991).

tourism. The PRACTICE of travelling for pleasure. The term was originally a derogatory one, and may still be used to distinguish between "frivolous" and "serious" travel. Tourism raises issues around CULTURE CONTACT: the tourist is out of context, in a situation where the OTHER is both near and distant, since communication may be hampered by linguistic and cultural misunderstandings—on both sides. The tourist may be resented for their wealth and cheated, or they may themselves exploit their hosts (e.g. in "SEX tourism"). Many of the ethical issues involved in anthropology apply with equal or greater sharpness to tourism—questions of intrusiveness, authenticity, POWER relations, and so on.

Further reading: Nash (2007); Scott & Selwyn (2010).

trade. EXCHANGE involving goods and services being given for either MONEY or BARTER (a person's trade may also be the craft they practice, their means of earning a living). Anthropologists and archaeologists have found trade of great interest as it often involves CULTURE CONTACT with a concomitant meeting of differing values. Throughout HISTORY, trade has been a motive for peoples to meet, and a spur for linguistic development (PIDGIN), MIGRATION, and (latterly) TRANSNATIONALISM; notable areas of study have included the fur trade, MARITIME trades, and so on. See also ASSOCIATION, COMMODITY, DRUGS, MARKET, POLANYI, TRAFFICKING.

tradition. The CUSTOMS and PRACTICES held to have been handed down from generation to generation within a CULTURE, or a particular instance of them. A tradition is often regarded as a cultural birthright; to label something "traditional" imbues it with significance. Tradition may be connected to RELIGION—the notion of a tradition that must be learned in order to participate in a faith occurs, for example, in CHRISTIANITY, ISLAM, JUDAISM.

Tradition, historically, has often been set against supposedly MODERN manners: this division underlies terms such as TRADITIONAL SOCIETY. More recent work in SOCIAL SCIENCES investigates the process by which traditional STATUS is claimed for certain practices, whether they are long-standing or not. See also GREAT TRADITION.

Further reading: Hobsbawm & Ranger (1983).

traditional knowledge (TK). See INDIGENOUS KNOWLEDGE.

traditional society. A problematic term that was used in the twentieth century to designate usually RURAL, non-industrial societies whose mode of life was assumed to change very little over time as against urban, fast-changing ("MODERN") industrial societies. While it works as shorthand, the term is inadequate to cover the range of societies it has been applied to, and overlooks complex reality. Recent work by anthropologists also tends to question the nature of TRADITION itself, and to see it as something claimed in all kinds of society. Compare NON-WESTERN. See also FOLK–URBAN CONTINUUM, PATRON–CLIENT RELATIONSHIP, TIME.

trafficking. TRADE in unethical or illicit goods, historically including arms, alcoholic DRINKS, and DRUGS. Latterly of great interest in SOCIAL SCIENCES regarding "trafficking in persons"—the movement of people (often WOMEN and children) for involuntary labor including PROSTITUTION. Hundreds of thousands of human beings are currently being trafficked around the world. Compare SLAVERY.

Further reading: Montgomery (2001).

trance. An altered state in which the subject appears semi-conscious, unaware of their surroundings, stimuli, or the passing of TIME. Often culturally associated with notions of POSSESSION and such figures as SHAMANS. A trance can be induced by drug or alcohol use, MUSIC, and dance; in some cases it can be willed by such acts as controlled breathing and meditation.

Further reading: Kapferer (1991).

trans-. A PREFIX from Latin usually meaning "across," "beyond."

transactionalism or **transactional analysis.** A THEORY of social EXCHANGE advanced by Fredrik BARTH that stressed the self-interested actions of INDIVIDUALS as opposed to the social factors assumed by FUNCTIONALISM and STRUCTURALISM. It was criticized for paying insufficient attention to cultural constraints on individualism but was influential on later thought. Compare SYMBOLIC INTERACTIONISM.

Further reading: Barth (2004, 1966); Kapferer (1976).

transformational analysis. A method of dealing with RELATIONSHIP TERMINOLOGY associated with Floyd Lounsbury (mid twentieth century) in which terms for close relations are seen as "extended" to draw in more distant individuals. Compare SKEWING, and see TRANSFORMATIONAL-GENERATIVE GRAMMAR.

transformational-generative grammar. A THEORY of LINGUISTICS developed by Noam CHOMSKY in the 1950s. Generative GRAMMAR defines the underlying *possible* sentence formations in a LANGUAGE (the "DEEP STRUCTURE") and transformational grammar according to the way they are *actually* adapted for use by native speakers (the "surface structure"). Since first definition these theories have evolved and the transformational part is now generally less stressed.

Further reading: Chomsky (2002).

transgender (noun and adjective). A person who adopts the attributes of the opposite GENDER from their apparent original one, or who assumes an ambiguous IDENTITY. In general use this term may be a neutral catchall for transsexuals (see TRANSSEXUALISM), transvestites (see TRANSVESTISM), and other groups.

Further reading: Shaw & Ardener (2005).

transhumance. A PRACTICE associated with PASTORALISM: the movement of livestock according to seasonal needs, for example from mountains to valleys. The term derives ultimately from Latin, "across ground."

translation. Translation has numerous meanings in several fields. In LINGUISTICS it usually means the process of transferring a TEXT from one language to another (as distinct from INTERPRETATION, which may imply *speech* in both directions). Translation itself is analogous to what anthropologists do: their work usually involves not only trying to literally comprehend other LANGUAGES or DIALECTS in the field but also digesting the meanings inherent in foreign cultural systems and then rendering these meanings comprehensible to an audience.

In PRACTICE, translation (on the literary level) may involve complications such as trying to render an oral performance as a written text. Traditionally, anthropologists had the same choice as general translators, between a literal rendering ("he take stick in field") or a "free translation" ("he takes the spear and goes to war"). Writers such as Dell Hymes and Dennis Tedlock have followed JAKOBSON in arguing that "poetic" features, as well as performance and context, are central to the meaning of the work being translated, and must be accounted for (see ETHNOPOETICS). Other questions include authorship and POWER: the imbalance between the observed and the observer (who represents the observed textually) needs to be acknowledged.

Further reading: Finnegan (1992); Becker (1995); Rubel & Rosman (2003).

transnationalism. The condition of having interests in two or more nations, which can apply to corporations as well as individuals or families. The issues raised are similar to those associated with the study of GLOBALIZATION and MIGRATION: the tensions of moving between different CULTURES, identities (see IDENTITY), and so on. See also DIASPORA, FORCED MIGRATION.

Further reading: Vertovec (2009).

transsexualism. Transsexual people often feel they inhabit the "wrong" BODY physically compared to the GENDER they feel themselves to be. They may switch sex by surgery, and/or dress in the CLOTHING of their preferred gender (see TRANSVESTISM). As with transvestites, they may be accorded a special social standing or vilified and abused, depending on their particular CULTURE. Transsexual people may prefer the term TRANSGENDER.

transvestism. The PRACTICE of wearing CLOTHING appropriate to the opposite GENDER. In the west, historically studied as a psychological or medical "problem," particularly with regard to male homosexuals and as a form of sexual gratification. Anthropologists have uncovered a variety of "transvestite" practices around the world, however, that may be socially accepted in a number of circumstances. Transvestism may be linked to the ROLE reversals of CARNIVALS, to certain kinds of RITUAL, and to groups of EUNUCHS or transsexuals (see TRANSSEXUALISM). Transvestites may want to change sex surgically, or they may not. See also BERDACHE.

Further reading: Suthrell (2004).

travel. See TOURISM.

travellers' tales. Early proto-anthropological writings from around the sixteenth century: usually reports of marvelous sights seen on sea voyages.

triad. A group of three (things, people). Studied sociologically by SIMMEL (compare DYAD).

tribe. A social group sharing common DESCENT and a common LANGUAGE, territory, and CULTURE. The term usually designates a historical community, or one in a NON-WESTERN context, with possibly derogatory overtones. In modern anthropology, it is mostly used to describe political formations rather than ethnic ones. Compare CLAN.

trickster. A character in MYTH and folk tales who deceives others and may take different shapes, for instance of an ANIMAL. One example is Anansi, an African and Caribbean spider. See also RADIN.

Trobriand Islands. A group of Pacific islands north-east of New Guinea. MALINOWSKI conducted FIELDWORK on the largest island, Kiriwina, between 1915 and 1918. The ideas he developed from this intensive period, and the primacy he attached to fieldwork, were very influential. See also MELANESIA.

trope. A figurative use of LANGUAGE (as in METAPHOR), or a motif.

tropics. The Tropics of Cancer (north) and Capricorn (south) are two parallels above and below the equator (around 23 degrees north and south, respectively); regions within them are characterized by high temperatures and heavy rainfall, with concomitant effects on plant life.

Trubetskoi, N. S., Prince (1890–1938). See PRAGUE SCHOOL.

Trucial states. The former name for the federation that became the United Arab Emirates in 1971. The federation includes the states of Abu Dhabi, Dubai, etc. The name derives from the truce with the British GOVERNMENT in the early nineteenth century.

Tswana. See COMAROFF.

Tuareg. A BERBER people of the west/central Sahara and Sahel deserts (North Africa) associated with nomadic (see NOMAD) PASTORALISM (though some are sedentary) and speaking Tamashek.

tundra. A large, very cold, and treeless region of northern America and Eurasia. The word is Sami in origin.

Tungus (Evenki). See SHAMAN.

turn. In LINGUISTICS, the transitions that occur between speaking and hearing in communication (or their equivalent online, for example). Thus, while Dick is speaking, Jane is listening for cues that prompt her turn.

Turner, Victor W. (1920–83). Scottish anthropologist, born in Glasgow. A product of the MANCHESTER SCHOOL, he is famous for a series of books about the Ndembu people of Zambia—including *Schism and continuity in an African society* (1957), *The forest of symbols* (1967), and others—and theoretical works such as *Dramas, fields, and metaphors* (1974). He taught in the US (at Cornell, Chicago, and Virginia) and became a major figure in SYMBOLIC ANTHROPOLOGY. Concepts associated with Turner's work include COMMUNITAS and LIMINALITY. See also DRAMA, DIVINATION, PILGRIMAGE, ROLE.

Turner's wife, Edith, has also published significant work.

tutelary. Of a SPIRIT or deity (usually): acting as protector or patron of a given person or PLACE. From Latin, "guardian."

twins. Two offspring conceived at the same time by the same mother. The BIRTH of twins may be regarded as good or bad fortune depending on their CULTURE, and may even be linked to INFANTICIDE. Twins also crop up in many MYTHS and legends.

Further reading: Ball & Hill (1996); Stewart (2003).

two-line prescription. A THEORY of ALLIANCE conventions developed by NEEDHAM and others, stipulating MARRIAGE between two halves of a MOIETY.

Tylor, E. B. (1832–1917). Anthropologist, often regarded as a founding figure. Born in Camberwell, Surrey, he was educated in London. Tubercular symptoms led Tylor to recuperate in the US; he explored Mississippi, then Cuba. In 1856 he travelled in Mexico with Henry Christy. He then researched deaf-mute patients in Berlin. Tylor became Keeper of the University Museum, Oxford in 1883 and reader in anthropology in 1884; he was the first Oxford professor of anthropology from 1896 to 1909. He was also president of the Anthropological Society in 1891.

Among his works are *Anahuac or, Mexico and the Mexicans, ancient and modern* (1861), *Researches into the early history of mankind* (1865), *Primitive culture: researches into the development of mythology, philosophy, religion, art and custom* (1871)—which contains the first anthropological definition of CULTURE—and *Anthropology: an introduction to the study of man and civilization* (1881).

In addition, Tylor contributed to the first edition of NOTES AND QUERIES ON ANTHROPOLOGY (1874) and to the ninth edition of the *Encyclopaedia Britannica* (1875–87).

Further reading: Balfour (1907); Marett (1936); Stocking (1987).

U

ultimogeniture. INHERITANCE or SUCCESSION by virtue of being the youngest child; a PRACTICE in parts of medieval England, for example. Compare PRIMOGENITURE, the condition of being first born.

Uluru (Australia). See PLACE.

umma or ummah. In ISLAM, the entire community of MUSLIM people.

unani or yunani. Indian medical system said to be derived from Greek roots and developed by Arab physicians. From the Arabic for "Ionian." Compare AYURVEDA.

underdevelopment. See DEVELOPMENT.

UNESCO. See BARTH.

ungulate (noun and adjective). Of an ANIMAL, characterized by having hoofs—for example, horses.

unilineal. Of a KINSHIP system, recognizing relationship, rights, or obligations based on a person's membership of *either* their mother's or their father's side of the FAMILY *only* (via MATRILINEALITY or PATRILINEALITY), as opposed to ambilineality (see AMBILINEAL), BILATERAL DESCENT, and MULTILINEALITY ("unilineality" is little used).

United Nations. See HUMAN RIGHTS, NGO, SUSTAINABLE DEVELOPMENT.

universal evolutionism. See EVOLUTIONISM.

universal kinship. A KINSHIP system that allocates a place to everyone in the "FAMILY" of a—usually fairly small—SOCIETY.

Concise Dictionary of Social and Cultural Anthropology, First Edition. Mike Morris.
© 2012 Michael Ashley Morris. Published 2012 by Blackwell Publishing Ltd.

universals. Characteristics of human societies that are believed to be found everywhere: it may be argued that all peoples have some concept of KINSHIP and of HUMOR, and some form of NUMBERS, for example. The exact nature of universals is disputed.

untouchable. See DALIT.

urban anthropology. The study of city life, which emerged as a field from the 1950s onward (though compare URBANISM). Areas of ethnological interest have included migrating RURAL populations and the SOCIAL NETWORKS they form, the study of SUBCULTURES, and problems associated with POVERTY, INEQUALITY, MARGINALITY, and VIOLENCE.

Further reading: Hannerz (1980); Low (1999).

Urban, Greg (1949–). See METACULTURE.

urbanism. Urbanism is primarily associated sociologically (it has related meanings in ARCHITECTURE and town planning) with the work of Chicago-based academics such as Park and Wirth around the 1930s (see CHICAGO SCHOOL). Wirth theorized that urbanism—a way of life characterized by living in a city, which historically has increased significantly in recent times—was responsible for phenomena such as breakdown of family ties and lack of community cohesion, thus leading to ANOMIE and lack of ethical restraint, CRIME, and other ills. This was an influential view but has been challenged by anthropologists offering examples of NON-WESTERN cities that do not match this MODEL, for instance in African cultures where strong bonds of KINSHIP persist.

Further reading: Wirth (1938).

urbanization. The process of becoming more urban. Specifically, growth in the proportion of people in a country or region who live in cities. In Europe and the US, associated with the growth of INDUSTRIAL SOCIETY in the nineteenth century (in Europe, particularly, large numbers moved from the country to the town); in NON-WESTERN cultures, where historically urban centers tended to be less central, cities such as Lagos, Nigeria have grown vastly in the twentieth century as urban populations have increased.

Ursprache. See PROTOLANGUAGE.

use value. In economics, as described by MARX and others, the practical worth of a particular COMMODITY or service. Compare EXCHANGE VALUE.

usufruct (noun and verb). The right to make use of others' PROPERTY or resources. From Latin, "use and enjoyment." Anthropologically it has been studied with regard to the use of land and natural features.

usury. See CULTURAL ECONOMY, MONEY.

uterine (noun and adjective). Literally, of the womb; used to describe offspring of the same mother but different fathers. In anthropology it is also a relationship term for DESCENT reckoned from the mother's side (MATRI-LINEALITY). The equivalent term for descent from the father's side is AGNATIC; the more general term is COGNATIC.

utilitarianism. A philosophical school associated with Jeremy Bentham and John Stuart Mill in the nineteenth century; influential in SOCIOLOGY and some anthropology. Utilitarians generally seek the greatest good for the greatest number of people, though this formulation raises a number of issues (e.g. how one balances conflicting "goods," what "good" means). As with many social and economic theories, utilitarianism presumes that people will usually be able to make purely "rational" decisions.

One prominent area for study within utilitarian thought is "rational choice theory"—loosely, the idea that people maximize their own benefits given the social constraints within which they operate—GAME THEORY being one further branch of this.

Further reading: Sen & Williams (1982).

utopianism. A concern with an ideal SOCIETY, as in Sir Thomas More's *Utopia* (1516). Supposedly utopian communities have been set up in numerous places on several occasions, and the idea has been discussed by many social thinkers including MARX and DURKHEIM. From Greek, "no place," with a pun on *eutopia*, "good place." See KIBBUTZ and compare MILLENARIANISM.

utrolateral. A KINSHIP term coined by Derek Freeman for the opposite of ambilaterality (see AMBILINEAL): utrolateral rights may be claimed via one parental LINE, but not both.

Further reading: Freeman (1958: 26–8).

utrolocal. A type of POST-MARITAL RESIDENCE, similar to AMBILOCALITY.

Further reading: Freeman (1958: 26–8).

uxoricide. Killing of one's own wife, or one who does this. See also MARITICIDE.

uxorilocality. The post-MARRIAGE CUSTOM of a couple living with, or near, the wife's family; sometimes termed "matrilocality." Living near the husband's family is termed VIRILOCALITY.

V

valorization. The process of fixing a value on a COMMODITY or currency; by extension, the setting of similar social worth.

value. See EXCHANGE VALUE, MONEY, USE VALUE.

Van den Berghe, Pierre L. (1933–). See PLURAL SOCIETY.

Van Gennep, Arnold (1873–1957). Ethnologist and folklorist; born Ludwigsburg, Germany but associated mainly with France. After gaining a doctorate in Paris, he taught at Neuchâtel, Switzerland (1912–15), thereafter mostly remaining outside academia. His influence on anthropology through his study of the RITE OF PASSAGE (*Les rites de passage*, 1909; English ed. 1960) has been seminal, particularly on authors such as TURNER.

variable. Anything with a range of possible values, such that it may change between being measured at different points. Thus, age is a variable: people inevitably have different ages. The opposite of a variable is a CONSTANT. Variables are of interest to social researchers as they may be set against other factors (including other variables) to produce insights: for example, age set against attitudes to MARRIAGE.

variation. In LINGUISTICS, the study of LANGUAGE variation reveals the diverse kinds of speech employed by individuals in differing contexts—for instance, street slang or DIALECT rather than standard forms of a dominant language. Such choices may be related to background or type of employment, and may encompass POWER relations. Variation is investigated in the work of William Labov and John Baugh. See also CODE-SWITCHING, DIGLOSSIA.

Concise Dictionary of Social and Cultural Anthropology, First Edition. Mike Morris.
© 2012 Michael Ashley Morris. Published 2012 by Blackwell Publishing Ltd.

vector. The Latin word for "agent." It has several meanings; in biology and medicine it denotes an organism (person, ANIMAL, or plant) that carries an agent that causes DISEASE to other species.

veda. Literally, "knowledge" in Sanskrit; the term can refer to all sacred TEXTS of the Hindu TRADITION, or, often, the main four (*Rig-Veda, Yajur-Veda, Sāma-Veda, Atharva-Veda*), which date from before 1000 BCE. See also HINDUISM.

vendetta. A protracted FEUD or (especially) BLOOD FEUD; originally specific to Corsica and areas of Italy. "Vendetta" is Italian for "revenge."

Verstehen. A concept from the German word for "understanding." Associated with Dilthey (see HUMAN SCIENCE(S)) and WEBER, it emphasizes the need to comprehend the motives and views of those studied, through empathy, rather than solely observing them externally, in a "scientific" way. *Verstehen* contrasts with *Erklärung* ("explanation").

Vico, Giambattista (1668–1744). Italian historical philosopher, whose ideas anticipated the development of SOCIAL SCIENCE as a separate discipline from physical sciences. He was interested in all facets of CULTURE, and suggested that societies could only be assessed in the context of the values of their own time and place (compare RELATIVISM). His major work was *Principi di una scienza nuova* (1725, revised 1730 and 1744; *The new science*, 1948).

Vidal de la Blache, Paul (1845–1918). See GENRE DE VIE, POSSIBILISM.

Vienna School of Ethnology. A group of anthropologists including Wilhelm Schmidt and Wilhelm Koppers, operating in the early-to-mid twentieth century and associated with ideas such as KULTURKREIS.

village. "Village studies" are particularly linked with the ETHNOGRAPHY of India and South Asia (especially of CASTE) in the period around 1950–1975.

Further reading: Srinivas (1976).

violence. The intentional use of physical force to injure people or damage PROPERTY. Western thought has a long TRADITION of seeing violence as a "natural" state that must be suppressed in order for CIVILIZATION to work (as in Thomas Hobbes' seventeenth-century writings), but anthropologists have undermined this picture. Some ethnographers have posited a cohesive role for violence itself, or suggested that a "natural" state would actually be peaceful (see PEACE). Issues in the study of violence include *legitimacy*—who is entitled to impose force on others? Is the STATE the only arbiter of violence? What is *defined* as violence? Most societies SANCTION force of some kind, ranging from corporal punishment of children and criminals up to execution, but they may also endorse CIRCUMCISION, the making of INITIATION marks, feuding (see FEUD), RITUAL violence, or SACRIFICE. Attitudes to domestic violence or inter-ethnic fighting may be ambiguous, and on the wider scale regional CONFLICTS and WARS may be endorsed. There is also the area of STRUCTURAL VIOLENCE or SYMBOLIC VIOLENCE. See also DAS, TERRORISM.

Further reading: Riches (1986); Strathern et al. (2006).

virilocality. The POST-MARITAL RESIDENCE practice of a couple living with, or near, the husband's family (sometimes termed "patrilocality"). Living near the wife's family is called UXORILOCALITY.

viri-patrilocal residence. The POST-MARITAL RESIDENCE practice of a couple living with, or near, the husband's father.

visual anthropology. Visual anthropology includes ethnographic film and PHOTOGRAPHY, which have been available since the late nineteenth century, and also other aspects of ART, MATERIAL CULTURE, and MEDIA, as well as consideration of how different cultures "see" the world.

Although early anthropologists harnessed still and moving images to record the "PRIMITIVE" (as travelers had produced drawings for centuries before), the discipline became more reflexive and collaborative—with its subjects—by the time of film-makers such as Jean ROUCH. Rouch was also an early user of cheaper and more available forms of TECHNOLOGY, which have allowed more of the world to tell its story directly, and to evaluate its own image in digital archives. With the rise of websites such as YouTube and the availability of cameraphones, visual material can be recorded and disseminated even in difficult circumstances and under repressive regimes.

Further reading: Banks & Morphy (1999); Ruby (2000).

vocabulary. The collective name for the words or phrases used in a specific LANGUAGE, profession, or interest group, or by an INDIVIDUAL. Also, a list of such terms in a written work (also called a "glossary").

voice. In PHONETICS, "voice" distinguishes sounds produced by passing air through the vocal organs, as opposed to "breath." In linguistic anthropology, voice can be said to be a persona presented by the speaker, an IDENTITY. This may be the speaker's "true" identity or it may be a representation of another person or group, as when the speaker reports the words of another. Following the work of BAKHTIN (see HETEROGLOSSIA) and V. N. Voloshinov, anthropologists have recognized the interplay of such ROLES. The concept of voice is important in DIALOGICAL anthropology and in SUBALTERN studies. From both perspectives, issues of POWER and REPRESENTATION are raised (condensed by Gyatri Spivak in the title of her 1988 paper "Can the subaltern speak?"). Compare VARIATION.

Völkerkunde. The German ethnological TRADITION (see GERMAN ANTHRO-POLOGY). *Völkerkunde* ("folks study") was from the eighteenth century distinguished from *Völkskunde* ("study of folk"). The former equates to social-cultural anthropology (though with distinctive features) of non-European peoples, and the latter to research on German-speaking folk CUSTOMS or ANTHROPOLOGY AT HOME. *Völkerkunde* has largely been superseded by *Ethnologie* as a working term.

volksgeist. The SPIRIT of a people. An idea in early German anthropological thought, shaped by the philosopher Hegel and J. G. Herder, among others, and with parallels in the thought of MONTESQUIEU.

Voloshinov, V. N. (1895–1936). See VOICE.

Voltaire (1694–1778). See ENLIGHTENMENT.

voodoo. A form of traditional RELIGION associated with West African peoples and blending Catholicism with elements of TRANCE and POSSESSION (see also SYNCRETISM). It is found in Africa, South America, the southern US, and the Caribbean, especially Haiti. The word *vodu* designates a SPIRIT or demon in several West African languages. See also ZOMBI.

W

W or **Wi** or **w**. In RELATIONSHIP TERMINOLOGY, the abbreviation for "wife."

Wahhabi or **Wahabi** (etc). A follower of Muhammad Abd al-Wahhab (1703–92), a conservative MUSLIM scholar and SECT leader. The Wahhabiyah are associated with the Saud family, who established Saudi Arabia.

Wallace, Alfred Russel (1823–1913). See DARWIN.

Wallace, Anthony F. C. (1923–). See NATIVISM, REVITALIZATION.

Wallerstein, Immanuel (1930–). See CENTER AND PERIPHERY, WORLD-SYSTEM.

war. Armed CONFLICT can be viewed as an essential part of political change, closely linked to the rise of STATES. Numerous theories have been advanced as to how wars start; the once-fashionable belief in innate AGGRESSION as an ultimate cause has been generally discredited. See also BORDER, PEACE.

Further reading: Haas (1990); Nordstrom (2004).

Warner, W. Lloyd (1898–1970). See AUSTRALIAN ANTHROPOLOGY, YOLNGU.

water. Fundamental issues concerning water include its availability, management, and control (through canals, dams, IRRIGATION, and so on— see also ORIENTAL DESPOTISM), and its EXPLOITATION for FISHING or as a means of navigation. Equally crucial is the *quality* of water available—the degree of POLLUTION, whether it spreads DISEASES, and so on. Water is increasingly important politically, for example in the MIDDLE EAST.

Further reading: Strang (2009[a]).

Watson, John B. (1878–1958). See BEHAVIORISM.

Concise Dictionary of Social and Cultural Anthropology, First Edition. Mike Morris.
© 2012 Michael Ashley Morris. Published 2012 by Blackwell Publishing Ltd.

Weber, Max (1864–1920). German sociologist, born Erfaut, Thuringia. Weber studied law at Heidelberg, Berlin, and Göttingen, gaining a doctorate in 1889. He became professor of political economy at Freiburg in 1894, soon moving to Heidelberg. He had a breakdown and was unable to teach from 1898. He traveled, wrote, and lectured, and co-founded the German Society for Sociology (1909). From 1919 he taught in Munich. Much of Weber's work was published after his death: key texts include *Die protestantische Ethik und der "Geist" des Kapitalismus* (1904; *The Protestant ethic*, 2009), *Konfuzianismus und Taoismus* (1920; *The religion of China*, 1951), *Theory of social and economic organization* (tr. Henderson & Parsons, 1947; originally part one of *Wirtschaft und Gesellschaft*, 1921), and Gerth and Mills' collection *From Max Weber* (2009 [1946]).

Crucial ideas developed by Weber include AUTHORITY, CHARISMA, the PROTESTANT (WORK) ETHIC, the IDEAL TYPE, and ROUTINIZATION. See also CAPITALISM, CLASS, CONFUCIANISM, DAOISM, FEUDALISM, POWER, PROPHECY, STATUS, VERSTEHEN.

Further reading: Käsler (1988).

well-being. Overall happiness, health, and/or prosperity; a quality dependent on subjective judgment that has been of interest to philosophers, psychologists, and economists for a long time and is beginning to emerge as a separate theme in SOCIAL SCIENCES, for instance comparatively between different societies. See ORIGINAL AFFLUENT SOCIETY for an early anthropological example.

Further reading: Corsín Jiménez (2008).

Weltanschauung. A WORLDVIEW, a philosophy of life. The word came into English directly from German in the late nineteenth century. It is associated with such writers as the philosopher Wilhelm Dilthey (see HUMAN SCIENCE(S)).

Westermarck, Edward (1862–1939). Finnish anthropologist and relativist social philosopher who studied comparative sexual behavior and morality (see e.g. PRIMITIVE PROMISCUITY). He was born, educated, and later taught in Helsinki; he also taught at the London School of Economics (1907–30). His works include *The history of human marriage* (5th ed. 1922) and *Ritual and belief in Morocco* (1926).

wetland. An area characterized by being saturated with WATER, for instance swamps and fens.

whaling. The pursuit and killing of whales to obtain meat, bones, and OILS. Traditionally practiced by many MARITIME peoples, whaling grew in scale and sophistication to become a global industry by the nineteenth century.

As whale stocks shrank, attempts were made to reduce overconsumption, culminating in the International Whaling Commission's commercial moratorium from 1985–6. Much energy has been expended by conservationists attacking countries that have rejected or circumvented the ban, such as Iceland, Japan, and Norway. Compare FISHING; see also SCRIMSHAW.

Further reading: Barnes (1996).

White, Leslie A. (1900–75). American cultural anthropologist, best known for his theories of TECHNOLOGICAL DETERMINISM—basically, White suggests that cultural EVOLUTION is tied to the ability to exploit energy sources. Born in Salida, Colorado, he was educated at Columbia University and Chicago (gaining his Ph.D. in 1927). He taught at the University of Michigan from 1930 to 1970. He did fieldwork among the Pueblo people; his publications include *The Pueblo of Santa Ana, New Mexico* (1942), *The science of culture* (1949), and *The evolution of culture* (1959).

Whorf, Benjamin Lee (1897–1941). American chemical engineer, born Winthrop, Mass. and educated at the Massachusetts Institute of Technology. Whorf worked in fire insurance but studied linguistics with SAPIR from 1930. He gave his name to the WHORFIAN HYPOTHESIS. A selection of his writings can be found in *Language, thought, and reality* (1956).

Whorfian hypothesis. An idea taken from the work of SAPIR and WHORF (sometimes called the "Sapir-Whorf hypothesis"—Harry Hoijer's term) that suggests a SOCIETY's WORLDVIEW is crucially influenced by its LANGUAGE, and that such worldviews are varied or discrete. Adherents of this type of LINGUISTIC RELATIVISM might hold either that only PERCEPTIONS are modified by language or that the deepest concepts one has are affected. Despite its permeation of popular thought (e.g. "Newspeak" in Orwell's *Nineteen eighty-four*) the idea has no real scientific evidence to support it.

Further reading: Sapir (1949); Hill & Mannheim (1992); Koerner (1992); Lucy (1992).

widow inheritance or **widow marriage.** A PRACTICE similar to LEVIRATE MARRIAGE (i.e. marriage of a man to his dead brother's wife) except that children of the new union are regarded as the offspring of the living, not the deceased, husband.

Wiener Schule der Völkerkunde. See VIENNA SCHOOL OF ETHNOLOGY.

wife-giver and **wife-taker.** A concept associated with LÉVI-STRAUSS and the study of ALLIANCE. Groups may both give wives (typically via the wife's brother) and receive them. Thus the husband is the wife-taker.

Wikan, Unni (1944–). See BARTH.

Wilson, Edward O. (1929–). See SOCIOBIOLOGY.

Wilson, Godfrey (1908–44). See RHODES-LIVINGSTONE INSTITUTE, WILSON [M. H.].

Wilson, Monica Hunter (1908–82). South African social anthropologist, born Eastern Cape Province. Educated at Cambridge, she did fieldwork in her native country and among the Nyakyusa of what is now Tanzania. She was married to the anthropologist Godfrey Wilson (of the RHODES-LIVINGSTONE INSTITUTE). After teaching at Fort Hare and Rhodes University, she became professor of social anthropology at Cape Town (1952–73). Noted for her studies of RITUAL and SOCIAL CHANGE, she produced *Reaction to conquest: effects of contact with Europeans on the Pondo of South Africa* (1936; 2nd ed. 1961), *Good company: a study of Nyakyusa age-villages* (1951), and *For men and elders: change in the relations of generations and of men and women among the Nyakyusa-Ngonde people, 1875–1971* (1977).

Further reading: Whisson & West (1975).

Winch, Peter (1926–97). See SOCIAL SCIENCES.

Winnebago. See RADIN.

Wirth, Louis (1897–1952). See CHICAGO SCHOOL, PLACE, URBANISM.

witch. See WITCHCRAFT.

witch doctor. One who professes to use MAGIC or SUPERNATURAL POWERS, for healing or to counter the effects of others' WITCHCRAFT and to discover witches. The term is associated with early popular writing on African tribal PRACTICES and is not much used in modern anthropology. Compare SORCERY, WIZARD.

witchcraft. The use of supposedly SUPERNATURAL POWERS. Witches may be considered powers for good or EVIL, and may be of either GENDER, despite the western ARCHETYPE of an unmarried elderly woman. Anthropologists have studied the use of witchcraft beliefs as a form of social SANCTION; Max Marwick saw them as an indicator of "social strain." Although witchcraft is generally synonymous with SORCERY, a distinction is made in the writings of EVANS-PRITCHARD and others based on INDIGENOUS notions: witchcraft is an inherited psychic ability that is not consciously sought; sorcery is a skill that is taught, and cultivated deliberately.

Further reading: Evans-Pritchard (1937); Douglas (1970); Marwick (1982); Kapferer (2003); Ashforth (2005).

Wittfogel, Karl (1896–1988). See ORIENTAL DESPOTISM.

Wittgenstein, Ludwig (1889–1951). Austrian-born philosopher; a key figure in twentieth-century thought. Born in Vienna, he was educated at Cambridge

(1912–13) under Bertrand Russell and later became professor of philosophy there (1939–47). Wittgenstein's later writings on language, such as those in *Philosophische untersuchungen* (*Philosophical investigations*, 1953; 4th ed. 2009), have influenced anthropologists as well as many other thinkers. For examples see FAMILY RESEMBLANCES, LANGUAGE GAMES.

wizard. A popular term for a male witch; sometimes used as a synonym for SHAMAN by anthropologists.

Wolf, Eric R. (1923–99). Austrian-born American anthropologist, noted for his work on PEASANTs and theories of the dynamic nature of CULTURE. Born in Vienna, he emigrated in 1940. Wolf served in World War II before taking his Ph.D. at Columbia in 1951. He taught at City University of New York from 1971 to 1992. Wolf's second wife is the anthropologist Sydel Silverman. His publications include *Peasants* (1966) and *Europe and the people without history* (1982; new preface 2010).

woman marriage. An institution reported among the NUER by EVANS-PRITCHARD (and subsequently in other East African locations by others) in which a woman may marry another woman and thereby acquire the STATUS and PROPERTY rights of a man. The woman is recognized as PATER (the socially acknowledged father) to any children conceived by her wife with a chosen male.

Further reading: Evans-Pritchard (1990).

women. Historically, women have usually been considered as adjuncts or chattels in male-dominated CULTURES. While this has not always and every-where been true (see e.g. MATRIARCHY), it probably also describes the approach of many early anthropologists. GENDER-specific expectations (in both many societies studied and those from which these anthropologists came) were developed chiefly by men, and only rejected by women at some risk. Latterly, with demands for female emancipation, the growth of the "women's movement," and a greater sensitivity to DISCRIMINATION in the west, feminist scholars (see FEMINIST ANTHROPOLOGY) have greatly stimu-lated debates around what women are, how they are socially constructed, the relationship between SEX and GENDER, and so on. Anthropologists have, for example, focused on how WORK is separated into jobs "for" men and women (see DIVISION OF LABOR). See also MISOGYNY.

Further reading: Ardener (1993)

Woodburn, James (1934–). See DELAYED-RETURN.

work. As a term it has many shades of meaning: it may be physical, mental, or a mixture of both. In the west it is commonly related to OCCUPATIONS: a job may give one STATUS, prestige, POWER, and income; conversely, working conditions may create POVERTY, INEQUALITY, and EXPLOITATION. Worse still,

Figure 26   Women. Nadine Beckmann in the women's section at a *hitima* (funeral rite) in rural Eastern Tanzania. Photo copyright: N. Beckmann.

one may be unemployed and lack the financial benefits and fulfillment work can provide.

In NON-WESTERN societies, work may not be geared to the MARKET so much as to the COMMUNITY. Classic ethnographies by MALINOWSKI, EVANS-PRITCHARD, and Audrey Richards are among those that study such work.

Questions raised by work—in either setting, though INDUSTRIAL SOCIETY has been much scrutinized recently—are of great interest also in SOCIOLOGY and economics. MARX and WEBER did influential work on work, and many writers have studied issues of GENDER. These include the question of what is "WOMEN's work," for instance, in the DIVISION OF LABOR, and "sex work" (PROSTITUTION), as well as matters of POWER, ETHNICITY, and IDENTITY. The effects of MIGRATION and GLOBALIZATION have also had an impact in the workplace. Sites for FIELDWORK have included factories, restaurants, medical facilities, banks, and many other institutions.

Further reading: Wallman (1979); Richards (2004); Weber (2009).

World Bank. See STRUCTURAL ADJUSTMENT.

world-system. A concept developed by Immanuel Wallerstein referring to large-scale economic groupings of STATES and smaller units. Within the world-system three types of societies emerge: *core* (or *center*) industrialized economies; *peripheral* less powerful (see POWER) ones; and *semi-peripheral* nations with characteristics in between. See also CENTER (OR CORE) AND PERIPHERY.

Further reading: Wallerstein (1974–89).

worldview. The English TRANSLATION of *WELTANSCHAUUNG*. Associated with the CULTURE AND PERSONALITY school, who followed SAPIR's view that different CULTURES live in different worlds, *not* the same world differently expressed. The term is less used recently as it may imply a unitary attitude within a given culture, as opposed to meanings being contested and in flux. Compare IDEOLOGY.

Further reading: Sapir (1949).

Wounded Knee (South Dakota) Massacre. See GHOST DANCE.

Wovoka ("Jack Wilson," 1856–1932). See GHOST DANCE.

writing. See LITERACY.

Writing culture. The title of an influential collection of essays (first published 1986) challenging then-conventional ways of writing ETHNOGRAPHY; among its concerns are the gap between anthropological THEORY and lived reality, cultural POETICS, and the limitations of the written TEXT. See also HERMENEUTICS, LITERARY ANTHROPOLOGY, POST-MODERNISM.

Further reading: Marcus (2007); Zenker & Kumoll (2010); Clifford & Marcus (2011).

writing systems. A writing system attempts to visually represent speech, provide cues for it, or record information. Early writing systems used PICTOGRAMS, which were capable of being interpreted in different ways; later HIEROGLYPHS, such as those found among the MAYA, incorporated some parts of speech to aid reading.

The most significant, and fully realized, systems developed from fourth millennium BCE Mesopotamia (corresponding partly to modern Iraq): they were based on CUNEIFORM characters representing whole words and included Sumerian-Akkadian and Chinese. Then came the representation of phonetic values, with characters based on sounds (see PHONETICS). By 1500 BCE, proto-Canaanite was developing as the first consonantal alphabet; later, Phoenician, Hebrew, and Aramaic scripts developed. By 750 BCE the Greeks were adding characters for vowel sounds. Most modern western writing systems derive ultimately from Phoenician; Aramaic has been widely influential in the east. Written information can be recorded in many media, and in numerous forms. See also LITERACY.

Further reading: Goody (1987); Coulmas (1996); Schmandt-Besserat (1996).

w.s. woman speaking (in KINSHIP accounts).

X

xenophobia. Hostility to, or fear of, foreigners or what is different.

Xhosa. See BANTU, MILLENARIANISM.

Y

y. A comparative KINSHIP abbreviation to denote that an INDIVIDUAL is younger than EGO: for example, yZ specifies "younger sister."

yagé. Another name for AYAHUASCA.

Yahi (Yana people). See ISHI.

Yanomami or **Yanomamö.** A South American Indian people of the Venezuelan/Brazilian RAINFOREST. Famously studied by Napoleon CHAGNON, they became better known in the west as their habitat was depleted by industrial encroachment.

Yaqui. See CASTANEDA.

yogi. A practitioner of yoga, originally in India; one who seeks thus to obtain "union" with his/her environment.

Yolngu. An ABORIGINAL people of Northeast Arnhem Land, Northern Territory of Australia. Famously studied (including their KINSHIP system) by W. L. Warner, who called them the "Murngin"; later also the subject of works by Howard Morphy and others. See also AUSTRALIAN ANTHROPOLOGY.

Further reading: Warner (1958).

Yoruba. See IFÁ, SANTERIA.

youth. The period following CHILDHOOD, or one who is in this state (the term is applied particularly to males). During youth or adolescence, social influences and activities reflect the physiological maturing of the BODY (attainment of PUBERTY, bringing with it questions of SEX and REPRODUCTION); a young person may begin preparation for their adult life (see INITIATION) in ways that reflect cultural expectations of their GENDER, for instance. (One relevant but contentious study is Margaret MEAD's of Samoan youth). In the industrial west, this transitional period may last longer than elsewhere; "youth CULTURE" may be a topic of interest (compare SUBCULTURE). See also AGGRESSION, EDUCATION.

Further reading: Alexander (1996); Mead (2001).

YouTube. See VISUAL ANTHROPOLOGY.

yunani. See UNANI.

Z

Z. In RELATIONSHIP TERMINOLOGY, an abbreviation for "sister"; Si, S or s can also be used.

Zafimaniry. A Malagasy people (i.e. from Madagascar), notably studied by Maurice Bloch.

zamindar or *zemindar*. The owner of an estate in some parts of India; in other parts (and originally everywhere) a collector of land revenue.

Zande or **Azande**. A Central African people described in detailed ethnographies by E. E. EVANS-PRITCHARD (most notably in *Witchcraft, oracles and magic among the Azande*, 1937).

Zār. A woman-centered phenomenon (or CULT) of Northern Sudan in which POSSESSION by a SPIRIT provides the subject with the opportunity to behave in unorthodox ways, adopting another ROLE. It may be regarded as a CULTURE-BOUND SYNDROME. Compare RITUAL OF REBELLION.

Further reading: Boddy (1989).

ZD marriage. See SISTER'S DAUGHTER'S MARRIAGE.

zero-equation. An occasionally used term for KINSHIP systems in which each KIN TYPE has a unique term (compare DESCRIPTIVE KINSHIP).

zombi or **zombie**. A human BODY lacking a soul; either a revived corpse or a living person whose soul has been removed by VOODOO. From Kongo, *nzambi* (god) and *zumbi* (FETISH).

Zoroastrianism. A dualistic RELIGION of the Parsees, a people who migrated from Persia (now Iran) to the region of modern Mumbai, India, around the eighth century CE. Its prophet, Zoroaster (active around 600 BCE) is sometimes called "Zarathustra."

Zulu. See BANTU.

Zuñi. See CUSHING.

Major Sources

Abercrombie, N. et al. *The Penguin dictionary of sociology.* 5th ed. London: Penguin, 2006.

Allen, R. E. (ed.) *The Penguin English dictionary.* 3rd ed. London: Penguin, 2007.

Barnard, A. & Spencer, J. (eds.) *The Routledge encyclopedia of social and cultural anthropology.* 2nd ed. London: Routledge, 2010.

Barfield, T. (ed.) *The dictionary of anthropology.* Oxford: Blackwell, 1997.

Chambers 21st century dictionary. London: Chambers, 2001.

Collins dictionary of sociology. Glasgow: Collins, 2006.

Crystal, D. (ed.) *The Crystal reference encyclopedia.* 2005. http://www.credoreference. com/entry/cre/the_crystal_reference_encyclopedia

Gregory, D. et al. (eds.) *The dictionary of human geography.* 5th ed. Oxford: Wiley-Blackwell, 2009.

Johnson, A. G. *The Blackwell dictionary of sociology: a user's guide to sociological language.* 2nd ed. Oxford: Blackwell, 2000.

Journal of linguistic anthropology, vol. 9, 1–2, 1999.

The Macmillan encyclopedia 2003. London: Macmillan, 2002.

McLeish, K. *Bloomsbury guide to human thought.* London: Bloomsbury Reference, 1993.

Morris, C. (ed.) *Academic Press dictionary of science and technology.* San Diego: Academic Press, 1992.

Mosby's dictionary of medicine, nursing & health professions. 8th ed. St Louis: Mosby, 2009.

Oxford English dictionary. http://dictionary.oed.com/, accessed 2008–10

Parkin, R. *Kinship: an introduction to basic concepts.* Oxford: Blackwell, 1997.

Palmisano, J. M. (ed.) *World of sociology.* Detroit: Gale, 2002.

Philip's encyclopedia 2008. London: Octopus, 2008.

Stone, L. *Kinship and gender: an introduction.* 4th ed. Boulder, Col.: Westview, 2010.

Concise Dictionary of Social and Cultural Anthropology, First Edition. Mike Morris.
© 2012 Michael Ashley Morris. Published 2012 by Blackwell Publishing Ltd.

References

Ahmed, A. S. *Journey into Islam: the crisis of globalization*. Washington, D. C.: Brookings Institution Press, 2007.

Aitchison, J. *The articulate mammal: an introduction to psycholinguistics*. 5th ed. London: Routledge, 2008.

Alcheringa [journal], 1970–80.

Alcock, J. *The triumph of sociobiology*. Oxford: Oxford University Press, 2001.

Alexander, C. *The art of being black: the creation of black British youth identities*. Oxford: Clarendon Press, 1996.

Alexander, C. et al. (eds.) *Urban life in post-Soviet Asia*. London: UCL Press, 2007.

Alexander, J. C. & Smith, P. (eds.) *The Cambridge companion to Durkheim*. Cambridge: Cambridge University Press, 2005.

American Anthropological Association. *Code of ethics of the American Anthropological Association*. 1998. [Available at http://www.aaanet.org/committees/ethics/ethcode.htm]

Amin, A. & Thrift, N. (eds.) *The Blackwell cultural economy reader*. Malden, Mass.: Blackwell, 2004.

Anderson, B. *Imagined communities: reflections on the origin and spread of nationalism*. Rev. ed. London: Verso, 2006.

Anderson, D. et al. *The khat controversy: stimulating the debate on drugs*. Oxford: Berg, 2007.

Anthropology in action [journal], 1991–.

Anthropos [journal], 1906–.

Antoun, R. T. *Understanding fundamentalism: Christian, Islamic, and Jewish movements*. 2nd ed. Lanham, Md.: Rowman & Littlefield, 2008.

Ardener, S. (ed.) *Defining females: the nature of women in society*. 2nd ed. Oxford: Berg, 1993.

Ardener, S. & Burman, S. (eds.) *Money-go-rounds: the importance of rotating savings and credit associations for women*. Oxford: Berg, 1995.

Arens, W. *The man-eating myth: anthropology & anthropophagy*. New York: Oxford University Press, 1979.

Arens, W. *The original sin: incest and its meaning*. New York: Oxford University Press, 1986.

Armbrust, W. *Mass mediations: new approaches to popular culture in the Middle East and beyond*. Berkeley, Calif.: University of California Press, 2000.

Asad, T. (ed.) *Anthropology & the colonial encounter*. Amherst, N. Y.: Humanity Books, 1998 [1973].

Asad, T. *On suicide bombing*. New York: Columbia University Press, 2007.

Ashforth, A. *Witchcraft, violence, and democracy in South Africa*. Chicago, Ill.: University of Chicago Press, 2005.

Atkinson, P. & Delamont, S. (eds.) *Narrative methods*. London: Sage, 2006.

Austin, J. L. (ed. Urmson & Sbisà) *How to do things with words: the William James lectures delivered at Harvard University in 1955*. 2nd ed. Oxford: Oxford University Press, 1975.

Baer, H. A. et al. (eds.) *Medical anthropology and the world system*. 2nd ed. Westport, Conn.: Praeger, 2003.

Balfour, H. (ed.) *Anthropological essays presented to Edward Burnett Tylor in honour of his 75th birthday, Oct. 2, 1907*. Oxford: Clarendon Press, 1907.

Ball, H. L. & Hill, C. M. Reevaluating "twin infanticide." *Current anthropology*, vol. 37, 1996, pp. 856–63.

Bamford, S. C. *Biology unmoored: Melanesian reflections on life and biotechnology*. Berkeley, Calif.: University of California Press, 2007.

Banerjee, M. & Miller, D. *The sari*. Oxford: Berg, 2003.

Banfield, E. C. *The moral basis of a backward society*. Glencoe, Ill.: Free Press, 1958.

Banks, M. *Ethnicity: anthropological constructions*. London: Routledge, 1996.

Banks, M. & Morphy, H. (eds.) *Rethinking visual anthropology*. New Haven, Conn.: Yale University Press, 1999.

Barber, K. *The anthropology of texts, persons and publics*. Cambridge: Cambridge University Press, 2007.

Barnard, A. J. (ed.) *Hunter-gatherers in history, archaeology and anthropology*. Oxford: Berg, 2004.

Barnes, R. H. *Kédang: a study of the collective thought of an eastern Indonesian people*. Oxford: Clarendon Press, 1974.

Barnes, R. H. *Sea hunters of Indonesia: fishers and weavers of Lamalera*. Oxford: Clarendon Press, 1996.

Barnes, R. H. Marriage by capture. *Journal of the Royal Anthropological Institute*, new series. vol. 5, 1999, pp. 57–73.

Barnes, R. H. *Two Crows denies it: a history of controversy in Omaha sociology*. Lincoln, Neb.: University of Nebraska Press, 2005 [1984].

Barth, F. *Political leadership among Swat Pathans*. Oxford: Berg, 2004 [1959].

Barth, F. The analytical importance of transaction. Part 1 (pp. 1–11) of *Models of social organization*. London: Royal Anthropological Institute, 1966.

Barth, F. (ed.) *Ethnic groups and boundaries: the social organization of culture difference*. Prospect Heights, Ill.: Waveland, 1998 [1969].

Bateson, G. Culture contact and schismogenesis. *Man*, vol. 35, 1935, pp. 178–83.

Bateson, G. *Naven: a survey of the problems suggested by a composite picture of the culture of a New Guinea tribe drawn from three points of view.* 2nd ed. Stanford, Calif.: Stanford University Press, 1958.

Bateson, G. *Steps to an ecology of mind.* Chicago, Ill.: University of Chicago Press, 2000 [1972].

Bauchspies, W. K. et al. *Science, technology, and society: a sociological approach.* Malden, Mass.: Blackwell, 2006.

Bauman, R. & Sherzer, J. (eds.) *Explorations in the ethnography of speaking.* 2nd ed. Cambridge: Cambridge University Press, 1989.

Baumann, G. *Contesting culture: discourses of identity in multi-ethnic London.* Cambridge: Cambridge University Press, 1996.

Baxter, P. T. W. et al. *Being and becoming Oromo: historical and anthropological enquiries.* Uppsala: Nordiska Afrikainstitutet, 1996.

Beattie, J. & Lienhardt, R. G. (ed.) *Studies in social anthropology: essays in memory of E. E. Evans-Pritchard.* Oxford: Clarendon Press, 1975.

Beck, L. *Nomad: a year in the life of a Qashqa'i tribesman in Iran.* Berkeley, Calif.: University of California Press, 1991.

Becker, A. L. *Beyond translation: essays towards a modern philology.* Ann Arbor, Mich.: University of Michigan Press, 1995.

Benedict, R. *Patterns of culture.* Boston, Mass.: Houghton Mifflin, 1934.

Benedict, R. *The chrysanthemum and the sword: patterns of Japanese culture.* Cambridge, Mass.: Houghton Mifflin, 1946.

Benthall, J. *Disasters, relief and the media.* Wantage: Sean Kingston, 2010 [reprint of 1993 ed. with new preface].

Berlin, B. *Ethnobiological classification: principles of categorization of plants and animals in traditional societies.* Princeton, N. J.: Princeton University Press, 1992.

Berlin, B. & Kay, P. *Basic color terms: their universality and evolution.* Berkeley, Calif.: University of California Press, 1991.

Bernard, H. R. *Research methods in anthropology: qualitative and quantitative approaches.* 4th ed. Lanham, Md.: Altamira Press, 2006.

Besteman, C. & Gusterson, H. (eds.) *Why America's top pundits are wrong: anthropologists talk back.* Berkeley, Calif.: University of California Press, 2005.

Béteille, A. *Caste, class, and power: changing patterns of stratification in a Tanjore village.* 2nd ed. Delhi: Oxford University Press, 1996.

Betts, A. *Forced migration and global politics.* Chichester: Wiley-Blackwell, 2009.

Blacking, J. *How musical is man?* Seattle, Wash.: University of Washington Press, 1973.

Black-Michaud, J. *Cohesive force: feud in the Mediterranean and the Middle East.* Oxford: Blackwell, 1975.

Bloch, M. (tr. Manyon) *Feudal society.* 2nd ed. London: Routledge, 1989. [*La société féodale*, 1939–40.]

Bloch, M. *Political language and oratory in traditional society.* London: Academic Press, 1975.

Bloch, M. (ed.) *Marxist analyses and social anthropology.* London: Routledge, 2004 [1975].

Bloch, M. *Marxism and anthropology: the history of a relationship* London: Routledge, 2004 [1983].

Bloch, M. *Essays on cultural transmission*. Oxford: Berg, 2005.

Bloch, M. & Parry, J. (eds.) *Death and the regeneration of life*. Cambridge: Cambridge University Press, 1982.

Blumer, H. *Symbolic interactionism: perspective and method*. Berkeley, Calif.: University of California Press, 1986 [1969].

Boas, F. Evolution or diffusion? *American anthropologist*, vol. 26, 1924, pp. 340–4.

Boas, F. *Race, language and culture*. Chicago, Ill.: University of Chicago Press, 1994 [1940].

Boas, F. (ed. Stocking) *The shaping of American anthropology, 1883–1911: a Franz Boas reader*. New York: Basic Books, 1974.

Boddy, J. *Wombs and alien spirits: women, men, and the Zār cult in Northern Sudan*. Madison, Wis.: University of Wisconsin Press, 1989.

Bosk, C. L. *What would you do? Juggling bioethics and ethnography*. Chicago, Ill.: University of Chicago Press, 2008.

Bourdieu, P. (tr. Nice) *Outline of a theory of practice*. Cambridge: Cambridge University Press, 1977. [*Esquisse d'une théorie de la pratique*, 1972.]

Bourdieu, P. (tr. Nice) *The logic of practice*. Cambridge: Polity, 1990. [*Le sens pratique*, 1980.]

Bourdieu, P. (tr. Nice) *Distinction: a social critique of the judgement of taste*. London: Routledge, 1999 [1984]. [*La distinction*, 1979.]

Bourdieu, P. & Passeron, J.-C. (tr. Nice) *Reproduction in education, society and culture*. 2nd ed. London: Sage, 1990. [*La reproduction*, 1977.]

Bowden, M. *Pitt Rivers: the life and archaeological work of Lieutenant-General Augustus Henry Lane Fox Pitt Rivers, DCL, FRS, FSA*. Cambridge: Cambridge University Press, 1991.

Bowen, J. R. *Why the French don't like headscarves: Islam, the State, and public space*. Princeton, N. J.: Princeton University Press, 2007.

Bowie, F. (ed.) *Cross-cultural approaches to adoption*. London: Routledge, 2004.

Boyden, S. *Western civilization in biological perspective: patterns in biohistory*. Oxford: Clarendon Press, 1987.

Bray, D. *Social space and governance in urban China: the danwei system from origins to reform*. Stanford, Calif.: Stanford University Press, 2005.

Brenneis, D. & Myers, F. R. (eds.) *Dangerous words: language and politics in the Pacific*. Prospect Heights, Ill.: Waveland Press, 1991 [1984].

Brewis, A. A. *Obesity: cultural and biocultural perspectives*. New Brunswick, N. J.: Rutgers University Press, 2011.

Brosius, C. *India's middle class: new forms of urban leisure, consumption and prosperity*. London: Routledge, 2010.

Bruce, S. *Sociology: a very short introduction*. Oxford: Oxford University Press, 1999.

Brummelhuis, H. ten & Herdt, G. (eds.) *Culture and sexual risk: anthropological perspectives on AIDS*. Amsterdam: Gordon & Breach, 1995.

Bryant, A. & Charmaz, K. C. (eds.) *The Sage handbook of grounded theory*. London: Sage, 2007.

Buckley, T. & Gottlieb, A. (eds.) *Blood magic: the anthropology of menstruation*. Berkeley, Calif.: University of California Press, 1988.

Burton, J. *An introduction to Evans-Pritchard*. Fribourg, Switzerland: University Press, 1992.

Buxton, L. H. D. (ed.) *Custom is king: essays presented to R. R. Marett on his seventieth birthday, June 13, 1936*. London: Hutchinson, 1936.

Byers, S. N. *Introduction to forensic anthropology*. 4th ed. Upper Saddle River, N. J.: Pearson Education, 2011.

Caillois, R. (tr. Barash) *Man, play, and games*. New York: Free Press, 1961. [*Les jeux et les hommes*, 1958.]

Campbell, J. R. & Rew, A. *Identity and affect: experiences of identity in a globalising world*. London: Pluto, 1999.

Campbell, L. & Poser, W. J. *Language classification: history and method*. Cambridge: Cambridge University Press, 2008.

Cancian, F. *Economics and prestige in a Maya community: the religious cargo system in Zinacantán*. Stanford: Stanford University Press, 1965.

Carneiro, R. L. *Evolutionism in cultural anthropology: a critical history*. Boulder, Colo.: Westview, 2003.

Carrier, J. G. *Occidentalism: images of the west*. Oxford: Clarendon Press, 1995.

Carrier, J. G. (ed.) *A handbook of economic anthropology*. Cheltenham: Elgar, 2005.

Carrithers, M. et al. (eds.) *The category of the person: anthropology, philosophy, history*. Cambridge: Cambridge University Press, 1985.

Carsten, J. & Hugh-Jones, S. (eds.) *About the house: Lévi-Strauss and beyond*. Cambridge: Cambridge University Press, 1995.

Cawte, J. E. Further comment on the Australian subincision ceremony. *American anthropologist*, vol. 70, 1968, pp. 961–4.

Celtel, A. *Categories of self: Louis Dumont's theory of the individual*. New York: Berghahn, 2005.

Chaianov, A. V. (ed. Thorner et al.) *A. V. Chayanov on the theory of peasant economy*. Manchester: Manchester University Press, 1986. [*Organizatsiia krestianskogo khoziaistva*, 1925.]

Chapple, E. D. & Coon, C. S. *Principles of anthropology*. New York: Holt, 1942.

Charbonnier, G. (ed. & tr. J. & D. Weightman) Clocks and steam-engines. In *Conversations with Claude Lévi-Strauss*. London: Cape, 1969. [*Entretiens avec Claude Lévi-Strauss*, 1961.]

Chomsky, N. *Aspects of the theory of syntax*. Cambridge, Mass.: MIT Press, 1965.

Chomsky, N. *Syntactic structures*. 2nd ed. Berlin: Mouton de Gruyter, 2002.

Christaller, W. (tr. Baskin) *Central places in Southern Germany*. Englewood Cliffs, N. J.: Prentice-Hall, 1966. [*Die zentralen Orte in Suddeutschland*, 1933.]

Clifford, J. & Marcus, G. E. (eds.) *Writing culture: the poetics and politics of ethnography*. 25th anniversary ed. Berkeley, Calif.: University of California Press, 2011.

Cohen, A. *Masquerade politics: explorations in the structure of urban cultural movements*. Oxford: Berg, 1993.

Cohen, A. P. *The symbolic construction of community*. Chichester: Ellis Horwood, 1985.

Cohen, R. *Global diasporas: an introduction*. 2nd ed. London: Routledge, 2008.

Cohn, N. *The pursuit of the millennium: revolutionary millenarians and mystical anarchists of the Middle Ages*. Rev. ed. New York: Oxford University Press, 1970.

Cole, D. *Franz Boas: the early years, 1858–1906.* Vancouver: Douglas & McIntyre, 1999.

Coleman, S. & Collins, P. (eds.) *Locating the field: space, place and context in anthropology.* Oxford: Berg, 2006.

Coleman, S. & Eade, J. (eds.) *Reframing pilgrimage: cultures in motion.* London: Routledge, 2004.

Collins, D. & Urry, J. A flame too intense for mortal body to support. *Anthropology today*, vol. 13, 1997, pp. 18–20.

Comaroff, Jean. *Body of power, spirit of resistance: the culture and history of a South African people.* Chicago, Ill.: University of Chicago Press, 1985.

Comaroff, Jean & Comaroff, John L. *Of revelation and revolution: Christianity, colonialism, and consciousness in South Africa.* Chicago, Ill.: University of Chicago Press, 1991–7.

Comaroff, John L. (ed.) *The meaning of marriage payments.* London: Academic Press, 1980.

Comaroff, John L. et al. (eds.) *Picturing a colonial past: the African photographs of Isaac Schapera.* Chicago, Ill.: University of Chicago Press, 2007.

Coote, J. & Shelton, A. (eds.) *Anthropology, art and aesthetics.* Oxford: Clarendon Press, 1992.

Corsín Jiménez, A. (ed.) *Culture and well-being: anthropological approaches to freedom and political ethics.* London: Pluto, 2008.

Coulmas, F. *The Blackwell encyclopedia of writing systems.* Oxford: Blackwell, 1996.

Crapanzano, V. *Tuhami, portrait of a Moroccan.* Chicago, Ill.: University of Chicago Press, 1980.

Creed, G. W. (ed.) *The seductions of community: emancipations, oppressions, quandaries.* Santa Fe, N. M.: School of American Research Press, 2006.

Critique of anthropology [journal], 1974–.

Crump, T. *The anthropology of numbers.* Cambridge: Cambridge University Press, 1990.

Czaplicka, M. A. (ed. Collins) *Collected works of M. A. Czaplicka.* Richmond: Curzon, 1999.

Das, V. (ed.) *The Oxford India companion to sociology and social anthropology.* New Delhi: Oxford University Press, 2003.

Davidson, J. S. & Henley, D. (eds.) *The revival of tradition in Indonesian politics: the deployment of adat from colonialism to indigenism.* London: Routledge, 2007.

Davies, C. A. *Reflexive ethnography: a guide to researching selves and others.* 2nd ed. London: Routledge, 2008.

Davis, J. (ed.) *Choice and change: essays in honour of Lucy Mair.* London: Athlone, 1984.

Davis, J. *Exchange.* Buckingham: Open University Press, 1992.

Davis-Floyd, R. E. & Sargent, C. F. (ed.) *Childbirth and authoritative knowledge: cross-cultural perspectives.* Berkeley, Calif.: University of California Press, 1997.

Dawson, W. R. (ed.) *Sir Grafton Elliot Smith: a biographical record by his colleagues.* London: Cape, 1938.

Day, S. et al. (eds.) *Lilies of the field: marginal people who live for the moment.* Boulder, Col.: Westview, 1999.

Deliège, R. (tr. Scott) *Lévi-Strauss today: an introduction to structural anthropology.* Oxford: Berg, 2004. [*Introduction à l'anthropologie structurale*, 2001.]

Derrida, J. (tr. Bass) *Différance*. In *Margins of philosophy*. Brighton: Harvester, 1982. [Address first published in French, 1968.]

De Waal, A. *Famine that kills: Darfur, Sudan*. Rev. ed. New York: Oxford University Press, 2005.

Diaspora: a journal of transnational studies. 1991–.

Dikötter, F. et al. *Narcotic culture: a history of drugs in China*. Chicago, Ill.: University of Chicago Press, 2004.

Dilley, R. (ed.) *Contesting markets: analyses of ideology, discourse and practice*. Edinburgh: Edinburgh University Press, 1992.

Dirks, N. B. et al. (eds.) *Culture/power/history: a reader in contemporary social theory*. Princeton, N. J.: Princeton University Press, 1994.

Dolgin, J. et al. (eds.) *Symbolic anthropology: a reader in the study of symbols and meanings*. New York: Columbia University Press, 1977.

Donham, D. *History, power, ideology: central issues in Marxism and anthropology*. Berkeley, Calif.: University of California Press, 1999.

Donnan, H. & Magowan, F. (eds.) *Transgressive sex: subversion and control in erotic encounters*. New York: Berghahn, 2009.

Donnan, H. & Magowan, F. *The anthropology of sex*. Oxford: Berg, 2010.

Donnan, H. & Wilson, T. W. *Borders: frontiers of identity, nation and state*. Oxford: Berg, 1999.

Douglas, M. *Purity and danger: an analysis of concepts of pollution and taboo*. London: Routledge, 2002 [1966].

Douglas, M. (ed.) *Witchcraft: confessions & accusations*. London: Tavistock, 1970.

Douglas, M. *Edward Evans-Pritchard*. London: Routledge, 2003 [1980].

Douglas, M. (ed.) *Constructive drinking: perspectives on drink from anthropology*. Cambridge: Cambridge University Press, 1987.

Douglas, M. *Risk and blame: essays in cultural theory*. London: Routledge, 1992.

Dove, M. *Swidden agriculture in Indonesia: the subsistence strategies of the Kalimantan Kantu'*. Berlin: Mouton, 1985.

Dresch, P. et al. (eds.) *Anthropologists in a wider world: essays on field research*. New York: Berghahn, 2000.

Drèze, J. et al. (eds.) *The political economy of hunger: selected essays*. Oxford: Clarendon Press, 1995.

DuBois, T. A. *An introduction to shamanism*. Cambridge: Cambridge University Press, 2009.

Dumont, L. (tr. Sainsbury et al.) *Homo hierarchicus: the caste system and its implications*. Rev. ed. Chicago, Ill.: University of Chicago Press, 1980.

Dunbar, R. I. M. *Grooming, gossip and the evolution of language*. London: Faber, 1996.

Dunbar, R. I. M. *The human story: a new history of mankind's evolution*. London: Faber, 2004.

Dundes, A. (ed.) *The evil eye: a casebook*. Madison, Wis.: University of Wisconsin Press, 1992 [1981].

Dundes, A. (ed.) *Folklore: critical concepts in literary and cultural studies*. London: Routledge, 2005.

Durkheim, E. (tr. Simpson) *The division of labor in society*. Glencoe, Ill.: Free Press, 1933. [*De la division du travail social*, 1893.]

Durkheim, E. (tr. Solovay & Mueller) *The rules of sociological method*. Glencoe, Ill.: Free Press, 1938. [*Les règles de la méthode sociologique*, 1895.]

Durkheim, E. (tr. Spaulding & Simpson) *Suicide: a study in sociology*. London: Routledge & Kegan Paul, 1952. [*Le suicide*, 1897.]

Durkheim, E. (tr. Fields) *The elementary forms of religious life*. New York: Free Press, 1995. [*Les formes élémentaires de la vie religieuse*, 1912.]

Durkheim, E. & Mauss, M. (tr. Needham) *Primitive classification*. 2nd ed. London: Cohen & West, 1969. [*De quelques formes primitives de classification*, 1901–2.]

Durrenberger, E. P. & Erem, S. *Class acts: an anthropology of service workers and their union*. Boulder, Col.: Paradigm, 2005.

Edwards, E. et al. (eds.) *Sensible objects: colonialism, museums and material culture*. Oxford: Berg, 2006.

Eicher, J. B. et al. (eds.) *The visible self: global perspectives on dress, culture, and society*. 3rd ed. New York: Fairchild, 2008.

Eickelman, D. F. *The Middle East and Central Asia: an anthropological approach*. 4th ed. Upper Saddle River, N. J.: Prentice Hall, 2002.

Eisenberg, L. Disease and illness: distinctions between professional and popular ideas of sickness. *Culture, medicine and psychiatry*, vol. 1, 1977, pp. 9–23.

Eliade, M. (tr. Trask) *Shamanism: archaic techniques of ecstasy*. Princeton, N. J.: Princeton University Press, 2004. [*Chamanisme et les techniques archaïques de l'extase*, 1951.]

Eliade, M. (tr. Trask) *The sacred and the profane: the nature of religion*. San Diego, Calif.: Harcourt Brace, 1987. [*Das Heilige und das Profane*, 1957.]

Ellen R. F. *The cultural relations of classification: an analysis of Nuaulu animal categories from Central Seram*. Cambridge: Cambridge University Press, 1993.

Ellen, R. F. et al. (eds.) *Malinowski between two worlds: the Polish roots of an anthropological tradition*. Cambridge: Cambridge University Press, 1988.

Ellen, R. F. et al. (eds.) *Indigenous environmental knowledge and its transformations: critical anthropological perspectives*. Amsterdam: Harwood Academic, 2000.

Eller, J. D. *Cultural anthropology: global forces, local lives*. New York: Routledge, 2009.

Emerson, R. M. et al. *Writing ethnographic fieldnotes*. Chicago, Ill.: University of Chicago Press, 1995.

Engels, F. (tr. Untermann) *The origin of the family, private property and the state*. Honolulu, Hawaii: University Press of the Pacific, 2001. [*Ursprung der Familie, des Privateigentums und des Staats*, 1884].

Epstein, A. L. *Scenes from African urban life: collected Copperbelt essays*. Edinburgh: Edinburgh University Press, 1992.

Eriksen, T. H. *What is anthropology?* London: Pluto Press, 2004.

Erneling, C. E. & Johnson, D. M. *The mind as a scientific object: between brain and culture*. New York: Oxford University Press, 2005.

Evans-Pritchard, E. E. Zande blood-brotherhood. In *Essays in social anthropology*. London: Faber, 1962 [1933].

Evans-Pritchard, E. E. *Witchcraft, oracles and magic among the Azande*. Oxford: Clarendon Press, 1937.

Evans-Pritchard, E. E. *The Nuer: a description of the modes of livelihood and political institutions of a Nilotic people*. Oxford: Clarendon Press, 1940.

Evans-Pritchard, E. E. *The divine kingship of the Shilluk of the Nilotic Sudan.* Cambridge: Cambridge University Press, 1948. [Reprinted in *Essays in social anthropology,* 1962.]

Evans-Pritchard, E. E. *Kinship and marriage among the Nuer.* Oxford: Clarendon Press, 1990 [1951].

Evans-Pritchard, E. E. *Social anthropology.* London: Cohen & West, 1951.

Evans-Pritchard, E. E. *The comparative method in social anthropology.* London: Athlone Press, 1963. [Reprinted in *The position of women in primitive societies,* 1965.]

Evans-Pritchard, E. E. *Theories of primitive religion.* Oxford: Clarendon Press, 1965.

Evans-Pritchard, E. E. (ed. Singer) *A history of anthropological thought.* London: Faber, 1981.

Evens, T. M. S. & Handelman, D. (eds.) *The Manchester School: practice and ethnographic praxis in anthropology.* New York: Berghahn, 2006.

Evolutionary anthropology [journal], 1992–.

Fassin, D. (tr. Jacobs & Varro) *When bodies remember: experiences and politics of AIDS in South Africa.* Berkeley, Calif.: University of California Press, 2007. [*Quand les corps se souviennent,* 2006.]

Faubion, J. D. & Marcus, G. E. (eds.) *Fieldwork is not what it used to be: learning anthropology's method in a time of transition.* Ithaca, N. Y.: Cornell University Press, 2009.

Feeley-Harnik, G. Issues in divine kingship. *Annual review of anthropology,* vol. 14, 1985, pp. 273–313.

Ferguson, C. A. Diglossia. *Word: journal of the International Linguistic Association,* vol. 15, 1959, pp. 325–40.

Finnegan, R. H. *Literacy and orality: studies in the technology of communication.* Oxford: Basil Blackwell, 1988.

Finnegan, R. H. *Oral traditions and the verbal arts: a guide to research practices.* London: Routledge, 1992.

Firth, R. (ed.) *Man and culture: an evaluation of the work of Bronislaw Malinowski.* London: Routledge & Kegan Paul, 1957[a].

Firth, R. *We, the Tikopia: a sociological study of kinship in primitive Polynesia.* 2nd ed. London: Allen & Unwin, 1957[b].

Flint, J. & de Waal, A. *Darfur: a new history of a long war.* Rev. ed. London: Zed, 2008.

Fournier, M. (tr. Todd) *Marcel Mauss: a biography.* Princeton, N. J.: Princeton University Press, 2006. [*Marcel Mauss,* 1994.]

Fortes, M. (ed.) *Social structure: studies presented to A. R. Radcliffe-Brown.* Oxford: Clarendon Press, 1949.

Fortes, M. The structure of unilineal descent groups. *American anthropologist,* vol. 55, 1953, pp. 65–95. [Reprinted in *Time and social structure and other essays,* 1970.]

Fortes, M. Kinship and the axiom of amity. In *Kinship and the social order.* Chicago, Ill.: Aldine, 1969.

Fortes, M. & Evans-Pritchard, E. E. (eds.) *African political systems.* London: IIALC/ Oxford University Press, 1940.

Foster, G. M. A second look at limited good. *Anthropological quarterly,* vol. 45, 1972, pp. 57–64.

Foucault, M. (tr. Sheridan Smith) *Archaeology of knowledge*. London: Routledge, 2002 [1972]. [*Archéologie du savoir*, 1969.]

Foucault, M. (tr. Sheridan) *Discipline and punish: the birth of the prison*. London: Allen Lane, 1977. [*Surveiller et punir*, 1975.]

Foucault, M. (tr. Hurley) *The history of sexuality: vol. 1, an introduction*. New York: Vintage, 1990 [1978]. [*La volonté de savoir*, 1976.]

Foucault, M. (ed. Faubion; tr. Hurley et al.) *Power*. London: Allen Lane, 2000. [selections from French originals]

Frankenberg, R. (ed.) *Displacing whiteness: essays in social and cultural criticism*. Durham, N. C.: Duke University Press, 1997.

Frazer, J. G. Sympathetic magic. In *The golden bough, vol. 1, part 1*. 3rd ed. London: Macmillan, 1911.

Freedman, M. (ed.) *Social organization: essays presented to Raymond Firth*. London: Cass, 1967.

Freeman, J. D. The family system of the Iban of Borneo. In Goody, J. (ed.) *The developmental cycle in domestic groups*. Cambridge: Cambridge University Press, 1958.

Fried, M. H. *The evolution of political society: an essay in political anthropology*. New York: Random House, 1967.

Fry, D. P. *Beyond war: the human potential for peace*. New York: Oxford University Press, 2007.

Fuller, C. J. *The camphor flame: popular Hinduism and society in India*. Rev. ed. Princeton, N. J.: Princeton University Press, 2004.

Furnivall, J. S. *Colonial policy and practice: a comparative study of Burma and Netherlands India*. Cambridge: Cambridge University Press, 1948.

Galaty, J. G. & Bonte, P. (eds.) *Herders, warriors, and traders: pastoralism in Africa*. Boulder, Colo.: Westview, 1991.

Galaty, J. G. & Johnson, D. L.(eds.) *The world of pastoralism: herding systems in comparative perspective*. New York: Guilford, 1990.

Gallie, W. B. Essentially contested concepts. In *Philosophy and the historical understanding*. 2nd ed. New York: Schocken, 1968 [1956].

[Galton, F.] Discussion. *Journal of the Anthropological Institute*, vol. 18, 1889, p. 270.

Galtung, J. Violence, peace and peace research. *Journal of peace research*, vol. 6, 1969, pp. 167–91.

Garfinkel, H. *Studies in ethnomethodology*. Expanded ed. Boulder, Col.: Paradigm, 2010.

Garine, I. de & Garine, V. de (eds.) *Drinking: anthropological approaches*. New York: Berghahn, 2001.

Geertz, C. *Agricultural involution: the process of ecological change in Indonesia*. Berkeley, Calif.: Association of Asian Studies/University of California Press, 1963.

Geertz, C. *The interpretation of cultures: selected essays*. New York: Basic Books, 2000 [1973].

Geertz, C. *Local knowledge: further essays in interpretive anthropology*. 3rd ed. New York: Basic Books, 2000 [1983].

Geertz, C. (ed. Inglis) *Life among the anthros: and other essays*. Princeton, N. J.: Princeton University Press, 2010.

Gellner, D. N. *The anthropology of Buddhism and Hinduism: Weberian themes.* New Delhi: Oxford University Press, 2001.

Gellner, E. *State and society in Soviet thought.* Oxford: Basil Blackwell, 1988.

Gellner, E. *Nations and nationalism.* 2nd ed. Malden, Mass.: Blackwell, 2006.

Gellner, E. & Waterbury, J. (eds.) *Patrons and clients in Mediterranean societies.* London: Duckworth/CMS, 1977.

Gilmore, D. D. *Manhood in the making: cultural concepts of masculinity.* New Haven, Conn.: Yale University Press, 1990.

Gilroy, P. *"There ain't no black in the Union Jack": the cultural politics of race and nation.* London: Routledge, 2002.

Gilsenan, M. *Recognizing Islam: religion and society in the modern Middle East.* Rev. ed. London: Tauris, 2000.

Gingrich, A. The German speaking countries. In Barth, F. et al. (eds.) *One discipline, four ways: British, German, French and American anthropology.* Chicago, Ill.: University of Chicago Press, 2005.

Ginkel, R. van. *Coastal cultures: an anthropology of fishing and whaling.* Apeldoorn: Het Spinhuis, 2007.

Glaser, B. G. & Strauss, A. L. *The discovery of grounded theory: strategies for qualitative research.* London: Weidenfeld and Nicolson, 1968.

Gluckman, M. Rituals of rebellion in South-East Africa. In *Order and rebellion in tribal Africa: collected essays, with an autobiographical introduction.* London: Cohen & West, 1963 [essay: 1954].

Gluckman, M. *The ideas in Barotse jurisprudence.* Rev. ed. Manchester: IAS, University of Zambia/Manchester University Press, 1972.

Godelier, M. & Strathern, M. *Big men and great men: personifications of power in Melanesia.* Cambridge: Cambridge University Press, 1991.

Goffman, E. *Stigma: notes on the management of spoiled identity.* Harmondsworth: Penguin, 1990 [1963].

Good, B. et al. (eds.) *A reader in medical anthropology: theoretical trajectories, emergent realities.* Chichester: Wiley-Blackwell, 2010.

Goodale, M. (ed.) *Human rights: an anthropological reader.* Chichester: Wiley-Blackwell, 2009.

Goodenough, W. H. Componential analysis and the study of meaning. *Language,* vol. 32, 1956, pp. 195–216.

Goodman, J. et al. (eds.) *Consuming habits: global and historical perspectives on how cultures define drugs.* 2nd ed. London: Routledge, 2007.

Gombrich, R. F. *Theravada Buddhism: a social history from ancient Benares to modern Colombo.* 2nd ed. London: Routledge, 2006.

Goody, J. (ed.) *The developmental cycle in domestic groups.* Cambridge: Cambridge University Press, 1958.

Goody, J. (ed.) *Succession to high office.* Cambridge: Cambridge University Press, 1966.

Goody, J. (ed.) *Literacy in traditional societies.* Cambridge: Cambridge University Press, 1968.

Goody, J. *Cooking, cuisine, and class: a study in comparative sociology.* Cambridge: Cambridge University Press, 1982.

Goody, J. *The interface between the written and the oral.* Cambridge: Cambridge University Press, 1987.

Goody, J. Towards a room with a view: a personal account of contributions to local knowledge, theory, and research in fieldwork and comparative studies. *Annual review of anthropology*, vol. 20, 1991, pp. 1–22.

Goody, J. *The expansive moment: the rise of social anthropology in Britain and Africa, 1918–1970.* Cambridge: Cambridge University Press, 1995.

Goody, J. *L'homme, l'écriture et la mort: entretiens avec Pierre-Emmanuel Dauzat.* Paris: Les Belles Lettres, 1996.

Goody, J. *Food and love: a cultural history of east and west.* London: Verso, 2009 [1998].

Goody, J. *The Eurasian miracle.* Cambridge: Polity, 2010.

Goody, J. & Tambiah, S. J. *Bridewealth and dowry.* Cambridge: Cambridge University Press, 1973.

Graeber, D. *Direct action: an ethnography.* Edinburgh: AK Press, 2009.

Gronhaug, R. et al. (eds.) *The ecology of choice and symbol: essays in honour of Fredrik Barth.* Bergen: Alma Mater, 1991.

Gudeman, S. *The demise of a rural economy: from subsistence to capitalism in a Latin American village.* London: Routledge, 2004 [1978].

Gudeman, S. *Economy's tension: the dialectics of community and market.* New York: Berghahn, 2008.

Gudeman, S. (ed.) *Economic persuasions.* New York: Berghahn, 2009.

Guha, R. (ed.) *A Subaltern studies reader, 1986–1995.* Minneapolis, Minn.: University of Minnesota Press, 1997.

Guibernau, M. & Rex, J. (eds.) *The ethnicity reader: nationalism, multiculturalism, and migration.* 2nd ed. Cambridge: Polity, 2010.

Guldin, G. E. *The saga of anthropology in China: from Malinowski to Moscow to Mao.* Armonk, N. Y.: M. E. Sharpe, 1994.

Gumperz, J. & Hymes, D. (eds.) *The ethnography of communication.* Special publication of *American Anthropologist*, vol. 66, no. 6, part 2, 1964.

Haas, J. (ed.) *The anthropology of war.* Cambridge: Cambridge University Press, 1990.

Haddon, A. C. et al. *Reports of the Cambridge anthropological expedition to Torres Straits.* Cambridge: Cambridge University Press, 1901–35.

Hall, S. & Jefferson, T. (eds.) *Resistance through rituals: youth subcultures in post-war Britain.* 2nd ed. London: Routledge, 2006.

Hallam, E. & Ingold, T. (eds.) *Creativity and cultural improvisation.* Oxford: Berg, 2007.

Hamilton, W. D. The genetical evolution of social behaviour, I. *Journal of theoretical biology*, vol. 7, 1964, pp. 1–16.

Hammersley, M. *Ethnography: principles in practice.* 3rd ed. London: Routledge, 2007.

Hann, C. M. (ed.) *Property relations: renewing the anthropological tradition.* Cambridge: Cambridge University Press, 1998.

Hann, C. M. & Hart, K. (eds.) *Market and society:* The great transformation *today.* Cambridge: Cambridge University Press, 2009.

Hann, C. M. & Hart, K. *Economic anthropology: history, ethnography, critique.* Cambridge: Polity, 2011.

Hannerz, U. *Exploring the city: inquiries toward an urban anthropology.* New York: Columbia University Press, 1980.

Haraway, D. *Primate visions: gender, race, and nature in the world of modern science.* New York: Routledge, 1989.

Harris, M. *The rise of anthropological theory: a history of theories of culture.* Updated ed. Walnut Creek, Calif.: Altamira, 2001[a] [1968].

Harris, M. *Cultural materialism: the struggle for a science of culture.* Updated ed. Walnut Creek, Calif.: Altamira, 2001[b] [1979].

Harris, M. *Good to eat: riddles of food and culture.* New York: Simon & Schuster, 1985.

Harris, M. *Our kind: who we are, where we came from, where we are going.* New York: Harper, 1990.

Harris, M. Cultural materialism. In Levinson, D. & Ember, M. (eds.) *Encyclopedia of cultural anthropology.* New York: Henry Holt and Co., 1996.

Harrison, G. A. & Waterlow, J. C. (eds.) *Diet and disease: in traditional and developing societies.* Cambridge: Cambridge University Press, 1990.

Hart, K. Informal income opportunities and urban employment in Ghana. *Journal of modern African studies,* vol. 11, 1973, pp. 61–89.

Harvey, D. *A brief history of neoliberalism.* Oxford: Oxford University Press, 2005.

Harvey, G. (ed.) *Shamanism: a reader.* London: Routledge, 2003.

Hastrup, K. *Action: anthropology in the company of Shakespeare.* Copenhagen: Museum Tusculanum Press, 2004.

Hausfater, G. & Hrdy, S. B. (eds.) *Infanticide: comparative and evolutionary perspectives.* New Brunswick, N. J.: Aldine Transaction, 2008 [1984].

Headland, T. et al. (eds.) *Emics and etics: the insider/outsider debate.* Newbury Park: Sage, 1990.

Hebdige, D. *Subculture: the meaning of style.* London: Routledge, 2003 [1979].

Hechter, M. *Internal colonialism: the Celtic fringe in British national development.* Rev. ed. New Brunswick, N. J.: Transaction, 1999.

Hefner, R. W. (ed.) *Conversion to Christianity: historical and anthropological perspectives on a great transformation.* Berkeley, Calif.: University of California Press, 1993.

Heller, M. (ed.) *Bilingualism: a social approach.* Basingstoke: Palgrave Macmillan, 2007.

Henley, P. *The adventure of the real: Jean Rouch and the craft of ethnographic cinema.* Chicago, Ill.: University of Chicago Press, 2009.

Herdt, G. *Guardians of the flutes: idioms of masculinity.* Chicago, Ill.: University of Chicago Press, 1994 [1981].

Héritier-Augé, F. & Copet-Rougier, E. (eds.) *Les complexités de l'alliance.* Paris: Éditions des Archives Contemporaines, 1990–4.

Herle, A. & Rouse, S. (eds.) *Cambridge and the Torres Strait: centenary essays on the 1898 anthropological expedition.* Cambridge: Cambridge University Press, 1998.

Herring, D. A. & Swedlund, A. C. (eds.) *Plagues and epidemics: infected spaces past and present.* Oxford: Berg, 2010.

Herskovits, M. The cattle complex in East Africa. *American anthropologist,* vol. 28 [4 parts], 1926.

Hertz, R. (tr. Needham) *Death and the right hand.* London: Cohen & West, 1960. [*Contribution à une etude sur la représentation collective de la mort,* 1907; *La prééminence de la main droite,*1909.]

Heusch, L. de (tr. O'Brien & Morton) *Sacrifice in Africa: a structuralist approach.* Manchester: Manchester University Press, 1985.

Hill, J. & Mannheim, B. Language and world view. *Annual review of anthropology*, vol. 21, 1992, pp. 381–406.

Hinton, A. L. & O'Neill, K. L. (eds.) *Genocide: truth, memory, and representation.* Durham, N. C.: Duke University Press, 2009.

Hobart, M. (ed.) *An anthropological critique of development: the growth of ignorance.* London: Routledge, 1993.

Hobsbawm, E. & Ranger, T. (eds.) *The invention of tradition.* Cambridge: Cambridge University Press, 1983.

Hocart, A. M. (ed. Raglan) *The life-giving myth and other essays.* London: Methuen, 1970 [1952].

Hocart, A. M. (ed. Raglan) *Social origins.* London: Watts, 1954.

Hockett, C. F. The origin of speech. *Scientific American*, vol. 203, no. 3, 1960, pp. 88–96.

Hoffman, S. M. & Oliver-Smith, A. (eds.) *Catastrophe & culture: the anthropology of disaster.* Santa Fe, Calif.: School of American Research Press, 2002.

Holy, L. (ed.) *Segmentary lineage systems reconsidered.* Belfast: Queen's University, 1979.

Holy, L. (ed.) *Comparative anthropology.* Oxford: Blackwell, 1987.

Homans, G. C. Social behavior as exchange. *American journal of sociology*, vol. 63, 1958, pp. 597–606.

L'homme: revue française d'anthropologie [journal], 1961–.

Hornborg, A. Learning from the Tiv: why a sustainable economy would have to be "multicentric." *Culture & agriculture*, vol. 29, 2007, pp. 63–9.

Howell, S. & Willis, R. (eds.) *Societies at peace: anthropological perspectives.* London: Routledge, 1989.

Howes, D. (ed.) *Empire of the senses: the sensual culture reader.* Oxford: Berg, 2005.

Hubert, H. & Mauss, M. (tr. Halls) *Sacrifice: its nature and function.* London: Cohen & West, 1964. [*Essai sur la nature et la fonction du sacrifice*, 1898.]

Huizinga, J. *Homo ludens: a study of the play-element in culture.* London: Routledge & Kegan Paul, 1949 [German: 1944].

Human fertility [journal], 1998–.

Huntington, S. P. *The clash of civilizations and the remaking of world order.* New York: Simon & Schuster, 1996.

Hymes, D. H. (ed. Gladwin & Sturtevant) The ethnography of speaking. In *Anthropology and human behaviour.* Washington, D. C.: Anthropological Society of Washington, 1962.

Hymes, D. H. *"In vain I tried to tell you": essays in Native American ethnopoetics.* Lincoln, Neb.: University of Nebraska Press, 2004 [1981].

Inda, J. X. & Rosaldo, R. (eds.) *The anthropology of globalization: a reader.* 2nd ed. Malden, Mass.: Blackwell, 2008.

Inhorn, M. C. (ed.) *Reproductive disruptions: gender, technology, and biopolitics in the new millennium.* New York: Berghahn, 2007.

Jackson, A. (ed.) *Anthropology at home.* London: Tavistock, 1987.

Jackson, M. (ed.) *Things as they are: new directions in phenomenological anthropology.* Bloomington, Ind.: Indiana University Press, 1996.

James, W. Sister-exchange marriage. *Scientific American*, vol. 233, 1975, pp. 84–94.

James, W. & Allen, N. J. (eds.) *Marcel Mauss: a centenary tribute.* New York: Berghahn, 1998.

James, W. & Johnson, D. H. (eds.) *Vernacular Christianity: essays in the social anthropology of religion.* Oxford: Journal of the Anthropological Society of Oxford, 1988.

James, W. & Mills, D. (eds.) *The qualities of time: anthropological approaches.* Oxford: Berg, 2005.

Jenkins, R. *Pierre Bourdieu.* Rev. ed. London: Routledge, 2002.

Jordan, B. *Birth in four cultures.* 3rd ed. Montréal: Eden Press, 1983.

Josselin de Jong, P. E. de (ed.) *Unity in diversity: Indonesia as a field of anthropological study.* Dordrecht: Foris, 1984.

Jourdan, C. & Tuite, K. (eds.) *Language, culture, and society: key topics in linguistic anthropology.* Cambridge: Cambridge University Press, 2006.

Journal for the anthropological study of human movement, 1980–.

Journal of the Anthropological Society of Oxford, vol. 18, no. 2, 1987.

Just, R. Methodological individualism and sociological reductionism. *Social analysis,* vol. 48, 2004, pp. 186–91.

Kalof, L. & Fitzgerald, A. (eds.) *The animals reader: the essential classic and contemporary writings.* Oxford: Berg, 2007.

Kammen, M. G. *Digging up the dead: a history of notable American reburials.* Chicago, Ill.: University of Chicago Press, 2010.

Kapferer, B. (ed.) *Transaction and meaning: directions in the anthropology of exchange and symbolic behavior.* Philadelphia: Institute for the Study of Human Issues, 1976.

Kapferer, B. *A celebration of demons: exorcism and the aesthetics of healing in Sri Lanka.* 2nd ed. Oxford: Berg, 1991.

Kapferer, B. (ed.) *Beyond rationalism: rethinking magic, witchcraft, and sorcery.* New York: Berghahn, 2003.

Karp, I. et al. (eds.) *Museum frictions: public cultures/global transformations.* Durham, N. C.: Duke University Press, 2006.

Käsler, D. (tr. Hurd) *Max Weber: an introduction to his life and work.* Cambridge: Polity, 1988 [German: 1979].

Keesing, R. Rethinking *mana. Journal of anthropological research,* vol. 40, 1984, pp. 137–56.

King, V. T. *The sociology of Southeast Asia: transformations in a developing region.* Honolulu, Hawaii: University of Hawai'i Press, 2008.

Kleinman, A. *Patients and healers in the context of culture: an exploration of the borderland between anthropology, medicine, and psychiatry.* Berkeley, Calif.: University of California Press, 1980.

Kleinman, A. et al. (eds.) *Social suffering.* Berkeley, Calif.: University of California Press, 1997.

Kloos, P. & Claessen, H. J. M. (eds.) *Contemporary anthropology in the Netherlands: the use of anthropological ideas.* Amsterdam: VU University Press, 1991.

Knight, C. *Blood relations: menstruation and the origins of culture.* New Haven, Conn.: Yale University Press, 1991.

Koerner, E. F. K. The Sapir-Whorf hypothesis: a preliminary history and a bibliographical essay. *Journal of linguistic anthropology*, vol. 2, 1992, pp. 173–98.

Koser, K. *International migration: a very short introduction*. Oxford: Oxford University Press, 2007.

Kottak, C. P. *Prime-time society: an anthropological analysis of television and culture*. Rev. ed. Walnut Creek, Calif.: Left Coast, 2009.

Kroeber, A. L. The superorganic. In *The nature of culture*. Rev. ed. Chicago, Ill.: University of Chicago Press, 1952 [1917].

Kroeber, A. L. & Kluckhohn, C. *Culture: a critical review of concepts and definitions*. Cambridge, Mass.: Peabody Museum, 1952.

Kroeber, A. L. & Parsons, T. The concepts of culture and of social system. *American sociological review*, vol. 23, 1958, pp. 582–3.

Krohn-Hansen, C. & Nustad, K. G. (eds.) *State formation: anthropological perspectives*. London: Pluto Press, 2005.

Kronenfeld, D. B. et al. (eds.) *A companion to cognitive anthropology*. Malden, Mass.: Wiley-Blackwell, 2011.

Kuhn, T. S. (ed. Conant & Haugeland) *The road since structure: philosophical essays, 1970–1993*. Chicago, Ill.: University of Chicago Press, 2000.

Kuklick, H. *The savage within: the social history of British anthropology, 1885–1945*. Cambridge: Cambridge University Press, 1991.

Kulick, D. & Meneley, A. (eds.) *Fat: the anthropology of an obsession*. New York: Jeremy P. Tarcher/Penguin, 2005.

Kuper, A. *Anthropology and anthropologists: the modern British school*. 3rd ed. London: Routledge, 1996.

Kuper, A. *The reinvention of primitive society: transformations of a myth*. 2nd ed. London: Routledge, 2005.

La Fontaine, J. S. *Initiation*. Harmondsworth: Penguin, 1985.

Lakoff, G. & Johnson, M. *Metaphors we live by*. Chicago, Ill.: University of Chicago Press, 2003 [1980].

Lambek, M. *Knowledge and practice in Mayotte: local discourses of Islam, sorcery, and spirit possession*. Toronto, On.: University of Toronto Press, 1993.

Landy, D. (ed.) *Culture, disease, and healing: studies in medical anthropology*. New York: Macmillan, 1977.

Latour, B. (tr. Porter) *We have never been modern*. Cambridge, Mass.: Harvard University Press, 1993. [*Nous n'avons jamais été moderns*, 1991.]

Latour, B. *Reassembling the social: an introduction to actor-network-theory*. Oxford: Oxford University Press, 2005.

Lawrence, P. *Road belong cargo: a study of the cargo movement in the Southern Madang District, New Guinea*. Rev. ed. Manchester: Manchester University Press, 1971 [1964].

Leach, E. R. *Political systems of Highland Burma: a study of Kachin social structure*. Oxford: Berg, 2004 [1954].

Leach, E. R. Anthropological aspects of language: animal categories and verbal abuse. In Lenneberg, E. H. (ed.) *New directions in the study of language*, pp. 23–63. Cambridge, Mass.: MIT Press, 1964.

Leach, J. W. & Leach, E. R. (eds.) *The kula: new perspectives on Massim exchange.* Cambridge: Cambridge University Press, 1983.

LeClair, E. E. & Schneider, H. K. (eds.) *Economic anthropology: readings in theory and analysis.* New York: Holt, Rinehart and Winston, 1968.

Lee, R. B. Demystifying primitive communism. In Gailey, C. W. (ed.) *Civilization in crisis: anthropological perspectives.* Gainesville, Fla.: University Press of Florida, 1992.

Lee, R. B. & DeVore, I. (eds.) *Man the hunter.* Chicago, Ill.: Aldine, 1968.

Lee, R. B. & DeVore, I. (eds.) *Kalahari hunter-gatherers: studies of the !Kung San and their neighbors.* Cambridge, Mass.: Harvard University Press, 1976.

Lem, W. & Leach, B. (eds.) *Culture, economy, power: anthropology as critique, anthropology as praxis.* Albany, N. Y.: SUNY Press, 2002.

Lewin, E. & Leap, W. L. *Out in public: reinventing lesbian/gay anthropology in a globalizing world.* Chichester: Wiley-Blackwell, 2009.

Lévi-Strauss, C. (tr. Russell) *A world on the wane.* London: Hutchinson, 1961. [*Tristes tropiques*, 1955.]

Lévi-Strauss, C. (tr. Jacobson & Schoepf) *Structural anthropology*, vol. 1. New York: Basic Books, 1963. [*Anthropologie structural*, 1958.]

Lévi-Strauss, C. (tr. Needham) *Totemism.* London: Merlin Press, 1991 [1964]. [*Le totémisme aujourd'hui*, 1962.]

Lévi-Strauss, C. *The savage mind.* London: Weidenfeld & Nicolson, 1966. [*La pensée sauvage*, 1962.]

Lévi-Strauss, C. (tr. J. & D. Weightman) *The raw and the cooked: introduction to a science of mythology.* New York: Harper & Row, 1969[a]. [*Le cru et le cuit*, 1964.]

Lévi-Strauss, C. (ed. Needham; tr. Bell & Sturmer) *The elementary structures of kinship.* Rev. ed. London: Eyre & Spottiswoode, 1969[b]. [*Les structures élémentaires de la parenté*, 1967.]

Lévi -Strauss, C. Reflections on the atom of kinship. In *Structural anthropology*, vol. 2. London: Allen Lane, 1977[a].

Lévi-Strauss, C. (tr. Layton) *Structural anthropology*, vol. 2. London: Allen Lane, 1977[b].

Lévi-Strauss, C. (tr. Willis) *Anthropology and myth: lectures, 1951–1982.* Oxford: Basil Blackwell, 1987.

Levine, N. *The dynamics of polyandry: kinship, domesticity, and population on the Tibetan border.* Chicago, Ill.: University of Chicago Press, 1988.

LeVine, R. A. (ed.) *Psychological anthropology: a reader on self in culture.* Chichester: Wiley-Blackwell, 2010.

Levinson, S. *Pragmatics.* Cambridge: Cambridge University Press, 1983.

Lewin, E. (ed.) *Feminist anthropology: a reader.* Malden, Mass.: Blackwell, 2006.

Lewis, O. The setting. In *Five families: Mexican case studies in the culture of poverty.* New York: Basic Books, 1959.

Lewis, O. Introduction. In *The children of Sánchez: autobiography of a Mexican family.* New York: Random House, 1961.

Linton, R. *The study of man: an introduction.* Student's ed. New York: Appleton-Century, 1936.

Linton, R. Nativistic movements. *American anthropologist*, vol. 45, 1943, pp. 230–40.

Littlewood, R. & Dein, S. (eds.) *Cultural psychiatry and medical anthropology: an introduction and reader*. London: Athlone, 2000.

Llamas, C. et al. (eds.) *The Routledge companion to sociolinguistics*. London: Routledge, 2007.

Llewellyn, K. N. & Hoebel, E. A. *The Cheyenne way: conflict and case law in primitive jurisprudence*. Norman, Okla.: University of Oklahoma Press, 1941.

Lock, M. & Nguyen, V.-K. *An anthropology of biomedicine*. Chichester: Wiley-Blackwell, 2010.

Loizos, P. & Heady, P. (eds.) *Conceiving persons: ethnographies of procreation, fertility and growth*. London: Athlone, 1999.

Low, S. (ed.) *Theorizing the city: the new urban anthropology reader*. New Brunswick, N. J.: Rutgers University Press, 1999.

Low, S. & Lawrence-Zúñiga, D. (eds.) *The anthropology of space and place: locating culture*. Malden, Mass.: Blackwell, 2003.

Lucy, J. A. *Language diversity and thought: a reformulation of the linguistic relativity hypothesis*. Cambridge: Cambridge University Press, 1992.

Luhrmann, T. M. *Persuasions of the witch's craft: ritual magic and witchcraft in present-day England*. Oxford: Basil Blackwell, 1989.

Lukes, S. Methodological individualism reconsidered. In *Essays in social theory*. London: Macmillan, 1977 [essay: 1968].

Lukes, S. *Émile Durkheim, his life and work: a historical and critical study*. Rev. ed. Harmondsworth: Penguin, 1992 [1973].

Luna, L. E. & White, S. F. (ed.) *Ayahuasca reader: encounters with Amazon's sacred vine*. Santa Fe, Calif.: Synergetic, 2000.

Lutz, C. A. *Unnatural emotions: everyday sentiments on a Micronesian atoll & their challenge to western theory*. Chicago, Ill.: University of Chicago Press, 1988.

MacClancy, J. *Consuming culture*. London: Chapmans, 1992.

Macdonald, S. (ed.) *A companion to museum studies*. Malden, Mass.: Blackwell, 2006.

MacLaury, R. E. et al. (eds.) *Anthropology of color: interdisciplinary multilevel modeling*. Amsterdam: John Benjamins, 2007.

McLennan, J. F. *Primitive marriage: an inquiry into the origin of the form of capture in marriage ceremonies*. Edinburgh: Adam and Charles Black, 1865.

McNeill, W. H. *Plagues and peoples*. New York: Anchor Books, 1998.

MacKenzie, J. M. *The empire of nature: hunting, conservation and British imperialism*. Manchester: Manchester University Press, 1988.

Maine, H. S. *Ancient law*. 10th ed. UK: Lightning Source, 2006 [1884].

Mair, L. P. *Primitive government: a study of traditional political systems in Eastern Africa*. Rev. ed. London: Scolar Press, 1977.

Makereti. *The old-time Maori*. Auckland: New Woman's Press, 1986 [1938].

Malinowski, B. *Argonauts of the western Pacific: an account of native enterprise and adventure in the archipelagoes of Melanesian New Guinea*. London: Routledge, 2002 [1922].

Malinowski, B. *Crime and custom in savage society*. London: Kegan Paul, Trench, Trübner, 1926.

Malinowski, B. The problem of meaning in primitive languages. Ogden, C. K. & Richards, I. A. (eds.) *The meaning of meaning: a study of the influence of language upon thought and of the science of symbolism*, supplement 1. 8th ed. London: Kegan Paul, Trench, Trübner, 1946.

Malinowski, B. *Magic, science and religion and other essays*. Boston, Mass.: Beacon Press, 1948.

Malinowski, B. (tr. Guterman) *A diary in the strict sense of the term*. 2nd ed. London: Athlone, 1989.

Marcus, G. E. *Ethnography through thick and thin*. Princeton, N. J.: Princeton University Press, 1998.

Marcus, G. E. Ethnography two decades after *Writing culture*: from the experimental to the Baroque. *Anthropological quarterly*, vol. 80, 2007, pp. 1127–45.

Marcus, G. E. & Fischer, M. M. J. *Anthropology as cultural critique: an experimental moment in the human sciences*. 2nd ed. Chicago, Ill.: University of Chicago Press, 1999.

Marett, R. R. *Tylor*. New York: John Wiley & Sons, 1936.

Marett, R. R. *A Jerseyman at Oxford*. London: Oxford University Press, 1941.

Martin, E. *The woman in the body: a cultural analysis of reproduction*. Rev. ed. Boston, Mass.: Beacon Press, 2001.

Marwick, M. (ed.) *Witchcraft and sorcery: selected readings*. 2nd ed. Harmondsworth: Penguin, 1982.

Marx, K. & Engels, F. (tr. Macfarlane) "Manifesto of the German Communists." In *Red Republican*, 1850. [*Manifest der Kommunistischen Partei*, 1848.]

Marx, K. & Engels, F. (tr. Moore & Engels) *The Communist manifesto*. London: Pluto, 2008. [*Manifest der Kommunistischen Partei*, 1848.]

Marx, K. & Engels, F. (ed. Dixon et al.) *Karl Marx, Frederick Engels: collected works*. London: Lawrence & Wishart, 1975–2004.

Mascia-Lees, F. E. (ed.) *A companion to the anthropology of the body and embodiment*. Chichester: Wiley-Blackwell, 2011.

Matory, J. L. *Black Atlantic religion: tradition, transnationalism, and matriarchy in the Afro-Brazilian Candomblé*. Princeton, N. J.: Princeton University Press, 2005.

Mattingly, C. *The paradox of hope: journeys through a clinical borderland*. Berkeley, Calif.: University of California Press, 2010.

Mauss, M. (tr. Cunnison) *The gift: forms and functions of exchange in archaic societies*. London: Cohen & West, 1954. [*Essai sur le don*, 1925.]

Mauss, M. (tr. Brewster) *Sociology and psychology: essays*. London: Routledge & Kegan Paul, 1979.

Mauss, M. (tr. Brewster) Techniques of the body. In Schlanger, N. (ed.) *Techniques, technology and civilisation*. New York: Durkheim Press/Berghahn, 2006. [*Les techniques du corps*, 1935.]

Maybury-Lewis, D. Parallel descent and the Apinayé anomaly. *Southwestern journal of anthropology*, vol. 16, 1960, pp. 191–216.

Mead, G. H. *Mind, self & society: from the standpoint of a social behaviorist*. Chicago, Ill.: University of Chicago Press, 1934.

Mead, M. *Coming of age in Samoa: a psychological study of primitive youth for western civilization*. New York: Perennial classics, 2001 [1928].

Mead, M. *Growing up in New Guinea: a comparative study of primitive education*. New York: William Morrow, 1930.

Mead, M. Socialization and enculturation. *Current anthropology*, vol. 4, 1963, pp. 184–8.

Mead, M. *Blackberry winter: my earlier years*. New York: William Morrow, 1972.

Mead, M. *Ruth Benedict: a humanist in anthropology*. 30th anniv. ed. New York: Columbia University Press, 2005.

Meillassoux, C. (tr. Dasnois) *The anthropology of slavery: the womb of iron and gold*. London: Athlone, 1991. [*Anthropologie de l'esclavage*, 1986.]

Melhuus, M. et al. (eds.) *Ethnographic practice in the present*. New York: Berghahn, 2010.

Merleau-Ponty, M. (tr. Smith) *Phenomenology of perception*. London: Routledge, 2002. [*Phénoménologie de la perception*, 1945.]

Merton, R. K. Manifest and latent functions. In *Social theory and social structure*. New York: Free Press, 1968 [1949].

Meskell, L. & Pels, P. (eds.) *Embedding ethics*. Oxford: Berg, 2005.

Metcalf, P. *They lie, we lie: getting on with anthropology*. London: Routledge, 2002.

Metcalf, P. & Huntingdon, R. *Celebrations of death: the anthropology of mortuary ritual*. 2nd ed. Cambridge: Cambridge University Press, 1991.

Migliore, S. *Mal'uocchiu: ambiguity, evil eye, and the language of distress*. Toronto, On.: University of Toronto Press, 1997.

Miller, D. *Material culture and mass consumption*. Oxford: Blackwell, 1994 [1987].

Miller, D. (ed.) *Anthropology and the individual: a material culture perspective*. Oxford: Berg, 2009.

Mills, C. W. *The power élite*. New York: Oxford University Press, 1999 [1956].

Milner, R. *Darwin's universe: evolution from A to Z*. Berkeley, Calif.: University of California Press, 2009.

Minnis, P. E. (ed.) *Ethnobotany: a reader*. Norman, Okla.: University of Oklahoma Press, 2000.

Missionaries, anthropologists, and human rights. Special issue of *Missiology*, vol. 24, 1996.

Montgomery, H. *Modern Babylon? Prostituting children in Thailand*. New York: Berghahn, 2001.

Montgomery, H. *An introduction to childhood: anthropological perspectives on children's lives*. Chichester: Wiley-Blackwell, 2009.

Moore, H. L. *A passion for difference: essays in anthropology and gender*. Cambridge: Polity, 1994.

Moore, H. L. *The subject of anthropology: gender, symbolism and psychoanalysis*. Cambridge: Polity, 2007.

Moran, E. F. *People and nature: an introduction to human ecological relations*. Malden, Mass.: Blackwell, 2006.

Morgan, L. H. *Systems of consanguinity and affinity of the human family*. Lincoln, Neb.: University of Nebraska Press, 1997 [1870].

Morgan, L. H. *Ancient society: or, Researches in the lines of human progress from savagery through barbarism to civilization*. New Brunswick, N. J.: Transaction, 2000 [1877].

Morphy, H. & Perkins, M. (eds.) *The anthropology of art: a reader*. Malden, Mass.: Blackwell, 2006.

Morris, B. *Anthropology of the self: the individual in cultural perspective.* London: Pluto, 1994.

Morris, B. *The power of animals: an ethnography.* Oxford: Berg, 1998.

Morris, B. & Bastin, R. (eds.) *Expert knowledge: First World peoples, consultancy and anthropology.* New York: Berghahn, 2004.

Morton, C. & Edwards, E. (eds.) *Photography, anthropology and history: expanding the frame.* Farnham: Ashgate, 2009.

Mundy, M. (ed.) *Law and anthropology.* Aldershot: Ashgate/Dartmouth, 2002.

Murdock, G. P. *Social structure.* New York: Macmillan, 1949.

Myerhoff, B. *Number our days.* New York: E. P. Dutton, 1978.

Nash, D. (ed.) *The study of tourism: anthropological and sociological beginnings.* Amsterdam: Elsevier, 2007.

Nash, J. *We eat the mines and the mines eat us: dependency and exploitation in Bolivian tin mines.* Centennial ed. New York: Columbia University Press, 1993.

Needham, R. *A bibliography of Arthur Maurice Hocart (1883–1939).* Oxford: Institute of Social Anthropology/Blackwell, 1967.

Needham, R. (ed.) *Rethinking kinship and marriage.* London: Routledge, 2004 [1971].

Needham, R. (ed.) *Right & left: essays on dual symbolic classification.* Chicago, Ill.: University of Chicago Press, 1973.

Needham, R. Polythetic classification: convergence and consequences. *Man,* new series, vol. 10, 1975, pp. 349–69.

Neumann, J. von & Morgenstern, O. *Theory of games and economic behavior.* 60th anniv. ed. Princeton, N. J.: Princeton University Press, 2004.

Nordstrom, C. *Shadows of war: violence, power, and international profiteering in the twenty-first century.* Berkeley, Calif.: University of California Press, 2004.

Nugent, D. & Vincent, J. (eds.) *A companion to the anthropology of politics.* Malden, Mass.: Blackwell, 2004.

Nugent, S. *Scoping the Amazon: image, icon, ethnography.* Walnut Creek, Calif.: Left Coast Press, 2007.

Nutini, H. G. & Isaac, B. L. *Social stratification in central Mexico, 1500–2000.* Austin, Tex.: University of Texas Press, 2009.

Obeyesekere, G. *The apotheosis of Captain Cook: European mythmaking in the Pacific.* Princeton, N. J.: Princeton University Press, 1997.

Obeyesekere, G. *Cannibal talk: the man-eating myth and human sacrifice in the South Seas.* Berkeley, Calif.: University of California Press, 2005.

Oceania [journal], 1930–.

Okely, J. *The traveller-gypsies.* Cambridge: Cambridge University Press, 1983.

O'Reilly, K. *Key concepts in ethnography.* Los Angeles: Sage, 2009.

Ortner, S. B. (ed.) *The fate of "culture": Geertz and beyond.* Berkeley, Calif.: University of California Press, 1999.

Ortner, S. B. & Whitehead, H. *Sexual meanings: the cultural construction of gender and sexuality.* Cambridge: Cambridge University Press, 1981.

Ottenheimer, H. J. *The anthropology of language: an introduction to linguistic anthropology.* 2nd ed. Belmont, Calif.: Wadsworth, 2009.

Otto, T. & Bubandt, N. (eds.) *Experiments in holism: theory and practice in contemporary anthropology.* Malden, Mass.: Wiley-Blackwell, 2010.

Overing, J. & Passes, A. (eds.) *The anthropology of love and anger: the aesthetics of conviviality in native Amazonia.* London: Routledge, 2000.

Paine, R. *Patrons and brokers in the East Arctic.* St. John's, Nfld.: Institute of Social and Economic Research, Memorial University, 1971.

Panourgiá, N. & Marcus, G. E. (eds.) *Ethnographica moralia: experiments in interpretive anthropology.* New York: Fordham University Press, 2008.

Parkin, D. (ed.) *The anthropology of evil.* Oxford: Blackwell, 1985.

Parkin, D. & Ulijaszek, S. J. (eds.) *Holistic anthropology: emergence and convergence.* New York: Berghahn, 2007.

Parkin, R. *The dark side of humanity: the work of Robert Hertz and its legacy.* Amsterdam: Harwood Academic, 1996.

Parry, J. & Bloch, M. (eds.) *Money and the morality of exchange.* Cambridge: Cambridge University Press, 1989.

Parsons, T. (ed. Turner) *The Talcott Parsons reader.* Malden, Mass.: Blackwell, 1999.

Parsons, T. & Shils, E. A. (eds.) *Toward a general theory of action.* Cambridge, Mass.: Harvard University Press, 1951.

Patterson, T. C. *Karl Marx, anthropologist.* Oxford: Berg, 2009.

Peacock, J. *Rites of modernization: symbolic and social aspects of Indonesian proletarian drama.* Chicago, Ill.: University of Chicago Press, 1987.

Peristiany, J. (ed.) *Honour and shame: the values of Mediterranean* society. Chicago, Ill.: University of Chicago Press, 1966.

Pinker, S. *The blank slate: the modern denial of human nature.* London: Allen Lane, 2002.

Polanyi, K. *The great transformation: the political and economic origins of our time.* 2nd Beacon pbk. ed. Boston, Mass.: Beacon Press, 2001 [1944].

Polanyi, K. et al. (eds.) *Trade and market in the early empires: economies in history and theory.* Glencoe, Ill.: Free Press, 1957.

Posey, D. A. (ed. Plenderleith) *Indigenous knowledge and ethics: a Darrell Posey reader.* New York: Routledge, 2004.

Post, J. C. (ed.) *Ethnomusicology: a contemporary reader.* New York: Routledge, 2006.

Pregadio, F. (ed.) *The encyclopedia of Taoism.* London: Routledge, 2008.

Prebish, C. S. & Keown, D. *Introducing Buddhism.* 2nd ed. London: Routledge, 2010.

Propp, V. I. (tr. Scott) *Morphology of the folktale.* 2nd ed. Austin: University of Texas Press, 1968. [*Morfologiia skazki,* 1928.]

Quigley, D. (ed.) *The character of kingship.* Oxford: Berg, 2005.

Rabinow, P. (ed.) *The Foucault reader.* New York: Pantheon, 1984.

Rabinow, P. *Making PCR: a story of biotechnology.* Chicago, Ill.: University of Chicago Press, 1996.

Rabinow, P. *Reflections on fieldwork in Morocco.* 30th anniv. ed. Berkeley, Calif.: University of California Press, 2007.

Radcliffe-Brown, A. R. A further note on Ambrym. *Man,* vol. 29, 1929, pp. 50–3.

Radcliffe-Brown, A. R. *Structure and function in primitive society.* London: Cohen & West, 1952.

Rappaport, R. A. *Pigs for the ancestors: ritual in the ecology of a New Guinea people.* 2nd ed. Long Grove, Ill.: Waveland, 2000 [1984].

Redfield, R. *The folk culture of Yucatan.* Chicago, Ill.: University of Chicago Press, 1941.

Redfield, R. *Peasant society and culture*. Chicago, Ill.: University of Chicago Press, 1989 [1956].

Reed-Danahay, D. E. (ed.) *Auto/ethnography: rewriting the self and the social*. Oxford: Berg, 1997.

Reyna, S. P. *Connections: brain, mind, and culture in a social anthropology*. London: Routledge, 2002.

Richards, A. I. *Hunger and work in a savage tribe: a functional study of nutrition among the southern Bantu*. London: Routledge, 2004 [1932].

Richards, A. I. *Land, labour and diet in Northern Rhodesia: an economic study of the Bemba tribe*. 2nd ed. Münster: LIT/IAI, 1995 [1961].

Riches, D. (ed.) *The anthropology of violence*. Oxford: Basil Blackwell, 1986.

Ridley, M. *The origins of virtue*. London: Viking, 1996.

Rio, K. M. & Smedal, O. H. *Hierarchy: persistence and transformation in social formations*. New York: Berghahn, 2009.

Rival, L. Androgynous parents and guest children: the Huaorani couvade. *Journal of the Royal Anthropological Institute*, new series. vol. 4, 1998, pp. 619–42.

Rivers, W. H. R. The genealogical method of anthropological inquiry. In *Kinship and social organization*. London: Athlone, 1968 [1910].

Robertson, A. F. *The dynamics of productive relationships: African share contracts in comparative perspective*. Cambridge: Cambridge University Press, 1987.

Robbins, J. & Wardlow, H. (eds.) *The making of global and local modernities in Melanesia: humiliation, transformation and the nature of cultural change*. Aldershot: Ashgate, 2005.

Robertson, J. (ed.) *Same-sex cultures and sexualities: an anthropological reader*. Malden, Mass.: Blackwell, 2005.

Robinson, R. & Clarke, S. (eds.) *Religious conversion in India: modes, motivations, and meanings*. New Delhi: Oxford University Press, 2003.

Rogers, S. C. Interesting friends and faux amis: an introduction to new directions in French anthropology. *Cultural anthropology*, vol. 14, 1999, pp. 396–404.

Rosen, L. *Varieties of Muslim experience: encounters with Arab political and cultural life*. Chicago, Ill.: University of Chicago Press, 2008.

Rosman, A. & Rubel, P. G. *Feasting with mine enemy: rank and exchange among Northwest coast societies*. New York: Columbia University Press, 1971.

Rosman, A. et al. *The tapestry of culture: an introduction to cultural anthropology*. 9th ed. Lanham, Md.: Altamira, 2009.

Rouch, J. (tr. Feld) *Ciné-ethnography*. Minneapolis: University of Minnesota Press, 2003.

Rousseau, J. J. (tr. Cranston) *The social contract*. Harmondsworth: Penguin, 2004. [*Du contrat social*, 1762.]

Rowley-Conwy, P. Time, change and the archaeology of hunter-gatherers: how original is the "original affluent society"? In Panter-Brick, C. et al. (eds.) *Hunter-gatherers: an interdisciplinary perspective*. Cambridge: Cambridge University Press, 2001.

Rubel, P. G. & Rosman, A. (eds.) *Translating cultures: perspectives on translation and anthropology*. Oxford: Berg, 2003.

Ruby, J. *Picturing culture: explorations of film & anthropology*. Chicago, Ill.: University of Chicago Press, 2000.

Russell, A. et al. (eds.) *Contraception across cultures: technologies, choices, constraints*. Oxford: Berg, 2000.

Sackman, D. C. *Wild men: Ishi and Kroeber in the wilderness of modern America.* New York: Oxford University Press, 2010.

Sahlins, M. D. *Social stratification in Polynesia.* Seattle, Wash.: University of Washington Press, 1958.

Sahlins, M. D. Poor man, rich man, big-man, chief: political types in Melanesia and Polynesia. *Comparative studies in society and history*, vol. 5, 1963, pp. 285–303.

Sahlins, M. D. Two or three things that I know about culture. *Journal of the Royal Anthropological Institute*, new series. vol. 5, 1999, pp. 399–421.

Sahlins, M. D. *Stone age economics.* New ed. London: Routledge, 2004 [1972].

Said, E. W. *Orientalism.* New ed. Harmondsworth: Penguin, 1995 [1978].

Sanjek, R. (ed.) *Fieldnotes: the makings of anthropology.* Ithaca, N. Y.: Cornell University Press, 1990.

Sanjek, R. *The future of us all: race and neighborhood politics in New York City.* Ithaca, N. Y.: Cornell University Press, 1998.

Sapir, E. The status of linguistics as a science. In *Selected writings of Edward Sapir in language, culture and personality.* Berkeley, Calif.: University of California Press, 1949 [1929].

Saussure, F. de (tr. Harris) The object of study. In *Course in general linguistics.* London: Duckworth, 1983.

Saville-Troike, M. *The ethnography of communication: an introduction.* 3rd ed. Malden, Mass.: Blackwell, 2003.

Schiffer, M. B. (ed.) *Anthropological perspectives on technology.* Albuquerque, N. M.: University of New Mexico Press, 2001.

Schmandt-Besserat, D. *How writing came about.* Austin, Tex.: University of Texas Press, 1996.

Schumaker, L. *Africanizing anthropology: fieldwork, networks, and the making of cultural knowledge in central Africa.* Durham, N. C.: Duke University Press, 2001.

Social studies of science [journal], 1971–.

Scott, J. & Selwyn, T. (eds.) *Thinking through tourism.* Oxford: Berg, 2010.

Scott, J. C. *The moral economy of the peasant: rebellion and subsistence in Southeast Asia.* New Haven, Conn.: Yale University Press, 1976.

Scott, J. C. *Weapons of the weak: everyday forms of peasant resistance.* New Haven, Conn.: Yale University Press, 1985.

Segal, R. A. (ed.) *The Blackwell companion to the study of religion.* Chichester: Wiley-Blackwell, 2006.

Sen, A. *Poverty and famines: an essay on entitlement and deprivation.* Oxford: Clarendon Press, 1982 [1981].

Sen, A. & Drèze, J. (eds.) *The political economy of hunger, vol. 1: Entitlement and well-being.* Oxford: Clarendon Press, 1990.

Sen, A. & Williams, B. (eds.) *Utilitarianism and beyond.* Cambridge: Cambridge University Press, 1982.

Social networks [journal], 1978–.

Shankman, P. *The trashing of Margaret Mead: anatomy of an anthropological controversy.* Madison, Wis.: University of Wisconsin Press, 2009.

Sharma, A. & Gupta, A. (eds.) *The anthropology of the state: a reader.* Malden, Mass.: Blackwell, 2006.

Shaw, A. & Ardener, S. (eds.) *Changing sex and bending gender.* New York: Berghahn, 2005.

Simmel, G. (tr. Bottomore & Frisby) *The philosophy of money.* 3rd ed. London: Routledge, 2004. [*Die Philosophie des Geldes,* 2nd ed. 1907.]

Singer, M. & Baer, H. *Introducing medical anthropology: a discipline in action.* Lanham, Md.: Altamira, 2007.

Singer, M. & Erickson, P. I. (eds.) *A companion to medical anthropology.* Malden, Mass.: Wiley-Blackwell, 2011.

Slobodin, R. *Rivers.* Rev. ed. Stroud: Sutton, 1997.

Smith, A. L. Heteroglossia, "common sense" and social memory. *American ethnologist,* vol. 31, 2004, pp. 251–69.

Smith, G. E. et al. *Culture: the diffusion controversy.* London: Kegan Paul, Trench, Trübner, 1928.

Smith, M. G. *The plural society in the British West Indies.* Berkeley, Calif.: University of California Press, 1965.

Spencer, P. (ed.) *Society and the dance: the social anthropology of process and performance.* Cambridge: Cambridge University Press, 1985.

Spencer, P. *Time, space and the unknown: Maasai configurations of power and providence.* London: Routledge, 2003.

Sperber, D. (tr. Morton) *Rethinking symbolism.* Cambridge: Cambridge University Press, 1975. [*Le symbolisme en general,* 1974.]

Sperber, D. & Wilson, D. *Relevance: communication and cognition.* 2nd ed. Malden, Mass.: Blackwell, 1995.

Spier, L. *The distribution of kinship systems in North America.* Seattle, Wash.: University of Washington Press, 1925.

Spindler, G. & Spindler, L. *Fifty years of anthropology and education, 1950–2000: a Spindler anthology.* Mahwah, N. J.: Lawrence Erlbaum, 2000.

Spiro, M. E. Cultural determinism, cultural relativism and the comparative study of psychopathology. *Ethos,* vol. 29, 2001, pp. 218–34.

Srinivas, M. N. *The remembered village.* Berkeley, Calif.: University of California Press, 1976.

Steiner, F. *Taboo.* London: Cohen & West, 1956.

Steward, J. H. *Theory of culture change: the methodology of multilinear evolution.* Urbana, Ill.: University of Illinois Press, 1976 [1955].

Stewart, E. A. *Exploring twins: towards a social analysis of twinship.* Basingstoke: Palgrave Macmillan, 2003 [2000].

Stocking, G. W. *Race, culture and evolution: essays in the history of anthropology.* Phoenix ed. Chicago, Ill.: University of Chicago Press, 1982.

Stocking, G. W. (ed.) *Functionalism historicized: essays on British social anthropology.* Madison, Wis.: University of Wisconsin Press, 1984.

Stocking, G. W. *Victorian anthropology.* New York: Free Press, 1987.

Stocking, G. W. (ed.) *Volksgeist as method and ethic: essays on Boasian ethnography and the German anthropological tradition.* Madison, Wis.: University of Wisconsin Press, 1996.

Stocking, G. W. & Handler, R. (eds.) *History of anthropology* [book series]. Madison, Wis.: University of Wisconsin Press, 1983–2010.

Stoller, P. & Olkes, C. *In sorcery's shadow: a memoir of apprenticeship among the Songhay of Niger.* Chicago, Ill.: University of Chicago Press, 1987.

Strang, V. *Gardening the world: agency, identity, and the ownership of water.* New York: Berghahn, 2009[a].

Strang, V. *What anthropologists do*. Oxford: Berg, 2009[b].

Strathern, A. et al. (eds.) *Terror and violence: imagination and the unimaginable*. London: Pluto, 2006.

Street, B. V. *Cross-cultural approaches to literacy*. Cambridge: Cambridge University Press, 1993.

Sumner, W. G. (ed. Sagarin) *Folkways and mores*. New York: Schocken, 1979.

Suthrell, C. A. *Unzipping gender: sex, cross-dressing and culture*. Oxford: Berg, 2004.

Sykes, K. *Arguing with anthropology: an introduction to critical theories of the gift*. London: Routledge, 2005.

Tattersall, I. *The fossil trail: how we know what we think we know about human evolution*. 2nd ed. New York: Oxford University Press, 2009.

Taussig, M. T. *The devil and commodity fetishism in South America*. 30th anniv. ed. Chapel Hill, N. C.: University of North Carolina Press, 2010.

Tcherkézoff, S. (tr. Thom) *Dual classification reconsidered: Nyamwezi sacred kingship and other examples*. Cambridge: Cambridge University Press, 1987. [*Le roi nyamwezi, la droite et la gauche*, 1983.]

Tedlock, B. (ed.) *Dreaming: anthropological and psychological interpretations*. Santa Fe, Calif.: School of American Research Press, 1992.

Tedlock, D. Questions concerning dialogical anthropology. *Journal of anthropological research*, vol. 43, 1987, pp. 325–37.

Tedlock, D. *2000 years of Mayan literature*. Berkeley, Calif.: University of California Press, 2010.

Tedlock, D. & Mannheim, B. (ed.) *The dialogic emergence of culture*. Urbana, Ill.: University of Illinois Press, 1995.

Tegnaeus, H. *Blood brothers: an ethno-sociological study of the institutions of blood-brotherhood with special reference to Africa*. Stockholm: Ethnographical Museum, 1952.

Thomas, N. *In Oceania: visions, artifacts, histories*. Durham, N. C.: Duke University Press, 1997.

Thompson, E. P. Time, work-discipline and industrial capitalism. *Past and present*, no. 38, 1967, pp. 56–97. [Reprinted in *Customs in common*, 1991.]

Tilley, C. Y. et al. (eds.) *Handbook of material culture*. London: Sage, 2006.

Tomlinson, M. Retheorizing *mana*: Bible translation and discourse of loss in Fiji. *Oceania*, vol. 76, 2006, pp. 173–85.

Tonkin, E. et al. (eds.) *History and ethnicity*. London: Routledge, 1989.

Tönnies, F. (tr. Loomis) *Community and association*. London: Routledge & Kegan Paul, 1955. [*Gemeinschaft und Gesellschaft*, 1887.]

Trautmann, T. R. *Dravidian kinship*. Cambridge: Cambridge University Press, 1981.

Trautmann, T. R. *Lewis Henry Morgan and the invention of kinship*. New ed. Lincoln, Neb.: University of Nebraska Press, 2008.

Turner, B. S. *The body & society: explorations in social theory*. 3rd ed. Los Angeles, Calif.: Sage, 2008.

Turner, V. W. *The forest of symbols: aspects of Ndembu ritual*. Ithaca, N. Y.: Cornell University Press, 1967.

Turner, V. W. *The ritual process: structure and anti-structure*. New York: Aldine de Gruyter, 1995 [1969].

Turner, V. W. *Dramas, fields, and metaphors: symbolic action in human society*. Ithaca, N. Y.: Cornell University Press, 1974.

Turner, V. W. *Revelation and divination in Ndembu ritual.* Ithaca, N. Y.: Cornell University Press, 1975.

Turner, V. W. *The anthropology of performance.* New York: PAJ, 1986.

Turner, V. W. & Turner, E. *Image and pilgrimage in Christian culture: anthropological perspectives.* New York: Columbia University Press, 1978.

Turney-High, H. *Primitive war: its practice and concepts.* 2nd ed. Columbia, S. C.: University of South Carolina Press, 1971.

Tylor, E. B. *Primitive culture: researches into the development of mythology, philosophy, religion, art and custom.* London: Murray, 1871.

Uberoi, P. et al. (eds.) *Anthropology in the east: founders of Indian sociology and anthropology.* Calcutta: Seagull, 2008.

Ulijaszek, S. J. & Komlos, J. From a history of anthropometry to anthropometric history. In Mascie-Taylor, C. G. N. et al. (eds.) *Human variation: from the laboratory to the field.* Boca Raton, Fla.: CRC Press, 2010.

Ulijaszek, S. J. & Strickland, S. S. *Nutritional anthropology: prospects and perspectives.* London: Smith-Gordon/Nishimura, 1993.

Urban, G. *Metaculture: how culture moves through the world.* Minneapolis, Minn.: University of Minnesota Press, 2001.

Urry, J. *Before social anthropology: essays on the history of British anthropology.* Chur, Switzerland: Harwood Academic, 1993.

Urry, J. The complexity turn. *Theory, culture and society,* vol. 22, 2005, pp. 1–14.

Van Gennep, A.(tr. Vizedom & Caffee) *The rites of passage.* Chicago, Ill.: University of Chicago Press, 1960. [*Les rites de passage,* 1909.].

Vayda, A. P. *Explaining human actions and environmental changes.* Lanham, Md.: Altamira, 2009.

Veblen, T. *The theory of the leisure class.* Oxford: Oxford University Press, 2007 [1899].

Verdery, K. *What was socialism, and what comes next?* Princeton, N. J.: Princeton University Press, 1996.

Vertovec, S. *Transnationalism.* London: Routledge, 2009.

Vertovec, S. & Cohen, R. *Migration, diasporas, and transnationalism.* Cheltenham: Elgar, 1999.

Volkov, V. *Violent entrepreneurs: the use of force in the making of Russian capitalism.* Ithaca, N. Y.: Cornell University Press, 2002.

Wacquant, L. Pierre Bourdieu (1930–2002). *American anthropologist,* vol. 105, 2003, pp. 478–80.

Wainwright, J. *Decolonizing development: colonial power and the Maya.* Malden, Mass.: Blackwell, 2008.

Walkowitz, D. J. & Knauer, L. M. (eds.) *Contested histories in public space: memory, race, and nation.* Durham, N. C.: Duke University Press, 2009.

Wallace, A. F. C. Revitalization movements. *American anthropologist,* vol. 58, 1956, pp. 264–81.

Wallace, A. F. C. *The death and rebirth of the Seneca.* New York: Knopf, 1970.

Wallerstein, I. *The modern world-system.* New York: Academic Press, 1974–89.

Wallman, S. (ed.) *Social anthropology of work.* London: Academic Press, 1979.

Warner, W. L. *A black civilization: a social study of an Australian tribe.* Rev. ed. New York: Harper, 1958.

Weber, M. (ed. Kalberg) *The Protestant ethic and the spirit of capitalism*. 4th ed. New York: Oxford University Press, 2009. [*Protestantische Ethik und der Geist des Kapitalismus*, 1904.]

Weber, M. (tr. & ed. Gerth) *The religion of China: Confucianism and Taoism*. Glencoe, Ill.: Free Press, 1951. [*Konfuzianismus und Taoismus*, 1920.]

Weber, M. (ed. & tr. Gerth & Mills) *From Max Weber: essays in sociology*. London: Routledge, 2009 [1946].

Weber, M. (tr. Henderson & Parsons) *The routinization of charisma*. Part III, section v of *The theory of social and economic organization*. New York: Free Press, 1964 [1947]. [*Wirtschaft und Gesellschaft*, Part 1, 1921.]

Weiner, A. B. & Schneider, J. (eds.) *Cloth and human experience*. Washington, D. C.: Smithsonian Institution Press, 1989.

Weiner, J. (ed.) *Aesthetics is a cross-cultural category*. Manchester: Group for Debates in Anthropological Theory, 1994.

West, H. G. & Raman, P. (eds.) *Enduring socialism: explorations of revolution and transformation, restoration and continuation*. New York: Berghahn, 2009.

Whisson, M. G. & West, M. (eds.) *Religion and social change in Southern Africa: anthropological essays in honour of Monica Wilson*. Cape Town: David Philip, 1975.

White, E. The cultural politics of the supernatural in Theravada Buddhist Thailand. *Anthropological forum*, vol. 13, 2003, pp. 205–12.

Whitehouse, H. & Laidlaw, J. (eds.) *Religion, anthropology, and cognitive science*. Durham, N. C.: Carolina Academic Press, 2007.

Whiting, J. W. M. (ed. Chasdi) *Culture and human development: the selected papers of John Whiting*. Cambridge: Cambridge University Press, 2006 [1994].

Whorf, B. L. (ed. Carroll) *Language, thought, and reality: selected writings of Benjamin Lee Whorf*. Cambridge, Mass.: MIT Press, 1956.

Widlok, T. & Tadesse, W. G.(eds.) *Property and equality*. New York: Berghahn, 2005.

Wilk, R. (ed.) *Fast food/slow food: the cultural economy of the global food system*. Lanham, Md.: Altamira, 2006.

Wilmsen, E. N. (ed.) *We are here: politics of aboriginal land tenure*. Berkeley, Calif.: University of California Press, 1989.

Wilson, E. O. *Sociobiology: the new synthesis*. Cambridge, Mass.: Belknap Press, 1975.

Wilson, T. M. (ed.) *Drinking cultures: alcohol and identity*. Oxford: Berg, 2005.

Wirth, L. Urbanism as a way of life. *American journal of sociology*, vol. 44, 1938, pp. 1–24.

Wirtz, K. How diasporic religious communities remember: learning to speak the "tongue of the oricha" in Cuban Santeria. *American ethnologist*, vol. 34, 2007, pp. 108–26.

Wiseman, B. (ed.) *The Cambridge companion to Lévi Strauss*. Cambridge: Cambridge University Press, 2009.

Wisnewski, J. J. *The politics of agency: toward a pragmatic approach to philosophical anthropology*. Aldershot: Ashgate, 2008.

Wittfogel, K. *Oriental despotism: a comparative study of total power*. New Haven, Conn.: Yale University Press, 1957.

Wittgenstein, L. (tr. Anscombe et al.) *Philosophical investigations*. 4th ed. Chichester: Wiley-Blackwell, 2009. [*Philosophische Untersuchungen*.]

Wolff, L. & Cipolloni, M. (eds.) *The anthropology of the Enlightenment*. Stanford, Calif.: Stanford University Press, 2007.

Womack, M. *Symbols and meaning: a concise introduction*. Walnut Creek, Calif.: Altamira, 2005.

Woodburn, J. African hunter-gatherer social organization: is it best understood as a product of encapsulation? In Ingold, T. et al. (eds.) *History, evolution and social change*. Oxford: Berg, 1988.

Worsley, P. *The trumpet shall sound: a study of "cargo" cults in Melanesia*. 2nd ed. London: MacGibbon & Kee, 1968.

Wulff, H. (ed.) *The emotions: a cultural reader*. Oxford: Berg, 2007.

Young, M. W. *Malinowski: odyssey of an anthropologist, 1884–1920*. New Haven, Conn.: Yale University Press, 2004.

Zeitschrift für Ethnologie [journal], 1869–.

Zenker, O. & Kumoll, K. (eds.) *Beyond* Writing culture: *current intersections of epistemologies and representational practices*. New York: Berghahn, 2010.